Forget the Alamo

FORGET THE ALAMO

THE RISE AND FALL OF AN AMERICAN MYTH

BRYAN BURROUGH, CHRIS TOMLINSON, AND JASON STANFORD

THORNDIKE PRESS
A part of Gale, a Cengage Company

**LIBRARY OF CONGRESS CIP DATA ON FILE.
CATALOGUING IN PUBLICATION FOR THIS BOOK
IS AVAILABLE FROM THE LIBRARY OF CONGRESS.**

ISBN-13: 978-1-4328-9285-2 (hardcover alk. paper)

Published in 2021 by arrangement with Penguin Press, an imprint of Penguin Publishing Group, a division of Penguin Random House LLC.

Printed in Mexico
Print Number: 01   Print Year: 2022

To John M. and Mary Burrough
of Temple, Texas,
Griffin Burrough of Seattle,
and Dane Burrough of Boston
— BB

To Shalini, who makes my
dreams come true
— CT

To Sonia Van Meter, my wife,
favorite reader, and partner.
While she changes the world, I get to
write about it and marvel at her.
— JS

CONTENTS

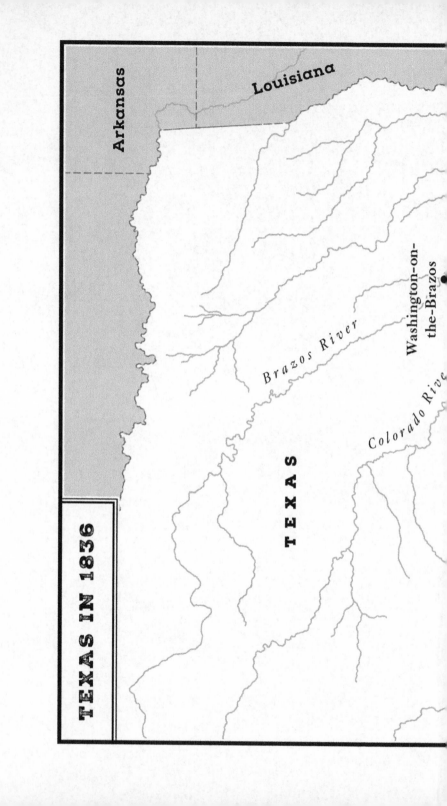

TEXAS IN 1836

Arkansas

Louisiana

Washington-on-the-Brazos

Brazos River

Colorado Rive

TEXAS

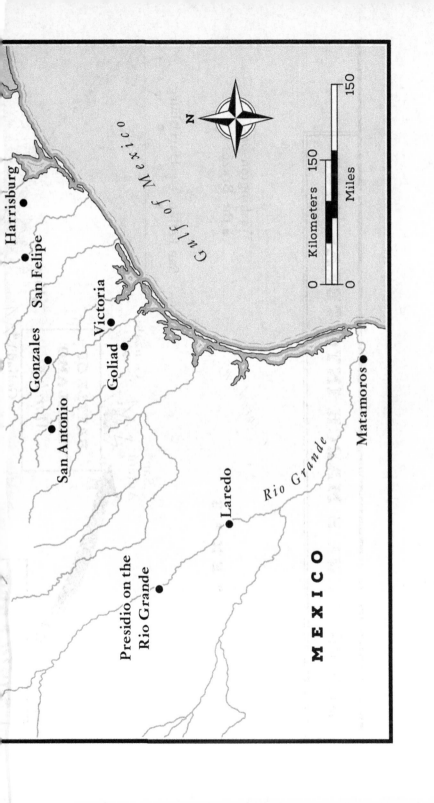

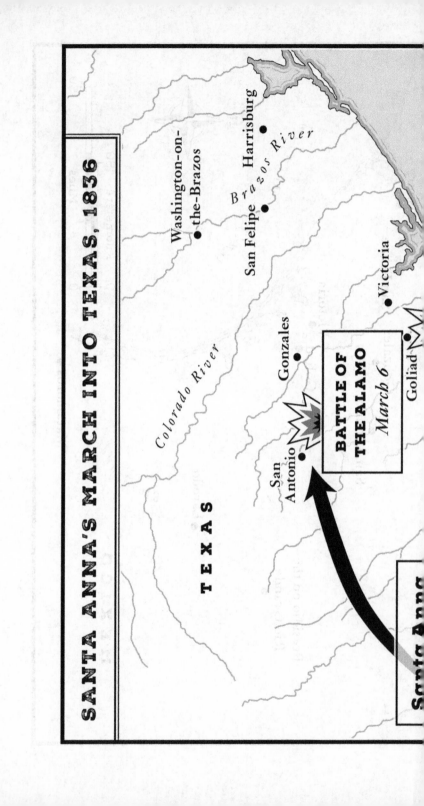

SANTA ANNA'S MARCH INTO TEXAS, 1836

Washington-on-the-Brazos

Harrisburg

Brazos River

San Felipe

Victoria

Colorado River

Gonzales

Goliad

BATTLE OF THE ALAMO
March 6

San Antonio

TEXAS

Santa Anna

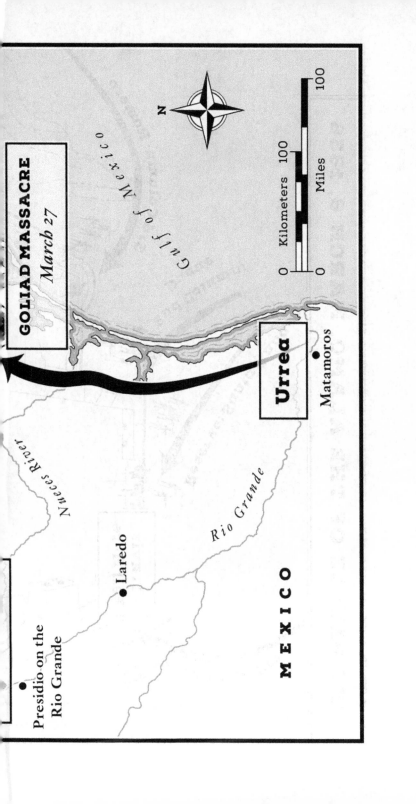

GOLIAD MASSACRE
March 27

Gulf of Mexico

N

Kilometers 0   100
Miles   0   100

Urrea

Matamoros

Nueces River

Rio Grande

Laredo

MEXICO

Presidio on the
Rio Grande

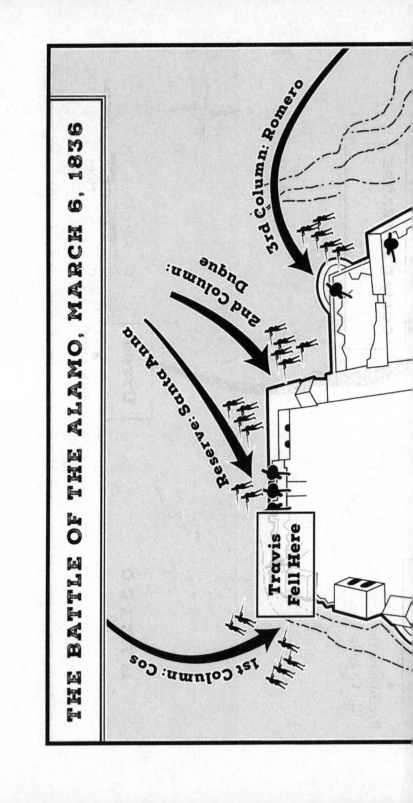

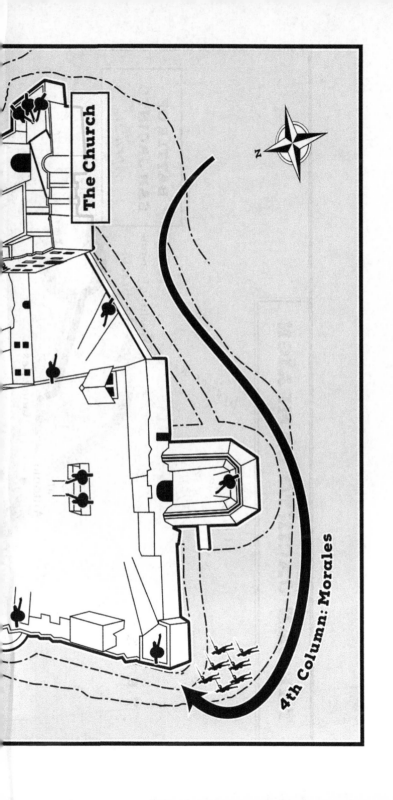

The Church

4th Column: Morales

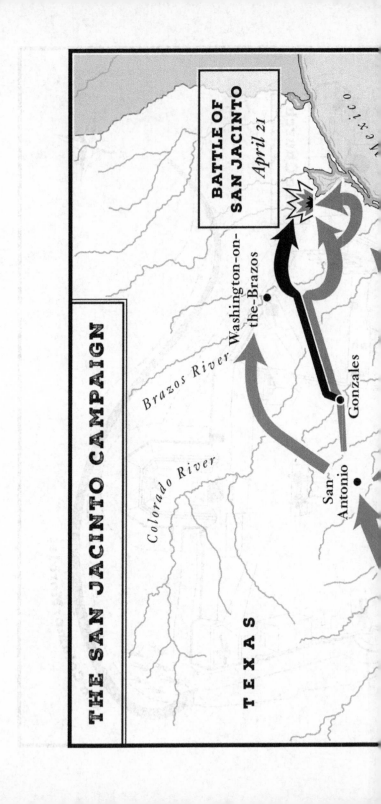

THE SAN JACINTO CAMPAIGN

BATTLE OF SAN JACINTO
April 21

TEXAS

Colorado River

Brazos River

Washington-on-the-Brazos

San Antonio

Gonzales

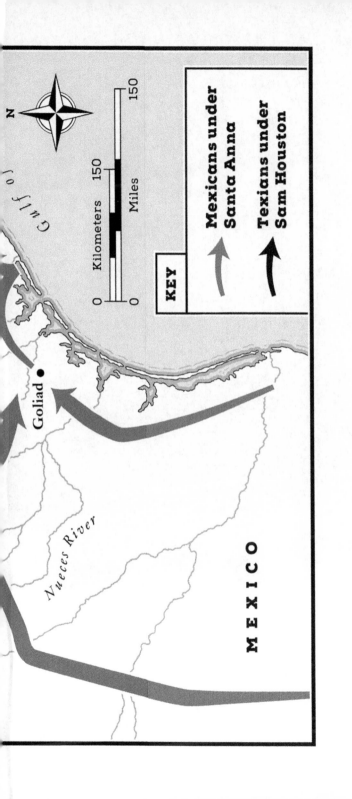

N

Gulf of

Goliad

Nueces River

MEXICO

Kilometers 150

0

0

Miles

150

150

KEY

Mexicans under
Santa Anna

Texians under
Sam Houston

INTRODUCTION

> I have said that Texas is a state of mind,
> but I think it is more than that. It is a
> mystique closely approximating a religion.
>
> — JOHN STEINBECK,
> *TRAVELS WITH CHARLEY:*
> *IN SEARCH OF AMERICA*

The story of the Alamo is simple, right?
Davy Crockett, Jim Bowie, William Barret
Travis, and a bunch of their friends come to
Texas to start new lives, suddenly realize
they are being oppressed by the Mexican
dictator Santa Anna, and rush off to do
battle with him at an old Spanish mission
in San Antonio. They are outnumbered but
fight valiantly and die to a man, buying Sam
Houston enough time to defeat Santa Anna
at the Battle of San Jacinto. As almost any
Texan will tell you, their sacrifice turned
the Alamo into the cradle of Texas liberty.

The problem is that much of what you

think you know about the Alamo is wrong. What you just read? That's the Alamo myth, the legend. The actual story, well, it's a lot more complicated.

These days there are essentially two schools of thought about the Alamo and what it means. A playful way to contrast them is through the stories of the two British rock stars most closely associated with all this. The first would be Phil Collins, who began his career drumming for the band Genesis and, as a solo singer, has sold millions of albums. Collins happens to be the world's greatest collector of Alamo artifacts. He owns Sam Houston's Bowie knife, a belt said to have been worn by Travis, and a shot pouch Crockett is said to have turned over to a Mexican soldier before dying. Not to mention Alamo-sourced cannonballs, maps, letters, muskets, powder flasks, bullets, swords, and even human teeth.

Like many aficionados of a certain age, Collins caught the Alamo bug as a boy watching Fess Parker's Davy Crockett on the small screen and John Wayne's on the big. He named his Jack Russell terrier Travis. He was once told that in a previous life, he'd been a courier dashing in and out of the old mission in the days before Santa Anna's soldiers stormed it. Collins wants to believe. He has hundreds of old Alamo photos, many flecked with small balls of white light. He believes these are "orbs," globs of paranormal energy. In London, the tabloids pretty much think he's lost his mind. The *Daily Mail* called him "one drumstick shy of a pair."[1]

In Texas, though, where he has donated his collection as the core of a grand new museum planned for San Antonio, Collins is a giant among men. He represents the apotheosis of Alamo "traditionalism," which is to say, he is deeply invested in the sanctity of the Texas shrine and its legends of heroism. He is the ultimate true believer.

If you position Phil Collins on one side of the Alamo seesaw, the other would be occupied by Ozzy Osbourne. Ozzy passed into Alamo lore on a Friday afternoon, February 19, 1982. At approximately 2:50 p.m., as San Antonio children were heading home from school, a thirty-three-year-old man wobbled unsteadily into Alamo Plaza. He was wearing a torn green evening gown and sneakers.* In his hand he carried a bottle of Courvoisier.

Ozzy was having a rough day. He and his

---

* There is at least one account that Ozzy was actually wearing pink tights and ballet slippers.

bandmates, scheduled to perform a set including their hits "Crazy Train" and "Paranoid" at the San Antonio Convention Center that night, were squabbling. His girlfriend, Sharon, was carping again about his drinking, which typically began when he rose in the morning, as it had on this day. In an effort to confine his drunken idylls to their hotel suite, Sharon had taken to hiding his clothes, hence the gown, which was hers.

Later, Ozzy would be hazy as to where he was heading that day. What he remembered clearly, though, was an overwhelming need to relieve himself. Frustrated by his inability to locate a suitable loo, he decided to do as inebriated rock stars have done since the dawn of time. He sidled up to what appeared to be a little-used section of wall, parted his dress, and proceeded, with a great sigh, to do his business. Suddenly he heard a voice behind him:

"You *disgust* me." (Italics his own.)

Ozzy turned, as one would, and said, "What?"

An older gent in a cowboy hat was staring at him. "You're a disgrace, d'ya know that?" he said.

Ozzy attempted to explain about the gown.

"It ain't the dress, you limey faggot piece of dirt," the man said. "That wall you're relieving yourself on is the Alamo."

"The Aala-wot?"[*][2]

Here we should insert a brief word in Ozzy's defense. He was not, after all, the first British rock star who failed to grasp the Alamo's sanctity. Seven years earlier, members of the Rolling Stones had posed for a set of louche photos on the plaza wrapped in the Union Jack and wearing coonskin caps. When a disapproving doyenne informed them that leaning against the Alamo walls was disrespectful, a puzzled Mick Jagger remarked, "I don't know what the Alamo is or where it is, but we'll never play it again."

That Ozzy Osbourne peed on the Alamo is a tale that passed into Texas legend. It has inspired everything from exchanges in mainstream movies (see: the Steve Buscemi character in *Airheads*) to journalistic investigations (see: "A Brief History of Peeing on

---

[*] Given the various chemicals involved, we would concede that this version of events, which Ozzy related in his 2009 autobiography, might not be 100 percent accurate, but it's the only detailed one that survives, and it doesn't conflict with a police report we've seen.

the Alamo," *Texas Monthly,* 2014) to an art installation in which a life-sized wax statue of Ozzy urinates on a wall once onlookers trigger an adjacent motion sensor. Alas, as with so much about the Alamo, the story is not exactly true. Ozzy didn't actually pee on the Alamo. He actually peed on the Cenotaph, a sixty-foot-high monument beside it, on which the names of all those killed are listed.[3] City fathers banned him from performing in San Antonio for years, until Ozzy apologized and donated $10,000 to charity.

Ozzy represents the flip side of Phil Collins's traditionalism, what people in Texas call Alamo "revisionism," an intellectual school that, metaphorically, amounts to peeing on the Alamo legend. Revisionists tend to think the entire Texas Revolt was a bit more about protecting slavery from Mexico's abolitionist government than it was about opposing Santa Anna's supposed tyranny. Some think the whole thing was an American conspiracy to steal Texas from Mexico. Many don't believe Crockett went down fighting, as John Wayne famously did in his 1960 movie *The Alamo.* Almost none of them believe Travis drew that fateful line in the Alamo sand.

And make no mistake: This is all very serious business in Texas. But then no other state prizes its history quite like Texas. Maybe it's the fact that it stood for a decade as an independent country. But once you get a certain kind of Texan talking about its history, well, you're not getting home soon. The first Texas-raised president, Lyndon Johnson, loved to entertain White House guests by reciting a poem about the Alamo his mother taught him. "The great difference between Texas and every other American state in the 20th century was that Texas had a history," one Texacentric chronicler, T. R. Fehrenbach, has written. "Other American regions merely had records of development."

The Alamo has always loomed at the center of the Texas mythos, a concrete link to the state's ten years as an independent nation. Its legends comprise the beating heart of Texas exceptionalism, the idea, deeply held among generations of Texans, that the state is special, somehow a cut above the Delawares and Rhode Islands of the world. Its story, as Steinbeck suggests, is thus prized as a kind of civic religion. It's not an overstatement to say the Alamo is the state's secular Western Wall, its secular Mecca. Somewhat as Jews and Muslims have struggled over the Temple Mount, so

Anglos, African-Americans, Mexican-Americans, Tejanos, and Native Americans are now debating the future of the Alamo, and its meaning.

It's more than a Texas symbol, of course. The Alamo is an American touchstone as well, a symbol of national resolve, looming during the 1950s as an embodiment of U.S. determination to halt the spread of Communism. During the '60s, LBJ repeatedly invoked it to generate backing for the war in Vietnam. In time it was embraced by "patriots" and right-wingers who viewed Santa Anna's Mexican army as a stand-in for all manner of threats, from Communists to brown-skinned immigrants pouring across the Mexican border.

And Texans are fiercely protective of it. Over the years, the state has gone to extraordinary lengths to safeguard the traditionalist legend against revisionist questioning. The State Board of Education actually has standing orders that schoolchildren must be taught a "heroic" version of Alamo history. In 2018, when a teachers' committee suggested this was a bit much, Governor Greg Abbott spearheaded a wave of online outrage that brought revisionists to their knees. Alamo "heroism" thus remains literally the law of the land. Those who challenge it have gotten a lot of hate mail, even death threats.

We intend this book to be a serious look at the Alamo and its legend, but we've tried not to take ourselves too seriously. We come in the spirit of patriotic Americans who prize their native land but still aren't quite sure that, you know, George Washington literally chopped down that cherry tree. We grew up with the myths and legends of Texas history, and we savor them for what they are: myths and legends. But as writers, we also love facts, especially the facts of history, and we don't believe knowing the truth about Texas history makes the state any less unique or important.

We are proud Texans. In fact, Chris is so proud of being a fifth-generation Texan he wrote a book about it, *Tomlinson Hill.* As a young man, he was one of the few soldiers (maybe ever) to get excited about a posting to Fort Hood. Later, as a foreign correspondent reporting from Afghanistan and thirty other countries, he carried a little Texas flag in his computer bag wherever he went, including Tora Bora. Jason's people moved to McLennan County from Arkansas during the Civil War in search of neighbors more welcoming to Confederate sympathizers. His great-grandfather, alas, left on a cattle drive soon after and never returned.

Jason didn't make it back until 1993. His oldest is now an Aggie. Bryan's family didn't get to Texas until 1969, but he wasted no time settling in. At college in Missouri he hung a Texas flag in his dorm room. His most valued possessions include the worn Tony Lamas he bought in Lott just after high school and a pair of "Come and Take It" socks.

While some points we make here may be new, we should be clear that Alamo revisionism, as a school of thought, is not. We trace its roots to the oral traditions of the Mexican-American community, elements of which have long viewed the Alamo as a symbol of Anglo oppression; one of our goals, in fact, is to highlight the often overlooked contributions of Mexican-Americans during Texas's early years, and the awful price they paid for them. We stand on the shoulders of revisionist authors such as Andrew Torget, Andrés Tijerina, Jesús F. de la Teja, Jeff Long, and Paul D. Lack, whose work is an antidote to the "Heroic Anglo Narrative" that's held sway in Texas for going on two hundred years.

The tension between traditionalism and revisionism has never been on more vivid display than it is today, at a moment when Latinos are poised to become a majority of

28

Texas's citizenry.* At such a fraught moment, one might have expected a sense of impending cultural change in the air. And yet, inexplicably, at a time when the United States is undergoing an unprecedented reassessment of its racial history, the Alamo and its heroes have essentially been given a pass. Given the fact that its defenders were fighting to form what became the single most militant slave nation in history, that men like Bowie and Travis traded slaves, and that the "father of Texas," Stephen F. Austin, spent years fighting to preserve slavery from the attacks of Mexican abolitionists, one would think the post–George Floyd era might have brought to Texas a long-overdue reevaluation of its history. By and large, that hasn't happened.

Part of it is the fervor with which many Anglo Texans still embrace the traditionalist narrative, and part of it, no doubt, the fact that Anglo writers, editors, and intellectuals

* We understand that much debate surrounds terms such as "Latino," "Latinx," "Mexican-American," "Chicano," "Hispanic," and "Tejano." We venture not to offend, and to apply as much specificity as possible for geographic accuracy and to reflect the personal preferences of those we interviewed.

still dominate the state's media, much as Anglo politicians still dominate state government. But really, one should ask, how on earth can Texas still defend naming dozens of schools, roads, and towns after a brazen slave trader and swindler like Jim Bowie? If there's ever been a moment for a spirited discussion about what the Alamo truly symbolizes, we'd suggest it's now.

Traditionalists, though, who tend to be older, conservative, and white, aren't terribly interested in reconsidering the Alamo's history, or its symbolism, which has fueled an intermittent debate that's been building in intensity for a good thirty years now. What began as a set of literary and scholarly discussions in the 1990s became a fight over education and textbooks in the 2000s, and has now engulfed the Alamo site itself. Blame Phil Collins: He made the donation of his collection dependent on the building of a "world class museum," which got the state government thinking of what changes to make, which got traditionalists up in arms. Literally. When state planners started musing about moving that hallowed Cenotaph, groups of angry traditionalists clad in Kevlar vests and armed with assault rifles began staging symbolic occupations of Alamo Plaza.

The presence of weekend soldiers aside, changes at the Alamo itself seem inevitable. The aging shrine has long been a disappointment to visitors — a dim church, a tiny museum, and a walled-in park plopped down in downtown San Antonio, all of it surrounded by the cheesiest possible tourist venues: a wax museum, a Ripley's Haunted Adventure, that kind of thing. Texans have debated how to spiff it all up for fifty years. Now that it might happen, it can sometimes seem that everyone in the state has an opinion on what to do. It's not just Anglos and Mexican-Americans. Native American groups want land set aside to honor ancestors buried beneath Alamo Plaza during the Spanish era. One set of plans would involve tearing down an old Woolworth's department store across the street; African-Americans are protesting this, explaining that the lunch counter there was one of the first public places in San Antonio where Black people were allowed to dine with whites. Stuck in the middle is a beleaguered state bureaucrat with a fine political pedigree, George P. Bush, son of Jeb. Just about no one in Texas envies poor George P. these days.

And, sad to say, this book won't make his job any easier. That vast collection of artifacts Phil Collins donated? The ones Bush is proposing to build a $400 million "world class" museum at the Alamo to house? Well, as we point out in chapter 23, our research indicates that a whole lot of items in the collection are, at best, of questionable provenance. At worst? A lot of them appear to be fakes.

The fight Bush is refereeing, of course, is not entirely new. But the squabbling today is far less about what happened in the nineteenth century than what's happening in the twenty-first. The world is changing. It's not as white as it used to be. As has become broadly evident, Brown and Black people aren't all that crazy about monuments built to the men who oppressed and enslaved them back in the day. Whether it's Maori activists defacing colonial-era statues in New Zealand or South Africans protesting monuments to the nineteenth-century racist potentate Cecil Rhodes, much the same thing is happening around the world.

No, history doesn't really change. But the way we view it does. In Texas, the history written by generations of white people is now being challenged by those who see the same events very differently. And man oh man, does that piss a lot of people off.

CHAPTER 1
BLOODY TEXAS

On March 6, 1836, during what's been known for almost two centuries as the Texas Revolution, around two hundred men were killed by Mexican troops at an old Spanish church outside San Antonio known as the Alamo. On this we can agree. But after that, pretty much everything — who died, how they died, why they died, and what they represented — has been a topic of debate ever since.

Granted, it's been a gradual thing. For the first 150 years after the battle, few disagreed — at least publicly — with the "traditional" notion that its defenders were fighting for their "freedom" against the "oppression" of a crazed Mexican tyrant, Antonio López de Santa Anna. Lots of folks still believe that.

After all this time, you'd think historians would have gotten together and agreed on the facts. Alas, no. We'll tell you more about this later, but suffice it to say, Texas history, and especially the Alamo's history, was not a high priority for serious academic study for a long time. A really long time. As late as 1986, in fact, on the occasion of the battle's 150th anniversary, one noted professor complained that the battle was still awaiting a decent academic analysis.[1] The truth is, the Texas Revolt, as we call it, didn't attract professional study because, until the last thirty years or so, it was considered hopelessly déclassé, an academic backwater best abandoned to amateur writers.

And so, beginning in the years after the Battle of the Alamo, amateur historians moved in and took over. It is these writers we can thank in part for the fact that the true history of the Alamo, and to an extent the secessionist revolt that led to it, remained obscured by a sooty veneer of myth and folklore. Certainly among American battlefields that attract millions of tourists every year, it remains the least understood. We know almost every intricate detail of Gettysburg, Antietam, and Yorktown, and a lot about Little Big Horn. The Alamo? It's mostly a guessing game.

What was the battle even about? The first professor to study the revolt in the early 1900s floated a strangled argument citing land speculation. The book Anglo Texans have long embraced as definitive, T. R. Fehrenbach's 1968 *Lone Star,* argued in favor of "ethnic hatred." In the fifty years since, most historians have thrown their hands up, chalking it up to "a clash of cultures."

Well, yeah.

Let's stipulate, if you'll allow, that every "revolution" has two causes: the proximate cause, the trigger that gets folks to fighting, and the underlying cause, the thing that got people so worked up in the first place. The proximate cause in Texas seems pretty clear. For those to whom all this is new, we won't give that away just yet. (Hint: If you're a Mexican general who wants to arrest a loudmouthed Texan, don't bring an army.)

It's the underlying cause that concerns us here. Ignore that and you end up believing the American Revolution was about tea. What, after all, had Texans and the Mexican government been squabbling about for years? Land speculation was part of it, sure, and for some, "ethnic hatred" was too. Anti-tax sentiment played a role, but no one has argued the Texas Revolt was about taxes. Certainly there was a clash of cultures. But the true underlying cause? The thing that got people worked up in the first place? That's something that still gets people worked up today.

At its roots, the Texas Revolt was about money, how Texans made it, and why the Mexican government objected. This line of thinking is neither far-fetched nor dry nor boring. It is solidly grounded in facts, especially the fact of why almost every American came to Texas in the first place: to make money. And make it in a specific way: planting and selling cotton.

The story of Texas's first fifteen years as an Anglo colony is the success story of a band of misfits and dreamers who came to forge sprawling cotton plantations. In just a scant few years, Texas cotton was being made into clothing as far away as England. The "Texians," as they called themselves, revolted because they believed a new Mexican government threatened this economic model.

What was it they feared losing? In the pamphlets and newspaper articles that swirled through the revolt, it was always called "property." The inarguable fact is that there was only one kind of property the Mexican government ever tried to take from its American colonists, and it tried to do so repeatedly. In the ten years before the Alamo, this single disagreement brought Texians and Mexican troops to the brink of warfare multiple times.

So, what did the Mexicans want to take? It wasn't the cotton. Or the land it was grown on. It was the third leg of the Texas economic stool, the "property" in which Texas farmers had invested more money, more working capital, than any other asset.

The slaves.

As hard as it may be to accept, Texas as we know it exists only because of slave labor. Southerners — and most Texians came from the South — wouldn't immigrate to Texas without it. Thousands didn't, in fact, worried that the Mexican government's ingrained opposition to slavery put their "property" at risk. For Mexicans, newly freed from Spanish oppression, abolishing slavery was a moral issue. For the American colonists, it was an issue of wealth creation. In the early years, as we'll see, each new Mexican effort to ban slaves got Texians packing to head back to America. In later years, many put away their suitcases and took out their guns.

For more than a century, historians tiptoed around the importance of slavery to the state's early development. Not until the 1980s did serious academic study of the subject really get under way, led by professors like Randolph B. Campbell at the

University of North Texas and Paul D. Lack at Stevenson University. And not until recent years have historians taken the next step, arguing that the need to protect slavery was a driving force behind the Texas Revolt. The most notable book to support this hypothesis, Andrew J. Torget's ground-breaking 2015 *Seeds of Empire,* proved enormously influential to our thinking. In these opening chapters, we draw heavily on its conclusions and research.

To understand what happened, as Torget demonstrates, it helps to understand how cotton and slavery transformed Texas almost overnight from a blood-drenched semi-wilderness — that's no exaggeration — into a place where fortunes were made. Talking about the U.S. economy back when this all got started, in the late 1700s, in the era before factories, is a short conversation. There was shipbuilding and whaling in New England, production of things like glass and iron ore in the mid-Atlantic states, and a smattering of plantations farming sugar, rice, tobacco, and indigo in Georgia and the Carolinas. None of it was wildly profitable.

And then two sets of inventions forever changed America and its economy, especially in the South. The first came in Britain, where advances in cotton spinning, steam power, and iron furnaces led to the first true textile factories, which turned out cotton clothing for people around the world. Then, in 1793, an American tinkerer named Eli Whitney invented the cotton gin, a machine that removes the seeds from cotton; "gin" is short for "engine," by the way. Before the cotton gin, a single person using her fingers could clean and produce a pound of cotton a day. Using a gin, she could generate up to fifty pounds a day.

The pairing of British textile mills and the cotton gin produced an industrial big bang whose shock waves shook economies around the world. Nowhere was its impact more dramatic than in the American South, whose long, hot summers and fertile river bottoms made it perhaps the single best place on earth to grow cotton. Thanks to the insatiable British appetite for raw cotton — by midcentury, textiles accounted for 40 percent of all its exports — American cotton production exploded.

Suddenly all anyone in the South wanted to farm was cotton. Between 1794 and 1800, as Andrew Torget notes, "virtually every tobacco planter in the territory around Natchez, Mississippi, converted his farm to cotton, and in only six years the Natchez

District increased its cotton production from 36,000 pounds annually to more than 1.2 million."[2] But production only truly took off after the War of 1812, when Andrew Jackson defeated the Creek Indians and made Alabama, Mississippi, and Louisiana safe for commerce. When the gun smoke cleared, the government put up for sale fourteen million new acres of prime cotton land — half the size of Alabama — at bargain prices. The price of cotton, meanwhile, soared.

This was the beginning of the "Gone with the Wind" South, of landed gentry building columned mansions and plantations. Cotton money made New Orleans the nation's largest slave port and third-largest city. Natchez was home to more millionaires per capita than New York or Boston. And of course, it was the birth of the slave boom. In 1800, America held almost 900,000 enslaved Black people. By 1860, there would be almost four million. Hundreds of thousands were marched in chains from the mid-Atlantic states to the Gulf Coast to pick King Cotton.

Every year more people trundled down the Natchez Trace seeking their share of this fabulous new wealth. Eventually the best land was all taken. What to do? Everyone in the South knew what needed to be done. There were thousands of acres of prime cotton land still available, after all, and all of it could be had for a song. It was right there, so close you could see it, just across the Sabine River on the western edge of Louisiana. In Spanish Texas.

Imperial Spain had been one of history's great bloody empires, its metal-plated conquistadors rampaging across the Americas, crushing the Aztec and Incan empires and chasing tales of treasure from Argentina to Kansas. But by 1800, after two centuries of corruption, inflation, and ill-conceived wars, Spain was the sick man of Europe, its far-flung American colonies bubbling with revolutionary resentments. The remote North American outposts, an archipelago of missions dotting California, New Mexico, Arizona, Texas, and Florida, were limbs on a dying tree, hungrily eyed by ministers in Russia, Great Britain, and the United States. Spain, which hadn't been able to coax more than a few thousand settlers into its desolate northern reaches, had never had the money or the men to defend them.

The Spanish first explored Texas in the 1500s, but for the next two hundred years dismissed it as untenable for settlement, oppressively hot and overrun by hostile Native American tribes. Not until the 1700s, when French traders established a few Texas outposts, did Spain make any real effort to colonize it, chasing off the French and sending priests to open lonely missions at Bexar, today's San Antonio,* and at Nacogdoches in the East Texas pines. Over the years the Spanish succeeded in settling five or six thousand colonists at new towns and missions across the province, but Native Americans killed or chased off almost everyone. By 1800, precisely three towns of note remained.

They were sad little places. Nacogdoches, reached by a rutted trail called El Camino Real, was so precarious that settlers abandoned it entirely every few years. San Antonio served as what passed for a capital, twenty-five hundred people, half Spanish soldiers, jammed into a dusty town of sunbaked adobe houses. A hundred miles down the San Antonio River stood La Bahía del Espiritu Santo, today's Goliad, with seven hundred people. The entire population of Texas amounted to maybe four thousand men, women, and children

* For simplicity's sake, we'll be using the modern names of these towns.

scratching out a living on subsistence farming, raising cattle outside San Antonio, and, in East Texas, smuggling anything that would sell to the French settlements in Louisiana. Because Spanish Texas had no port, all supplies had to be walked in from faraway Mexico. From food to rifles, there was never enough of anything. Governors paid off the Native Americans and prayed for the best.

The first hint of change came in 1803, when Napoleon sold Thomas Jefferson the French claims on Louisiana and all the western lands between the Spanish settlements and Canada. At the stroke of a pen, America found itself with a new international border with Spain, at the Sabine River. When the two countries set to squabbling over the precise boundary in 1805, both rushed a few hundred troops to the border, but Jefferson decided to let the matter drop. Other Americans wouldn't.

The real trouble began five years later, in 1810, when a crusading Spanish priest named Miguel Hidalgo raised an army of peasants in Mexico intent on overthrowing the colonial government. A year later, rebel soldiers stormed the governor's house in San Antonio and took him prisoner; La Bahía and Nacogdoches surrendered without a fight. But two months after that, when Hidalgo's army disintegrated in Mexico, loyalist Tejanos easily retook San Antonio.

The whole thing might have ended there if not for the Americans. Rebels still fighting in Mexico decided to ask for Washington's help. They sent an emissary named José Bernardo Gutiérrez de Lara to Louisiana to meet with the governor, who gave him money and a letter of introduction to the secretary of state, James Monroe. Gutiérrez proceeded to Washington, where in December 1811 he met with Monroe. The details are instructive given the myriad intrigues that would engulf Texas in coming years. Long story short, every time anyone so much as imagined a revolt in Texas, the authorities in Mexico came to see it as a U.S. government plot. As Monroe's involvement with Gutiérrez illustrates, there was ample reason for these suspicions.

Monroe, it is clear, was keen to snap up territorial acorns that might fall from the Spanish colonial tree, and if he could shake the tree a little, well, so much the better. In their first meeting, Gutiérrez wrote in his diary, Monroe agreed to a request for money and arms to invade Texas. He mused about sending an American army to invade Mexico. Gutiérrez supposedly promised to give him Texas if he did, though Gutiérrez would later deny it. Afterward, Monroe apparently realized he was getting ahead of himself. In a second meeting he made it clear, apparently without furnishing specifics, that while America remained eager to help, its contributions would be more subtle.[3]

And they were, a bit. Two weeks later, Gutiérrez met with Monroe's chief clerk, who gave him $200 and a letter asking the Louisiana governor to give him more. When he reached New Orleans, the governor handed him off to a government "commercial agent" — read: spy — who stayed at Gutiérrez's side for months, detailing their work together in letters to Monroe.

All this amounted to a kind of Bay of Pigs, 1812-style. The staging area for the invasion Gutiérrez planned was the western Louisiana town of Natchitoches, which served as a kind of log-cabin Miami. To lead his forces, Gutiérrez hired an army officer named Augustus Magee, who helped raise a motley battalion of 130 or so smugglers, adventurers, and the occasional man of good breeding. Monroe, it's clear, was briefed every step of the way.

In August 1812, the little army crossed into Texas. Four days later Nacogdoches surrendered without a fight; almost all its soldiers joined the invaders, as did a few settlers, bringing their numbers to maybe three hundred. Magee led them toward Goliad, whose defenders retreated to San Antonio, allowing him to occupy the town in November. The Spanish governor did his best to rally folks against the rebels, managing to get a few hundred men into the field; when they appeared outside Goliad, Magee lost hope. Negotiations on a surrender stretched for weeks, during which time Magee dropped dead. A bellicose type named Samuel Kemper took command. He must have been quite a leader: Under Kemper's command, his men repelled two attacks, then chased the retreating Spaniards back toward San Antonio, where they thrashed them in March 1813. Twenty-three years before the Alamo, an American force marched into the capital, occupied the Alamo, and took control of Texas.

The joy of victory lasted barely two days, dissolving once a group of soldiers slit the throats of the Spanish governor and a dozen officers. Gutiérrez then declared Mexico independent from Spain and wrote a new constitution making Texas forever a part of Mexico. This was not what his Anglo troops had in mind, and they began to melt away.

Gutiérrez would later say he had been foolish to believe them when they claimed to support his revolution, when all they really wanted was to make Texas part of the United States.[4]

Down in Mexico City, the Spanish swore revenge. The remaining rebels, their numbers now swollen to a thousand or more, managed to beat back the first Spanish troops sent north that June. But the second column, commanded by a severe Barcelona-born general named José Joaquín de Arredondo y Mioño, routed the rebels south of San Antonio at the Battle of Medina, a bloody four-hour brawl in the August heat. It degenerated into a slaughter; maybe a hundred rebels survived. Thus ended the rebellion.

But that was only the beginning. Arredondo was renowned in Mexico for killing every prisoner he took, no matter the number, no matter the conditions. After securing San Antonio, he embarked on a reign of terror to make Genghis Khan proud. In San Antonio, as Torget and other historians have detailed, his men lined up and shot forty residents, three a day for almost two weeks. He put more on a chain gang. Down the river, the people of Goliad fled east toward Louisiana. Arredondo's cavalry ran them down, killing every man they found, seventy-one in all, then captured the main group of 150 refugees at a Trinity River crossing. They killed a hundred. Among the officers under Arredondo's command was a young Antonio López de Santa Anna, who was taking careful notes of his mentor's tactics.

When Spanish troops reached Nacogdoches, they found that all but a handful of families had fled. Leaving the town empty, they took the last people in chains to San Antonio, where the men were executed, the women put to work, and the children left to the streets. By the time Arredondo returned to Mexico, half the province's prewar population was dead or gone. Texas lay in ruins.

The story of the Texas revolt really begins with the end of this carnage in 1813. What remained of the province began to change. With East Texas practically empty, a vacuum arose that was soon filled by all manner of smugglers and pirates. The best known, Pierre and Jean Lafitte, transformed Galveston Island into a buccaneer base to raid Spanish shipping. Most everything the Lafittes took — from dry goods and liquor to rifles and enslaved Black people — they sold into the booming Louisiana cotton economy. For American plantation owners looking for bargains, Galveston became a kind of backwoods Walmart. The Lafittes sold enslaved Black people for a dollar a pound, meaning a slave that fetched $1,500 in New Orleans could be had for $150 in Galveston. Finally, someone was making money in Texas.

The turning point, the thing that would lead the Spanish government to invite American colonists into Texas, seemingly had nothing to do with cotton, slavery, or Americans. It was an onslaught of attacks by Native Americans. Warriors of the Comanche empire, which sprawled north of Spanish Texas, had raided Texas intermittently for years. But in the winter of 1813, the Comanche launched a blitzkrieg unlike anything seen before. Ranches and farms went up in flames. Families were murdered, women raped. Down in Monterrey, General Arredondo, now military commander for the north, realized he couldn't win a war with the Comanche. He ordered the countryside evacuated.

The Comanche raids were not some Hollywood-style orgy of random bloodlust. The chiefs were skilled politicians who practiced a sophisticated diplomacy to sustain their economy. They despised the

Spanish and had given shelter to several exiled Tejano rebels who had fought with Gutiérrez, including San Antonio's Francisco Ruiz, who lived with them for eight years. Ruiz and other would-be insurgents encouraged the Comanche to conduct their raids, which had the added benefit of bringing in the resource the Comanche sought above all: horses and mules. There was only one thing all those planters in Mississippi and Louisiana needed as much as slaves, and it was horses and mules. American horse buyers opened trading posts on the Red River to swap guns for every animal the Comanche and their Wichita allies herded their way.

Inside two years the Comanche and their allies had stolen seemingly every horse in Texas not protected within a settlement and sold them into Louisiana. With Texas stripped bare, they forged an alliance with the Apache and began raiding below the Rio Grande. Thanks to the thousands of new guns they were receiving as payment, the tribes were able to mount ever larger and more ambitious raids; in 1817, a force of a thousand Comanche and Apache stole ten thousand horses around the town of Refugio in a single raid. A year later, a Tejano trader testified that the Comanche were pushing three thousand horses into Louisiana every month.[5]

When a new governor, Antonio Martínez, arrived in San Antonio, he found the town under virtual siege. Supplies rarely got through. The townspeople were on the verge of starvation. Few of the soldiers left had shoes, horses, or weapons; many had deserted. When Mexico City ordered him to evict the Lafittes from Galveston, all Martínez could do was laugh.

As Spanish colonies from Colombia to Argentina convulsed with revolution, Martínez's plight emboldened the American politicians and adventurers now calling for Texas to be "freed" from Spanish rule. In the mid-1810s, arranging invasions of Spanish colonies emerged as a favorite Washington parlor game. Most of these efforts never got off the ground, but a few did, as with a Mexican revolutionary named Francisco Mina. Over the futile squeaks of the Spanish ambassador, Mina toured Washington and other cities, receiving encouragement from an American general and ships and arms from merchants in New York, Baltimore, and Philadelphia. After mustering on Galveston Island, he landed a few hundred men in Mexico. But, like armchair revolutionaries before and since, he proved a better talker than fighter, and ended up in front of a firing squad.

Eventually someone wearied of all this amateur pussyfooting and simply grabbed a Spanish colony — Andrew Jackson, who got tired of fighting Seminole along the border of Spanish Florida and decided to invade the thing himself in 1818. There was the predictable pearl-clutching in Washington and Madrid, but Spain was in no position to argue, much less take Florida back. Instead it cut a deal, selling Florida to the United States in exchange for a promise from now-president Monroe to recognize Spain's claims to Texas.

This did not go over well in Mississippi and Louisiana, where just about everyone had designs on all that cotton land in Texas. The citizens of Natchez were so incensed they decided to invade Texas themselves, treaties be damned. A couple hundred Southern adventurers, including a shady Louisiana slave trader named Jim Bowie, rallied to the cause. What became known as the Long Expedition — after its commander, James Long — crossed into Texas in June 1819. At Nacogdoches they declared Texas an independent nation, chose a provisional government, and decried "Spanish rapacity" and "odious tyranny." Long promised chunks of land to any man who joined up.

By July, his force had grown to three hundred men. But Long had misread the political winds. A government spokesman, perhaps mindful of the treaty Monroe had just signed, issued a statement reminding everyone this kind of thing was actually, you know, illegal. From Monterrey, Arredondo dispatched a column of 550 men. On its approach, Long and his people turned tail and headed back to Natchez.

As pitiful as its ending, the Long Expedition was nevertheless something like a last straw for poor Antonio Martínez, Texas's embattled governor. If it wasn't whooping Comanche and wild-eyed American invaders, it was Mother Nature; a flood nearly wiped out San Antonio in 1819. In letters to the viceroy in Mexico, Martínez threw his hands up. "From now on," he wrote, "I am not responsible for defending and controlling this province." The people were "so distressed, dejected, and desperate" that he feared they might begin leaving. "And I am in a quandary," Martínez concluded, "because I do not consider that I have a right to stop them."[6]

One month later, as luck would have it, a man on horseback arrived on the outskirts of San Antonio, offering the promise of salvation. His name was Moses Austin.

CHAPTER 2
THE AMERICANS, THEIR COTTON, AND WHO PICKED IT

Nothing is wanted but money, and negros are necessary to make it.
— STEPHEN F. AUSTIN, 1832

The Florida treaty and the failure of the Long Expedition dampened the American clamoring for Texas among newspapers and most politicians. A few diehards, notably Senator Henry Clay, denounced the treaty, but most reluctantly agreed with the expansionist Andrew Jackson, who sighed, "For the present we ought to be content with the Floridas." The thirst for Texas land, however, remained unquenched among Southerners. It only grew after an economic panic in 1819 wiped out hundreds of American businesses and prompted Washington to demand cash up front to buy government land, something few could afford to do.

Fifty-nine years old the day he rode into San Antonio, Moses Austin, like many who would follow him to Texas, was a hard-pressed economic refugee desperate for a new start. The son of an old New England family, ambitious, diligent, and a tad high-strung, Moses was a serial entrepreneur who began his career with a Philadelphia dry goods store before moving to Richmond, Virginia, in 1784 to open a second store. A few years later, spying a new opportunity, he and his brother bought and began working an abandoned lead mine in a remote corner of southwest Virginia. The village that grew up around it is called Austinville to this day.

The mine struggled, the brothers fell out, and once again Moses found himself looking for something new. He found it in distant Missouri, then still a Spanish province, where lead deposits had been discovered. After wrangling a concession from Spanish authorities in 1798, Moses led a group of friends, slaves, and family members, including his wife and two young children, onto a flatboat that, in a calamitous trip marked by disease and drownings, brought them down the Ohio River to southeastern Missouri, where the survivors began settling into new homes near the old French village of Ste. Genevieve.

Here, in what became U.S. territory after

the Louisiana Purchase, the Austins thrived; their mines produced lead that was made into bullets and nails that sold all across the frontier. Moses and the Austins lived in a fine frame mansion they built, called Durham Hall. By 1816, now among the wealthier men in Missouri, Moses joined a group of businessmen who founded the Bank of St. Louis. But in the Panic of 1819, Moses lost everything.

Like many across the frontier, he cast his eyes toward Texas. He had charmed Spanish authorities once and was confident he could do so again with an offer to found a colony for American settlers and farm cotton. In San Antonio he got off to a rough start: Governor Martínez, in fact, ordered him back across the border. Then, as Austin walked in dejection across the main plaza, came one of those serendipitous moments that twinkle across Texas history like stars. He spied a familiar face, someone he had met exactly once, in a Louisiana tavern twenty years before. A man who called himself the Baron de Bastrop.

His real name was Philip Hendrik Nering Bögel. His title was a fake: He had fled the Netherlands after being charged with embezzlement. In San Antonio, Bastrop was poor but respectable and had served as second alcalde, or vice mayor. He persuaded the governor to see Austin again and forward his request to the government in Monterrey to settle three hundred families in Texas. Bastrop also introduced Austin to San Antonio's Tejano elite, including Juan Martín de Veramendi, a prominent merchant and rancher, and Erasmo Seguín, who dabbled in postal work and insurrection.* The Seguín family was destined to play a vital role in Texas history. Seguín's grandparents had immigrated to Mexico from France, and his parents were among the earliest settlers in San Antonio. A cattle rancher, he helped open the first public school in Texas, served as postmaster from 1807 to 1835, and frequently visited the United States to trade animal skins and other goods.

After a bit, Austin decided to return to the United States to await word on his application. The trip, though, nearly killed

* In addition to trading dry goods, Veramendi loaned money to help finance the Lafitte brothers in their piracy enterprise. He also raised cattle, sheep, and goats on a ranch along Cibolo Creek. The son of a Spanish merchant, he was well educated, and he served on the city council and as an officer in the local militia.

him; when a traveling companion disappeared with their mounts, he and another man had to trudge back to Louisiana on foot, barely surviving frigid weather and a panther attack. Austin took to his bed, feverish.

Ironically, it was the man who had single-handedly depopulated Texas eight years earlier, Joaquín de Arredondo, who gave the go-ahead to repopulate it with Americans. He really had no choice. If someone couldn't be plunked down in Texas to ward off the Comanche and their allies, Spain risked losing all its northern provinces. Why not some Americans? As a Mexican commission put it the following year, "It would be an irreparable loss to the Empire if this beautiful Province is lost. In order to save it there remains only one recourse — to populate it."[1]

Moses Austin, however, would not lead the effort. On June 10, 1821, he died in bed in Missouri. As morbid as it sounds, Austin's death was probably one of the best things to ever happen to Anglo Texas. It's doubtful a man of his age and uncertain health could have made his dream of a Texas colony come true. But his replacement, his twenty-seven-year-old son Stephen, could. Stephen F. Austin, who would go down as "the Father of Texas," was a slender, smart, thoughtful man with wavy hair and liquid brown eyes. He was that rare thing, a frontier intellectual, as driven as his father but a loner and a brooder, reserved and prone to depression. After the family business failed, he had washed up in New Orleans, and was planning to study law when his father asked him to help out with his Texas venture. He was in the town of Natchitoches, in fact, when Moses died.

General Arredondo appointed Seguín to oversee Austin's colony and dispatched him and Veramendi to deliver the news. When the two found Stephen Austin in Natchitoches instead of his father, they decided to move forward with their plans anyway. They rode to San Antonio via the Colorado and Brazos river valleys to explore potential areas for the colonists to settle. But while they were looking at real estate, a messenger arrived with momentous news: After years of revolution, Spain had finally lost control of Mexico, which had declared independence. In Mexico City, a general named Agustín de Iturbide was taking over.

At first, independence had little impact on Texas. In San Antonio, Austin found the authorities willing to allow him to take his father's place. Seguín welcomed him into his home, and his family taught him Spanish. When Austin tried to pay for his room and board, Seguín waved away his money. Years later, Austin repaid the favor by taking in Seguín's son, Juan, to teach him English and law.

The people of San Antonio welcomed Austin and his plans because they saw a chance to calm the countryside, and everyone knew that more people meant more commerce, more money. An independent Mexico, they hoped, meant an end to crippling government corruption and considerably more freedom. San Antonians, in fact, seized on the chaos in Mexico City to chart their own course. They welcomed home several insurgents, including Francisco Ruiz.* For the first time in a long time, they

---

* A charming rogue, Ruiz is one of those Tejano players largely forgotten to history, but prized by modern-day Tejano activists and scholars. Born in 1783 to one of San Antonio's wealthiest families, he had been a schoolmaster, soldier, and freedom fighter. Tall, with a goatee and long black hair parted across his forehead, Ruiz moved effortlessly across cultural and political lines, charming those he had doubled-crossed just months before. Soon after returning, he was sent to negotiate a

saw something like hope.

Stephen F. Austin chose to establish his colony away from the Tejano lands, in southeast Texas, in the rich bottomlands west of modern-day Houston, an area stretching from the Gulf of Mexico to today's towns of Brenham, Navasota, and La Grange.* After securing his approvals, Austin returned to Louisiana and placed newspaper advertisements in search of settlers, promising virgin cotton land at bargain prices. By the time he returned to Texas in early 1822, the first hundred settlers had already appeared.

Austin had been back in Texas barely ninety days, however, when his friends in San Antonio passed along devastating news. The new Mexican government had inexplicably put his plans on hold. Settlers could stay for the moment, but Austin was prevented from distributing more land until a

---

peace treaty with the Comanche, Cherokee, and Apache.

* The land Austin chose was far from the Comanche lands in west and northwest Texas. The Spanish let him have it anyway. But they did not allow Americans to colonize the coast, which they considered important for security.

new congress approved it. When Austin asked what he should do, Governor Martínez helpfully suggested he try straightening it out in Mexico City himself.

And so Austin and two companions found themselves riding southwest out of San Antonio in March 1822; it took six weeks to make the two-thousand-mile trip. Austin figured he would need ten to twelve days to clear things up. In fact, it would take a solid year. Some of the delay was the chaos of a new government, some the bureaucratic snafus one might expect, plus another change of government or two. But that wasn't the real problem. Nor, it turned out, was the idea of colonization. Austin discovered that few in Mexico City had any real concerns about admitting American settlers. No, the real problem was something entirely new. The real problem, it turned out, was slavery.

From the beginning, the prospect of American settlements in Texas was entirely dependent on slavery. It was no secret. Everyone knew it. Austin would say it over and over and over: The only reason Americans would come to Texas was to farm cotton, and they would not do that without slaves. They really didn't know any other way.

Slavery hadn't been an issue under Spanish law, which allowed it. Wealthy Tejanos like the Seguíns owned slaves themselves. But slavery would be a problem in the new country of Mexico. As backward as many Americans liked to portray it, the new Mexican government was dedicated to liberal ideals. Equal rights for all races had been the revolution's rallying cry; in a land where 60 percent of the population was of mixed race, this was a powerful message. A new wave of liberal legislators, many committed to liberty and equality for all, thought slavery an abomination. There were only eight thousand slaves left in Mexico anyway. Who really cared if they were set free?

Stephen F. Austin, that's who. Not that you'd know it from most history books. The best biography of Austin devotes fifteen pages to the year he spent lobbying in Mexico City, but of his efforts attempting to make sure his people could keep their slaves, there is but a single sentence.[2] Austin was not some pro-slavery zealot. He belonged to a long line of Southern intellectuals going back to Thomas Jefferson who understood slavery was morally repugnant but who nevertheless owned slaves because it was the best way to make money. In other words, Stephen F. Austin was a sellout, a not-uncommon kind in his day.*

The bizarre thing was that Austin's professed opposition to slavery wasn't based on morality. He detested slavery because he felt its growth would inevitably lead to slave revolts. "The idea of seeing such a country as this overrun by a slave population almost makes me weep," he wrote a cousin in 1830. "It is in vain to tell a North American that the white population will be destroyed some fifty or eighty years hence by the negros, and that his daughters will be violated and Butch[er]ed by them."[3]

In Mexico City, Austin proved a natural and energetic diplomat, perfecting his Spanish as he buttonholed legislators. He drew plenty of allies, including emissaries from another two dozen or so would-be empresarios hoping to bring their own settlers to Texas. The most important, though, were influential Mexican politicians such as the congressional leader Lorenzo de Zavala, a vocal supporter of immigration, and Juan N. Almonte, a savvy military man known for his intellect and discretion. Both de Zavala and Almonte were to play outsized roles in Texas's future.

* One biographer, Gregg Cantrell, terms this "Austin's great moral shortcoming."

By that summer, three colonization bills were working their way through congress. All three gave native Mexicans priority in claiming Texas land — not that any much wanted it — and all insisted that migrants be good Catholics. And all envisioned either the immediate or eventual abolition of slavery. Austin could see he had his work cut out for him. "The principal difficulty is slavery," Austin wrote a friend back home. "This they will not admit."[4]

The man in charge, General Iturbide, spent the fall jailing his enemies and dissolving congress, as despots do. He then reopened it with handpicked legislators and called for a constitutional convention. Texas chose Seguín to serve as its delegate, and he joined Austin in Mexico City to lobby for colonization and slavery. In addition to the three anti-slavery bills, they faced a new threat, a bill that called for freeing slaves within ten years.

"I am trying to have it amended," Austin wrote at one point, "so as to make them slaves for life and their children free at 21, but I do not think I shall succeed." Still, he refused to give up. "I talked to each individual member of the junta of the necessity which existed in Texas . . . for the new colonists to bring their slaves."[5]

66

Iturbide's junta faced a conundrum: Either allow slavery or surrender an empty Texas to the Comanche and, down the line, the seemingly inevitable onrush of American squatters, who were erecting little farms all over East Texas's empty expanses. In the end, Iturbide accepted a compromise, allowing the Americans to bring in their slaves while outlawing the commercial "trade" in slaves; the children of enslaved parents were to be free at fourteen. Austin, exultant, believed his efforts alone had won the day. To those who fretted about the law's restrictions, he insisted it was the best deal possible. "No article of any kind permitting slavery in the Empire would ever have been passed by Congress for a time," he wrote a supporter.[6]

The law passed in early 1823. Shortly afterward, Austin returned north to Texas, his new colony good to go.

One could argue that all this was beside the point. No central government had ever had enough influence in faraway Texas to enforce its laws, and Mexico would prove no different; few if any of Austin's colonists were Catholic, for instance, and no one did a thing about it. But Austin's lobbying efforts were less about reality on the ground than his own advertising. Cotton growers had an awful lot of money invested in slaves, and they depended on supportive laws to protect that investment. Austin was keenly aware that few slave owners would come to Texas if he couldn't guarantee the sanctity of their property, their slaves.

Now that he had, Americans hungry for cotton land streamed into Texas. By the time Austin returned, another thirty-nine families had arrived. By the following summer, Austin had distributed almost all his three hundred land titles; for a modern Texan, tracing one's ancestry to these "Old Three Hundred" families is akin to a New Englander tracing his roots to the *Mayflower.* The Old Three Hundred planted the first cotton, and when it was harvested in the autumn, it was with Black hands. Of the 1,800 people living in Austin's colony in 1825, one in four was enslaved.[7]

Austin was a force of nature in those early days, arranging the first overland shipments of Texas cotton to New Orleans and pestering merchants there and in New York to buy more. He petitioned the government to build a port on Galveston Island, the better to export cotton, and wrote the colony's legal code, which set out slavery laws in detail. Any slave who left a plantation without permission was to be tied up and whipped. A slave who stole was to receive ten to a hundred lashes. Harboring a runaway slave meant a $500 fine; helping one escape was a $1,000 fine. He received permission to begin settling more families.[8]

The colony thrived. But nothing in early Texas was ever easy. The trouble began in 1824. It was Mexico. Again. General Iturbide was overthrown, and his sudden exit prompted a wholesale rethinking of the government. Out went monarchists, conservatives, and those who wanted a strong central government; in came liberals, democrats, and those who sought a weaker one, i.e., federalism. No one knew it at the time, but the concept of federalism would prove a crucial factor in triggering the Texas Revolt.

The new congress passed several measures that gave Austin fits. One outlawed "commerce and traffic in slaves," which was nothing new, but it also stated that any enslaved person brought into Mexico would be deemed free by "the mere act of treading Mexican soil." In San Antonio, the governor promised Austin the law wouldn't be enforced. None of this, however, reassured many prospective colonists.

Austin was deluged with letters from worried would-be immigrants. From a writer in

Mississippi: "Nothing appears at present to prevent a portion of our wealthy planters from emigrating immediately to the province of Texas, but for the uncertainty now prevailing with regard to the subject of slavery." And from Alabama: "Our most valuable inhabitants here own negroes. . . . Our planters are not willing to remove without they can first be assured of their being secured to them by the laws of your Govt."[9] Immigration began to slow. Of the dozen or so other empresarios who tried to establish colonies during this period, all failed. Austin had no answers for those seeking assurances about the safety of their slaves. "At the moment," he wrote in late 1824, "I cannot give them a definitive response."[10]

The question of slavery arose again during debates over a new Mexican constitution. Austin begged Seguín to do everything possible to preserve slavery. Thanks in part to Seguín's lobbying, in fact, the new Constitution of 1824 ended up saying nothing about slavery. Rather, in the new spirit of federalism, it delegated any decision to the states. Texas didn't have enough people to be its own state, so it was merged into the northeastern state of Coahuila. The Coahuila y Tejas capital was the Mexican town of Saltillo, which now became the focus for the slavery debate.

Seguín, for one, was overjoyed, assuring Austin a new state government would be more responsive to their needs than Mexico City. "They will put an end to your problems," he promised. Publicly, Austin agreed, issuing a proclamation promising the new Mexican federalism would ensure the "prospects of Freedom, Happiness, and Prosperity."[11] Privately, he wasn't so sure. It all depended on how an entirely new and unknown group of legislators in backwater Saltillo felt about slavery. For without it, Austin wrote, "we will have nothing but poverty for a long time, perhaps the rest of our lives."[12]

The first test came in 1825, when delegates convened to write a state constitution in Saltillo. The debates over slavery that ensued mirrored those that would consume U.S. politics for the next forty years. Liberals formed a vocal anti-slavery bloc that argued for "the universal rights of men." Tejanos, led by San Antonian José Antonio Navarro, argued that without slavery, Texas would wither and die.*

In June 1826, to Austin's dismay, the

* Navarro, a self-taught lawyer who did legal work for Austin, was among the Anglos' strongest

liberals appeared poised to win. Article 13 of the constitution's final draft read: "The state prohibits absolutely and for all time slavery in all its territory, and slaves that already reside in the state will be free from the day [the constitution becomes law]." The Tejano leaders in San Antonio fired off an exasperated letter to Saltillo, terming Article 13 a "deathblow" and demanding that debate on the measure be halted until Texas could be heard. "Otherwise," one wrote Austin, "all is lost."

This was the true crisis of Texas's first years, though not one that's often emphasized to the state's present-day seventh graders. Austin and his Tejano allies again mobilized their lobbyists, but for Austin, as in 1822, the immediate risk was not actually losing slavery. It was the *appearance* of losing slavery. Immigration would grind to a halt. His settlers would leave. The slaves could revolt.

Furious settlers confronted Austin at every turn. Many in the colony began preparing to leave. Austin could feel everything beginning to slip away. "Fathers tell me that I have reduced their children to a life of

---

defenders. He had served alongside his uncle Francisco Ruiz during the Gutiérrez rebellion.

poverty," Austin fretted. "A weeping widow berates me for having robbed her of her only means of subsistence."[13] In desperation he dispatched his younger brother Brown to Saltillo. "Try and Keep the Slave holders from going until they hear the result of the Slave question," Brown pleaded.

In the end, Austin's lobbyists appeared to win the day with a legalistic compromise. Once again it all came down to money. Legislators feared that if they freed the slaves, the settlers would deluge them with lost-property lawsuits. Texas slaves were worth a half million or so dollars; that was money the rickety state government couldn't repay. But if the government lost the battle, it won the war. Texans were given six more months to bring in slaves, but then no more. Liberals were satisfied. "Because the legislator cannot cut the tether of slavery all at once," one wrote, "he unties it little by little over time, and the march of liberty is no less safe for being slow."[14] The new constitution was made law in early 1827.

In Texas, the panic subsided. But for Austin, the writing was on the adobe. No more slaves meant no more immigrants, or at least far fewer. Austin told colonists it was the best deal they could get, but he would spend the next years doing everything possible to fix the problem.

No sooner did the Coahuilan constitution pass than Saltillo fired another legal shell across the Texas skies. This one introduced a flurry of laws curbing slavery, outlawing the export of pregnant slaves to America, mandating the emancipation of 10 percent of an owner's slaves upon his death, and, most important, ordering a census of Texas slaves to be undertaken every three months. This last regulation was especially ominous because it suggested the government might actually begin enforcing its laws. Austin shot off letters of outrage, but it was no use. The restrictions became law in September 1827.

Austin's Tejano allies told him to ignore the census. He did, and it wasn't enforced. When someone in Mexico City politely inquired why, a Tejano bureaucrat sent along a note from Austin explaining that none of the Americans knew of the requirement because they, um, didn't speak Spanish.

This kind of arrogance wasn't making the American colonists many friends in Mexico. Events in another part of Texas, meanwhile, only made things worse. Over on the Louisiana line, a hothead named Haden Edwards had received permission from Mexico City to settle families around Nacogdoches. When Edwards nailed up notices demanding that all landowners in the area provide proof of ownership or face eviction, skirmishing broke out between settlers new and old. At one point Edwards declared himself head of a new independent nation he grandly dubbed Fredonia. It was a measure of how eagerly Austin sought the Mexican government's favor that when San Antonio dispatched Francisco Ruiz with a column of troops to East Texas, Austin raised a militia to join it. When they got within shouting distance, Edwards fled to Louisiana. Fredonia was no more.

The incident might have been dismissed as seriocomic but for the reaction in Mexico City, where it fed a growing sense of alarm. These Americans, people began saying, weren't just law-breaking whiners. They could be dangerous.

CHAPTER 3
THE AMERICAN MIDDLE
FINGER, EXTENDED

Screw you, we're from Texas.
— RAY WYLIE HUBBARD

By the spring of 1828, Austin's colony had
built a capital of sorts in San Felipe de Austin, a muddy village of forty or fifty houses
along the Brazos River.* It was here that he
convened a group to confront their future.
Those in attendance had achieved a kind of
miracle, in seven years transforming a
corner of the Texas wilderness into cotton
plantations that now annually shipped to
New Orleans a half million bales of cotton.
But without slaves, their children wouldn't
be able to do the same. Without slaves, there
would be few if any more immigrants.
Without slaves, Anglo Texas was doomed.

But what to do? The idea they came up
with that day was a bit of twisted frontier

* San Felipe de Austin is today's San Felipe,
population 838.

76

genius, something that had been kicking around a few years. What if, they reasoned, a slave wasn't technically a slave? What if they called it something else? Say, an indentured servant? Or a really, really loyal servant?

As harebrained as it sounds today, Austin thought it just might work. Each incoming slave would be forced to sign an employment contract with his owner. The slave would be paid twenty dollars a year, and in return could buy his freedom for $1,200, i.e., after sixty years. The catch was, the slave would also be charged for food and housing, making emancipation all but impossible.*

To make the scheme work, they would need the Coahuilan legislature to guarantee that such contracts would be honored in Mexico. Austin sent a proposed bill to the Tejanos in San Antonio, who sent it on to their delegates in Saltillo, José Miguel de Arciniega and José Antonio Navarro. These two must have been real gems. Everyone involved in this scheme realized that the

---

* This practice was not much different from the Mexican peonage system, and Texas landowners would use a similar scam after the Civil War, calling it sharecropping.

legislature would never pass the law if they knew its true purpose. So Navarro and Arciniega came up with an ingenious plan. It must surely go down as one of the sneakier dodges in northeastern Mexican provincial legislative history.

In April 1828, the two rose on the floor of the legislature; at the moment, its members were distracted by a debate over the budget. Almost apologetically, one imagines, Navarro and Arciniega explained that their proposal was intended to benefit a small group of American settlers, "principally those from Ohio." These Ohio people, they explained, had a tradition of hiring men for years at a time. They wouldn't come to Texas unless they were sure the contracts would remain in force. Amazingly, though not a word of this was true, the measure passed.[1]

Austin rushed the news to New Orleans, where a newspaper ran a story announcing the Texas slavery problem had been solved. And for some, it was. Across the South, would-be immigrants began signing up their slaves as indentured servants. A fellow named James Morgan walked into a Florida courthouse and signed his slaves to ninety-nine-year contracts; in return, the men were to be taught "the art and mystery of farming and planting," the women "the art and mystery" of cooking and housekeeping.[2]

But of course, this kind of thing was too clever by half. To many, it just seemed too risky, too complicated. As a result, it did not lead to the river of colonists Austin wanted; what he got was a babbling brook. His mail continued to sag with letters from Southerners seeking guarantees the Mexicans wouldn't free their slaves, and for good reason. Every time Austin turned around, some Mexican politician was pushing another law to ban slavery. When the new Mexican president, Vicente Guerrero, was granted emergency powers to fend off a feeble Spanish invasion attempt, to Austin's horror, he used them to announce that all slaves in Mexico were to be freed.

When the decree arrived in San Antonio, the authorities refused to enforce or even publish it, warning the governor, José María Viesca, of "the fatal consequences that will result." Viesca rallied legislators in Coahuila, one of his allies firing off a letter of protest against "fulfillment of a tyrannical, cruel, illegal and monstrous order." In Texas, panic set in. "In the Name of God what Shall we do?" a Nacogdoches settler wrote Austin. "We are ruind for ever [sic] Should this Measure be adopted."[3]

Guerrero's decree was a turning point. For the first time, some Texians began talking openly of rebellion. The Mexican commander at Nacogdoches overheard insurrectionary chatter and reported it. "Many have announced to me that there will be a revolution if the law takes effect," he wrote a superior. "Austin's colony would be the first to think along these lines. It was formed for slavery, and without it her inhabitants would be nothing."[4]

It wasn't intended as a threat, but no doubt many in the Mexican government took it that way. That December, President Guerrero gave in, exempting Texas from the decree. But the contretemps was to have lasting consequences. In Texas it reinforced the settlers' fervor for federalism, which became a kind of code word for slavery. But the real damage was done in Mexico City, where a line had been crossed. It was one thing for Texians to thumb their noses at the government by blithely ignoring its laws. It was another to threaten armed rebellion.

In the ten years after independence, Mexican politics was a chaotic mess, a blur of elections, coups, and revolts in which emperors, presidents, and generals took turns stumbling through the revolving door of power. Much of it came down to a contest between federalists and centralists. When Guerrero was ousted in 1829, centralists took over. Their ideological leader was the conservative intellectual Lucas Alamán. A cut above the Guerreros and Iturbides of the world, Alamán was not someone to mess with. Deeply skeptical of American power, he wanted to bring Texas, and every other province, under tight central control.

If he needed a pretext, he got it two weeks after taking office. After the Edwards rebellion, a general named Manuel de Mier y Terán had been dispatched to Texas to assess the state of the American settlements. What he saw alarmed him. Outside San Antonio, Mexican officials were almost nowhere to be seen. In southeast Texas the Americans had built a world all their own, bustling villages and plantations and cotton warehouses where the only language one heard was English and no one paid the slightest attention to the government in far-off Mexico City. If the government didn't find a quick way to reassert control over these people, Terán reported in early 1830, it never would. "Either the government occupies Texas *now,*" one official summarized Terán's report, "or it is lost forever."[5]

Alamán seized on Terán's report to push

through congress a game-changing plan for Texas. The law authorized the government to build new military posts and tax offices. To pay for them — the Mexican government was virtually bankrupt throughout this period — new taxes would be placed on cotton. The ban on importing slaves was confirmed, but what became known as the Law of April 6 went even further, banning all American immigration. The border was now officially closed.

Austin, for once, reacted with something like resignation. Always a brooder, it was almost like he was giving up. He fired off the angry letters you'd expect, but his heart clearly wasn't in it. His allies in San Antonio and Saltillo could almost understand; they sensed a conviction in Alamán's orders they hadn't felt before. "I do not know what to tell you," a Tejano friend in San Antonio wrote Austin, "except to agree with your opinion and have the displeasure of informing you that it is now impossible to do anything to counteract the proposed law, which is bound to retard the growth of Texas."[6]

Austin could see now that Mexico City would never allow unfettered slavery. For the first time he allowed himself to believe that maybe Texas could survive without it.

It was during this period, feeling out friends and correspondents, that Austin fretted about the danger that a mushrooming slave population would inevitably revolt and murder its masters. "Satan entered the sacred garden in the shape of a serpent," he wrote at one point, and "if he is allowed to enter Texas in the shape of negros it will share the fate of Eden."[7] Most thought Austin had lost his mind. "Do you believe that cane and cotton can be grown to advantage by a sparce [sic] white population?" a Pennsylvania immigrant asked. "It is impossible!"

It was the only moment in Austin's life where you sense real doubt. Within weeks, though, it passed. To surrender slavery was to surrender Texas, to surrender everything he and the settlers had built. His people, after all, hadn't come to Texas to retire. They had come to make money. "Nothing is wanted but money," Austin wrote in one letter, adding in another, "and negros are necessary to make it."[8]

And then, as fate would have it, the cotton market went into overdrive. Early in 1831, prices in New Orleans and Liverpool began to go up, and would rise steadily for the next four years, reaching fifteen-year highs by 1835. While overall Southern production rose 37 percent during this period, Andrew Torget estimates that Texas production shot up an incredible 600 percent. Higher production in Texas, despite the Mexican government's new laws against immigration, lured a flood of illegal immigrants across a border Mexico was never able to control. In four years, from 1831 to 1835, the population of Texas would more than double, from ten thousand to twenty-one thousand. In the 1820s many Southerners didn't think Texas worth the risk. But when cotton prices soared, it became another story. Americans, still a minority in Texas at this point, were fast on their way to becoming an overwhelming majority.[9]

Let us pause for a moment to consider the irony of a Mexican government determined to stop the flow of illegal American immigrants. You just have to relish it. The only thing missing is a Mexican president promising to build a wall. Of course, to Mexico City there was nothing funny about any of this. In New Orleans, the Mexican consul sent a stream of reports detailing the Americans now streaming toward Texas, many with slaves — uh, contract workers — in tow. (The Texians had taken to calling them "indentures.")

Alamán and his centralist allies, though, weren't fooling around. They were determined to close the border once and for all, and this is where things begin to go seriously downhill. Texians had already come close to rebellion a time or two over slavery, and many, it's clear, never stopped looking for a reason to fight. Alamán would give them plenty. He was poised to introduce a seismic change in government policy, and when combined with the sudden boom in American immigrants, it would put Mexico and the Texians on a course toward war.

It began in October 1830, with the sudden arrival of Mexican soldiers, the first to take up station beside the American colonies. The Trinity and Brazos Rivers served as the main arteries of commerce for the colonists, and the first forty soldiers disembarked at the mouth of the Trinity. They set to work building a fort and a village, Anahuac, on a bluff overlooking Galveston Bay, east of modern Houston. A second outpost was later built at the mouth of the Brazos, at Velasco, today's Surfside Beach. More soldiers arrived in San Antonio, Nacogdoches, and Goliad as well.

For the moment, no one got too worked up. In San Felipe, in fact, Austin was actually satisfied. But then no matter how restrictive the laws, no one worked the Mexican bureaucracy like Austin. Over the years he had wheedled permission to build four more colonies and had managed to exploit a loophole in the Law of April 6 to convince the Mexicans that immigrants headed for an existing colony — i.e., his — would be allowed into the province.*

But Texas was changing. Everyone could

* Even better, after years of his begging them to come, his beloved sister Emily and her husband, James Perry — who had delayed making the move over his concerns about slavery's legitimacy — arrived with their seven children to begin new lives in Texas. Austin, who had lived alone since his brother's passing, intended to live with them in a grand, three-thousand-square-foot mansion he planned to build overlooking Galveston Bay. He began musing about retirement as a gentleman planter. Perry would run everything.

Austin's cousin Henry came with his own family soon after, and with them arrived a young woman with a special place in Stephen's heart, a distant cousin, Mary Austin Holley. Mary was every bit Stephen's intellectual equal, and he was clearly smitten, sitting for hours with her relating stories of Texas for a book she intended to write. They sang and went to dances together, and Mary urged Stephen to lighten up, to "laugh away care."

feel it. For ten years it had been a small place with little Mexican presence. Now, practically overnight, it was becoming a big place with serious in-your-face government authority: tax collectors, forts, and soldiers. There was a time when Austin could have kept things under control. But there were too many newcomers now, people he didn't know, and they were laying out farms all across southeast Texas, a handful with permission, many without. Most had little regard for Mexican authority. While ignoring laws they disliked, Austin and the Old Three Hundred were at least respectful. Some of these new people, many of them racist Southerners, would just as soon punch a Mexican as look at him.

You could see the newcomers' loyalties in the names of the new towns they began founding: Liberty, Columbia, Washington-on-the-Brazos. And the people, the men especially, those who had written "G.T.T." — Gone to Texas — on the homes they left behind, were different. Austin had been careful about the colonists he accepted; many were economic refugees, it's true, but he insisted on men of high character. These new immigrants? Not so much. The truism, in fact, was that any man coming to Texas was running from something, an arrest warrant sometimes, but more often debts. After an Arkansas newspaperman toured Texas, he wrote that everywhere he went, people asked what he had done to force him to Texas. As one professor has put it, "For any man to go to Texas, in those days, meant his moral, mental, and financial dilapidation."*[10]

The crisis, when it came, arrived in two acts. The first opened in October 1831, after a Mexican tax collector arrived at Anahuac with orders to stop illegal immigration and

* Any number of men at the Alamo, as you may know, had questionable pasts. Sam Houston and Davy Crockett were fleeing failed political careers. One of these checkered Texas leaders is Robert Potter, a onetime North Carolina congressman who, upon suspecting that a teenager and a fifty-year-old minister had affairs with his wife, hogtied both men and castrated them. On his release from prison he was elected to the state legislature, only to be expelled for cheating at cards and brandishing a knife and a pistol. Potter came to Texas in 1835, joined forces fighting Santa Anna, and ended up a signer of the Texas Declaration of Independence and later secretary of the Texas Navy. Potter County, up in the Texas Panhandle, is named for him. He ended up getting murdered by his next-door neighbors.

levy customs taxes on all incoming ships. One night that December, three captains tried to run the fort without showing their papers. Shots were fired. A Mexican soldier was wounded. Then, when a governor in Coahuila inexplicably allowed a group of migrants to cross the border and form the town of Liberty, the military governor in Monterrey objected, sending in troops, who broke up the settlement. When the settlers protested, the commandant at Anahuac retaliated by shutting down both ports, freezing commerce, including cotton shipments. The Texians, predictably, went nuts. Austin fired off some of his angriest letters. On December 31, Americans assembled in the community of Brazoria, vowing to oppose this "tyranny." Act one of the crisis passed only when the ports were reopened.

The second act opened weeks later. It revolved around a pair of malcontents at Anahuac, that imperious commandant, who was an American expatriate named Juan (né John) Davis Bradburn, and one of the chest-thumping newcomers, a twenty-two-year-old Alabama lawyer named William Barret Travis. Yes, that Travis. The one destined for history.

The Americans around Anahuac, including a pack of irritable illegal immigrants and those who had lost their land at Liberty, despised Bradburn. Runaway slaves had taken to seeking shelter at his barracks, and rather than return them, Bradburn outraged settlers by keeping them and putting them to work. Some of his soldiers were Black, and that spring a rumor circulated they had raped an American woman. When a settler who had supposedly witnessed the attack refused to give witness, a crowd of angry newcomers tarred and feathered him. Soldiers came to break it up. Punches were thrown, and a few shots were fired in the air.

Outraged, Bradburn blamed Travis and his wingman, a bellicose Georgian named Patrick Jack. Travis and Bradburn had been at it awhile by this point. They had first clashed when a Louisiana slave owner hired Travis to retrieve two runaways from Bradburn; Bradburn told him to get lost. The two had taken to exchanging insults around town. Tensions escalated on May 1 when Travis and Jack helped organize an American militia, even though this was patently illegal under Mexican law. Bradburn arrested Jack, its would-be leader, only to release him a few days later.

Now things got strange. First came a rumor that slave owners were gathering forty miles away on the Louisiana border and were preparing to march on Anahuac and recapture the two runaways. Bradburn put his men on high alert, only to discover the rumor was false. It was then, on a dark and rainy night that May, that "a tall man, wrapped in a big cloak" approached a Mexican sentry and, before melting back into the darkness, handed over two letters for Bradburn. Both warned again of a hundred Louisiana slave owners heading for Anahuac. Bradburn smelled a hoax.

The dark stranger was probably Travis. Bradburn certainly thought so. Days later Mexican soldiers burst into Travis's office and arrested him. When Patrick Jack angrily confronted Bradburn, Bradburn tossed him in the guardhouse too and began making noises about shipping both to Monterrey to face charges of attempting to foment a rebellion. Desperate, Travis tried to smuggle a note to friends urging them to "come and rescue [us] from the claws of thirsty ra[s]cally and convict soldiers."

A group of armed settlers responded, exchanged a few shots with Bradburn's men, then retreated with a pen and paper, drafting a set of resolutions declaring they were only supporting the federalist side in the latest Mexican civil war. As they waited, a Mexican relief force arrived from Nacog-doches and relieved Bradburn of command, defusing the situation. By then, though, Jack's brother had ridden to San Felipe and called for men to attack Anahuac and free the prisoners. Some 160 Texians gathered at Brazoria, loaded three cannon onto a ship, and then sailed down the Brazos intent on attacking Anahuac from the bay.

The Mexican fort at Velasco, at the river's mouth, blocked the way. When it refused to surrender, the Texians attacked, firing cannon from the ship while riflemen disembarked and began sniping at the Mexicans from the fort's unprotected landside. Five Mexicans were killed, seven Texians. The fort surrendered when it ran out of ammunition. The Texians were readying for the attack on Anahuac but called it off at the last minute.

The Battle of Velasco, on June 25, 1832, might have gone down as the first battle of the Texas Revolt. Certainly one would have expected a bloody retaliation. Three weeks later, in fact, a Mexican squadron packed with soldiers appeared offshore. But who should disembark but Stephen F. Austin, followed by the Mexican commander, an old friend. The troops were federalists. The Texians cheered, throwing a "grand ball" to celebrate. At the ball, and for weeks afterward, all anyone wanted to talk about was their new savior, the Mexican general who appeared poised to win the war for the federalists.

His name was Antonio López de Santa Anna. At San Felipe, Austin and the Texians toasted to his victory. Patrick Jack and his belligerent newcomers renamed their militia the Santa Anna Volunteer Company.[11] Santa Anna would save them, people were saying. He would save Texas.

Privately, Austin had his doubts. He had heard things.

Chapter 4
"The President Santana is Friendly to Texas . . ."

The Texians had gotten lucky. Twenty years earlier Mexican cavalry would have ridden in and started executing people. With civil war between centralists and Santa Anna's federalists engulfing Mexico, however, the government dismissed the mini-rebellion as another regional flare-up. For the Texians, though, Anahuac and Velasco demonstrated that the status quo was unsustainable. Something had to be done.

Federalism seemed to offer the answer, holding out the hope of preserving Texas's slave-based economic model. But the state government in Saltillo was no longer a reliable ally, a realization hammered home in April 1832 when anti-slavery legislators passed a law closing the indentured servant loophole. For Austin, this was the last straw. "Texas must be a slave country," he wrote a friend, "circumstances and unavoidable necessity compels it."

The answer, most Texians saw, was to make Texas a state of its own. And so on October 1, 1832, three months after the Battle of Velasco, colonists held a convention in San Felipe to craft a message for Mexico City. The fifty-five Anglo delegates passed several resolutions. The most important, drafted in respectful and deferential language, called for repeal of the Law of April 6, and for statehood. The state government ignored it, sending a letter to San Antonio asking the Tejanos to remind the Americans that this kind of thing was illegal and "represented a disturbance of good order."[1] The Texians, raised under U.S. law, were dismayed, believing this was how democracy worked. Alas, they were playing by American rules on a Mexican field.*

The Texians held a second convention on

---

* Austin's Tejano allies in San Antonio, curiously, were not invited to the convention, even though they favored federalism every bit as much as the Anglos. Austin tried to make up for the slight by writing that his colonists would "harmonize" with the Tejanos going forward. Seguín, Navarro, and four other Tejano leaders drafted a petition to the state legislature condemning the Law of April 6 and defending Anglo immigration as necessary for future prosperity.

April 1, 1833. They repeated their resolutions, this time adding a draft constitution for the new state. Austin, though exhausted by years of grappling with the bureaucracy, volunteered to take them to Mexico City. He had little choice. Angry newcomers were beginning to question his cozy ties with the government. He had been president of the first convention; at the second, delegates replaced him with a fire-breathing newcomer. Slowly, Austin was losing control of his beloved Texas.

As he rode south into Mexico, he sensed what was at stake — either statehood or rebellion. There was "no middle course left," Austin wrote his cousin Henry that April. And while he loathed the idea of war, he knew he would side with his people if it came.[2] The trip to Mexico City, then, amounted to Austin's Hail Mary pass. If he succeeded in gaining statehood, he would retire to life as a gentleman planter. If war came, he wrote, "I will take a hand in that, and enter the ranks as a soldier of Texas."

Reaching the capital, Austin had one solid reason for hope: Santa Anna. This is one of Texas history's great ironies. This, after all, is the man generations of Texas politicians have compared to every loathsome dictator from Adolf Hitler to Saddam Hussein, the

Voldemort of Texas schoolchildren's nightmares, the great Mexican bogeyman, a blood-thirsty killer, a fiendish, mustache-twirling despot guilty of every conceivable crime from mass murder to body odor. Okay, that's overdoing it. But not by much. If Texans could elect a National Villain, and we're a little surprised they haven't tried, it would be Santa Anna hands down. Lee Harvey Oswald couldn't even force a runoff.

Yet few remember today that before Santa Anna was Texas's enemy, he was its friend. He is a singular figure in Mexican history, a man who held the presidency eleven times in twenty-two years. In person he was nothing special, wavy black hair, sallow complexion, a man of breeding and bearing and unswerving confidence. Despite all the bad movies you've seen, he was not flamboyant or a shouter; he was usually the quietest man in the room.

Born into the country's elite criollo class of Mexican-born Spaniards, Santa Anna began his career in 1810 at fifteen by joining the Spanish army. No stranger to Texas, he fought under Arredondo against the Gutiérrez expedition in 1813 and was cited for bravery at the Battle of Medina. He was on hand for the subsequent butchery, which presumably did not repel him. Some, in fact, speculate that Santa Anna modeled his career on Arredondo's.

As he ascended the military ladder, Santa Anna remained loyal to the Spanish government until the last minute, expertly crossing to the rebel side on the eve of Mexican independence in 1821. When troops under his command drove the Spanish out of his native Veracruz, the not-quite-emperor Iturbide made him a general. He was twenty-five. Santa Anna first led his troops in revolt a year later, joining the federalists against Iturbide. When they won, he was given command of the Yucatán. How ambitious was Santa Anna? While there, he moved to invade Spanish Cuba. On his own. He only held off when the Spanish rushed in reinforcements.

Santa Anna took part in another two or three rebellions in the 1820s — you almost lose count — but he made his name repelling that bumbling Spanish invasion in 1829, after which he began calling himself "the Savior of the Motherland" and "the Napoleon of the West." In this latest rebellion, against Lucas Alamán's conservatives, he led the victorious federalists into Mexico City in January 1833, five months before Austin arrived. While he assumed the presidency as a federalist, his real allegiance was to himself; his followers would be known as "Santanistas." The details of governance seemed to bore him; he spent much of his time at his estate outside Veracruz, allowing his number two, a reformer named Valentín Gómez Farías, to run things.

It was Gómez Farías who Austin saw first. If Texas wasn't granted statehood, Austin said, it would organize a state government of its own. Gómez Farías took it as a threat. Both men got angry. Afterward, in a "moment of irritation and impatience," as Austin put it later, he fired off a letter to San Antonio urging Erasmo Seguín to begin laying the groundwork for a state government.

Two weeks later Santa Anna arrived in Mexico City and, as he sometimes did, tried a little governing. He met with Austin twice, and to Austin's surprise, proved the soul of reason. After several hours of debate, Santa Anna agreed to remove restrictions on American immigration, halt tax collection for a year, and give thought to statehood. Austin was impressed. "He speaks very friendly about Texas," he wrote in one letter. "I am of [the] opinion that if you all keep quiet and obey the state laws that the *substance* of all Texas wants will be granted."[3] When Austin headed home on December 10, he was pretty pleased with himself.

What happened next came out of the blue. On January 2, 1834, Austin reached Saltillo, and the next day ducked in to pay his respects to the commanding general, Pedro Lemus. Lemus shook his hand, apologized, and placed him under arrest. Austin was gobsmacked. One imagines him demanding an explanation: "What are the charges?" As Lemus explained, it was the letter he had written to San Antonio, suggesting the Tejanos begin work on a state constitution. A new San Antonio *ayuntamiento,* or town council, had judged it an act of treason, as it kind of was, and forwarded it to officials in Mexico City, who agreed.

Two weeks later, armed guards returned Austin to Mexico City, where he was taken to an aging stone prison on Santo Domingo Plaza and led into cell fifteen, a windowless thirteen-by-sixteen-foot chamber with a skylight high overhead. He was only allowed out for short walks in the prison yard. Guards slipped him meals through a slot in the door. Austin took to feeding his crumbs to a mouse.[4]

By this point, in the spring of 1834, with Santa Anna finally on the stage, the first deadly battle on Texas soil, and momentum seemingly rushing inevitably toward insurrection, you might be expecting a full-blown war to break out, right? Heroic Texians riding against the evil Mexican dictator, right? Well, it doesn't happen.

This is in large part because Austin urged everyone to stay cool. "The people must keep quiet, obey the state authorities and law, harmonise fully with Bexar and Goliad and with the Mexican population," he wrote a friend, "and discountenance all violent men or measures."[5] Santa Anna, meanwhile, actually followed through on his promises, withdrawing government tax collectors from Texas for a year. Then, that April, he had the Coahuilan legislature allow Anglos to buy cheap land from the government, extend several empresario contracts, make English a state language, and even allow trial by jury. Austin was overjoyed, judging that "every evil complained of has been remedied — this fully compensates me for all I have suffered."[6] Statehood, he decided, could wait.

If Austin was thrilled, Santa Anna remained suspicious. Many in Mexico City believed Texas a swarming hive of rebels. To assess the situation, Santa Anna dispatched Austin's old friend Juan Almonte.

Allow us to pause for a moment to tell

you about Almonte, a key cog in Santa Anna's political machine. And because he has a Zelig-like presence throughout our story — you'll see him at the Alamo — he's a good lens through which you can appreciate Mexican perspectives.

In a political world run by light-skinned criollos like Santa Anna, Almonte was mixed-blood and brown, a mestizo, and a bastard to boot, the son of a union between an Indigenous woman and a charismatic warrior priest named José María Morelos y Pavón. When Father Hidalgo rallied Mexicans to arms against the Spanish in 1810, he asked his protégé Morelos to raise an army on the west coast and take Acapulco, which he did. When Hidalgo was captured and executed, Morelos took command of the rebellion; when the rebels formed a provisional government, he was named its first president. Alas, Morelos too was captured and killed when Spain quelled the revolt in 1815.

The rebels employed child soldiers, and Juan Almonte was said to be one, fighting savagely in any number of his father's battles, suffering his first combat wound at the age of ten. Before his death, his father sent him to safety in New Orleans, where he was raised by expatriate Mexican revolutionaries, received a quality education, and learned English. After independence in 1821 he returned to Mexico City, where he was quickly dispatched to Texas as the governor's assistant. In both Mexico and San Antonio his brown skin made him a regular target of racist taunts; one Anglo memorably called him the "copper colonel."[7]

An intensely patriotic nationalist and abolitionist, Almonte survived the political tumult of the 1820s with relative ease, arranging arms shipments while a military attaché in London and only once going briefly into exile in New Orleans, which is saying something given the times. As he crept up the military ladder, he maintained friendships in Texas and New Orleans, making him a natural for the not-quite-secret mission Santa Anna sent him on in 1834.

Officially, he was to perform a statistical survey, but just about everyone realized he was coming to take Texas's temperature. Santa Anna correctly suspected President Andrew Jackson had designs on Texas, and Mexican spies in New Orleans regularly reported on the covetous intrigues of the city's merchants. When Almonte arrived in New Orleans, someone slid him a pair of anonymous letters mailed by someone in

Mexico City that called on wealthy Texas cotton planters to take up arms against the central government. More on this a bit later.

From New Orleans, Almonte was given a tour of the U.S. Army's Fort Jesup, near the border, which Santa Anna suspected would be the staging area for any invasion. Almonte was relieved to find a drowsy backwoods base holding barely three hundred men and six artillery pieces. But with no Mexican soldiers stationed along it, the border alarmed him. It was wide open, Americans pouring across at will. Almonte would later recommend trying to settle free American Black people along it or giving land grants to the Creek or Choctaw to form a kind of buffer zone.

At Nacogdoches, he was relieved to find no signs of rebellious sentiment. The settlers seemed far less concerned with Mexican politics than basic government services and protection from occasional Indian raids, land swindlers, and smugglers. If Mexico could just guard the border and provide basic protections, Almonte wrote Santa Anna, Texas should be fine. There were troublemakers, it was true, but not many, although if Mexico couldn't protect the people, they might find fertile ground for some kind of revolt.

What horrified Almonte were the abuses rooted in slavery, including an influx of illegal African slaves imported from Cuba. He wasn't the only traveler so startled. In San Felipe, as he prepared to return to Mexico, Almonte found a sympathetic ear in the form of another voice in Texas affairs, a Baltimore abolitionist and writer named Benjamin Lundy. A vocal critic of Southern designs on Texas, Lundy was on his way to Mexico City to seek approval for a plan to settle free Black people in the Mexican state of Tamaulipas, where slavery was outlawed.

The report Almonte wrote for Santa Anna is regarded as the most comprehensive description made of early Texas. In it, he worried that a rebellion would probably draw U.S. troops across the border. It was Santa Anna's nightmare scenario. But Almonte cautioned it needn't happen. Give the Texans statehood, he advised, curtail immigration, send in troops, and work to integrate the existing Americans into Mexican society. Texas could be saved. Almonte also weighed in on Austin's imprisonment, advising Santa Anna that Austin's release might tamp down any rebel sentiments.

It was enough. After a year in prison, Austin was freed on Christmas Day 1834. Until his case could be resolved, he remained in the capital. That spring, when he met one last time with Santa Anna, the generalissimo assured him of the government's goodwill toward the Anglo Texans. Austin urged him to visit. "He is very friendly to Texas," Austin wrote a friend, "and it would be an advantage to that country if he would pay it a visit."[8]

These words were written ten months before the Battle of the Alamo, suggesting how out of touch Austin had grown after his time away, and how swiftly things were changing. But in fairness, few saw what was coming.

As 1835 dawned, Texas had been calm for two and a half years. Santa Anna was giving the Americans almost everything they wanted. The borders were now wide open, and cotton shipments were at record levels. Though many were uneasy that the government remained philosophically opposed to slavery, most Texians were satisfied. As long as Santa Anna remained committed to federalism, the planters were confident he would stay out of their hair.

The trouble actually began before Austin headed home. Santa Anna had spent much of early 1834 at his estate in Veracruz while his second-in-command, Valentín Gómez Farías, passed a series of liberal reforms aimed at corralling the power of the church and the military. But as the year wore on, conservatives felt the reforms were going too far. Contrary to myth, Santa Anna was not some bloody tyrant, nor even a dictator; that would come later. At this point, he was an astute politician who needed the support of congress, the church, the military, and the people, and thus remained keenly alert to ripples in the Mexican political pond.

Santa Anna warned that Gómez Farías's reforms were moving too fast, but congress ignored him. A group of influential conservatives called for the reversal of reforms and asked for Santa Anna alone to be given the power to do it. Whether he orchestrated all this or simply surfed the political wave — his biographers appear divided — Santa Anna accepted his new powers and moved forcefully to dismiss Gómez Farías, reverse his reforms, and dissolve congress. Allies urged him to declare himself dictator. Santa Anna demurred. He had all the power he needed.

By January 1835, federalism was all but dead, which put local governments across Mexico, including Texas, on edge. When the Mexican congress passed a law banning state militias, one of the most liberal state governments, in the mountainous central province of Zacatecas, rose in revolt. Santa Anna took four army divisions and easily routed the defending force. He then stood by as his soldiers embarked on a daylong orgy of rape and plunder.

If this was intended as a message to other provincial governments, not everyone was listening. No sooner was Zacatecas sacked than trouble erupted in Coahuila. Since Santa Anna had reopened the American border a year earlier, the state government had descended into a cesspool of corruption as the government put thousands of leagues of state-owned land up for sale. All manner of promoters and speculators, both Mexican and American, flocked to Saltillo to grab what they could, often with the help of bribes. The governor and his rivals inevitably began fighting over the spoils, until something like a little civil war broke out. When one side tried to establish a second state capital, Santa Anna decreed they would do no such thing. The state legislature passed a measure boldly telling the generalissimo to mind his own business. Bad move.

Santa Anna sent in his brother-in-law, a callow young general named Martín Perfecto de Cos, to reestablish order. As Cos and his troops approached in April 1835, the governor and his cronies began packing, thinking they would reestablish the state government at San Antonio. Across the Rio Grande, Texians began exchanging nervous glances.

If you're like many casual students of Texas history, you may believe, as we did, that the American colonists more or less instigated the secessionist revolt that led to what happened at the Alamo. And while yeah, they kind of did, they actually weren't the first Texians to raise arms against Santa Anna. That honor belongs to the criminally overlooked Tejanos of San Antonio and South Texas. To this day, in fact, you can find a historian or three who will argue it was the Tejanos who really started the Texas Revolt; the Anglos simply piled on a little later.

Why the Tejanos of yore matter today is that the decisions they made in the 1830s would have profound repercussions for their descendants. By the time Santa Anna rose to power, there were maybe five thousand Tejanos in Texas, most in and around San Antonio, the rest scattered along the coastal plains and the Rio Grande Valley. Many could trace their roots to the founding of the first Spanish mission in San Antonio a century earlier, in 1718, and the formation of the actual town in 1731. Tejano society was diverse but highly stratified, an upper crust of ethnic Spaniard criollo families governing lower-caste mestizos, Native Americans, and a smattering of European adventurers and exiles. Most grew up in constant fear of Native American attack. Many were seasoned fighters as a result.

They were also, at least in Mexico City's eyes, chronic malcontents, a remote, hard-pressed outpost always pestering the government for food and protection. What they got instead was higher taxes and micro-management. By the 1830s, what San Antonio wanted most was just to be left alone, which made them ardent federalists. All in all, the arrival of the Americans had been good for Tejanos, especially moneyed families like the Seguíns and Navarros. Austin's people mostly stayed over in southeast Texas with their slaves, which didn't bother the Tejanos a bit.

The Tejanos, as we've seen, became Austin's reliable allies, mostly because it was profitable. The two even did a little business, the slyest bit a real estate dodge the Tejanos perfected. Because the government limited how much land the Americans could buy, Tejano brokers sprang up, buying tens of thousands of acres they resold to Americans. When Mexico City objected, the Tejanos ignored it.

By the fall of 1834, the most visible Tejano leader was twenty-eight-year-old Juan Seguín, Erasmo's son. Lean, handsome, and more than a little dashing, Seguín was destined to become the true tragic hero of early Texas. He married at nineteen and eventually fathered ten children. After helping his parents run the San Antonio post office, he was elected to the city council in 1828, and then alcalde in 1833. When the area's political chief fell ill the following year, Seguín took his place for a time.

Like most of those in the old San Antonio families, Seguín was a liberal federalist who loved Mexico but loathed the authoritarian impulse Santa Anna represented. He was also not the kind of leader to sit on the couch during troubled times. His first move, acting as interim political chief in October 1834, had been to call for a statewide convention to reexamine the issue of splitting off from Coahuila to form a new state. It was met by a crashing silence, from Tejanos and Anglos alike. Irked, Seguín sat and simmered, waiting for the right moment.

Six months later, in April 1835, it seemed to come. When the Coahuilan governor called for help against the approaching General Cos, Seguín was asked to lead a San Antonio–area militia — 150 Tejanos and twenty-five Anglos, including Jim Bowie. These were actually the first Texas troops to raise arms against Santa Anna. Seguín rode with them to Coahuila, just in time to watch the governor surrender. Disgusted, most returned to San Antonio in June, determined to take the fight to Santa Anna in Texas.

The Mexican colonel in charge of the San Antonio garrison, suspicious of Seguín, ordered two men to watch him at all times. Quietly, Seguín sent a message to San Felipe to see if the Americans were ready to join him in revolt. The answer: nope. As Seguín wrote in his memoir years later, "We were apprised that there was a great deal of talk about a revolution, in public meetings, but that the moment for an armed movement was still remote."[9]

And to most in Texas, it was. But not to everyone.

As fate would have it, some of Seguín's men managed to get arrested in Coahuila. One was a future hero of the Alamo, Jim Bowie.

We'll tell you more about him later, but suffice it to say, Bowie was a seasoned swindler, always on the make, a man who fled to Texas rather than face the consequences of a series of land frauds he had attempted back in Arkansas and Louisiana. In Coahuila, Bowie managed to bribe his way to a massive land grant, only to have Santa Anna annul all such sales. It was at this point that he started badgering folks to try to take Santa Anna down. The Mexican crackdown made a deep impression on Bowie, who was taken with other prisoners to a jail in Matamoros. He became convinced Cos was about to invade Texas to reassert government control. In June, he managed to escape, riding a horse north across the Rio Grande, and, like a latter-day Paul Revere, proceeded to spread the alarm.

As Bowie raced into Texas, a Mexican court finally allowed Stephen F. Austin to return home as well. He sailed from Veracruz on July 23, 1835, for New Orleans. Maybe it was all that time alone in a prison cell. Maybe it was the new and unsettling news from Texas. No doubt Santa Anna's grasp for power contributed. But by the time he reached Louisiana, Austin had undergone a profound change of heart. For the first time he began musing about Texas somehow separating from Mexico. "A gentle breeze shakes off a ripe peach," he wrote a cousin. "Can it be supposed that the violent political convulsions of Mexico will not shake off Texas as soon as it is ripe enough to fall[?]"[10]

Truer words were seldom written. On August 25, with both Jim Bowie and Juan Seguín already agitating for a revolution, Austin embarked on the schooner *San Felipe* for his return to Texas. It was an uneventful voyage until the ship neared the mouth of the Brazos, when the sound of gunshots rang out across the water. On deck, Austin could see a Mexican schooner and a pair of small Texas ships. They were firing on each other. It was beginning.

CHAPTER 5
THE WAR DOGS

After Austin's arrest, no one had seemed to know what to do; at least at first, no one filled the leadership vacuum. One or two hotheads urged Texas town councils to draft calls for statehood, and while a few did, the issue appeared moot. The big cotton planters, meanwhile, wanted little to do with anything that would upset the apple cart. They were making too much money. Unless Santa Anna marched in and began taking their slaves, most Texians did not feel strongly about statehood, much less insurrection.

Other than Juan Seguín, among the few who backed the idea was the same little group of angry young men who had been bitching about the Mexican government for years. Later they would be known as the War Party, or the War Dogs. They had little in the way of public support; one history puts their number at barely two dozen. A century ago the first significant Texas historian, Eugene C. Barker, thought the group even smaller, maybe a dozen malcontents in all.

They were mostly young bachelors, passionately pro-slavery Southerners deeply suspicious of seemingly all authority, Mexican or Anglo. Several were lawyers. Most, like Jim Bowie, were involved in land speculation. The loudest and most persistent of the embryonic War Dogs, though, was young William Barret Travis. If ever a man could be said to have single-handedly started the Texas Revolt, it was the histrionic, melodramatic, oversexed, underprincipled "Buck" Travis. A lawyer raised in small-town Alabama, Travis represented a certain type of "elite" frontier Southerner, bright, well-read, and hugely ambitious, yet haughty, humorless, and quick to take offense, the kind of man you'd expect to see challenge someone to a duel. More than one modern observer has suggested he was a classic victim of what Mark Twain called "Sir Walter disease," that is, the social code of chivalry, formality, and ornate speechifying found in Walter Scott's novels such as *Ivanhoe* that proved wildly popular in the antebellum South and probably inspired many of its social mores.

Travis was young, even for the times, all of twenty-one when he arrived in Texas in 1831, twenty-five when things got busy in 1835; at the Alamo, he was barely half the age of Jim Bowie and Davy Crockett. He had a big chip on his shoulder, some of it his prickly personality, much of it the result of the events that brought him to Texas as a fugitive. We have no photos of Travis, but contemporaries describe him as of medium height, with reddish-brown hair and sideburns framing a full face.*

By nineteen, he not only had hung out his own shingle but had started an Alabama newspaper, the *Claiborne Herald.* Neither venture thrived. By that point Travis had a teenaged wife, Rosanna, a baby, another on the way, and several slaves to feed. His debts mounted. It's a measure of his low esteem in Claiborne that the man with whom he "read the law" came forward to prosecute his debts.

* While researching this book, coauthor Chris Tomlinson learned that Travis was his great-great-grandmother's cousin and that they grew up together in Alabama. That Travis's physical description approximates Tomlinson's when he was a similar age is deeply disturbing to the Tomlinson household.

Like many Southern men who faced reversals in those years, he thought of Texas. Travis slipped out of Claiborne in the spring of 1831, promising his wife he would return for her once he could repay his debts. He never would. He reached San Felipe in six weeks and found legal work within days. His first clients, as fate would have it, were War Dogs: Frank Johnson and the Jack brothers, who shared Travis's evident distaste for the Mexican government. He opened a law office in Anahuac, where he crossed Juan Bradburn and ended up in 1832, barely a year after arriving in Texas, playing a leading role in the Anahuac "disturbances" that climaxed in the Battle of Velasco.

There's one more thing to keep in mind about Travis, and it's a little speculative. He kept a diary in which, among other things, he listed his sexual dalliances, of which there were many. "I fucked the fifty-sixth woman in my life," he wrote on September 26, 1833.[1] For this, Travis apparently earned a nasty case of venereal disease, probably syphilis. The only treatment at the time was liquid mercury, sometimes taken as a blue pill, and we know Travis took it. Mercury's side effects ranged from tremors and bloody diarrhea to emotional instability and irritability. Travis was certainly high-strung; in one memorable court appearance, he pulled a knife on an opposing attorney. Could mercury poisoning explain such behavior? Maybe. Maybe not. We'll probably never know.*

What we do know is that, during Austin's time in prison, Travis had emerged as probably the loudest, angriest voice in Texas, intent on driving the Mexicans out of his adopted home. When Seguín called for a convention to consider statehood in October 1834, a few towns responded, but most ignored him. Travis was disgusted. "Public opinion runs so high against any change that I doubt whether anything can be done towards an organization of Texas at this time," he wrote a fellow War Dog. "As long as people are prosperous they do not desire a change."2

There matters lay until January 1835, when the Mexican government finally re-opened its customs houses at Anahuac and Velasco. This time the Mexicans were very serious and very well armed; naval schooners cruised offshore, alert for smugglers, of

* As we say, this is speculative. There is but a single reference to venereal disease in Travis's diary, though several about buying mercury.

which there were many. The tax collectors were zealous and thought little of impounding goods and even entire ships until the appropriate tax was paid.

Several of Travis's clients had goods impounded, and he wanted to strike back. To him, this was tyranny. But he was torn. This was in May, when Austin remained in Mexico. Attacking soldiers, or even calling for resistance, could be held against Austin. But Travis couldn't help himself. He called for resistance "to the oppressions of a govt. that seems determined to destroy, to smash & to ruin us," he wrote a friend, terming Santa Anna's "a *plundering* robbing, autocratical, aristocratical jumbled up govt. which is in fact no govt. at all — one day a republic — one day a fanatical heptarchy, the next a military despotism — then a mixture of the evil qualities of all."*[3] Reading his letters, you get the real sense of a man chomping at the bit.

And in short order, he found his excuse to act. Two messages arrived from Mexico.

* We had to look up "heptarchy." The dictionary calls it a "government by seven rulers." Not quite sure what Travis was going for here, but as one of our grandfathers used to say, that's a real hundred-dollar word.

The first, some hotheads seized from a courier dispatched by General Cos; they suggested Santa Anna was sending soldiers into Texas, as in fact he was. A few nights later a letter from Bowie arrived; it warned, prematurely, of three thousand soldiers already heading into Texas. In Travis's fevered mind, Texas was on the verge of an invasion. There was no time to lose.

After a gathering of locals in San Felipe approved his plan, it was decided they would attack Anahuac. Travis and a group of twenty men loaded cannon onto a friendly ship and on June 28 crossed Galveston Bay and disembarked there. When the Mexican commander sent a note asking his intentions, Travis demanded his surrender. They met on the shore under a bright moon. Travis gave the commander fifteen minutes to respond or, he swore, he would kill every man. The Mexicans surrendered. Exultant, Travis put them on his ship and took them back to the new town of Harrisburg, inside modern Houston's city limits.

Travis, it turns out, was way out over his skis; Texians were aghast. A number of locals denounced him. One of Travis's opponents suggested he be arrested. Travis was floored. He issued a notice to the Brazoria paper asking everyone to calm down until he could explain himself. "The people are much divided here," he wrote Bowie, who had last been seen heading for Nacogdoches. "Unless we could be united, had we better not settle down and be quiet for a while."[4]

Much the same happened to Bowie, who reached Nacogdoches a few days after the Anahuac attack. Alarmed by his warning of an imminent invasion, a hundred men gathered in the city square, elected Bowie their "colonel," and broke into a Mexican arms warehouse, emerging with armloads of muskets. And then: nothing. If Bowie thought Texas on the verge of revolution, like Travis, he was mistaken. Even when he too managed to seize a Mexican courier's orders, which included hints of the coming troops, the townspeople yawned. Bowie, irked, rode off to pursue business ventures in Louisiana and Mississippi until things blew over.

In their wake, he and Travis left a group of prominent planters and businessmen stunned at the turn of events. Members of this "Peace Party," as it was sometimes called, slipped the Mexican authorities in San Antonio a list of the troublemakers' names, including those of Travis and other rabble-rousers. "Till they are dealt with," one wrote another on July 25, "Texas will never be quiet."[5]

So true. And that's when it happened. On August 1, 1835, General Cos issued an arrest order for Travis and others who had taken part in the Anahuac attack, terming him "the ungrateful and bad citizen W. B. Travis who headed the revolutionary party," adding, "He ought to have been punished long since."

It was then, during the months of August and September, that the most extraordinary thing occurred. As news of the arrest order raced from town to town, people reacted with outrage — not at Travis now, but at the Mexicans. Travis's actions may have been impetuous and unprovoked, but few Texians, it turns out, were willing to hand over a fellow American, even one as deluded as Travis, to be executed by the Mexican government. This, coupled with rumors of a coming invasion, spurred public meetings in town after town. On August 15, the War Dog William H. Wharton chaired one at Columbia that called for a "consultation" of all Texas citizens at Washington-on-the-Brazos on October 15. Its aim was to secure peace if peace was achievable, and prepare Texas for war if it wasn't.

A natural question on everyone's lips was how Austin felt. He had been greeted warmly on his return. At a gala ball in Brazoria, Austin stopped short of calling for rebellion, instead endorsing the October "consultation." But as invasion rumors flew, his mood darkened. A week later, he learned that Cos and his troops had boarded ships to arrest Travis and his fellow troublemakers.

This set off all manner of wild rumors. Austin fired off a letter to the War Dogs in Columbus claiming the "real object" of Cos's move was "to destroy and break up the foreign settlements in Texas." This was far from true, but it didn't matter. War fever was sweeping Texas, and Austin got caught up in it. "Conciliatory measures with Gen Cos and the military at [San Antonio] are hopeless," he wrote. "WAR is our only resource."[6]

And that was all it took. A call to arms went out, electrifying the colony. An army was to be raised.

In San Antonio, the Seguíns and the Navarros were preparing for the town's Diez y Seis de Septiembre celebration of Mexican independence. Erasmo Seguín, José Antonio Navarro, and his brother Ángel were in charge of organizing floats for the parade, while Juan Seguín helped with the dance in the town's Plaza de Armas, where Comandante Domingo de Ugartechea awaited Cos's arrival.

Throughout the preparations, the Tejano elites conferred on politics and next steps. They feared Santa Anna would become a centralist dictator if left unchecked, but should they join the Anglos? Seguín, Navarro, and the others wanted autonomy just as badly as the Texians, but they wanted it as part of Mexico. They dreamed of a nation where the Anglos called themselves *mexicanos* with pride. But they also understood that economic prosperity could only come from closer relations with the United States.

Austin understood this tension, and in his letters to Tejanos in San Antonio suggested that everyone unite to defend the federalist Constitution of 1824. He convinced his Tejano correspondents that his goal was merely to help the republic reach its potential, not to secede from Mexico. He was not completely forthcoming about his intentions to his old friends.[7]

On September 20, the day after the call to arms, Cos and five hundred troops landed at Copano, north of modern-day Corpus

Christi. To Cos, and to generations of Mexicans since, his mission was a matter of justice, of arresting Travis and the War Dogs who had attacked Anahuac without cause. But to Texians, it was an invasion. As Cos headed inland toward San Antonio, 150 miles north, men across the colonies grabbed their guns.

Cos knew what he was walking into. He sent word ahead to San Antonio that he wanted all available arms seized, especially cannon. The nearest cannon in American hands was at Gonzales, seventy miles east; it had been given to the town to ward off Comanche attacks years earlier. Ugartechea sent a squad to fetch it, but the American alcalde refused to hand it over, then buried it. On October 1, a Mexican force of two hundred arrived, upping the ante. Texas militiamen, smelling a fight, were already pouring into Gonzales. There was a lot of yelling back and forth. Some smart-aleck American made a flag with a picture of the cannon and the words "Come and Take It." Thus was born the Texas T-shirt industry; to this day, it's hard to spend a half hour in Dallas or Houston without seeing a "Come and Take It" tee.

The next morning the Texians opened fire, and the Mexican commander, after politely asking why he was being attacked, headed back to San Antonio. Ugartechea sent an equally polite letter to Austin asking for the cannon. A few days later General Cos and his men arrived, bringing the number of Mexican troops to eight hundred. The Mexicans then retreated to San Antonio. As word spread of their "victory" at Gonzales, Texas gunmen began swarming the countryside. The Mexicans in San Antonio found themselves in a de facto siege.

The Tejanos, meanwhile, found themselves in a bind. When Ugartechea asked the Navarros and the Seguíns to open their homes to Cos and his officers, they declined. But neither did Navarro throw his support behind the Texians, instead telling the people of San Antonio that the Anglos appeared to be the aggressors. Young Juan Seguín, on the other hand, rode off to join the Anglos.[8]

Named to lead the aborning Texian army, Austin joined the men gathering at Gonzales. He knew little about running a military campaign, but he remained an important symbol. A few hundred militiamen were camped around the town on October 11 when Austin arrived to cheers and shouts of "On to San Antonio!" More joined every day. Austin, while working furiously to form some sort of unity government, decided to move decisively. The next day he led his motley troops out of Gonzales and up the river road, toward San Antonio.

It was slow going, as new groups arrived each day. Travis rode in from San Felipe, Jim Bowie too. On October 17, after some shots were exchanged with Mexican scouts, Austin sent a message to General Cos offering to negotiate peace. Cos told him to get lost. His confidence was actually rising. More Mexican troops were trickling into town every day. But Austin's forces were also growing. Seguín raised a company of Tejanos; Austin made him a captain.

By this point bickering had broken out in the Texian camp. The Consultation, already delayed once, was to be held in a week, and half the men wanted to disband and attend; the rest wanted to attack San Antonio. On October 25, Austin gathered his officers to decide what to do.

There was a new face around the campfire that evening: Sam Houston, who had wobbled into camp on a tiny yellow stallion. Everyone knew Houston's tale of woe, if not the man himself. He was hands down the most famous person in Texas, a politician once considered so gifted that, had he not blown up so spectacularly, he might have reached the White House. Instead, he ended up a blackout drunk living with the Cherokee in what is now Oklahoma.

Born in Virginia in 1793, the same year as Austin, Houston grew up in frontier Tennessee. No fan of working the family farm, he ran away to live with a Cherokee family at sixteen. He later joined the army and was severely wounded during the Creek War while serving under Andrew Jackson, who became his mentor. After the army, he became a lawyer, got himself named Tennessee's solicitor general, and was then elected to Congress in 1823. With Jackson's backing, he was elected governor in 1827.

He was a rising star on the national stage. People whispered he might succeed Jackson as president. But then, in 1829, he married a plantation owner's daughter named Eliza Allen. Weeks later she left him — apparently for another man — and Houston fell apart. He resigned as governor and decamped to live with Cherokee friends in Oklahoma. He never again talked about what had happened.

With the Cherokee, Houston drank so heavily he acquired the nickname "Big Drunk." In time, he recovered his senses, married a Cherokee woman, and began representing the tribe in dealings with

Washington. After three years, his ambitions once more began to stir. His logical move, as disgraced men as varied as Travis and Bowie had learned, was to Texas, the place everyone went to start their second act. One of the War Dogs invited him; a pal in New York offered money for land. Houston crossed into Texas in December 1832, settling in Nacogdoches, where he opened a law office.

He was thirty-eight now, a big man, well over six feet, with a Roman nose and a billboard forehead. His arrival in Texas was the source of some speculation. Given his relationship with President Jackson, with whom he kept up a correspondence, some thought him a spy, perhaps intent on fomenting rebellion. For the most part, Houston kept his head down that first year or two. Mostly, he seemed to be waiting. For what he wouldn't say, although friends thought they knew. Upon leaving the Cherokee, one had given him a razor. "I except [sic] your gift," Houston famously replied, "and mark my words, if I have luck this razor will some day shave the chin of a president of a republic."

That night in Austin's camp, several officers argued that they should attend the Consultation. Others argued for an advance on San Antonio. Houston, who had left Nacogdoches to take part in the Consultation, made a speech too. His words are lost to history, but he apparently urged caution. He had little regard for the War Dogs. And he couldn't see routing Mexican regulars in fortified positions without more artillery. To him, storming San Antonio seemed like suicide.

In hindsight, the gathering that night could be viewed as the first hint of a baton's passing, of Texas leadership ebbing from Austin and flowing toward Houston. For now, Austin remained in charge, but he was in a bind. His men were undertrained and outnumbered, facing professional troops with plenty of big cannon. Worse, most of the militiamen had only signed on for two months. If the Texian "army" didn't attack now, there might not be an army by Christmas. Austin decided to allow a few dozen men to attend the Consultation. He kept the rest. With a little pressure, he might persuade Cos to return to Mexico.

Austin sent Bowie, Seguín, and a man named James W. Fannin Jr., a slave trader who had trained at West Point, with ninety men, including thirty-two Tejanos, to find a campsite closer to San Antonio. They found one at the abandoned Mission Concepción, on a wooded bend of the San Antonio River three miles outside town. Against Austin's directive, the group stayed there overnight.

At dawn, amid a thick fog, a guard heard the sound of troops approaching. A flurry of shots was exchanged. The Texians took up positions, Bowie lying on the riverbank. Through the fog, he could just make out the ghostly outlines of Mexican horsemen. They were coming.

CHAPTER 6
SAN ANTONIO

"Keep under cover, boys, and reserve your fire. We haven't a man to spare," Jim Bowie shouted.[1]

The Texians were in a bad spot in the fog at Concepción that morning. For two hours the Mexican forces, four hundred strong, crept into positions encircling Bowie's men. When the fog lifted, the Mexican artillery opened fire and the infantry charged. The rebels, many of them lying flat behind fallen trees and brush, fired accurately, picking off several men. The Mexicans fell back, but in the next half hour charged twice more, before a bugle sounded retreat. The Mexican force then withdrew.*

The sharp little fight at Concepción that morning had lasting consequences. While General Cos's army could easily rout the

---

* The Mexicans suffered at least fourteen dead and thirty-nine wounded. One Texian was killed.

Texians in a set-piece battle, the insurgents' guerrilla tactics and especially their excellent long-range riflery convinced him he couldn't get one; from here on, Cos and his men mostly stayed bottled up in San Antonio.

In the next week, reinforced by two hundred volunteers from Nacogdoches, sixty Tejano militiamen from surrounding towns, and three artillery pieces, Austin slung a loose cordon around the town. Cos and his soldiers were hunkered down in fortified positions. If things got nasty, he could withdraw to an old Spanish mission four hundred yards east of town, the Alamo, a massive compound lined with high stone walls. In the American camp, a few firebrands argued for an immediate assault, but most, including Austin and Bowie, demurred. It was the original Mexican standoff.

Volunteer militias, alas, don't do well in sieges. They get bored, they gripe, they pine for home. Within days, many of Austin's men began to leave. Seguín and the Tejanos hung on; they were fighting for their hometown. When Cos learned that Seguín was among the rebels, he forced his father, Erasmo, to leave San Antonio. The old rebel went to his ranch and ordered his vaqueros to herd cattle to the rebel camp. He also sent along some weapons.

So what to do? This was a volunteer army, and in the 1800s that meant that tough decisions were often put to a vote. After Bowie left in a huff, the army of five hundred men decided to stay with Austin and besiege San Antonio.

The consultation, and the weeks that followed, brought profound changes to the Texian war effort. They formed a provisional government, and its most important job was funding and peopling the army. To this point, almost all the men at San Antonio were volunteers. Sam Houston, after a determined lobbying effort, was elected chief of a "regular" Texas army, that is, the state's official army. The problem was that there was no regular army. Despite pleas from just about everyone associated with leadership, just about no one was signing up. Most Texians and Tejanos had farms and businesses to run; they didn't need jobs as soldiers. Most hadn't asked for this fight anyway.

The government's calls for men were met with enthusiasm outside Texas, however, especially in the South, where hundreds of idle young men thought shooting Mexicans sounded like the adventure of a lifetime, especially with the promise of decent pay and a few hundred acres of land thrown in. As one particularly effusive columnist urged:

> Now is the moment for all young men, who want to create a name, and make a fortune, to bestir themselves. Go to Texas. Enroll yourselves in the brave army. . . . A splendid country is before you. You fight for a soil and a name that will become your own. . . . Texas must soon become the second great republic.[2]

Some rode in across Louisiana or Arkansas; others gathered at New Orleans and sailed to Galveston. Still others formed militias. From Mississippi came the Natchez Mustangs, from St. Louis the Missouri Invincibles, from Alabama the Huntsville Rovers and Mobile Greys. One of the most prominent groups was the New Orleans Greys, 120 or so men who made it to San Antonio in November.

This was all, of course, blatantly illegal, a violation of U.S. neutrality laws, not that anyone listened to the complaints of Mexican ambassadors. So too was the war's financing, a collection of loans the provisional government arranged from big New

Orleans cotton importers secured by thousands of acres of Texas land.

The Consultation signaled an end to Austin's time on the battlefield. It elected him one of three commissioners to be dispatched to the United States to raise more money and support — an honor, to be sure, but a nudge off his perch atop the largest grouping of Texian troops. The decision made sense — Austin's talents were certainly of more use in diplomacy than battle — but it stung nevertheless.

Okay, so now that the revolt is under way, let's take a breath and consider what's really going on here. By this point, we can safely set aside some of the hoariest Texas myths. Santa Anna was not some blood-thirsty tyrant; in fact, he had given the colonists almost everything they wanted short of guaranteeing the sanctity of their slaves. The Americans were free men and women, by no means "oppressed," and thanks to Santa Anna, possessed of more rights than other Mexican citizens. "The people of Texas had received much from the government of Mexico and had not been badly treated," the historian Paul D. Lack wrote in 1992. "Seldom has the ruling hand been felt so lightly as in Texas in the period 1821–35."[3]

In return, the Americans had ignored Mexican laws, evaded taxes, and, when the government had the temerity to insist they actually pay them, attacked and killed Mexican soldiers. Imagine if the United States opens interior Alaska to colonization and, for whatever reason, thousands of Canadians pour in and establish their own farms, hockey rinks, and Tim Hortons stores. When we insist they follow American laws and pay American taxes, they refuse. When we try to enforce the laws, they shoot and kill American soldiers. When we insist on arresting the murderers, the Canadians take up arms in open revolt. How would you feel? Well, that's how Santa Anna felt.

Then, of course, there was the question of slavery. Mexicans were ardently abolitionist. They had lived under Spanish rule and experienced its caste system, its bigotry, discrimination, and oppression. They knew the rest of the world was abolishing slavery; allowing a group of white Americans to install it in their new republic felt backward and hypocritical. Southerners, on the other hand, believed slavery was ordained by God. They had always depended on enslaved Black labor and believed that not just God but science was on their side. Some of Europe's most esteemed thinkers had established a natural hierarchy of man, with white people on high. Therefore, Southern whites believed they held a sacred duty to spread the American democratic system — and slavery — far and wide, and they were not going to let people of color stand in their way.

The proximate cause of the revolt, as we've seen, was the Mexican "invasion" whose goal was arresting Travis and other troublemakers. But the underlying cause was Santa Anna's abolition of federalism, which became official in October 1835, when his handpicked congress abolished the Constitution of 1824 and decreed that all Mexican states would be converted into military departments overseen by the government. With the central government firmly in control of their fates, many Texians believed it was inevitable that it would finally take away slavery for good. "If the Federal system is lost in Texas, what will be our situation?" asked one prominent colonist, Ben Milam. "Worse than that of the most degraded slaves."[4]

There was reason for these fears. As war approached, a host of Mexican voices prophesied the end to slavery in Texas. Cos, for one, warned that "the inevitable consequences of war will bear upon [Texians] and their property." In Matagorda, the safety commission declared that "merciless soldiery" was coming "to give liberty to our slaves, and to make slaves of ourselves."

Perhaps unsurprisingly, few in the Texian leadership were willing to publicly declare this a revolt over the peculiar institution. Even in 1836 this was not the way to attract widespread support, especially international support in a world increasingly rallying against slavery. Instead, code words were used. Plantation owners referred to their labor as "hands" or "negroes," never as slaves. Time and again, from the Consultation onward, you see the Texas leadership justifying the war as a fight to preserve their "natural rights" and — that word again — their "property." For Texians, any effort to abolish slavery was really about taking their "property." It was always an economic rather than a moral issue.

Tejanos, meanwhile, were fighting for federalism. Santa Anna's suspension of the constitution was about the future of their country. Their dream was to join federalists in other parts of Mexico to restore the constitution. At least that was their plan in 1835, when the Anglos made for a marriage of convenience.

In an effort to rally American support,

Texian war advocates wrapped themselves in the Stars and Stripes, describing the revolt as the second coming of the American Revolution, part of what would later be called manifest destiny. By and large, this propaganda worked, but it wasn't universal. Northern abolitionists denounced the Texas insurgency as the world's first pro-slavery rebellion, a conspiracy intended to preserve the rights of slaveholders. A Massachusetts paper, for instance, editorialized that Texians were fighting on behalf of "the perpetuity of slavery throughout the world."[5] Santa Anna and Mexican politicians would agree.

The loudest such voice, the abolitionist Benjamin Lundy, had traveled widely in Texas between 1832 and 1835, and knew many of those involved, from Juan Almonte to Sam Houston. When the war was over, he would write a pamphlet alleging that it was initiated by a conspiracy of Northern land speculators and Texas slaveholders whose intention was to bring Texas into the United States — but only after chopping it into as many as fifteen states, thereby upsetting the country's fragile balance of free and slave states.

Lundy would find an adherent in the former president John Quincy Adams, by then a Massachusetts congressman and a leading abolitionist. "The war now raging in Texas," Adams charged, "is a Mexican civil war, and a war for the re-establishment of Slavery where it was abolished. It is not a servile war, but a war between Slavery and Emancipation, and every possible effort has been made to drive us into this war, on the side of slavery."[6]

The Texas Revolt may have been brought on by a ham-handed Mexican "invasion," but the underlying cause, the one thing Americans and Mexicans had disagreed on since the beginning, remained the preservation of slavery.

For going on two hundred years, Mexicans and Americans have viewed the Texian secession in very different ways. What Texans would view as a glorious revolution about liberty and freedom, many Mexicans have always seen in much darker terms: a revolt of ungrateful foreigners intent on stealing their sovereign land. Still others have long believed something more insidious was at work. To many in Mexico, including its leading newspapers, the revolution from start to finish was a secret plot of the American government. U.S. historians, by and large, have scoffed at the idea. Yet there was, and still is, some evidence for these suspicions. So the question becomes: Did Andrew Jackson and his government plot or otherwise influence the revolution? Could the conspiracy theories be true? Even just a little?

American presidents, after all, had never given up dreams of getting their hands on Texas. In 1825, President John Quincy Adams sent the first U.S. minister to Mexico, a South Carolinian named Joel Roberts Poinsett; in his pocket was the authority to offer $1 million for Texas. Poinsett, alas, was a deep-seated racist who viewed Mexican politicians as bickering children. For the next four years Poinsett would try to buy Texas. He got nowhere, in large part because he could never fathom Mexico's new and blossoming national pride; about the only thing all Mexican politicians could agree on, in fact, was a burning desire never to sell land to the Americans.*

Poinsett, however, was a veritable Winston Churchill compared with his successor, a bumpkin named Anthony Butler. The expansionist President Jackson, who would

* That's not entirely true. He did bring back to the United States a pretty Mexican flower, which proved so popular it was named for him: the poinsettia.

spend the next few years fumbling after Texas like a bear cub in a trout stream, became president in 1828, and Butler was Jackson's man. Orphaned as a boy, he had actually grown up the president's ward. As an adult, his comportment was, shall we say, lacking. One historian terms Butler "hopelessly vulgar, corrupt and insolent." A fellow diplomat termed him "a disgrace."[7] He had tried with little luck to speculate in Texas land deals. Sam Houston would call him a swindler and a cheat.

Jackson sent Butler to Mexico City with orders to offer $5 million for Texas. "Let a listening ear, a silent tongue and a stefast [sic] heart, the three jewels of wisdom, guard every advance you make on the subject of Texas," he wrote his former ward.[8] Butler ignored the advice. In fact, he boasted of the $5 million offer so often as he rode across Texas that a Mexican newspaper learned of it and printed it. Before Butler set foot in Mexico, his offer was already being viewed as the worst American insult yet.

Butler met over and over with the Mexican foreign minister, who firmly told him Texas was not for sale. This went on for three solid years. Finally, in early 1834, with insurrectionary talk rising in Texas, Butler tried to gain some leverage with a scheme of breathtaking audacity.

What was needed, Butler decided, was for Texians to get serious about an armed rebellion. He wrote a pair of anonymous letters, signed "O.P.Q.," to a Texas planter urging them to do so. In one, he termed the Mexicans "an ignorant, fanatical and arrogant race." Nothing came of the letters; apparently even Texians had Butler pegged as a nincompoop. Jackson recalled him the following year.

If Poinsett's and Butler's intrigues ended up sideshows in the conspiracy carnival, the main event has always featured Sam Houston. Here the plot thickens a bit. What, after all, was Jackson's longtime protégé actually doing twiddling his thumbs in Texas? While there had been hints and murmurs for years, the question really burst into the open in 1838 during a speech by John Quincy Adams. Houston, Adams charged, had been a secret agent sent by Jackson to ignite rebellion and steal Texas for the United States.

Adams's evidence was thin, but it posed a question Houston's biographers have struggled to answer for more than a century. Pretty much everyone agrees that Houston dreamed of some kind of political glory in

Texas, whether as president of an independent republic or as conqueror of a new slave state he could present to Jackson. Some believe Jackson quietly egged him on; others think Houston kept his own counsel. According to an 1891 biography, "Houston went forth to Texas with a conditional authorization from Jackson, 'Good luck to you in any case; recognition if you succeed.' "[9] In his Pulitzer Prize–winning 1929 biography of Houston, Marquis James suggested his dreams were hazy other than "to do something grand" and perhaps "capture an empire and lay it at his old Chieftain's feet."[10]

In fact, Houston's friends were questioning his motives even before he left Tennessee. In June 1829, mere weeks after the collapse of Houston's marriage, Jackson's private secretary, A. J. Donelson, received an eye-opening letter from his brother Daniel in Nashville. Daniel claimed that the collapse of Houston's marriage was a hoax designed to obscure his real motive for leaving the United States, a "grand scheme" to incite revolution in Texas. Donelson claimed that Houston told him he had actually sent the War Dog William Wharton to Texas and that Wharton was to notify Houston once "everything was properly arranged."[11] After this letter, in fact, Jackson wrote Houston asking, in essence, if he had lost his mind.

A fervent conspiracy theorist could view Jackson's letter as an effort to disassociate himself from Houston's schemes. Whatever its motive, Houston denied everything. The incident might have been forgotten except for a bizarre incident in 1830 in which a Washington doctor named Robert Mayo claimed that after befriending Houston in a hotel, Houston had confided that he planned to lead a Cherokee invasion of Texas. Mayo, armed with all sorts of details of the supposed invasion, forwarded them to President Jackson, who in turn asked the governor of Arkansas to investigate. Nothing came of it; that is, until 1837, when Jackson, clearing out his desk at the end of his presidency, mistakenly mailed Mayo's letter to a man in Memphis, who got it to John Quincy Adams, who then revealed it all in his 1838 speech on the House floor. Most historians paint Mayo as a kook.

The Mexican government was suspicious of Houston from the start. Its ambassador protested through diplomatic channels that Houston was conspiring with Jackson to steal Texas in 1833, a full two years before fighting broke out. Jackson got worried this kind of talk would undercut his efforts to buy it. In a bizarre coda seemingly ripped from an episode of *The Wild Wild West,* he actually wrote his bumbling ambassador Butler in Mexico City that he had a "secret agent watching [Houston's] movements and preparing to thwart any attempt to organize within the United States a military force to aid in the revolution of Texas."

There's one last piece of the conspiracy puzzle to consider, and here we jump ahead a bit in our story. It centers on American troops on the Louisiana border. In January 1836, after the Texians captured the Alamo, Jackson placed his old pal General Edmund Gaines, like Jackson an ardent expansionist, in command of them; Secretary of War Lewis Cass ordered Gaines to take the Sixth Infantry to Fort Jesup and mass his troops on the Sabine River. The river that was the key to the conflict, however, was the Neches, fifty miles west in Texas, which the U.S. government claimed as the true border. If Santa Anna crossed the Neches, Gaines's orders clearly indicate, Gaines had permission to attack the Mexican army and occupy East Texas as far as Nacogdoches.

Did Sam Houston, who was by then leading the Texian army, know of this? Did he attempt to lure Santa Anna across the Neches, thus bringing the United States into the war? Political rivals would later claim so. Houston never said. Whatever the case, it never happened. Instead, four months after the war's end, Gaines dispatched a force of U.S. troops across the border to secure Nacogdoches for the Texians. They stayed there for five months. The Mexican press viewed this occupation as an American invasion of Mexican territory, and an attempt to prop up the Texas government when it still seemed an uncertain proposition. The Mexican ambassador in Washington protested again and again. The Jackson administration politely told him to jump in a lake.

Afterward, all through 1836 and 1837, Mexican newspapers loudly blamed Washington for the loss of Texas, one terming Texians "a gang of thieves" controlled by the "true enemy," the American people, who were hiding their complicity behind "the evil mask of scandalous hypocrisy."[12] John Quincy Adams and other abolitionists opposed to Jackson and the spread of slavery raised their voices in agreement, but nothing ever came of it.

Yet there remains no smoking gun. While we agree there was likely no overt U.S. involvement, the evidence does suggest some kind of "wink-wink-nudge-nudge" conspiracy, one that allowed Houston to win a war while giving Jackson deniability. We're generally skeptical of conspiracy theories, but in this case, we'd say the Mexicans' accusations shouldn't be dismissed so easily.

CHAPTER 7
THE WORST KIND OF VICTORY

By the time Austin left San Antonio, the army's ranks were already filling with American adventurers, most of them spoiling for action. In early December 1835, in the little-remembered Battle of San Antonio, this unlikely bunch managed to storm the town and, after four days of vicious house-to-house fighting, force General Cos back into the Alamo. There, confronted by mutinous aides, Cos surrendered, and was allowed to return to Mexico.

It was a stunning upset victory, but it came at a cost. We're not huge fans of the historian T. R. Fehrenbach, but he was correct in his judgment that the win was "almost fatal to the Texas cause."[1] Why? Because Texans being Texans, a lot of folks started getting awfully cocky.

Several things happened after the battle that, taken together, thoroughly weakened the Texian war effort. Almost all the Texas volunteers, for one, went home. With the province now free of Mexican soldiers, there seemed little reason to hang around. A big chunk of those who remained, taking a hard left turn toward Crazy Town, rode off to try to sack the border city of Matamoros; most would end up dead. Those who stayed in San Antonio were mostly American adventurers, who promptly set to chasing señoritas and insulting the Tejanos, whom they termed "greasers."

In San Felipe, the new governor, Henry Smith, got into an ugly power struggle with his governing council. When Smith tried to disband the council, it impeached him. He refused to leave office. Instead, he seized the state archives and swore he would shoot "any son of a bitch" who attempted to retrieve them. On January 17, 1836, when the council was unable to raise a quorum, the government effectively ceased to exist, though everyone continued to bicker as if nothing had changed. The resulting leadership vacuum was to have serious implications for the men who remained in San Antonio.

Sam Houston, meanwhile, got to squabbling with the politicians about what to do with the old town. Houston wanted nothing to do with the place. He thought it indefensible, as it pretty much was, and argued for establishing a defensive line across the rivers to the east. Almost no one listened. Give up San Antonio after fighting so hard to get it? Plus, the town did have some strategic importance, lying astride the road from Mexico.

Houston took matters into his own hands. He took Jim Bowie aside, asked him to assess the situation and, should he too judge the situation untenable, consider destroying the Alamo and beating a retreat eastward. Bowie took thirty men and left the next day. Houston, meanwhile, still a commander with no troops, got so sick of all the infighting he rode to Nacogdoches to negotiate a treaty with the Cherokee. He would be gone for much of what happened.

Bowie arrived in San Antonio on January 19 and found the garrison a mess. There were barely a hundred fighting men, low on powder, food, and supplies, unpaid and angry about it. They were all outsiders; the only Texian was the new commander, an artilleryman named James Clinton Neill. In mid-January, Neill fired off a letter to Houston: "[The men] are almost naked . . . and almost every one of them speaks of going home, and not less than twenty will leave to-morrow. We are in a torpid, defenseless condition."

Bowie had little sense of the danger he was riding into. Just the day before, a scout named José Cassiano had trotted into the hills above the old Spanish town of Presidio on the Rio Grande. Below, he was startled to see Mexican troops on parade. Hundreds of them. Infantrymen in navy tunics. Dragoons in high hats and red sashes. Cannon.

Cassiano counted the men and stopped at two thousand, then wheeled north to warn San Antonio.[2]

There's really no better way to put it:

Santa Anna was *pissed.*

It wasn't just that another province was revolting, it's that it was the ungrateful Americans. It's difficult to overstate how thoroughly the Mexican intelligentsia loathed the high-handed *norteamericanos,* so arrogant, so cocky, so condescending. And the Texians were the worst of the lot, traitors Santa Anna had gone out of his way to coddle. He had given them everything they asked for, even allowing their wretched slaves, and this was the thanks he got.

Santa Anna sent for his expert on Texas, Colonel Juan Almonte, who was at the embassy in Washington. "The audacity of those colonists is now intolerable, as is the

154

protection given them by the authorities," Almonte wrote to Mexico's secretary of foreign affairs on October 2, 1835. "It is necessary for the Government to assume all the vigor sufficient to repress the excesses of these adventurers and to severely criticize this [U.S.] Government, whose treacherous conduct I am confirming more each day."[3] The evidence of White House involvement was overwhelming, Almonte believed. He knew that if Mexico did not act quickly, it would lose Texas. He booked himself on the first available ship and caught up with Santa Anna, already on the march.

There were stories later that Santa Anna was so apoplectic he intended to kill every American he encountered, much as his mentor Arredondo had done in 1813. By seizing government property and attacking the state, the Texians were now considered "pirates," which, under international law, meant that Santa Anna could summarily execute them. Austin and others heard rumors that Santa Anna intended to drive every American from Texas. Some scholars believe Almonte kept Santa Anna's angrier instincts in check. In a letter to the Mexican congress, Santa Anna asked for clarity on whether Anglos who rebelled had violated the terms under which the government had granted them land. Santa Anna had the right to seize the land, goods, and slaves of every Texian who had taken up arms.[4] The general also intended, it's clear, to free all slaves.

"There is a considerable number of slaves in Texas also, who have been introduced by their masters under cover of certain questionable contracts, but who according to our laws should be free," Santa Anna wrote to the congress before crossing into Texas. "Shall we permit those wretches to moan in chains any longer in a country whose kind laws protect the liberty of man without distinction of caste or color?"[5]

When Texas revolted, Santa Anna had expected to respond in the spring, when military campaigning was the easiest. But the fall of San Antonio changed everything. This was an embarrassment that had to be countered immediately. In mid-December he ordered the army to gather, the first elements of a force that would grow to almost six thousand men. They mustered at San Luis Potosí, 260 miles north of Mexico City. Roughly half were professional soldiers, veterans who had fought at Zacatecas and elsewhere; the rest were last-minute conscripts, frightened peasants who barely knew how to handle a gun and had little interest other than returning to their villages in one piece.

In January, Santa Anna force-marched his army to the village of Presidio on the Rio Grande, where Texian scouts watched it drill. A second, smaller force was dispatched to Matamoros, where it linked up with troops arriving from the south. Santa Anna gave a rousing speech explaining how this was more than a simple campaign to put down an insurrection. This, he said, was a defense against foreign invaders.

"Soldiers! Our comrades have been shamefully sacrificed at Anáhuac, Goliad and Béxar, and you are the ones destined to punish these murderers," Santa Anna said. "The pretenders to our acres of Texas land will soon learn to their sorrow that their reinforcements from New Orleans, Mobile, Boston, New York and other ports [of the] North — whence they never should have come — are insignificant."[6]

Just a glance at the two armies makes you wonder what on earth the Texians were thinking when they rose in revolt. Not a soul doubted Santa Anna would retaliate. Not a soul failed to understand what that meant. There was no reasonable scenario in which this was not a complete mismatch. Santa Anna was bringing six thousand soldiers to

Texas. On a good day the Texans had maybe a thousand, split among several squabbling groups, with no unified leadership. More could join at any moment, it's true, but on the face of it, this was shaping up to be a slaughter.

Of the Alamo's Holy Trinity, Jim Bowie was the first to ascend its stage. In the Heroic Anglo Narrative of the Alamo Texans would come to embrace, Bowie would go down as the Alamo's tragic hero, a swashbuckling American archetype of romance and adventure brought low by bad luck and the bottle. In legend, he was everything Travis and Davy Crockett were not, a wounded man of action and violence and poor choices. The reality? Bowie may have been a heck of a fighting man, but it's also clear he was an amazingly brazen swindler. Had he stayed in the United States, there's a decent chance he'd have ended up swinging from a rope.

Tall, sandy-haired, and charismatic, Bowie was an early prototype, perhaps the first, of the roaming western gunfighter who sought to parlay his fame — and he was famous in his day — into the big score he never quite pulled off. Raised in a large frontier Louisiana family, he grew to become a strapping backwoodsman adept with guns and knives.

After surviving the 1819 Long Expedition, he went into business with two of his brothers, and here his story darkens considerably. The Bowies' big moneymaking scheme, the venture that defined Jim's early adulthood, revolved around two unsavory projects, smuggling illegal African slaves into the United States and flat-out real estate fraud.

The importation of enslaved people into the United States had been illegal since 1808, but as we've seen, that created an opportunity for Jean and Pierre Lafitte, who smuggled African slaves from Cuba and sold them for a pittance at their base on Galveston Island. The Bowies signed on as middlemen, driving groups of emaciated, enslaved Black people into Louisiana. At the border they cloaked themselves as customs officers, earning a reward of half their purchase price. Their costs halved, they then swooped in and bought their own slaves at auction, giving them legal title to resell them. The profits were huge.

Jim Bowie used his share of the profits to launch a land fraud "on an almost industrial scale," as one biographer, William C. Davis, put it.[7] In 1821 he forged dozens, perhaps hundreds, of deeds and used them to snatch up thousands of acres in unclaimed land all across northern Louisiana. A lengthy investigation ensued, but at some point all of Bowie's paperwork mysteriously disappeared from the investigators' offices, ending the probe.

Amazingly, he then began doing the exact same thing in Arkansas, forging dozens more deeds and filing claims there, rumors of which quickly made the rounds back in the town of Alexandria, Louisiana, where Bowie was actively wooing potential investors and mulling a run for Congress. When the local sheriff, Norris Wright, began raising questions, Bowie confronted him in a saloon; when Bowie raised a chair to bash Wright over the head, the sheriff drew a pistol and shot Bowie through the chest. Somehow, he lived.

This, however, was mere prelude to the duel of September 19, 1827, that would catapult Bowie to national fame. Two Alexandria political opponents faced off on a sandbar in the Mississippi River. Bowie and Norris Wright were among the seconds. Firing pistols, both duelists missed, then shook hands, at which point all hell broke loose. One of the first shots struck Bowie in the hip and he fell, at which point Wright lunged at him, driving a sword cane into his chest. Rising, Bowie grabbed Wright by the shirt and jerked him down onto his massive knife, killing him.

Not much Louisiana news reached the East Coast press in those days, but somehow this did. In short order the "Sandbar Fight" made Bowie — who got shot a second time; oh, and knifed again too — and his enormous "Bowie knife" into national celebrities. The knife was more than twelve inches long, practically a short sword. Armories everywhere soon produced their own. None of it made Bowie much money. It was at this point he decided to discreetly try a second act in Texas, sniffing around land deals in Coahuila before settling in San Antonio in 1828.

The Tejano elite welcomed him with open arms. Renouncing his American citizenship and joining the Catholic church, Bowie struck up a partnership with San Antonio's wealthiest man, Juan Martín de Veramendi; then, using his worthless Arkansas land claims as a dowry, he romanced and married Veramendi's teenaged daughter, Ursula. This was a sweet, sweet deal for a penniless land swindler. The newlyweds moved in with her parents. For much of the next two years Bowie turned his attention to the sulfurous land grab going on in Coahuila. This was work he knew well. Veramendi advanced him $10,000, which may have gone toward bribes or ended up in Bowie's pocket. Plying the town's darker corners, Bowie managed to amass wobbly claims to nearly a million acres of land in Texas.

It was then that Bowie's run of luck came to its end. Santa Anna annulled almost all of his land "purchases," fueling Bowie's sudden zeal for an independent Texas; it appeared to be the only way he would ever see all that land again. But then, in 1833, came the real tragedy. While Bowie was off on one of his U.S. business trips, the Veramendis were at their summer home in Coahuila when a cholera epidemic struck. Within days Ursula Bowie and her parents were dead.

Some said Bowie was never the same after that. He was stricken by cholera too, nearly dying in a friend's bed in Natchez. But say what you will about Jim Bowie, he was one tough SOB. He made it back to San Antonio in the spring of 1834, but he had no money. The stories of his drinking ramped up. And the fights. Folks in San Antonio were onto him now; some began calling him *"fanfarron Santiago Bowie,"* or "James Bowie the Braggart."[8]

When war came, though, Bowie found himself back in demand. After all, there was no more renowned gunman in Texas. He had met Sam Houston in San Felipe, and the two struck up a fast friendship; Houston needed a man he could count on, and Bowie was among the few. Once again men were marveling at Bowie's bravery, his head-shaking aggression, his coolness under fire. The fact was, Bowie had little left to lose. One senses he knew it. When he wasn't on the battlefield, he could often be found drinking.

History, though, wasn't done with Jim Bowie yet.

CHAPTER 8
COUNTDOWN

When Jim Bowie arrived back in San Antonio, he found the defenders focusing almost all their energies on defending the Alamo itself. James Neill and his engineer, Green Jameson, were keeping the men busy patching up walls, building gun emplacements, and hauling most of their cannon into place. Jameson was feeling pretty happy with himself, boasting in a letter to Sam Houston that the Alamo's troops could "whip" a Mexican force ten times their size.

Bit by bit, Bowie was growing aware that they might need to. Every few days he received some new rumor or report, often from travelers coming up the road from Laredo, of a Mexican army massing at the Rio Grande. José Cassiano's sighting was but a single voice in a chorus of ominous confusion. A priest whispered that the Mexicans would come via Goliad. Bowie couldn't be sure what to believe.

What he did know was that no matter how and when Santa Anna came for revenge, a hundred men had little chance of fighting him off. Forget Santa Anna: A hundred men could not defend the sprawling Alamo from Santa *Claus.* A quarter mile around, it was simply too big. Bowie and Neill fired off a letter almost every day begging San Felipe to send them men and money. For two long weeks, what they got instead was a steady trickle of American volunteers.

There are those who believe Sam Houston never really wanted Bowie to blow up the Alamo, that he only said so later to rationalize his lethargy. But there are real-time letters that make clear he did, and that he allowed Bowie to make the decision. When Governor Smith learned this, in fact, he sent a letter to Bowie countermanding Houston's order. Whether it was this letter, his admiration for Neill's work, his love for the town, or his appreciation of its strategic value, Bowie decided to stay in San Antonio, fortify the Alamo, and, if necessary, defend it.

"The salvation of Texas depends in great measure on keeping Bexar out of the hands of the enemy," he wrote Governor Smith on February 2. "We would rather die in these ditches than give it up to the enemy." No matter how hard they fought, though, he wrote, "it would be a waste of men to put our brave little band against thousands. . . . Again we call loud for *relief.*"

The very next day, in fact, reinforcements arrived, the first of thirty men from the new "regular" army sent from San Felipe. But they came with complications, for they were led by none other than William Barret Travis. Having started this whole thing, Travis hadn't really known what to do with himself once the actual fighting started. Austin had given him a cavalry company during the march on San Antonio, but Travis quit for some reason, staying on as Joe Cavalryman, a role in which he took several scouts with Juan Seguín's riders. He quit again after that, only to accept a lieutenant colonel's commission in the embryonic Texas army, taking his oath on Christmas Eve. When word of Mexican troops massing on the Rio Grande reached San Felipe, his cavalrymen were among the first regulars dispatched to reinforce San Antonio.

With him Travis brought his slave, a young African-American man named Joe. As one of only a handful of enslaved Black people at the Alamo, Joe would play an outsized role in its history. Oddly, he may have come

166

from among the most prominent families represented at the Alamo. According to a 2015 book, *Joe: The Slave Who Became an Alamo Legend,* by Ron L. Jackson Jr. and Lee Spencer White, there is evidence Joe was an illegitimate grandson of Daniel Boone. Of mixed race, he was born in Kentucky, probably in 1815. His mother gave birth to seven children by seven fathers. One, Joe's likely father, was Boone's illegitimate son.

One of Joe's half brothers, William Wells Brown, escaped to the North and went on to a distinguished career as an abolitionist and man of letters; his 1853 novel *Clotel* is regarded as the first written by an African-American. Joe, however, remained enslaved, and in the late 1820s, when he was twelve or thirteen, he was sold to a St. Louis factory owner named Isaac Mansfield, who, like the Austins, fell on hard times and immigrated to Texas, in 1832. Mansfield's farm was wiped out in a flood two years later, and he died shortly thereafter, in 1834.

Travis was the Mansfield estate's lawyer. That December, when Joe, now nineteen, was put up for sale, a Travis pal named John Cummings bought him for $410. Even though this was obvious self-dealing, Travis purchased him from Cummings and brought him to the Alamo. He would be at Travis's side for the duration.

Two of the three pillars of the Alamo legend — Travis and Bowie — had now ascended the final stage. On February 8, five days after Travis's arrival, Bowie was summoned to a graveyard outside San Antonio to greet the third, the most famous new arrival in Texas: Davy Crockett.*

After Andrew Jackson, Crockett may have been the most famous man in America in 1836, a fact that had almost nothing to do with anything he had actually done. Crockett was a middling Tennessee congressman whose penchant for tall tales led Jackson's opponents to briefly consider him a candidate for the White House; Crockett wasn't quite Sam Houston's doppelgänger, but there were obvious parallels in their careers. Crockett the man, however, was almost completely overshadowed by his alter ego, the Davy Crockett of popular lore, the bear-battling, alligator-wrestling, Indian-fighting hero of Broadway plays and cheap novels

* To be fair, he preferred to be called David, but hagiographers have made sure he'll always be Davy.

168

that Crockett inspired but had little control over.

Born into a frontier family in what's now eastern Tennessee in 1786, Crockett spent his early years driving cattle and serving as a scout during the Creek War and Jackson's Florida invasion. Afterward, settling as a farmer near the Alabama border, he gained election to the state legislature in 1821. When a flood wiped out the farm, Crockett and his family — now deeply in debt — were forced to move into a cabin in northwest Tennessee. This was serious frontier living, and it was there that Crockett displayed a keen talent for, of all things, killing bears. By one count he shot 105 during a single season.

History would have forgotten Crockett had he not developed his second talent: telling people about killing all those bears. It began, we are told, when a dandyish legislator teased Crockett as "the gentleman from the cane" — "cane" apparently being an obscure Tennesseeism for a heavy forest. Crockett capitalized on the incident by turning his teasing image as a backward backwoodsman into a strength, pouring it on thick with tales of killing "bahrs" and "Injuns" and river pirates, at the same time making fun of the rich and pompous. Once this act caught on, he adopted a syrupy drawl and syntax; the word "known," for instance, became "know'd."

Crockett's was a gentle kind of frontier populism, and it worked. He leveraged his popularity into a seat in the U.S. House of Representatives in Washington. But what would transform Crockett from a curiosity into a celebrity was Americans' newfound appetite for tales of life along the growing country's frontiers. The 1820s brought a flowering of such literature, notably James Fenimore Cooper's Leatherstocking Tales, featuring the woodsman Natty Bumppo and including *The Last of the Mohicans,* one of the century's most popular books. These books renewed interest in Daniel Boone, who became America's first popular hero.

Crockett cannily developed his act to exploit this fascination. He seemed to be a living, breathing Natty Bumppo, and far more fun and accessible than the taciturn Boone, who was dead anyway. The turning point came in 1831, during Crockett's second term in Congress, with the New York debut of a wildly popular play called *The Lion of the West,* a farce starring a dim-witted congressman named Colonel Nimrod Wildfire, clearly modeled on Crockett. The play, the most popular American production until *Uncle Tom's Cabin* twenty years later, made Crockett a celebrity at a time when celebrity was still a very rare thing in America.

As such, it caught the eye of the Whigs, who began grooming Crockett for higher office, possibly the presidency. Whig politicians began ghost-writing Crockett's speeches and a book or two, most notably a madly exaggerated 1833 biography, *Sketches and Eccentricities of Colonel David Crockett of West Tennessee*. It was the "biography" that made Crockett a true national figure, its most memorable lines enshrining him as a bighearted, boastful, cartoonish caricature of Daniel Boone:

> I'm that same David Crockett, fresh from the backwoods, half-horse, half-alligator, a little touchéd with the snapping-turtle; can wade the Mississippi, leap the Ohio, ride upon a streak of lightning, and slip without a scratch down a honey locust; can whip my weight in wild cats — and if any gentleman pleases, for a ten dollar bill, he may throw in a panther.

In the pantheon of American celebrity frontiersmen circa 1833, Crockett probably ranked second only to Boone; if there was a third, it might have been Jim Bowie. Crockett the man, alas, proved no match for the Crockett of the public imagination. The size of his crowds mushroomed, but his alter ego's buffoonery irked him, and besides, neither the book nor the biography made him a cent. At the very peak of his fame, though, Crockett suffered a Sam Houston moment and walked away from it all. The trouble began after he wrote a competing autobiography and embarked on a three-week book tour while Congress was in session. His political opponents attacked him as an ineffectual truant — he hadn't managed to get a single bill passed during his three terms — and in August 1835, just as secessionist passions ignited in Texas, he was defeated for reelection.

Crockett was tired, unwelcome in Washington, and nearly broke, and clearly longing for something like a new start, if not redemption. In interviews after his defeat, he spoke the words still excerpted on bumper stickers from Brownsville to Dalhart: "I told the people of my district that, if they saw fit to re-elect me I would serve them as faithfully as I had done; but if not, they might go to hell, and I would go to Texas."

And so he did, heading west with a band of pals barely ninety days after the election.

They arrived in Nacogdoches in January 1836. There, in return for a six-month stint in the new Texas army, Crockett received 4,600 acres of land. Of course, he had no intention of actually fighting anyone. After all, there were no Mexican troops left in Texas to fight. No, like Sam Houston, what Crockett wanted was an entrée into politics. He wrote his children he had "little doubt" he would be elected to the upcoming constitutional convention. After that, who knew? Governor? President?

A fleshy forty-nine years old, Crockett was certainly more suited to politics than soldiering. But if it took a six-month stint to get into the game, he was up for it. The army was at San Antonio. Barely a month after arriving in Texas, Crockett and his friends met Bowie on the outskirts of town. His arrival at the Alamo is one of history's great juxtapositional flukes, as if Teddy Roosevelt or Mark Twain had darted onto the *Titanic* at the last minute. The man and the place had almost nothing to do with each other, yet their stories would now be forever intertwined.

His arrival prompted the stir you'd expect. He gave a speech atop a packing crate on the Plaza de las Yslas, telling his favorite tales as he had a thousand times before, and then became a private in the Alamo garrison. What little we know of Crockett's time in San Antonio suggests he was a popular, easygoing, courteous fellow, a fist-bumper to the bros, a hat-tipper to the señoritas. Two nights after Crockett's arrival, the officers threw a fandango in his honor. It went into the early hours. At one point, Bowie noticed Juan Seguín studying a letter. He read it, then handed it to Travis, who translated the Spanish for Crockett. It was yet another scout's report, putting Santa Anna himself at the head of the Mexican army massing at Presidio. Travis famously waved it off. "Let us dance to-night," he said, "and to-morrow we will make provisions for our defense."[1]

The next day brought more pressing troubles. James Neill learned of a family illness and left, promising to return in three weeks. Neill's departure left Travis in overall command, which was a problem. Maybe half the men had signed up since December, making them beholden to the Texas government, such as it was, and Travis was its representative at the Alamo. But the other half were volunteers who had no interest in joining an actual army. Two companies, in fact, announced that they wouldn't. The volunteers elected Bowie their commander.

Both Travis and Bowie were notoriously headstrong. Bowie was thirty-nine, Travis twenty-six, and Bowie made clear that he had little intention of listening to any order from another officer, especially one as wet behind the ears as Travis. The garrison divided into grumbling camps.

The election, in turn, triggered one of the Alamo legend's stranger episodes, Bowie's colossal drunk. Bowie was a brooder, his motivations typically opaque, to his peers and to later historians. Whatever its cause, Bowie showed up deeply drunk the day after the election, February 12. When he spied a group of Tejanos leaving town with their carts, he ordered them forcibly detained. Then, inexplicably, he ordered a thief released from jail. When the judge, Erasmo Seguín, sent the thief right back, Bowie and a group of his equally plastered volunteers paraded in front of the jail, an obvious intimidation attempt. After that, Bowie ordered all the prisoners released.

By the next day, anarchy reigned. Many of the volunteers remained drunk, and some began selling their guns to buy more liquor. Bowie had clearly lost his mind. Travis certainly thought so. Things got so bad Travis led his men out of the Alamo and into an encampment on the Medina River.

He fired off a letter to his law partner, who took it to the governor. Bowie "has been roaring drunk all the time," Travis wrote, "turning everything topsy-turvy." He offered to resign, begged for more men, and explained, "I am unwilling to be responsible for the drunken irregularities of any man."[2]

And then, as suddenly as it arose, the crisis passed. On February 14, Bowie sobered up and apologized to Travis, who returned to town. The two agreed to share leadership of the garrison, an awkward proposition to be sure, but workable, and not a moment too soon. Almost every day now brought another rider with news of the Mexican army at Presidio. And almost every day Travis or Bowie, and often both, sent letters begging for reinforcements.

Historians agree that Travis's melodramatic messages were intended for public consumption; having lost confidence in the Texas government, he was resorting to public appeals via the newspapers. His language would grow steadily more florid. "We hope that our Countrymen will open their eyes to the present danger," he beseeched the governor in one missive. "I fear [that] The Thunder of the Enemy's Cannon and the pollution of their wives and daughters — The Cries of their Famished Children, and the Smoke of their burning dwellings, will only arouse them."

And still the warnings came. On February 16 a rider appeared from Laredo. Santa Anna, he claimed, was already crossing the Rio Grande. If true, this meant that Mexican troops could be only a week away. Travis, in the words of one historian, was "politely skeptical."[3] Two days later came an identical report. One of the Tejanos urged Travis to abandon San Antonio. But Travis still didn't believe Santa Anna would be in a position to invade for weeks. The Mexicans, he argued, would surely wait for the spring grasses to sprout before bringing their cavalry north. By that point, Travis expected reinforcements.

Seguín's scouts had been riding the roads south and west of San Antonio for weeks. On Saturday, February 20, he heard that Santa Anna's vanguard, a force of fifteen hundred cavalry under the command of General Joaquín Ramírez y Sesma, had crossed into Texas three days earlier. They were force-marching to San Antonio in an attempt to catch the garrison by surprise. They could make it in a matter of days.

Travis and Bowie called a council of war that night. They debated for hours, the details lost to time. In the end, the doubters

177

won; after all, several Anglos reasoned, they'd be fools to trust a Mexican. But even had they believed Seguín's report, it's not clear it would have altered their fate. Because Travis and Bowie, for whatever reason — honor, duty, ego, overconfidence, or strategy — were determined to defend the Alamo, no matter what. It was, in every respect, a questionable decision.

The next day, Sunday, February 21, San Antonio was on edge. But by nightfall there was no sign of Mexican cavalry. Monday too passed with no news or sightings. That evening Travis and Bowie saw no reason to cancel a fandango to celebrate George Washington's birthday. Generations of writers have imagined that Crockett played his fiddle, that Travis danced with the señoritas, that everyone enjoyed a festive evening. One final night of cheer.

Then, the next morning, Travis was at his headquarters on the Plaza de las Yslas, preparing for a minor court-martial proceeding, when he noticed a Tejano family loading their belongings onto a cart. Glancing about, he saw others doing the same, still others huddled in worried conversation. When Travis asked what was going on, he was told the families were leaving for spring planting. Skeptical, he sent men into the streets to discern the truth. A friendly Tejano relayed the news: Mexican cavalrymen had been spotted five miles south of town. Impoverished Tejanos, who didn't care anything about politics, did know one thing. They wanted to be far away when Santa Anna arrived.

Travis hustled to the San Fernando church, whose belfry commanded views to the south and west. Studying the chaparral intently, he saw nothing suspicious. Travis left a man in the tower, praying this was a false alarm. Around two came the sound of the church bell, suggesting it wasn't. Again, Travis raced up to the church and up the belfry stairs. The lookout insisted he had just seen a cavalry column that had disappeared into a mesquite break.

Travis sent two riders out to check. He watched as they cantered a mile down the road, then crested a low rise. Suddenly they whirled; one horse stumbled, throwing its rider to the ground, where he writhed in pain. The second rider helped him remount, and they raced back to the edge of town, where Crockett ran out to meet them. Above, the lookout began frantically ringing the church bell.

Travis sprinted to his headquarters and

penned a dispatch to the government pledging to defend the Alamo and begging for reinforcement. Bowie and others, meanwhile, began breaking into houses, gathering up food and bringing it to the fort. Another group rounded up cattle. Men who had sold their rifles for drinking money now frantically ran to buy them back. By two thirty that afternoon everyone was swarming up Potrero Street toward the footbridge that led across the San Antonio River to the Alamo. A Tejano woman, in a rueful comment included in most every account, was overheard saying, "Poor fellows, you will all be killed."

By three, after penning a second demand for reinforcements, this one to James Fannin, who commanded four hundred men at Goliad, Travis and many of his men were standing high on the Alamo's western wall, studying the town for signs of Mexican troops. It was then that they glimpsed the cavalrymen — flags flying, lances flashing in the sun — trot into Military Plaza. There were hundreds of them.

Atop the wall, anxious glances were exchanged. This was no longer playtime. This was real. This was happening. The Mexicans' first communication came not long after. Soldiers climbed the belfry. From eight hundred yards away, Travis watched as they unfurled a bloodred flag. Everyone knew what it meant. The Mexicans would take no prisoners. Travis, famously, ordered a single cannon shot in defiant response. The Mexicans answered with four of their own.

Travis and Bowie decided a parley was in order but couldn't agree on what to say. They ended up sending separate messengers. Bowie's went first, riding out beneath a white flag. The messenger returned with a note demanding the Texians surrender unconditionally.[4] Travis then sent out a man named Albert Martin, who was met by none other than Juan Almonte, who repeated the demand to surrender.[5] When Martin returned, Travis sent him back to the bridge to promise an immediate answer. If the Texians refused, he would fire a single cannon shot.

Travis assembled the troops and gave a stirring speech — its details lost to history — and the men reportedly responded with huzzahs. Travis ordered the cannon shot: They would not be surrendering. From the town a howitzer replied, then commenced a random bombardment. (The Mexican artillery did little damage at first. It mostly fired solid cannonballs. When Travis wanted to return fire, he simply asked a man to pick one up and shoot it back.)

That night Travis and his men stood atop the walls studying the Mexican soldiers as they moved through San Antonio, making themselves at home. One man was missing: Bowie. Something was wrong with him, and not just the drinking. For days he had been quiet and listless. By that night Bowie had taken to bed, lying in a room inside the Alamo's southern wall, where his sister-in-law and another Tejana ministered to him. He was running a temperature, estimated between 101 and 104 degrees. Within days there would be vomiting and bloody diarrhea. Historians speculate that he contracted typhoid, likely from something he drank.

For better or worse, Travis was now in full command, which would have an incalculable impact not only on what happened at the Alamo but on how history would remember it. Travis and the letters he would write from the old Spanish mission have been held up for nearly two hundred years as heartbreaking evidence of his selfless bravery, and that of his men. And to many they still are.

But it's equally true that none of this needed to happen — none of the Alamo's defenders needed to die — and they only did so because Travis and Bowie ignored every warning of Santa Anna's approach and inexplicably remained in San Antonio to defend an indefensible outpost. And, sad to say, how anything that happened after Santa Anna's appearance on February 23 can be held up as "bravery" is beyond us. Once Santa Anna appeared, Travis and his men were trapped. Despite the legends, there was never any conscious decision or vote in which the defenders elected to stay and fight. They had simply lingered too long, and now they were trapped. Every one was a dead man walking.

CHAPTER 9
THE FINAL DAYS

The next morning, February 24, dawned warm and drizzly. It was a good time for the American rebels to take stock of the fort they would now defend. In 1836 the Alamo appeared nothing like you see today. If you've visited San Antonio only a time or two, you might be under the mistaken impression that "the Alamo" refers to the iconic stone church that remains its most striking remnant. In fact, the church was just one building of several that lined a three-acre open-air compound whose features have long since been destroyed or paved over to make way for downtown streets.

The Alamo compound was a rectangle the size of a city block, its long western wall facing San Antonio a few hundred yards away and lined along the inside by a row of adobe huts.* The western and northern

* The western wall faced what today is the Ripley's

184

walls were made of stone, twelve feet high. The south side was composed of a long, low building chopped into rooms, half on either side of the main, arched entranceway. The east side of the compound — the "back" of the Alamo, facing away from town — was dominated by the two sturdiest buildings: the church, with four-foot-thick walls but no roof, much of it piled with debris after a misguided Mexican effort to strengthen it; and the two-story "Long Barrack," a strong stone building bordered by corrals on two sides. All this surrounded an open "plaza" of sunbaked hardpan.

The Alamo was never intended to be an actual fort. The walls, for one thing, had no holes through which to fire a rifle. Atop them, there were no parapets riflemen could use for cover. A bigger problem was a gaping fifty-yard hole at the plaza's southeast corner, between the church and the southern wall. Cos's troops had thrown up a wooden palisade to fill it, but it was the kind of thing a few cannonballs could smash to pieces. All told, the Alamo was almost a

---

Believe It or Not! store, across Alamo Plaza. The southern wall faces what is today the Menger Hotel. The northern wall ran through what is today the lobby of the federal courthouse.

quarter mile around. Even Travis, a military novice, saw there was no way 150 men could defend it. If the Mexicans attacked with scaling ladders from all sides, many could hop inside unopposed.

The Texians had a few things going for them, though. For one, they had a great number of cannon, twenty-one in all, many of them seized from Cos in December. There were actually too many: a single gun needed a six-man crew for peak performance, which would require almost every man Travis had. Most ended up with three-man crews, meaning they would fire far less frequently. The biggest gun, an eighteen-pounder, was mounted at the southwest corner of the walls facing San Antonio. Travis personally commanded a battery of smaller guns on the north wall. The Alamo had plenty of powder, but it was poor quality, presumably leading to a fair share of misfires and dribbles.

Several of the guns were mounted atop makeshift firing platforms, basically high heaps of dirt Cos's engineers had built. But just as riflemen on the walls had little protection from incoming fire, so did the platforms. Early on, members of Santa Anna's staff noted the Texian crews were silhouetted against the sky, making them easy targets.

The Texians used a variety of guns, but by far their best was the Kentucky long rifle. Four to six feet long, with spiral grooving within the bore, this gun could fire accurately at distances well over two hundred yards; it had killed many a bear on the western frontier. Most of Santa Anna's infantry, meanwhile, carried a vastly inferior India Pattern musket, a ten-pound behemoth with a thirty-nine-inch barrel; in perfect conditions, it could hit a target at maybe a hundred yards. But the barrels fouled easily, and in practice the guns were wildly inaccurate. In combat Mexican officers were often obliged to wait until a charging enemy was upon them before ordering men to fire.

Even with little experience in combat, Travis had a decent grasp of the Alamo's strengths and weaknesses. In fact, other than some obvious rookie mistakes, he would prove a capable enough commander. But as a lawyer and orator who had been trying to shape public opinion in Texas for years, his real strength was communications. His shining legacy, and a major factor in the Alamo's enduring popularity, was the dramatic letters he wrote. More than anyone else fighting this little war, Travis had a vivid sense of the place he might occupy on not just the national but the world stage. Time and again, he portrayed himself as a lone beacon of civilization facing the insurmountable odds of a barbarian invasion. In true Walter Scott style, his letters drip with chivalry, glory, and duty. He was at heart a politician, no doubt with an eye on spurring reinforcements from the United States; as such, Travis repeatedly invoked "American character" and ideals.

His most famous letter, penned on February 24, the first full day of the siege, was cannily addressed "To the People of Texas and all Americans in the World."

I am besieged by a thousand or more of the Mexicans under Santa Anna — I have sustained a continual Bombardment & cannonade for 24 hours & have not lost a man — The enemy has demanded a surrender at discretion, otherwise, the garrison are to be put to the sword, if the fort is taken — I have answered the demand with a cannon shot, & our flag still waves proudly from the walls — *I shall never surrender or retreat. Then,* I call on you in the name of Liberty, of patriotism & . . . everything dear to the American character, to come to our aid, with all dispatch — The enemy is receiving reinforcements daily & will no doubt increase to three or four thousand in four or five days. If this call is neglected, I am determined to sustain myself as long as possible & die like a soldier who never forgets what is due to his own honor & that of his country —

Victory or Death.

The next morning, no doubt testing the Alamo's defenses, Mexican soldiers emerged from San Antonio and took positions in bushes along the river barely a hundred yards off the southwest corner of the compound. Travis had them blasted with cannon fire, and after a bit they scurried off, carrying a few bodies. The skirmish convinced Travis that an attack was imminent. "If they overpower us, we fall a sacrifice at the shrine of our country, and we hope posterity and our country will do our memory justice. Give me help, oh my Country!" he wrote Houston.

In San Felipe, the governor began publishing Travis's missives in the newspapers, urging Texans to "fly" to his aid. And then: nothing. It is one of the Texas Revolt's dark little secrets that, even after the Mexican "invasion" — or perhaps because of it —

the great mass of Texians and Tejanos wanted nothing to do with Travis or the Alamo or fighting Mexican soldiers. Most had never wanted to revolt in the first place. Others, it's clear, were downright skeptical of Travis's pleas. He was, after all, a known troublemaker and propagandist with a track record of putting his causes before the truth.

Foremost among Travis skeptics was none other than Sam Houston, who returned from East Texas on February 29 for a constitutional convention. The problem seems to have been politics: Houston suspected that both Travis and James Fannin at Goliad were angling to replace him as head of the army. One delegate at the convention later quoted Houston as saying that Travis's letters were "a damned lie, and that all those reports from Travis & Fannin were lies, for there were no Mexican forces [at San Antonio] and that he believed that it was only electioneering schemed [by] Travis & Fannin to sustain their popularity."[1]

By the Siege's third morning, Thursday, February 25, the days began to take on a familiar rhythm. It was a strange kind of siege. The Mexican soldiers stayed mostly in town, sallying out on cavalry patrols or to establish gun emplacements closer to the walls; initially, the Mexican cannon were set up roughly 250 yards out, at the outside range of the Texian riflemen.

In those first few days, civilians could file in and out of the Alamo's gate pretty much at will. Seguín actually had his meals delivered. Santa Anna never bothered to physically encircle the fort. There was no need. Escape was never a serious option. Even if every man in the Alamo had a horse, the Mexican cavalry could have easily ridden down the entire force of 150 or so men. Couriers came and left with ease, at least at first.

On the fourth day, Friday, February 26, the Mexican cannon fired through the afternoon. At one point cavalry circled off the east side of the fort, again testing its defenses. A few shots from the Texian cannon scattered them. On Saturday it rained. The Mexican cannonade was intermittent. Travis was able to send men outside the compound to repair damage to the north walls, and dispatch yet another messenger, James Bonham, to Goliad with yet another plea for reinforcements. On Monday, February 29, a cold front blew in, bringing hail and high winds and driving the temperature down almost to freezing. Sometime around three in the morning, Travis was summoned to the main gate. What he encountered must have warmed his heart: his first reinforcements, a contingent of thirty-two mounted men from Gonzales who had managed to elude the Mexican patrols.

No doubt Travis thought it the vanguard of incoming aid. It wasn't. In fact, it was the last.

Travis's letters should have made clear to any reader that his troops were doomed without reinforcement. Yet other than this single group from Gonzales, none came. To this day, historians debate why. Much of the discussion centers on Sam Houston and James Fannin. Houston, having spent a solid month dallying with the Cherokee in East Texas, returned for the convention and, true to his critics' caricature, promptly set to drinking himself into an eggnog stupor. Yes, one can say Houston didn't have an army to send. But had he rallied to Travis's cause, no doubt he could have raised at least *some* men. His skepticism had a dampening effect on all.

Fannin, at Goliad, commanded the nearest force, about four hundred men. At least once, Travis sent Seguín there asking for reinforcement. Fannin's men, it's clear, were skeptical about the wisdom of marching to the Alamo. "The force of the enemy is possibly 3000 — a vast disparity," one wrote his father. "We are almost naked and without provisions and very little ammunition. We are undisciplined in a great measure; they are regulars, the elite of Santa [Anna's] army. . . . I frankly confess that without the interposition of Providence, we can not rationally anticipate any other result to our Quixotic expedition than total defeat."[2]

From surviving correspondence, it's clear that Fannin himself was freaking out. Even in a land that prized slavery, his illegal trafficking in African slaves was considered unsavory. He was unpopular with the adventurers in his command, and despite his pleas, hadn't managed to attract many actual Texians to join his forces. In letter after letter, he wrote San Felipe begging to be relieved of his command. In one, he actually pleaded his own incompetence.

In the end, Fannin was practically shamed into the rescue mission. At dawn on February 26, hours after the cold front roared in, Fannin's little force trundled up the river road toward San Antonio a hundred miles northwest. Almost from its first steps, it was a disaster. Most of the men had no shoes;

three wagons broke down in the first two miles. The men muscled the cannon across the San Antonio River, but couldn't get the ammunition wagon across. Several of the oxen wandered off that first night. The next morning, no one wanted to go on. They unanimously decided to call the whole thing off and return to Goliad.

Later, apologists would insist that Fannin decided to wait for a shipload of supplies said to be landing on the coast. But to his critics, and there have been plenty over the years, Colonel James Fannin simply chickened out.

While all this was going on, the constitutional convention opened on March 1 in the ramshackle settlement of Washington-on-the-Brazos, the convention's fifty-nine delegates milling about inside a wooden hall. You may already know that they ended up declaring independence. What you may not know is that the most experienced delegate in the hall was not one of the American colonists but a Mexican, Stephen F. Austin's old pal Lorenzo de Zavala, and his actions there would make possible perhaps the greatest tragedy of early Texas history.

Depending on whom you talk to, de

Zavala is viewed today as a traitor, a naïf, or an Uncle Tom. In fact, much like his Tejano cousins, he is probably best understood as a well-meaning political player. Little remembered today, de Zavala was a very big deal at the time, a Mexican legislator and diplomat whose fame was on a par with Sam Houston's. Born in the Yucatán in 1788, the grandson of Spanish immigrants, he was raised upper class and as a young writer managed to get himself thrown into prison for demanding democratic reforms from the Spanish.

Released at twenty-nine, he entered politics, winning a seat in the Spanish legislature in Madrid and, after the revolution, rising to become presiding officer of the Mexican congress. Somewhat like Santa Anna, he was a political chameleon, moving from monarchist to republican with ease. Unlike much of the Mexican intelligentsia, de Zavala admired the U.S. political system, enough that he pushed to adopt American-style federalism. He was a key figure in the writing of the 1824 Mexican constitution.[3]

A reliable supporter of American immigration, de Zavala and his allies had been instrumental in orchestrating the legal and legislative changes Austin needed to build his colony. There is a good argument that de Zavala and his ilk are far more important to the narrative of early Texas than eleventh-hour arrivals like Crockett. There is a good argument, in fact, that without de Zavala's support in passing pro-colonization laws and regulations in Mexico City, and his unflagging friendship with Austin, Anglos might never have settled in Texas.

He certainly wanted to be part of it. In 1829, looking to make some money, de Zavala wrangled an empresario grant to settle five hundred families on a strip of land in the far corner of southeast Texas. He was heading there when he was named Mexico's finance minister, only to lose the job in a government change six months later. Placed under house arrest, he fled to Washington, where he had dinner with President Jackson.[4] Then he headed to New York, where he sold much of his land to New York real estate speculators.[5] One of his new partners was a man named David G. Burnet, a U.S. senator's brother who was on his way to Texas.

Settling in New York, de Zavala spent the next two years authoring a pair of well-received books, including a U.S. travelogue, *Journey to the United States of North America,* that's sometimes compared to Alexis de Tocqueville's *Democracy in America.* He returned to Mexico City when Santa Anna took power in 1832, serving as a provincial governor and then congressman. His advocacy of land reforms made him so popular, in fact, there was speculation he might run for president. At that point Santa Anna sent him off to be Mexico's ambassador to France. De Zavala was in Paris in 1834 when Santa Anna assumed his quasi-dictatorship. He denounced him, at which point Santa Anna ordered him home, at which point de Zavala headed to America to see if he could incite rebellion in the one corner of Mexico he bet Santa Anna couldn't defeat: Texas.

After stopping in New Orleans, where he plotted with other exiles, de Zavala sailed to Galveston, disembarking there in July 1835, just days before Austin returned from imprisonment. Austin and David Burnet welcomed him warmly. When word reached Santa Anna, he was not pleased. To him, de Zavala was easily the most prominent of the rebels, a candidate to replace him if the wider rebellion succeeded.

In San Felipe, where he briefly shared a house with Austin, de Zavala was a curiosity, a slight, effete intellectual plunked down in a world of buckskin, bullets, and mud.[6] A year before, he was hobnobbing with the king of France; now, when he walked into a room, white men grew silent. He had never experienced such abject racism, and struggled to address it. Burnet and Austin alone appeared to understand his value. Texas would need a constitution soon, and de Zavala was the only man around who had helped write one. He could quote Thomas Jefferson and John Locke, and often did. His presence alone gave the Texians credibility, especially with Mexican federalists.[7]

De Zavala, meanwhile, was playing a bit of a double game. In New Orleans, a group of exiles planned to mount an invasion of the northern province of Tampico. A group of U.S. businessmen had agreed to fund it, on the condition they receive a chunk of Texas if it succeeded.[8] De Zavala's job was to egg on the Texas rebellion and draw Santa Anna north to quell it, at which point he would be sandwiched between hostile forces in Tampico and Texas. He told Austin of the invasion but assured him Santa Anna was a paper tiger. "Texas," he promised, "is his certain death."[9]

By the time de Zavala arrived in Texas, though, the rebellion was well on its way. The Tampico invasion fizzled. De Zavala fell back on plan B, making sure the Texian revolt remained part of the broader federalist rebellion to topple Santa Anna. Already, though, there were many in the Texian leadership, including Burnet, who wanted independence. The two men debated it around the clock.[10]

A man of proven diplomatic skills, de Zavala might have been more effective but for a sickness, probably malaria, he picked up soon after his arrival; he never really shook it off. Still, invited to the Consultation that October, he successfully pushed to have the revolt characterized as an effort to preserve the 1824 Mexican constitution. Austin thought so highly of de Zavala that he appointed him to the twelve-man Permanent Council that oversaw Texas that winter. When troops were raised, Austin made him a general.[11] That interim governor, though, the bellicose Henry Smith, was a thoroughgoing racist and barred de Zavala from leading troops because he was Mexican. When Smith fell out with the council, de Zavala was in the thick of it. He got invited to the Washington-on-the-Brazos convention to sort it all out.[12]

De Zavala was encouraged to find a pair of Tejanos, San Antonio's Ángel Navarro and Francisco Ruiz, who were in attendance. He bunked with them in a rented carpentry shop. But on the very first day, the trio realized they had been badly out-flanked. A delegate named George Childress presented the convention with a declaration of independence; to the surprise of almost everyone, and the evident dismay of de Zavala, it was adopted unanimously the next day. De Zavala signed it too. He had little choice. It was clearly going to pass anyway.[13] Afterward, there was a constitution to write. De Zavala took the lead crafting its section on executive powers, and sat on the defense and flag-design committees.[14]* The Texas constitution remains the only one in world history to guarantee slavery and actually outlaw any and all emancipation. No free Black people were to be allowed. In a direct reflection of cotton's wholesale dependence on slave labor, Texas was to be the most militant slavocracy anywhere.

But if de Zavala was crestfallen at his failure to head off independence, he took solace in accepting the vice presidency of

* There are people who sell something called the Zavala flag, which features a white star on a navy field with letters spelling "Texas" placed in a circle around the star. It is a fraud. We know that de Zavala designed a flag, but there are no records revealing what it looked like, other than that the convention voted to add a rainbow to it.

the new Republic of Texas; Burnet was named president. His appointment was an effort to ensure the San Antonio Tejanos' loyalty to the rebels. De Zavala yearned to be president of Mexico, not the number two man of a breakaway province. But he took the job. It kept him in the game.

It wouldn't take long, though, for de Zavala to realize his mistake. The Texians were not quite what they seemed, at least as far as their Latino allies were concerned. For Tejanos, living in an Anglo-run independent nation would never be quite the same as a Mexican state, and de Zavala would go down as the man who failed to prevent it, with disastrous consequences for his people.

Life for the men and women at the Alamo, meanwhile, had devolved into waiting for Santa Anna — or for reinforcements. On March 3, the siege's tenth day, a rider was spotted approaching from the east. It was James Bonham, with letters from San Felipe. The most important came from one of the War Dogs and painted a portrait of reinforcements streaming toward San Antonio. Sixty had just left San Felipe. Fannin had left Goliad, and should arrive any day. Another three hundred were due in San Felipe at any moment and would rush to the Alamo's defense.

Travis, historians agree, probably read the letter to the men. No doubt it buoyed morale. Privately, though, he was growing increasingly fatalistic. He wanted to believe men were coming, but he already sensed Fannin wasn't.

The next morning, Friday, March 4, the Mexican guns seemed angrier, more insistent. Every shot, it seemed, brought a shower of rocks and dirt into the plaza. This was the roughest day. Even the affable Crockett, always eager to cheer the men, appears to have realized this wasn't sustainable. "I think we had better march out and die in the open air," a soldier's wife named Susanna Dickinson heard him say. "I don't like to be hemmed up."[15]

Bowie, some say, came out of his sickroom at least once to boost morale, but it was hard now. From up on the walls, they could see Mexican reinforcements streaming into town. They could see the soldiers building scaling ladders. A number of the Tejanos and their wives melted away in these final days, leaving maybe nine Tejano fighters among the defenders. One young woman who fled, it's said, gave Santa Anna's officers detailed information on the Alamo's ramshackle defenses.

Saturday, March 5, a beautiful day with temperatures rising into the upper sixties, brought more of the same, the Mexican cannon on the north now barely two hundred yards away. The northern wall was crumbling by this point. That night Travis sent a messenger — it would be his last — to Goliad, begging Fannin to come to his aid. He wouldn't.

It was then, according to separate accounts by two of Santa Anna's officers, that Travis sent a messenger to Santa Anna offering to surrender. It was a Tejano woman, we're told, her name unknown. As General Vicente Filisola put it in a memoir years later, Travis, "through the intermediary of a woman, proposed to the general in chief that they would surrender arms and fort with everybody in it with the only condition of saving his life and that of all his comrades in arms."[16] According to Mexican accounts, Santa Anna replied that the only surrender he would accept was unconditional. No deal.

If these accounts are to be believed, and there's little reason they shouldn't, it puts the lie to the legend of Travis's resolute bravery, his insistence on fighting to the end. The evidence suggests he offered to give up, but Santa Anna wouldn't guarantee the men's lives. He wanted to make Travis, and the entire garrison, a bloody example.

That night the Alamo was quiet. Overhead, the moon rose, almost full, peeking in and out of thickening clouds. Travis, his slave Joe by his side, dozed in his quarters. Bowie slept in his sickroom on the south wall. No one can be sure where Crockett laid his head. Atop the walls, the officer of the watch, Captain John J. Baugh, had just begun his rounds at five o'clock, when he heard the notes of a lone bugle out in the darkness. It was followed by distant cries of "Viva!" and "Viva Santa Anna!"

Baugh peered into the darkness. The cries and shouts continued. One can only imagine the adrenaline that must have surged through the man. A moment later, Baugh turned, took a deep breath, and yelled the words everyone had been expecting for weeks: "The Mexicans are coming!"

CHAPTER 10
THE BATTLE OF THE ALAMO

Santa Anna lived for moments like this. The details of military maneuver and assault thrilled him as government never would. His orders covered every detail: which soldiers would attack and where, how much ammunition each would carry, even which headgear would be worn and how. But he wasn't perfect; far from it. Some officers privately wished they would hold off the assault a few more days. Portions of the walls, especially on the north, seemed ready to fall. But Santa Anna chose to silence his guns that night. Rather than further soften the defenses, he decided to try to catch Travis and his men by surprise.

As the Texians well knew, Santa Anna planned for his men to scale the walls with high ladders. Even a commander as meticulous as Santa Anna had limits, and at the Alamo, the Mexican ladders would be one. Twenty-eight were built, we are told.[1] Santa

Anna issued orders explaining how each was to be carried — by hand, with guns slung across shoulders — but no one spent much time examining their quality. Each ladder was made of sticks bound together by rawhide, but they were rickety, as battle would show.

About eighteen hundred men, roughly three-quarters of the Mexican force, would make the assault. Santa Anna chose veteran soldiers to do it, ordering new recruits to remain behind. All day Saturday, and into the evening, officers circulated among the troops still bunked in town, giving patriotic pep talks and making sure the guns and bayonets gleamed. At nightfall many tried to sleep. Most dozed fitfully.

A little after midnight, it was time. Officers began rousing the men, gathering them in the moonlight. No torches were lit, little noise made. By two the assault force had been formed into four columns. One by one, they filed across the river and veered into the darkness away from the Alamo, then looped back to take their positions, each a musket shot from the wall. General Cos, returning from his Mexican exile, lay down opposite the west wall with five hundred men. Colonel Francisco Duque took another five hundred men and positioned them opposite the north wall. Three hundred men would attack from the east. The final hundred were positioned to attack the south wall's main gate. On the high ground above, cavalry took up positions, ready to ride down anyone who tried to escape.

Santa Anna and his staff rode to positions alongside the cannon to the north. With them was the Mexican reserve, elite engineers, and five companies of grenadiers, around four hundred men. The men sat, or lay, in silence in the dark, forbidden from smoking or talking audibly.

Then, around five, came the sound of a bugle. In the darkness, the Mexican soldiers rose. After a few moments, the officers led them forward in a walk, then a trot, then a dead run, many of them pumping themselves up with shouts of "Viva Santa Anna!" As the men rushed forward in the gloom, Santa Anna had his band begin playing the "Degüello." The old Spanish cavalry tune dated to Moorish times, the title translated as the action of cutting a throat, or beheading. Every man in the Alamo was to be killed.

You'll sometimes hear people say that no one will ever know exactly what happened during the battle, because everyone died. But of course, this is not true. Several Mexican soldiers and officers would eventually leave accounts, and there would be a handful of Texian survivors with stories as well. Many writers have attempted to piece all these tales together into a believable story of what happened that morning. But even at their most vivid, these individual accounts only provide flashes of memory in the narrative darkness. We know a little, but not much.

One thing we do know is that the assault caught the defenders by surprise. Travis had posted three sentries outside the walls. They were either asleep or killed before they could raise a warning; none was given. Those inside the mission were mostly asleep. Inexplicably, Travis hadn't introduced the military custom of sleeping in shifts. The first man to raise the alarm, Captain Baugh, ran down into the compound, shouting to rouse the men. He raced to Travis's room. "The Mexicans are coming!" he yelled.

Out in the darkness, 1,400 soldiers were running toward the Alamo. By the time Travis stirred, the first were already approaching the walls. As they did, men across the Alamo rose, snatched up rifles, and found their positions. Travis and Joe were among them, sprinting atop the northern wall. "Come on, boys!" Travis hollered. "The Mexicans are upon us, and we'll give them hell!"[2]

All around the compound, men aimed their rifles and fired downward toward the onrushing troops. Each man had three or four rifles at his position, and according to Mexican accounts, much of this fire was accurate and deadly, killing dozens of men. The Texian artillery seems to have been slower to react — each gun, after all, needed several men in place — and had difficulty selecting targets in the night. Musket flashes helped to pinpoint some, but the real targeting aid came when Mexican soldiers shouted, "Viva Santa Anna!" Gunners beside Travis on the north wall loosed a blast of grapeshot at one such grouping, which seems to have killed at least a dozen soldiers, including a captain. Of the cheers that gave them away, one soldier wrote later, "The officers were unable to repress this act of folly, which was paid for dearly."[3]

All this happened in the battle's opening moments. Just about every account agrees that in those first few minutes, Travis was an energetic leader atop the northern wall. As soldiers approached, he fired his shotgun down into them. It may have been the only shot Travis got off. A moment later, a bullet struck him flush in the forehead. Joe watched as he toppled backward down a dirt ramp. At the bottom, he managed to pull himself to a sitting position, his sword in his hand, then slumped over, dead.

Mexican accounts paint a nightmarish picture of what happened next. You'd think that outnumbering the enemy fifteen to one would have made this something of a cakewalk for Santa Anna's troops. Yeah, no. The problems began at the north wall. By far the best account comes from a young Mexican officer named José Enrique de la Peña, whose long-forgotten diary first surfaced only in the 1950s.

Fire from the Texian rifles and artillery was so murderous, de la Peña tells us, that few of the first ladder carriers made it to the base of the wall. The first wave of men, in fact, wavered and had to be egged on by the cries of their officers. Precisely one ladder made it to the north wall in a timely fashion; many others fell apart once men put their weight on them. After maybe ten minutes of fighting, a massive tide of Mexican soldiers, probably numbering in the hundreds, was jammed against the northern wall, with nothing to climb, unable to move, exchanging wild shots with the Texian riflemen on the wall above. The situation grew worse, de la Peña tells us, when Texian guns atop the church splintered the three hundred Mexican soldiers charging from the east, forcing them to seek cover along the north wall as well. Mexican soldiers coming from the west also sought shelter on the north side. "All united at one point," de la Peña writes, "mixing and creating a confused mass."[4] For the Texians atop the north wall — twenty men? fifty? — it was like shooting the proverbial fish in a barrel.

Then Santa Anna made it worse. From his position several hundred yards north, the generalissimo viewed the trapped mass of soldiery beneath the northern wall with justifiable alarm. He called to the colonel commanding his four-hundred-man reserve and ordered him to charge. The entire general staff followed. As this group ran toward the compound, it fired its blunderbusses and pistols wildly. In his own memoir, General Filisola described how much of this fire ended up killing cornered Mexican troops.

But the Mexican fire, however haphazard, took its toll, and soon there simply weren't enough defenders. The turning point, says de la Peña, came when the desperate soldiers began climbing the damaged wall.

Fortunately the wall reinforcement on this front was of lumber, its excavation was hardly begun, and the height of the parapet was eight or nine feet [actually twelve]; there was therefore a starting point, and it could be climbed, though with some difficulty. But disorder had already begun; officers of all ranks shouted but were hardly heard. The most daring of our veterans tried to be the first to climb, which they accomplished, yelling wildly so that room could be made for them, at times climbing over their own comrades. Others, jammed together, made useless efforts, obstructing each other, getting in the way of the more agile ones and pushing down those who were about to carry out their courageous effort. A lively rifle fire coming from the roof of the [Long Barrack] and other points caused painful havoc, increasing the confusion of our disorderly mass.*

The first to climb were thrown down by bayonets already waiting for them behind the parapet, or by pistol fire, but the cour-

* We've added a paragraph break to make this easier to follow.

age of our soldiers was not diminished as they saw their comrades falling dead or wounded, and they hurried to occupy their places and to avenge them, climbing over their bleeding bodies. The sharp reports of the rifles, the whistling of bullets, the groans of the wounded, the cursing of the men, the sighs and anguished cries of the dying, the arrogant harangues of the officers, the noise of the instruments of war, and the inordinate shouts of the attackers, who climbed vigorously, bewildered all and made of this moment a tremendous and critical one. The shouting of those being attacked was no less loud and from the beginning had pierced our ears with desperate, terrible cries of alarm in a language we did not understand.[5]

Over on the south wall, a hundred soldiers under Colonel Juan Morales had also seen their initial charge repulsed. The traditional story is that Crockett and a group of Tennesseans led the south wall's initial defense with deadly efficient fire. Whoever was responsible, Morales quickly withdrew beneath the massive eighteen-pounder at the compound's southwest corner and regrouped his men.

By this point, it appears that at least some

of the rebels at this end of the compound had left their posts to help out on the northern wall. If so, this could explain why Colonel Morales's second charge, apparently against the main entrance, succeeded. In minutes, Morales and his men had rushed into the compound and charged up onto the western wall, taking control of the eighteen-pounder.

Mexican soldiers now had control of the northern and western walls, roughly fifteen minutes into the battle. Inside the church, Susanna Dickinson cowered with her baby and other women. At one point, her husband, Lieutenant Almaron Dickinson, burst into the room where she hid.* "Great God, Sue," he blurted. "The Mexicans are inside our walls! All is lost! If they spare you, save my child." He gave her one last kiss, drew his sword, and rushed back outside.†

Many of the defenders retreated inside the compound's strongest building, the Long Barrack, a narrow two-story structure beside the church that extended at an angle

* The name is sometimes spelled Almeron. Some sources cite his last name as Dickerson.
† Dickinson told this story many times later in life, sometimes in return for payment. She may have romanticized things just a bit.

toward the northern wall. Soldiers rushed the doors, and here the battle degenerated into the ugliest kind of hand-to-hand fighting. People desperately grappled for their lives in shadowy stone rooms, men killing one another with flashing knives, bayonets, and point-blank pistol fire.

We do not have detailed accounts of what must have been frenzied fighting. The closest we come is de la Peña:

> Our soldiers, some stimulated by courage and others by fury, burst into the quarters where the enemy had entrenched themselves, from which issued an infernal fire. Behind these came others, who, nearing the doors and blind with fury and smoke, fired their shots against friends and enemies alike, and in this way our losses were most grievous. . . . The tumult was great, the disorder frightful; it seemed as if the furies had descended upon us; different groups of soldiers were firing in all directions, on their comrades and on their officers, so that one was as likely to die by a friendly hand as by an enemy's.[6]

The fighting at the Long Barrack was the battle's dramatic climax. It ended only after Mexican soldiers on the walls swiveled the

Texian cannon and began firing down at the building. This fire not only killed some of the defenders, it opened gaping holes through which Mexican soldiers charged. It was a slaughter. There were simply too many soldiers. Up on the church's roof, meanwhile, Lieutenant Dickinson turned his guns in place and loosed several rounds of grapeshot at the Mexican troops swarming the compound.

All around, other crews tried to do the same. One by one, though, the Texian cannon were overrun. When Mexican soldiers finally burst into the church, they killed a number of men begging for their lives, then bayoneted a group of boys, several as young as twelve. Susanna Dickinson listened in horror at their screams.

Some accounts of the battle, especially older accounts, suggest the fighting essentially ended once the Mexicans took the Long Barrack and the church. We now know that's not true. In fact, new scholarship demonstrates that scores of men, perhaps as many as half the rebel defenders, were still alive after Mexican soldiers took the Long Barrack, throwing new light on the Alamo legend.

Of all the Alamo myths, the most enduring

216

has been the notion that those inside fought valiantly to the death. Given that none survived, it seemed self-evident. A classic version was offered by T. R. Fehrenbach, who wrote in 1968 that once the Mexicans made it over the walls,

the defenders no longer fought to win. They charged into the Mexican soldiery to kill as many as they could. These troops had seen much cruelty and understood it. . . . They smashed, butted, used tomahawks and knives. They had fought as paladins, each touchy of his rights and his own section of the wall. Now, they died as paladins, each with his ring of surrounding dead.[7]

Some of this was no doubt true; but recent scholarship has shown that a large number of the Alamo's defenders did not make a last stand inside the walls. Call it a retreat, an escape attempt, a dash for safety, or a "breakout" — no one survived to explain — but once confronted by overwhelming numbers, many of the men cut and ran.

This was never exactly a secret. There were hints of it in several Mexican accounts, including Santa Anna's. More than one nineteenth-century account, in fact, mentions fighting outside the walls. In 1961's *A Time to Stand,* Walter Lord wrote that "a few" defenders leapt a palisade "and raced pell-mell into the graying dawn."[8] Most historians, however, ignored the issue until 1992, when an Alamo enthusiast named Wallace O. Chariton published a little-remembered 1878 interview in which a Mexican sergeant named Manuel Loranca claimed that sixty-two defenders "sallied" from the east side of the compound. All but one were run down and killed by lancers. The last man, it was said, hid under a bush and was shot.[9]

Lord, the first twentieth-century writer to address the episode in any detail, presumably used the Loranca account as the basis for his single paragraph on it.

The [elite] Dolores cavalry had been waiting for just this moment. Sweeping down on the scene, they hacked away at the fleeing men. Here and there a cornered Texan fought back — one man killed a lance corporal with a double-barreled shotgun — but mostly it was child's play. The superb Mexican horsemen simply toyed with the fugitives, slashing them with sabers or running them through with brightly decked lances. Only two men

218

escaped immediate slaughter. One Texan wriggled under a bush, where he was ultimately found and shot; another hid beneath a small bridge, where he was later reported by a local woman washing laundry. He too was executed.[10]

It makes sense: In various letters written before the battle, any number of defenders had expressed frustration with being cooped up inside a fort, pining for a battle in the open field. Then, while researching his 1998 book *Three Roads to the Alamo* in a Mexico City archive, a Virginia Tech professor named William C. Davis stumbled on a report from one of Santa Anna's generals he hadn't seen before. Davis wasn't the first to read it; there were modern ink notations in the margins. But he was the first modern researcher to appreciate its significance.

The report, dated March 11, 1836, was written by General Joaquín Ramírez y Sesma, who commanded Santa Anna's cavalry. It noted that while the compound was being stormed,

as many of them believed their retreat was secure they left the fort from the right, and so many came out that they marched organized on the plains trying to take advantage of the nearby *brañal* [a rocky outcrop]. As soon as I observed this, I sent a company . . . so that they would harass the enemy from the side of the *brañal* and charge them with valiant officers' short lances/spears, and in this way the troop that they commanded charged and knifed them in moments, without letting the desperate resistance of [the enemy] make them vacillate for a moment.[11]

But Sesma's account went further. No sooner was this group run down than a larger group of defenders emerged from the main gate at the southern end of the compound.

Another group of around fifty men then came from the center of the fort, and I ordered [a company of lancers] to charge them. And upon seeing this movement, the enemy availed themselves of a trench/ ditch and made such a vigorous defense that I had to send [another forty-seven lancers] in order to defeat the [enemy]. All of these officials executed the movement with such decision and exactitude that some men truly barricaded in that position and resolved to lose their skins only at great expense, were run over in just a few minutes and knifed.[12]

Sesma concludes with mention of yet another, third group of defenders who fled "from the left," probably through an opening in the compound's west palisade.

What seems clear from Sesma's account is that as fighting raged inside the Long Barrack, a sizable number of defenders avoided the fighting inside. It appears they gathered into at least three groups. At this point it must have been clear that the battle was degenerating into a slaughter. The remaining defenders were outnumbered twenty to one. Travis and Bowie were dead or about to be. The Texian cannon were silent. The sun was rising. In the darkness outside the Alamo's walls, there were no Mexican troops in sight, and barely three hundred yards from the main gate there was high ground and trees. Beyond that was the road toward Gonzales, toward safety.

It would be wrong to suggest that the men in any of these "breakouts," as they are sometimes known, were cowards, or unwilling to fight. Rather, "they had no plan and no hope," writes William C. Davis. "They had simply been forced out of the fortress by overwhelming numbers. It was either go over the walls to fight and live a little longer, or else stand and be swarmed where they were."[13]

We know a few men surrendered. Some accounts say seven. But all were then killed, several apparently on Santa Anna's direct orders. Almost all the fighters died anonymous deaths, shot or bayoneted by soldiers who had no clue whom they were killing. Other than Travis, the only defender whose death can be described with any certainty is Bowie. Almonte's journal[14] and other Mexican accounts say he was killed in his sickbed, where he lay covered with heavy blankets, unable to defend himself. There are second- and thirdhand accounts of his body's mutilation, and of his corpse being raised on Mexican bayonets.

Crockett's fate has long fascinated historians. Some accounts, especially many written in the first decades after the battle, assumed he went down fighting. It was certainly what many wanted to believe. His death, inevitably depicted as at the center of a ring of fallen Mexican soldiers, would be celebrated in paintings, songs, and literature for years. Yet other accounts, including ones that circulated within days of the battle and one written by Almonte years later,[15] say he surrendered and was executed. For decades those versions were ignored. Not until the 1970s would the questions surrounding Crockett's death explode into a full-blown controversy.

Whatever his precise fate, Crockett's was no doubt one of the bodies that afterward were assembled into three piles. Tejanos with carts were sent into the countryside to gather wood, and when they returned it was used to build two or three funeral pyres, the wood and the bodies stacked in alternating layers. The fires burned into the night. The next morning all that remained were piles of ashes and charred bones, each pyre surrounded by a darkened ring of dirt, the result of fat cooked out of the corpses.

In later years, Santa Anna would downplay the battle. Whatever you think of San Antonio's strategic importance, it was clearly of significance. Somewhere between 180 and 250 Texians and Tejanos died, but at the price of an estimated six hundred or so Mexican soldiers. Nearly a quarter of Santa Anna's assault force was, in fact, wounded, no small number. In terms of scale and one-sidedness, the battle could be compared to the Battle of Fort Pillow in Tennessee in 1864, when two thousand Confederate troops under the command of Nathan Bedford Forrest defeated six hundred Union soldiers and massacred many of the survivors. Or the Battle of Rorke's Drift in 1879, when 140 British regulars successfully fought off more than four thousand Zulu warriors.

The legacy of the Alamo dwarfs those encounters, though, as it does that of most other battles in modern history. In art, in literature, and in history books, it has been imbued with the kind of potent symbolism bestowed on few other battlefields in the world. How that happened, how the story of this single hourlong mismatch came to mean so much to so many, is a fascinating story.

For the longest time, the Alamo was all but forgotten. But once rediscovered, it would emerge as the great creation myth of Texas, a heroic narrative written and shaped by men — and a few women — who instilled in it the values of their times. Their efforts would prove remarkably enduring. For 150 years, the world pretty much agreed on what the Alamo symbolized, what it meant.

But values change. Symbols change. Our understanding of history changes. The truth is, the Alamo has always meant different things to different groups. Only in recent years have these other voices, long ignored, begun to be heard.

CHAPTER 11
A FIRST DRAFT OF HISTORY

The moment the battle ended, the Alamo became a story, and a story told in times of war can be a powerful thing. It becomes propaganda, and in this way it can be viewed almost as a weaponized virus, something that can be contained or spread, something that can trigger panic or destroy an enemy's morale, even prompt defections.

The Alamo narrative would never be as important as it was in those first weeks after the battle. From the outset, Santa Anna and Sam Houston understood its potential impact and strove to mold it for their own uses. Santa Anna hoped the tale of a crushing loss would sap the will of Houston's fighters. Houston would shape it into a rallying cry.

The first carriers of the Alamo "virus" were the battle's few survivors, and none was as crucial to Santa Anna as the lone Anglo, Susanna Dickinson. Even before the battle, he knew of her existence from Tejanos who had fled the mission, and understood her significance. Soldiers were still roaming the compound, in fact, bayoneting the last defenders, when Almonte poked his head into the church room where Dickinson was hiding, her arms wrapped around her toddler.[1] A stray bullet had struck her in the leg, and she was sobbing. "Are you Mrs. Dickinson?" he asked in English. When she nodded, Almonte helped her hobble outside, past dozens of fallen bodies, where a doctor gently wrapped her wound.

Other officers went in search of the enslaved, whom Santa Anna intended to free. "Are there any Negroes here?" they shouted. They found Bowie's two slaves, and fished Travis's servant, Joe, from his hiding place. That afternoon, Santa Anna summoned Dickinson, Joe, and the other survivors, almost all Tejano women and children who had hidden in the church. To the Tejanos, he offered two pesos, a blanket, and amnesty in return for an oath of loyalty. He made a show of treating Dickinson and the slaves with respect. He then released the Tejanos but kept Dickinson and Joe in custody. With Almonte translating, he quizzed them on whether U.S. troops were fighting with the rebels.* On several occasions he tried to persuade them to build a new life in Mexico rather than return to the Americans.[2] Both declined.

A few nights later, Joe escaped. Bowie's slaves are lost to history. Dickinson, though, was someone Santa Anna could use. Almonte persuaded him to release her five days after the battle, arranging for a servant to escort her to Gonzales, where Sam Houston's Texian army was finally gathering.[3] With her she took a demand that Houston surrender, and her story.

Volunteers were streaming into The Hamlet of Gonzales, seventy miles east, when Houston rode in on March 11. The volunteers, energized by Travis's letters and the government's call for troops, were finally mustering to relieve the Alamo. No one knew it had already fallen. Houston, we are told, still didn't believe any of it.

Arriving late in the afternoon, Houston was reluctantly planning a relief expedition when he heard women shrieking. Two of Seguín's Tejano cohorts, Andrés Barcena

* Three of the dead at the Alamo are listed as "deserters" on U.S. Army muster rolls in Louisiana. More on this later.

and Anselmo Bergara, had arrived with news that the Alamo had fallen. Barcena had slipped out of San Antonio the night before the attack; Bergara was one of Seguín's scouts. They had been at a friend's ranch the night of March 6 when a rider appeared with the news. The rider's description of the fighting, the number of casualties, Bowie's death, the execution of those who surrendered — it was all fairly accurate. His one piece of misinformation was a story that Travis had committed suicide.[4]

For Houston, this was the worst possible news — not just a calamitous loss, but the deaths of the Alamo's best-known fighters. If the story spread, Houston knew, there would be panic. He told everyone it was an obvious lie. Privately, Houston wrote to Fannin, "I fear a melancholy portion of it will be found too true."[5] He ordered Fannin to blow up the Goliad presidio and retreat.

Everything now depended on discerning the truth of Barcena and Bergara's story. If the Alamo had fallen, Santa Anna's army could be on them at any moment, and his forces outnumbered Houston's nine to one. When the next day passed with no news, Houston sent a trio of scouts west toward San Antonio. To his surprise, they returned that same evening with Dickinson, her Mexican escort, and Joe, who encountered them on the road. Dickinson's dress was still splashed with blood. When her story spread through town, panic broke out. Men and women were running everywhere, shouting, abandoning camp, packing wagons. Amid the chaos, Houston learned that twenty volunteers had disappeared into the night. In a booming voice, he hollered for someone to find them and bring them back. But it was too late.

Houston's first impulse was to cover his rear. He fired off letters to several politicians blaming Travis and Fannin for the disaster. Yet he also understood the need to turn Travis's tactical foolishness into martyrdom. Within forty-eight hours of learning the news, he struck upon an analogy to the Battle of Thermopylae, where Spartans and other Greek soldiers fought to the death against an invading Persian force of a hundred thousand troops in 480 BCE — a battle especially prized in nineteenth-century America.* "The conduct of our brave men in the Alamo," he wrote, "was only equaled by Spartan valor."[6]

* Contemporary audiences will know the story from the 2006 movie *300*.

Within two hours of Dickinson's arrival, Houston declared a retreat. By eleven o'clock that night everyone was on the road streaming east and Gonzales was in flames, torched on Houston's orders. Those twenty deserters, meanwhile, spread the story into the heart of the colonies. Thus began what's known in Texas as the "Runaway Scrape," the mass evacuation of pretty much all Anglo Texans toward Louisiana. It was utter chaos. Riders galloped from farm to farm, shouting, "The Mexicans are coming!" Families evacuated so fast one house was discovered with fried chicken, a pitcher of milk, and a coffeepot still on the kitchen table. Heavy rains turned the roads into mud pits; mothers trudged knee-deep through it, infants in their arms. Some of the weak got sick and died. The strong headed for Galveston Island, hoping to catch a boat to New Orleans, or scurried toward the East Texas pines, hoping to hide from the Mexican cavalry.

If Santa Anna's approach spelled doom for the Anglo colonists, though, it meant freedom for Texas slaves, still a full 10 percent of the population. Already a group on the Brazos had tried to revolt; a number were hanged or whipped to death. Now, as Anglos streamed east, many broke free and headed west, where the Mexican troops held out the hope of freedom. Some joined up as spies and scouts.

As the grumbling Texian army retreated toward San Felipe, Houston struggled to regain control of the narrative. The first step was a debriefing of Dickinson and Joe. An officer named William Fairfax Gray sat down with them on March 20. Their stories were generally accurate and aligned, though there is evidence Houston's men massaged their accounts to inject a bit more heroism.

Because Dickinson had remained inside the church, Joe had the more compelling story. He told of witnessing Travis's sudden death[7] at the wall, ruling out the suicide rumor. Later, however, under questioning by George Childress, a secessionist politician, he gave an entirely different account, this one claiming that Travis rose after being shot and valiantly used his saber to slash a Mexican general named Mora with his final breath. The only Mora at the Alamo, unfortunately, was a cavalry general who remained outside the compound during the battle. No one knew that then, of course. In one fell swoop, Houston's men transformed Travis's reported suicide into a heroic death.[8]

Dickinson, meanwhile, first said she had

seen none of the fighting. Later, though, two accounts by men who heard her story claimed she witnessed Crockett fighting to the death, using his rifle Old Betsy as a club when he ran out of bullets. Given the evidence that Crockett likely surrendered, either Dickinson or her interlocutors were embellishing things. Her story would change still more over the years. But for the moment one senses Houston and his men had enough to assemble the story they wanted told. What they needed now was to find someone to publish it.

On March 17, four days after retreating from Gonzales, the Texian army and hundreds of anxious settlers paused at the Colorado River. Houston decided to wait for Fannin and his men from Goliad. They never made it. No sooner had Fannin's four hundred men left the town than they were surrounded by General José de Urrea's cavalry. After a skirmish, Fannin surrendered, meekly marching his men back into town. They spent a week there as prisoners, until March 27, when soldiers divided them into three groups, marched them down three different roads, and then opened fire. Three hundred ninety men were massacred. Fannin, it's said, only asked not to be shot in the face, and to be given a decent burial. He was shot in the face; his body was then burned. General Urrea had asked Santa Anna to spare the Texians, but he ordered their execution.

The days after Goliad were the revolt's darkest hours. Grumbling among Houston's men grew worse, bordering on mutiny. As the army retreated east, the Runaway Scrape spread into the rich cotton lands astride the Brazos; hundreds more families abandoned their farms, slopping east through the mud and rain. The new Texas president, David Burnet, beseeched Houston to stop and fight. "The enemy are laughing you to scorn," he wrote in a letter. "You must retreat no further. The country expects you to fight. The salvation of the country depends on you doing so."

But Houston knew he was not ready. Men were pouring into the ranks now; in just three weeks, the size of his force tripled, to around fourteen hundred men, including a large contingent of Seguín's Tejano cavalry. But the new soldiers were raw and badly in need of training, so Houston marched them north twenty miles to Jared Groce's plantation on the Brazos, made camp, and began drills. Discipline alone, however, would not defeat Santa Anna. What Houston's army needed, he knew, was confidence. And inspiration. And purpose. His men would find them in the story of the Alamo.

The first published account of the Alamo's fall appeared March 24, eighteen days after the battle, in a Harrisburg newspaper, the *Telegraph and Texas Register,* the Texians' reliable propaganda arm. It used the narrative lumber supplied by Joe and Dickinson to build a mansion of bravery, heroism, and sacrifice. In the *Telegraph*'s hands, every defender valiantly falls inside the walls; only one surrenders. Here is Crockett surrounded by Mexican dead — a "glorious death"; here is a man named Robert Evans blowing up the Texian powder magazine — and himself — which most certainly never happened; here is Travis getting shot not once but twice. And — still not dead! — using his last breath to kill that Mexican officer.[9]

The *Telegraph* account is more than a news story. It is a straightforward effort to build a legend. In perhaps its best line, one that would be repeated often in years to come, the article's unidentified author endorses Houston's comparison of the Alamo to Thermopylae. He termed its fall an "event so lamentable, and yet so glorious to Texas . . . that we shall never cease to celebrate it."

And he was right. But in the near term, what the *Telegraph* article did best was distract people from the uncomfortable truth of what a boneheaded loss the Alamo actually was. Houston had wanted Bowie to destroy the old mission and then failed to send him reinforcements. The *Telegraph*'s big lie was that the Alamo fighters were serving a strategic purpose as a rear guard, that their deaths had purchased precious time for Houston's army. This myth persists to this day. In fact, Santa Anna had told Mexico City he planned to secure San Antonio by March 2. In the end, the siege ended up delaying him all of four days. The fact is, as painful as it may be to hear, the Alamo's trapped defenders died for pretty much nothing.

The legend really began to grow, though, when news hit the U.S. press. On March 28, four days after the *Telegraph* story, the first news of the Alamo's fall appeared in a New Orleans newspaper, brought in by Texians fleeing via Galveston. That initial account was spotty, as first reports typically are; sourced to Joe and Dickinson by name, it claimed that both Travis and Bowie had killed themselves. But the details didn't much matter. What mattered was that Mexican troops had killed nearly two hundred men, most of them Americans. As the news spread to Natchez, then Nashville, then finally to the East Coast, Santa Anna was pilloried as a "tyrant" and a "butcher."

Across America, the press exploded in grief and outrage. Crockett remained a beloved figure in most quarters; news of his death drove the coverage. "David Crockett (now rendered immortal in glory) had fortified himself with sixteen guns well charged, and a monument of slain encompassed his lifeless body," read the *Richmond Enquirer.*[10] A notable lamentation was a bit of doggerel penned by an editor at the *New-Orleans Commercial Bulletin:*

Vengeance on Santa Anna and his
    minions,
Vile scum, up boiled from the infernal
    regions,
Dragons of fire on black sulphuros
    pinions,
The offscouring baseness of hell's
    blackest legions,
Too filthy far with crawling worms to dwell
And far too horrid and too base for hell.[11]

Even those papers that had criticized the Texas war backed it now. "We have been opposed to the Texan war from first to last," the *Memphis Enquirer* editorialized, "but our feelings we cannot suppress — some of our own bosom friends have fallen in the Alamo. We would avenge their death and spill the last drop of our blood upon the altar of Liberty."[12] States and cities fell all over themselves pledging money, men, and guns to avenge the dead. The state of Alabama sent every musket in its arsenal. Slaveholders in Natchez assembled an expedition — again — that set off for the Texas border within days.

Among the new arrivals, historians have determined, were an estimated two hundred American soldiers, who had quietly crossed the border from posts in Louisiana. Some came on their own, others came in groups. No one knows whether they were on a covert mission or responding to the offer of pay and free land. U.S. commanders officially listed them as "deserters,"[13] but they were a godsend to the Texians, who desperately needed training to face Santa Anna's professional soldiers. Among the new recruits were expert cannoneers from Fort Jesup, Louisiana, who wore buckskin accessories over their U.S. Army uniforms.*

As these U.S. regulars drilled the militia at the Groce plantation, those who remained discovered within themselves something new, something that every army badly needs — a cause, a purpose, a fiery new commitment. And there's no doubting what it was: the Alamo narrative. It's not an overstatement to venture that the gently massaged story of its heroic fall emerged as the single most powerful weapon in Houston's arsenal. Part of it was a thirst for revenge, no doubt. Part of it was what the historian Walter Lord termed a "deep, gnawing shame" at failing to rally to Travis's defense. What happened at the Alamo proved this was a "kill or be killed" situation if the Mexican army caught them. They would beat Santa Anna, or die. "We ask nor expect no quarter in the future," one man wrote home. What Hous-

* Some of the so-called deserters chose to remain in Texas, but many returned to their U.S. Army units in Louisiana, where their desertions were punished with a proverbial slap on the wrist. In one case, the muster rolls for an entire thirty-man company based at Fort Jesup is missing for the month of April 1836. Mexican scholars consider their deployment proof that the United States was behind the Texas Revolt all along.

ton's army found was a spirit of desperation, and desperate armies can do amazing things.

Back in San Antonio, a satisfied Santa Anna was convinced the war was over. All that remained, he told his aides, was securing the province. He sent his first troops — General Sesma's cavalry — east from San Antonio on March 11. In the following days, others marched to Goliad and elsewhere. Santa Anna was actually planning to return to Mexico City, but he agreed to stay, just to make sure Texas was pacified. It couldn't have been hard to persuade him. Santa Anna loved this kind of victory-lap campaigning.

Riding east with 750 men on March 31, Santa Anna's own column reached the ruins of Gonzales in three days, then forged on to San Felipe on April 7, only to discover that Houston had destroyed boats he needed to cross the river. It took a week to get everyone across, at which point a friendly Tejano relayed the news that the new Texas government was at Harrisburg, thirty miles east.

Santa Anna, sensing the chance to capture Lorenzo de Zavala, lunged forward. But when he reached Harrisburg, he discovered the government had fled to Galveston.

Enraged, he had the *Telegraph*'s presses thrown into Buffalo Bayou and burned the town. Belatedly, he sent out scouts in search of Houston's army. It was time to end this thing.

By this point, Santa Anna had pushed far past the Texians, who remained up the Brazos, fifty miles to the northwest. Houston drilled his men there for two solid weeks before finally stirring. Finally, on April 12, the Texians broke camp, marched south, and then swung east, falling in behind Santa Anna and effectively cutting him off from the rest of his army, now spread across the Texas plains far behind. Houston may have been heading for the U.S. border, where General Edmund Gaines had reinforcements waiting if Mexican troops crossed the Neches.[14] Santa Anna, catching wind the Texians were moving east once more, struck out blindly through the marshlands north of Galveston Bay, checking each of the river crossings for sign of them. Behind him, Houston reached Buffalo Bayou, across from the ashes of Harrisburg, where on April 18 he sent out scouts. The turning point came when they reported back that Santa Anna himself was leading the force ahead of them, with maybe a thousand men. If he hadn't known it by that point, Houston

240

knew it then: His nine hundred had a chance to win, and they were eager to fight.

The hunted Texians now became the hunters. At daybreak on the nineteenth, Houston assembled his men beside the bayou, explained the situation, and for the first time — that we know of — invoked the Alamo. "Victory is certain!" Houston bellowed. "Trust in God and fear not. And remember the Alamo! Remember the Alamo!"

Leaving the wounded behind, Houston force-marched his men east, taking with him two newly arrived six-pounders, dubbed the "Twin Sisters," a gift from the people of Cincinnati. They were commanded by American artillerymen who had "deserted" from Fort Jesup.[15] After midnight they camped, then moved out at dawn. That morning Mexican scouts spotted them. By afternoon Houston's own scouts reported Santa Anna was moving toward them. Stopping beside a wide field of high grasses, Houston unfurled his men into a line at one end, atop a gentle rise fronting a wood, Buffalo Bayou to one side, the San Jacinto River on the other.

When Mexican lancers cantered into view, the Twin Sisters opened fire. Santa Anna's cannon returned the volleys. After a bit, his infantry came up and mounted a desultory charge. By nightfall the two armies had withdrawn into camps a thousand yards apart across open prairie.

The next morning, Thursday, April 21, 1836, dawned clear and warm, a picture-perfect spring day. In his camp, Santa Anna was in no hurry to attack Houston's well-positioned line along the trees. He had sent word for other Mexican units to hurry forward. Around nine, General Cos trotted in with four hundred more troops. More were expected at any moment. On the off chance the Texians did something foolish, Santa Anna had breastworks erected in front of the camp. In early afternoon, satisfied, the general lay beneath a spreading oak to take a siesta.

In the Texian camp, Houston held a council of war — his first ever, it's said — at noon. If Santa Anna didn't attack, he was considering an assault the next morning. His men, however, were chomping at the bit. Houston, seeing their resolve, shrewdly went along. By two the men were moving into a line about a thousand yards across; sixty cavalrymen on the right; next, two companies of Texas "regulars"; the Twin Sisters in the middle; Burleson's First Regiment to their left; and on the far left, the

Second Regiment, many of its men from Kentucky.[16]

Houston initially did not want to use Seguín's Tejano cavalry for fear the Anglos would mistake them for Mexican troops, but relented when Seguín agreed his men would wear distinctive pieces of cardboard in their headbands. At four, Houston, riding his gray stallion, Saracen, raised his sword, and his men began trotting forward through the grass. A German gent played a fife, a Black man a drum. Ahead, in the distant Mexican camp, nothing moved.*

Incredibly, Santa Anna had posted neither pickets nor scouts to watch the Texian

* One of the most enduring legends of the Battle of San Jacinto is that Santa Anna was distracted while enjoying a tryst with a mulatto woman named Emily Morgan in his tent that afternoon. The story comes from a British traveler's diary, in which he records hearing the story in 1842 while visiting Texas. There are no other sources, but it quickly became folklore. A hotel across the street from the Alamo today is even named for Emily Morgan, the so-called Yellow Rose of Texas. But while Morgan was a real person who was captured by Mexican forces, there is no evidence that she ever met Santa Anna, let alone distracted him so that Houston could launch a surprise attack.

camp. As Houston's men trotted across the grassy plain, the Mexican camp remained entirely still. Not until they were practically within musket range did a Mexican bugle sound. It was answered by a shout from the Texas left, said to be Colonel Sidney Sherman: "Remember the Alamo! Remember Goliad! Remember the Alamo!"

At barely twenty yards, as Mexican infantrymen struggled to form a line, the Texians opened fire. Dozens of Mexican soldiers fell. Only a few managed to loose shots in return: Houston's horse shrieked and fell. He grabbed the reins of another. In a flash the onrushing Texians crashed into the milling Mexicans, bayonets thrusting, tomahawks hacking, men screaming. Hundreds of soldiers turned and ran, many of them cut down by Texian cavalry.

Things got nasty fast. For those of you who believe the Texians were paragons of virtue, you might want to skip to the next paragraph. "Take prisoners like the Meskins do!" the scout Deaf Smith was heard hollering. Dozens of Mexicans fell to their knees, some mouthing, "Mi no Alamo" or "Mi no Goliad." Houston's men clubbed and stabbed many to death as they knelt. The Texians massacred hundreds of men, while others pillaged Santa Anna's camp and raped Mexican women who were camp followers. One of the U.S. Army deserters later wrote that he used his pistol to force a group of Texians to free several women they seemed ready to rape, and turned them over to Seguín's men for protection.[17]

The whole thing was over, famously, in eighteen minutes. Six hundred Mexican soldiers, nearly half of Santa Anna's command, were dead. Nine Texians died in battle; six more would die of their wounds. Houston was shot in the leg. They captured Santa Anna the next day wearing a private's gray trousers and a silk shirt. A downcast Lorenzo de Zavala, already thoroughly frozen out of the new Texas government, showed up soon after, greeting his old friend Juan Almonte and icily agreeing to serve as Houston's translator. The generalissimo and his staff were then transported to Velasco, where de Zavala and Santa Anna spent the next month negotiating the treaties that would end the war and grant Texas its independence.

The Battle of San Jacinto would go down as perhaps the most decisive in North American history. Men and guns fought it, of course, but make no mistake, the spanking new myth of the Alamo was decisive. The Mexican generals understood this. The

245

loss at San Jacinto represented "the consequences of the executions of the Alamo, of Refugio, Goliad," General Filisola wrote in his memoir thirteen years later. "The rebels saw that with such conduct and design there could be no hope for a peaceful understanding."[18]

The Alamo legend wasn't solely created by the battle in San Antonio. It was given flight at San Jacinto. Had Texas remained a Mexican province, would we still be remembering the Battle of the Alamo? Maybe. But what gives the Alamo its resonant symbolism is the power its story had on the men who won at San Jacinto. It was there the words "Remember the Alamo" entered history, which the victors would now sit down and begin to write.

CHAPTER 12
REMEMBER THE ALAMO?

As legends go, the story of the Alamo was not exactly an overnight sensation. Even in the first years afterward, there weren't a lot of people around with firsthand knowledge of what happened that fateful morning in 1836. The rebels were dead. Mexican accounts, by and large, wouldn't come to light for years. So while there were plenty of books and monographs examining the strange new independent nation of Texas, the Alamo was not a big part of them. The first significant history of Texas, issued in 1855, devoted exactly six of its thousand-plus pages to it.

The years that followed the siege were tumultuous in Texas. Under its first president, Sam Houston, the new country made a stab at going it alone, but pretty much everyone was glancing at their watches to see when the United States would invite them in. The Mexican government, meanwhile, never gave up hollering about getting Texas back. When Santa Anna retook the Mexican presidency in 1841, he ordered troops to harass the frontier. One group of seven hundred crossed the Rio Grande and, finding no opposition, kept marching until it reached San Antonio, waltzing in and occupying the town for two days in March 1842. Houston raised a militia, and there was some skirmishing down in South Texas, but still, no one was prepared six months later when a larger Mexican force, under a general named Adrián Woll, swept into San Antonio. Once the militia responded, there was a battle at Salado Creek, after which Woll too scurried back south.

At this point Houston, now in his second term, decided to knock a little harder on the White House door. The United States, though, jittery about provoking a war with Mexico, and facing sectional opposition to creating a new slave state, passed. But after a few years of vigorous back-and-forth, Texas became the twenty-eighth American state on December 29, 1845. And indeed, war with Mexico ensued in 1846. It lasted three years. Barely a decade later came the Civil War. As a slave state, Texas seceded and fought with the Confederacy for five long years. You can understand if folks had better things to do than write about what happened at the Alamo.

And yet they did, a handful of authors anyway. The publishing business was beginning a massive boom — in dollar terms, the industry quintupled between 1820 and 1850 — and Texas, first as an independent nation, then as a shiny new state, was the subject of thirty or so books and monographs during this period, mostly travelogues written by outsiders. By today's standards, their work was, well, jingoistic crap. Typical in tone was a two-volume history written in 1841 by a Mississippi legislator named Henry Foote, who had a good word for seemingly every filibuster from Aaron Burr to the East Texas pooh-bah Haden Edwards. Mexican authorities, Foote judged, were "vulgar tyrants," their soldiers "unprincipled renegades." Travis and Fannin, he concluded, "are not censurable for *anything.*"

Many of these books suffered from the twin sins of florid romanticism and score settling. Amateurs ruled the day; the kind of professional historian we take for granted would not exist for decades. As bad as they were, these authors' works established the foundation of what we call the Heroic Anglo Narrative of Texas history. They portrayed

Anglo Texans as God's righteous democratic warriors, exemplars of progress, patriotism, and morality, two-legged arguments for American expansionism and manifest destiny. Maybe the best of a bad lot, written by Austin's cousin Mary Holley, noted, "The Anglo-Saxon American race are destined to be forever the proprietors of this land of promise and fulfillment," adding: "The righteous cause, the cause of LIBERTY, PHILANTHROPY, and RELIGION — shall prosper. Such is the cause of Texas." And the Mexicans? Holley judged them "very indolent, of loose morals, and if not infidels, of which there are many, involved in the grossest superstition."[1]

We could cite another dozen examples along these lines, but this stuff gets pretty tiresome. Not all such early books were so doctrinaire, though. One or two were actually critical, most notably *The History of Texas,* written by a caustic Gonzales seminarian named David Barnett Edward. A rare Texas Tory, Edward was no fan of Texans or their revolt. He praised Santa Anna's immigration policies as "enlightened," going on to proclaim the Americans had "by their perverse conduct, forfeited every claim to protection from civil law." Published in 1836, Edward's book prompted Texas's first literary uproar, and not only because it plagiarized sections of Mary Holley's work. Stephen F. Austin termed it "a slander on the people of Texas."[2]

The Alamo did not figure prominently in any of this work. Where it was mentioned, authors had little to offer beyond what had been in the newspapers. With historians stymied, at least for the moment, writers of fiction filled the void, which by and large was not a good thing; Mary Holley was practically Chaucer compared with this crew. Much of this "literature" consists of trashy potboilers written by outsiders using the Texas Revolt as a fresh backdrop, typically with Santa Anna or a stand-in portrayed as a Mexican version of Snidely Whiplash. The late University of Texas professor Don Graham points out the startling number of early Texas novels used as vehicles for anti-Catholicism, the Texians fighting the "dark designs of priests and the hierarchical and undemocratic structure of the Catholic church." Forget Santa Anna; the real enemy was Father Tim. The evil priest in 1888's *Remember the Alamo,* to cite but one example, is consumed with hatred for Texas Protestants. "If these American heretics were only in my power!"

he seethes. "I would cut a throat — just one throat — every day of my life."[3]

It's a short hop from anticlericalism to overt racism, which would infuse Alamo-based fiction after the mid-1800s. In these books the Mexican characters are inevitably cruel, dirty, and treacherous. In many they are referred to as "greasers." An 1856 "historical romance" set during the revolution helpfully imagines how visitors to Matamoros coined the term: "The people look greasy, their clothes are greasy, their dogs are greasy, their houses are greasy — everywhere grease and filth."[4]★ (You know racists are pretty serious when they start in on pets.) It just goes on and on. In a 1909 Texas novel, *The Trapper's Bride,* the author calls the Mexican army "savage legions . . . given to every kind of horrible excesses, and whose arms were deeply stained with the blood of helpless old men, feeble women and innocent children."

And we're not even getting to nineteenth-century Alamo poetry. There's a lot of it, typically replete with classical references; Thermopylae is a staple, of course. The very

★ It's been suggested the term may actually derive from Mexican laborers tasked with the greasing of wagon axles.

worst manages to combine elements of classicism and racism, as in Horace Claflin Southwick's "The Alamo."

> Say, you talk of Balaklava,
>   And the bloomin' British
> Square, Of Waterloo and Ballyhoo,
>   Why, that's nothin' but hot air;
> Like the story of Thermopelae,
>   An' yarns about the Greeks,
> An' Persians and Egyptians —
>   Not to speak of other freaks.
> Why, sonny, down in Texas
>   Not so very long ago,
> They had a scrap with Greasers,
>   At a place called Alamo . . .[5]

Had enough?

If the Alamo narrative was initially neglected by anyone like a serious historian, that neglect was symbolized by the Alamo itself. Almost overnight, the old mission had become a ruin. Retreating Mexican cavalry had torn down the walls and set fire to everything that would burn. For years the only remaining structures, the church and the Long Barrack, sat roofless and filled with rubble; the town began selling wagonloads of Alamo stone for five dollars a pop.

Slowly everything returned to nature, grass and weeds sprouting everywhere, vines snaking up over the barracks. By the 1840s the Alamo's only permanent occupants were a colony of unruly bats.

Every now and then the curious, often a traveler, would appear and wander the grounds, snatching up a souvenir rock much as latter-day tourists did at the Berlin Wall. The soldiers who occasionally camped at the site — Texas troops in 1836 and 1839, those raiding Mexicans in 1842 — were less reverential, etching their names into the walls and using the stone carvings and little statues that dotted the old compound for target practice.

The first hint of change arrived in 1841, when a squat, balding clerk with the splendid name of Reuben Marmaduke Potter visited the site. Potter, who was destined to become the first serious student of the Alamo, already knew more about the battle than almost anyone who hadn't fought there. The first serious "Alamo-head," as modern-day enthusiasts are known, he considered the compound hallowed ground and was stunned by its condition. There was nothing — no marker, no monument — to mark the battle. Potter located the spot where Juan Seguín, upon returning to San

Antonio, had buried the ashes of the dead. Someone had planted a peach orchard atop it. "This," Potter wrote in his journal, "is too sad to comment."[6]

Potter's interest arose from firsthand experience. Born in New Jersey in 1802, he was managing a warehouse in Matamoros, just across the Rio Grande, when the Texas war broke out. When a group of Texians was jailed there during the Runaway Scrape, a Mexican general asked the expatriate community to look after them. Potter delivered their meals and listened, fascinated, to their stories of the war. When Santa Anna ordered them executed, Potter argued for due process, buying them time until the fighting ended.[7] Later he helped a pair of Texas prisoners smuggle a message to Texas in the handle of a whip.[8] Of all the stories he picked up in those eventful months during and after the war, none fascinated Potter as much as the Alamo. He was so inspired he scribbled down a poem, "Hymn of the Alamo."★

Potter thought so highly of his work he had it published as sheet music; in time, it caught on. Though little remembered today,

★ The poem read, in full, can be found at the end of the chapter.

"Hymn of the Alamo" emerged as Texas's "Star-Spangled Banner" in the mid-1800s.[9]

After the revolt Potter moved to Texas, working as a tax collector. Startled at the Alamo's condition, he checked to see whether anyone in local government would address it. No one would. At one point he paid to have a memorial made; when no one in San Antonio wanted it, he ended up selling it to the state. It stood in the Texas Capitol until the building was destroyed in an 1881 fire.[10]

In 1846, Potter went to work as a wandering aide to several U.S. Army quartermasters, which seems to have diverted him from his Alamo interests for the next decade or so. In his absence, a Tennessee-born lawyer named Henderson K. Yoakum began years of work on what would become the first definitive history of Texas. Yoakum had settled in the town of Huntsville in 1845, where his legal clients included none other than Sam Houston, who became one of the state's senators after Texas joined the United States. In his downtime, Houston, like aging politicians and cops everywhere, loved to tell war stories, to which Yoakum would listen, rapt. He began taking notes, then started poring over Houston's papers, and at some point realized there was a book in it.

The volume that resulted, 1855's massive *History of Texas,* was the first of its kind to employ anything like professional methods. Yoakum spent long periods in state archives, making sure he got names and dates as accurate as he could. Though criticized at the time for its slavish adoration of Houston, the book's reputation would flourish in the years to come; as late as 1935, one writer still judged it "the standard for the period it covers."[11]

It was Yoakum, like Houston a slave owner, who as much as any other nineteenth-century author enshrined the myth of the Heroic Anglo Narrative. He portrays the Texian revolt as an organic continuation of the American Revolution, arguing it was the rightful extension of Anglo-American culture.[12] Each time the Mexican government attempts to enforce a law in Texas, Yoakum evokes tyranny. When Travis and others overrun Mexican outposts, he sees an act in furtherance of "liberty."[13] Yet Yoakum was surprisingly upfront about matters that might seem revisionist today. He cites Mexico's abolition of slavery as a cause of the revolution. He was equally candid about the importance of U.S. support, detailing how Americans sent men, money, and weapons in violation of U.S. law.

It was Yoakum who devoted only six of his thousand-plus pages to the Alamo, which makes sense given it wasn't exactly Houston's finest hour. What little he does say only reinforces the myth of supreme, selfless heroism. "The defenders of Texas did not retreat, but lay there in obedience to the command of their country; and in that obedience the world has witnessed among men no greater moral sublimity," he wrote.[14]

Potter didn't much care for Yoakum's book. In 1858, when he took an army quartermaster's post and returned to San Antonio, he got a unique chance to craft a reply. The army had rescued the church and the Long Barrack from ruin, turning them into a supply depot; army engineers put a new roof on the church, creating that signature hump beloved by Alamo enthusiasts to this day. Potter's office was inside. While overseeing the distribution of supplies, he spent every extra minute poring over the compound and interviewing anyone who had a role in the battle, from Tejano rebels to Mexican soldiers to civilian witnesses. Fluent in Spanish, he befriended

Seguín and Santa Anna's onetime chief of staff. He even hired as a servant a Mexican soldier who fought in the battle.

What Yoakum did for the Texas Revolt, Potter did for the Alamo. His account of the battle, printed in a San Antonio newspaper in 1860 and later published as a sixteen-page monograph, was the first that approaches anything like modern professional history. Having debriefed Mexican generals and soldiers, Potter was the first Anglo historian to describe the mash-up at the north wall; the fighting in the Long Barrack; the Mexican soldiers turning the Texians' own cannon on them. Potter made detailed measurements of the old compound and drew maps and diagrams that stand up to this day. And he was the first to correctly report the number of men in Santa Anna's army. He had been at Matamoros when it returned across the border, and once said he knew its size because, as he put it, "I counted."[15]

Yet Potter's monograph also serves as a veritable petri dish of Alamo folklore. He accepts details that Sam Houston's men had massaged into the first eyewitness accounts offered by Susanna Dickinson and the enslaved Joe. In Potter's version, Davy Crockett charges into a line of Mexican troops and dies fighting, while Almaron Dickinson leaps to his death with his child strapped to his back.[16] Jim Bowie is laid up not by disease but by injuries he suffered in a fall from the ramparts, a story Potter would sheepishly admit creating from whole cloth years later. He conjures an image of Bowie going out guns blazing from his sickbed, even though he must've known better.

As flawed as his work was, Potter should be applauded for hauling the historical Alamo out of the literary darkness. By the time of the Civil War, he was universally recognized as its leading authority. When the state commissioned the Irish-born artist Henry McArdle to create an epic painting of the battle, Potter was called in to consult. The work that resulted, McArdle's massive 1905 *Dawn at the Alamo,* which today hangs in the Senate Chamber of the Texas Capitol, is a detailed panorama, hailed for correctly depicting topography, weaponry, and portraiture, even as it shows Travis and company in heroic gestures bathed in light and includes some obvious boners. Bowie, for instance, is shown in the thick of the fighting.

Potter never stopped writing about the Alamo, even after Confederate soldiers marched into the church in 1861 and had him deported to New York. In later years he wrote articles excoriating Yoakum and was honored by Texas veterans' groups. But he would never return to Texas. He died in Brooklyn in 1890.

One thing that's notable about these early histories is the wholesale absence of Tejano figures like the Seguíns. You can debate the centrality of Tejano contributions all you want, but they were undeniably key figures in the Austin colony's early successes and, later, in the success of the Texas Revolt. What the Tejanos got in return, alas, and this is one of the great injustices of Texas history, was uneasy membership in a new Anglo society of grinding racism that marginalized everyone who wasn't white. It's a kind of betrayal, really, one that is reflected in how thoroughly Tejanos were written out of the emerging Heroic Anglo Narrative.

You can see the stirrings of racism during the revolt, when a handful of Texian leaders, most notably Austin, began rationalizing the rebellion as a struggle against a "mongrel race." The Alabama-born Travis, for one, didn't trust San Antonio's brown-skinned residents, and said so more than once. And it only got worse once the fighting stopped. To that point, Anglos and Tejanos hadn't mixed all that much, the Anglos concentrated in the southeast, the Tejanos in San Antonio and South Texas. But with the war's end, Anglos old and new surged into Tejano Texas, crowding the coast, establishing ranches around San Antonio, and eventually surging into the Rio Grande Valley.

Unlike the Spanish-bred San Antonio elites, most Tejanos were mixed-blood mestizos, and incoming Anglos, many of them Southern racists, saw little difference between their dark skin and that of Native Americans and African Americans. They tended to view Tejanos, many of whom spoke little English, as lazy, stupid, and filthy. "You will hear many say that you must treat them like dogs," one Anglo sheepherder wrote, "but that depends upon how you treat your dogs."[17]

But it was more than simple bigotry. In those early years, when another Mexican invasion always seemed around the corner, many Anglos suspected that Tejanos sympathized with Mexico. In the months after San Jacinto, they forcibly expelled them from the towns of Victoria and Goliad, taking their homes and stealing their livestock. In the 1840s and '50s, any number of Texas counties and towns expelled Tejanos for fear they would help slaves escape to Mexico. Across antebellum Texas, Tejanos were murdered for crimes actual and imagined, a phenomenon that soared after the Civil War.[18]

The classic victim of all this was Juan Seguín. As one of the rebels' most effective commanders, Seguín had overseen a network of scouts and spies, fought at Concepción and San Antonio, and, after leaving the Alamo as a messenger, led cavalry at San Jacinto. Afterward, the government named him military commander of San Antonio. But from the outset, Seguín felt slighted. He noticed how Anglo soldiers and militiamen carried the newest guns and rode the best horses. Many, he felt, treated him with little respect. Elected to the Texas Senate, he sought to have the new constitution and laws translated into Spanish. Anglo lawmakers more or less rolled their eyes.

Again and again, Seguín found himself clashing with incoming Anglos. The Mississippi planter who replaced Houston as the army's commander, Felix Huston, had little use for Tejanos. When rumor of a Mexican invasion circulated in February 1837, Huston ordered Seguín to evacuate San Antonio and burn it behind him. Seguín saved the town by appealing to Houston. Seguín was repeatedly called on to settle disputes between Anglos and Tejanos, the worst coming in 1842, when a pair of troublemakers named Smith and Goodman began laying claims to San Antonio's Tejano-owned lots and buildings, insisting they were spoils of war. Seguín put a stop to it. They swore revenge.

Everything came to a head after that first Mexican raid in March 1842. Seguín, commanding only a small militia, had fled the town. When the Mexicans retreated, they left behind a pair of Texas prisoners who wasted no time telling everyone that Seguín — along with virtually every other prominent Tejano in San Antonio — was secretly in league with Santa Anna. Though blatantly untrue, the charge gained purchase amid wartime hysteria. Smith and Goodman publicly vowed to kill Seguín. Though still an army officer, Seguín was the last Tejano holding so high a post, and Anglo generals like Huston were eager to be rid of him.[19]

Fearing for his life, Seguín took refuge in a series of Tejano homes and ranches around San Antonio, sleeping in a new bed almost every night for weeks. Anglo mobs were soon on his trail, burning several haciendas suspected of sheltering him. Out of options, Seguín fled to Mexico, where the authorities threw him in prison. He was given a choice: Fight the Texans who had taken his homeland, or rot in a dungeon. Seguín chose to fight, raising a militia of onetime San Antonio residents. When General Woll rode into the city, Seguín was there at his side, where he proudly took Goodman prisoner, which of course only appeared to confirm the duplicity the Anglos suspected. When Woll's troops returned south, more than two hundred Tejano families followed, seeing no future for themselves in San Antonio.[20]

In the wake of the Mexican raids, Anglos appropriated much of the town from the Tejano families who had lived there a century or more. It was the turning point in what amounted to a kind of ethnic cleansing. Anglos commandeered San Antonio's political structure; another Tejano wouldn't serve as mayor until the twentieth century. Laws were passed allowing Anglo men to marry Tejano women, but Tejano men were forbidden from mingling with Anglo women.

During the Mexican War, Seguín's militia fought once more, this time against American troops. But after years of political upheaval in Mexico, Seguín wanted to rejoin his family in Texas, and the state eventually granted him amnesty, allowing him to quietly return to Texas. He settled in the town north of San Antonio that bore his name, and ran for local office, including justice of the peace. He lived until 1890, long enough to see a string of Texas histories published that ignored or downplayed the Tejano contributions to early Texas.

While Seguín generally declined to correct them, his longtime friend and legislative wingman, the state legislator José Antonio Navarro, tried. In articles written for San Antonio newspapers in the 1850s, Navarro emerged as the first Tejano historian, and the last for a very long time. In one article, he urged Anglos to "regard with more indulgence this race of men, who, legitimate lords of this land, lost it together with their lives and their hopes, to follow in the footsteps of those very ones who enjoy the land in the midst of peace and abundance."[21]

No one really noticed. For much of the next century, Anglo historians would mostly ignore the Tejanos, preferring what one modern writer terms the "binary" story of a war, and a siege, fought by all whites against all Latinos. Generations of Texans would grow up under the impression that many

266

Mexican Texans had sided with Santa Anna, an impulse, as we'll see later, that has often been viewed as justification for their oppression. Of the early Texas historians, only Potter made any serious effort to celebrate the lives of men like Seguín and de Zavala, Navarro and Ruiz. Yet even Potter was not above the era's racist tropes. In one article he noted that all four were "Mexicans of respectable Spanish descent," meaning they were not brown-skinned mestizos.[22] It would be decades before Mexican-American writers would begin setting the record straight.

The American Centennial in 1876 prompted a wave of interest in the nation's history, and in the state's. Texas war veterans were getting up there in years and turning nostalgic. The Texas Veterans Association was formed in Houston in 1873 to celebrate those who fought Santa Anna.

One of its charter members had been a fifteen-year-old guarding the Texian baggage train at San Jacinto. His name was William Physick Zuber. In the intervening years Zuber had fought against General Woll and the Comanche, served in the Confederate Army, and taught in Huntsville-area schools, where he developed an interest in

267

history. He was an odd-looking chap, gaunt, with crossed eyes, splayed ears, and a scruffy beard. Late in life he posed for a photograph, which included a jaunty ear horn he used as a hearing aid.

It was Zuber's destiny to conjure one of Texas's most cherished myths. In 1873, after publishing a memoir, he began writing articles about Texas history, many published in the *Texas Almanac* and *The Quarterly of the Texas State Historical Association*. By far the most significant was a story Zuber wrote in the *Almanac*'s 1873 edition that he had heard from his parents, Mary Ann and Abraham Zuber.

As Zuber told it, his parents were at their farmstead in March 1836 near present-day College Station when an old friend, a French immigrant named Louis (Moses) Rose, staggered to their door. Rose's clothing was bloodstained. He was exhausted, malnourished, and covered with infected wounds. As the family nursed Rose back to health, he told them he had escaped from the Alamo. He had quite a story to tell.

According to Zuber, Rose had been friends with Jim Bowie and had accompanied him to the Alamo in late 1835. After fighting in the Battle of San Antonio, Rose stayed on, and remained in the garrison when Mexican troops appeared. On March 3, Rose claimed, three days before the Alamo's fall, Travis mustered the garrison and delivered a fateful speech. Travis, Zuber wrote, announced that their chance of survival was nil. Reinforcements were not coming. For his part, Travis said he would fight to the death.

At this point, writing thirty-seven years later, Zuber quoted Travis at length. "I am sure that Santa Anna is determined to storm the fort and take it," he said. "Then we must die! Our speedy dissolution is a fixed and inevitable fact. Our business is, not to make a fruitless effort to save our lives, but to choose the manner of our death. . . . When, at last, they shall storm our fortress, let us kill them as they come! kill them as they scale our wall! kill them as they leap within! kill them as they raise their weapons, and as they use them!"[23]

After a bit more like this, Zuber wrote, Travis dramatically unsheathed his saber and traced "a line upon the ground." "I now want every man who is determined to stay here and die with me to come across this line," Travis asked. "Who will be first?"

Moses Rose, Zuber wrote, told his parents that a man named Tapley Holland crossed first and was followed by dozens of others.

Bowie asked his men to carry him. After a moment, every single man in the garrison had stepped across the fateful line in the sand — every man, that is, except Rose himself. He froze. He didn't want to die. In Zuber's telling, Rose buried his face in his hands. When he looked up, the rest of the rebels had returned to their posts.

Zuber then described Bowie and Crockett walking up.

"You seem not to be willing to die with us, Rose," Bowie said.

"No . . . I am not prepared to die, and shall not do so if I can avoid it," Rose answered.

Then Crockett chimed in: "You may as well conclude to die with us, old man, for escape is impossible."

Well, apparently not. As Zuber told it, Rose grabbed his things, scaled a wall at night, and leapt over, landing, inexplicably, in a pool of Mexican blood. Zuber describes how Rose ran through a field filled with Mexican corpses — corpses? before the battle itself? — and reached the San Antonio River, slipping away under the cover of darkness. When he finally reached the Zuber homestead, the Alamo had fallen. He found a newspaper that listed a "Rose, of Nacogdoches" among the dead. Rose stayed with his family nearly three weeks before leaving, Zuber wrote. His wounds never healed, it was said, and he died a few months later.

Heckuva story, right? The editors at the *Texas Almanac* sure thought so. They published Zuber's account as a letter to the editor, complete with a note from his elderly mother attesting to its accuracy. The story, as they say, quickly went viral. Texans just loved it — still do, in fact. And why not? It had everything Texans wanted in an Alamo story: heroism, sacrifice, drama, courage in the face of insurmountable odds. The heart of its appeal was that it gave Texans something they had always desperately wanted but never had, a glimpse into what really happened inside the Alamo. Best of all, to those who might have believed the garrison was surprised by Santa Anna's appearance and had no option but to fight, here was concrete evidence that they stayed and died by choice. Plus, it kind of felt like something the histrionic Travis might actually have done.

At this point, you may be expecting us to body-slam poor Zuber as a nutty, ear-horned fabulist. On its face, the story is too good to be true, right? Certainly it didn't fit the known facts. The only Rose listed among the dead was a James M. Rose, a nephew of the founding father James Madison. Travis's letters clearly show he had not lost all hope by March 3; he was still listing the supplies that reinforcements should bring. And a courier who left the mission that night never mentioned the story.

So yes, almost from the beginning, there were skeptics. Among the first was the state's adjutant general, William Steele, who, in an 1877 letter asking Zuber for help in developing an accurate list of the Alamo's dead, mentioned that the story didn't match any told by Susanna Dickinson. In his reply, Zuber explained that Santa Anna had allowed Dickinson, and presumably other women, to leave the Alamo days earlier.[24] This was utter claptrap, and sent any number of journalists in search of Dickinson.

Hers was a sad story. She had settled in the Houston area. Her first husband beat her, and she filed for divorce in 1838, one of the first divorces granted in what became Harris County. She ended up marrying four more times. One husband accused her in court papers of running a brothel, though friends insisted she was its housecleaner. The fifth marriage apparently stuck, and Dickinson was living with this gent in Austin when the writers came calling.

Her stories, alas, were all over the map. Sometimes she confirmed Zuber's tale, sometimes she denied it. In an interview two years before her death in 1883, Dickinson actually told the story backward — Travis had asked those who wanted to *leave* to cross the line, not those who wanted to stay. And she couldn't remember Rose at all.

Reuben Potter thought the whole thing was a figment of Zuber's imagination. In an 1878 letter, Potter conceded that someone named Rose might have escaped the Alamo, but there was no evidence of it. The night of March 3, Potter wrote, "was not a time when Travis would have demoralized his band by an offer for skulking which would have enabled the few cowards in it, if there were any, to subvert the determination of the rest. . . . I gave my reasons (to other Texas historians) for discarding both stories."[25]

By the 1880s, then, the verdict on Zuber's story was pretty well split. Scholars dismissed it as a fable, while the public overwhelmingly embraced it as a treasured bit of Texas lore. It would be cited for years in newspapers and more than a few books. Zuber never disavowed it, though at least twice he made what seemed like significant alterations. When confronted about his liberal use of quotations, he admitted he might have improvised Travis's dramatic oratory, you know, just a tad. But he insisted, as "the ideas are precisely those [Travis] advanced, and most of the language is also nearly the same."[26]

All this might have passed into legend if not for a young woman named Anna Hardwicke Pennybacker. Pennybacker, who would go on to a distinguished career of public service that included a long friendship with Eleanor Roosevelt, was fresh out of the state's first teacher certification classes in 1888 when she authored a textbook called *A New History of Texas for Schools*. When she couldn't find a publisher, she and her husband issued the book themselves. Surprisingly, it found an audience, proving so popular it became the state's standard Texas History textbook.

The centerpiece of Pennybacker's section on the Alamo was Travis's "line in the sand" speech, "one of the grandest scenes in history." She quotes Zuber's version of the speech almost word for word, throwing in an additional stirring line: "Those who wish to die like heroes and patriots," Travis is quoted telling his men, "come over to me."[27] The book did supply a helpful footnote explaining that most historians doubted the story, to which Pennybacker added, "We deem it to the interest of the student to let him investigate the matter for himself."[28]

A shot across Pennybacker's bow was fired in 1903, when a University of Texas professor named George Garrison published a Texas history that pointedly excluded the Travis speech. Garrison's implicit challenge appears to have stung; the book's next edition appeared without any mention of the Travis speech. Finally, in 1913, after a quarter century as the standard Texas History textbook, the state shelved the Pennybacker book and replaced it with one authored by three of Garrison's skeptical colleagues. The new book included mention of the Travis speech only in a section on page 120 titled "Some Old Errors."

Even then the story refused to die. It was just too good, and Texans clearly, desperately, wanted to believe it, wanted to believe in their founders' heroism. As the folklorist J. Frank Dobie put it, the Travis story "may be expurgated from histories, but it can no more be expunged from popular imagination than the damned spots on Lady Macbeth's hands. Teachers of children dramatize it in school rooms; orators on holidays silver and gild it; the tellers of historical anecdotes — and there are many of them in Texas — sitting around hotel lobbies speculate on it and say, 'Well, we'll believe it whether it's true or not.' "[29]

But wait, there's more. Twenty-five years later, in 1939, a Nacogdoches court reporter named Robert Blake discovered records indicating there actually had been a Frenchman named Moses Rose who claimed to have been at the Alamo. In the cozy corridors of Texas history, this amounted to earth-shattering news, on a par with archaeologists discovering a triceratops hibernating in Waxahachie. Rose's real name, it turns out, was Louis; he got the nickname "Moses" while at the Alamo, he claimed, because he was among the oldest defenders and wore a white beard.[30] Rose claimed to have fought in the Napoleonic Wars; he may have been the Louis Rose who became a lieutenant in Napoleon's armies, earning the French Legion of Honor after fighting in Portugal, Spain, and Russia. Whatever his origins, by 1827 he was working at a Nacogdoches sawmill.[31]

In the years after the rebellion, many Texas veterans needed to document their service to gain government land and benefits. As a Nacogdoches butcher during the 1840s,

Rose often testified on friends' behalf. He always claimed he had stayed at the Alamo until the final days, finally managing his escape because, as he said more than once, "By God, I wasn't ready to die." He passed away in 1851.

So Moses Rose did exist. Yet there was no evidence in 1939, and still none today, that he fought at the Alamo, much less that he watched Travis draw any line in its sand. Despite all the times he claimed to have been there, there is no other record, nor even a secondhand account, that he ever told the story the Zubers attributed to him.

Modern Alamo enthusiast Thomas Ricks Lindley has uncovered a couple of stories that might have inspired Zuber. Lindley describes in his 2003 book *Alamo Traces* an 1844 interview Mary Holley conducted with a colonial-era innkeeper named Angelina Eberly. Eberly claimed that one of Houston's officers related an anecdote said to have occurred in the final days before the Battle of San Jacinto. In it, Houston drew a line in the dirt and demanded that those willing to fight step across it. Could fifteen-year-old William Zuber, attending Houston's supply train, have been there to witness it? Or hear about it?

What we know is that, remarkably, despite

no credible evidence to support its existence, Travis's famous line is still celebrated to this day — even at the Alamo itself. If you visit, you may not even notice it. Many people don't. Just in front of the church entrance, look down. Sunk into the stonework is a brass line about five feet long, a tribute to what a nearby plaque terms the "legend" of Travis's line. The Alamo's former longtime official historian, Bruce Winders, tells us that the brass line was installed in 1988 by the Daughters of the Republic of Texas, despite a good deal of internal criticism that doing so would lend credibility to the legend. But as so often happens with all matters Alamo, the legend won out.

■ ■ ■ ■

"Rise, man the wall, our clarion's blast
Now sounds its final reveille;
This dawning morn must be the last
Our fated band shall ever see.
To life, but not to hope, farewell!
Yon trumpet's clang, and cannon's peal,
And storming shout, and clash of steel,
Is ours, but not our country's knell!
Welcome the Spartan's death —
'Tis no despairing strife —

We fall! we die! but our expiring breath
Is Freedom's breath of life!"

"Here, on this new Thermopylae,
Our monument shall tower on high,
And 'Alamo' hereafter be
In bloodier fields the battle cry."
Thus Travis from the rampart cried;
And when his warriors saw the foe,
Like whelming billows move below,
At once each dauntless heart replied,
"Welcome the Spartan's death —
'Tis no despairing strife —
We fall! we die! but our expiring breath
Is Freedom's breath of life!"

They come — like autumn's leaves they
   fall,
Yet, hordes on hordes, they onward rush;
With gory tramp they mount the wall,
Till numbers the defenders crush —
Till falls their flag when none remain!
Well may the ruffians quake to tell
How Travis and his hundred fell
Amid a thousand foemen slain!
They died the Spartan's death,
But not in hopeless strife —
Like brothers died, and their expiring
   breath
Was Freedom's breath of life!

CHAPTER 13
THE SECOND BATTLE
OF THE ALAMO

The Texas veterans and historians who began gathering to celebrate and write about the Texas Revolt in the late 1800s were typically male, but the work of commemoration often fell to women. In the 1860s and 1870s, widows dressed in black formed myriad groups to remember the dead and build monuments. At the same time, excluded from politics and business, women of all stripes found purpose and power in social clubs. At a time of dizzying change, they organized temperance movements, hereditary societies, and memorial organizations to try to keep America from losing touch with a past whose conflicts, from the American Revolution to the Texas Revolt, seemed far more heroic than those of the day.

You'd think all this would've led to a focus on the Alamo. At least initially, it didn't. When the battle's fiftieth anniversary arrived in 1886, there was no commemoration, no services, no fireworks, no nothing, nor the slightest impulse toward historical preservation: At that point the largest building of the old compound — the Long Barrack — had been turned into a grocery store.

The U.S. Army had outgrown the Alamo in the 1870s and returned it to the Catholic diocese, which kept the church but sold the Long Barrack to a grocer named Honoré Grenet. Grenet turned it into a garish little castle, adding crenellated cornices and faux towers, from which he did a fine business selling watermelons, lettuce, and whiskey.[1] The first hints of change came in 1883, when a mercantile firm, Hugo & Schmeltzer, purchased the building and leased the empty church as a warehouse. It soon noticed a stream of tourists asking to see where Crockett, Bowie, and Travis had died, and began charging a penny a tour. A group of war veterans and widows persuaded state lawmakers to purchase the church. The state asked the city to manage it, and it hired Tom Rife, a Texas Revolt veteran, to lead tours, while Hugo & Schmeltzer provided lunch.

Then, in 1886, when the fiftieth anniversary passed without commemoration, the *San Antonio Daily Express* called for the formation of an organization that would "see that the prominent anniversaries of Texas histories are observed."[2] The newspaper's call was answered by a twenty-five-year-old San Antonio schoolteacher named Adina De Zavala.* De Zavala, who grew up beside the San Jacinto battlefield, had just moved to San Antonio to care for her ailing father, the son of Lorenzo de Zavala. She had only learned of her grandfather's importance in her late teens, after which she developed an interest in teaching a more accurate version of Texas history that included the Spanish colonial period and preserving its documents and relics.[3]

Smart, educated, and passionate, with lustrous black hair and blue eyes, De Zavala carried herself with a regal bearing. At a time when women were expected to know their place, she didn't, and more than a few in San Antonio would view her as a tad difficult. She had a temper.[4] Making matters worse, she was Catholic, unmarried, and not wealthy. So De Zavala proudly held tight to her one advantage, a last name important to Texas history.†

---

* De Zavala began capitalizing the "De" to confer aristocracy to which she was not entitled.

† De Zavala spent her time and teacher's salary

The decrepit condition of all five of San Antonio's Spanish missions irked her.[5] In 1889, in an effort to preserve them, she organized the De Zavala Daughters to keep "green the memory of the heroes, founders, and pioneers of Texas." The group's few dozen members dedicated themselves to rehabilitating the missions. Studying the Alamo, De Zavala wondered why the state had purchased the church, where little of the fighting occurred, instead of the Long Barrack, the site of the battle's bloodiest fighting, and to her mind, far more deserving of preservation. The church? That was where the women hid till it was over.

On her walks through the city, she studied the Long Barrack and despaired. It was hard to recognize under Hugo & Schmeltzer's rococo facade. By the 1890s the grocer had added porches and balconies and covered the walls with billboards. De Zavala grew emotional thinking that flour sacks, corn

---

caring for her father, financing her brother's education, preserving Texas history, and trying to reclaim her family's land, which the Republic of Texas had awarded her grandfather and father for their service. Still, Anglos had tied up the family's estate in years-long litigation, just as they had that of other Tejano families.

bushels, and beer kegs covered the ground stained with the blood of Texas patriots. She extracted a promise from the owners that if and when they were ready to sell, she and her friends would get first dibs.

Meanwhile, two years after De Zavala began her efforts, another, larger preservation group sprang up. The Daughters of the Republic of Texas, often referred to as the DRT or simply the Daughters, was formed by a group of Houston women seeking an exclusive club for those whose ancestors took part in the Texas Revolt. At their inaugural convention in 1892, the Daughters declared that their mission was to acquire and preserve historic sites and "implant in the minds and hearts of succeeding generations a desire to emulate the example and maintain the high principles of patriotic devotion bequeathed them by their ancestors." Excited by this boom in preservation efforts, De Zavala folded her group into the Daughters, creating the "De Zavala Chapter" to restore San Antonio's missions.

And then, well, not much happened. For ten long years, the Daughters held meetings, and De Zavala made a few repairs on the other San Antonio missions, but in terms of actual efforts to preserve the Alamo buildings, it was mostly talk and tea parties.

And then, suddenly, on a single day, February 9, 1903, everything changed.

One of De Zavala's friends was Lizzie Coppini, the wife of an Italian sculptor living in San Antonio. That afternoon in 1903, Harvey L. Page, a San Antonio architect, invited Pompeo Coppini to discuss a potential commission for a new downtown hotel. An "Eastern syndicate" had offered $75,000 for the Hugo & Schmeltzer building[6] — the Long Barrack — and wanted a statue of Crockett for the lobby.

"I made a beeline for Miss Adina De Zavala's home on Fourth and Taylor," Coppini wrote later. De Zavala "seemed to be much affected when I told her how I had found out, and of what [was] offered me, but she remained calm as one does sometimes when stunned by an unexpected blow."[7]

De Zavala knew this had to be stopped, and fast. Searching for options, she recognized that a new hotel would take business from the adjacent Menger Hotel. If she could convince the Menger's owners that their business was threatened, she might be able to persuade them to buy the Long Barrack and block the new hotel. De Zavala found the owning family's sister at the front desk, but she said the rest of the family was in Europe. There was a guest at the hotel, however, who might help instead, she added.

Her name was Clara Driscoll.[8]

And that's how it started.

Clara Driscoll would go down as one of the unstoppable forces of Texas history. That day at the Menger, she was all of twenty-one, restless, unmoored, and in mourning, searching for a purpose in life. Like De Zavala, she had an impeccable Texas pedigree; both her grandfathers had fought at San Jacinto. Unlike De Zavala, she had the social class, the political skills, and — most important — the money to make dreams come true. Her father was one of the state's richest men, having used the family's early land grants to build up a fortune in cattle, railroads, and oil.

Driscoll grew up on her family's ranch outside Corpus Christi, where she learned to speak Spanish, ride a horse, and fire a pistol as well as the ranch hands. She was sent to a private academy in San Antonio, then to a top Catholic school in New York City, and finally a junior college in France. By the age of eighteen she was as comfortable wandering the Louvre as the back forty. And she was flat-out charming. One San

Antonio reporter[9] described her as "small, dainty, gracious always, with sensitive mouth and eyes that twinkle on the slightest provocation."

After completing her education in 1899, Driscoll and her mother journeyed to India, where they lived on a luxurious houseboat for a year. During their travels, her mother taught her of architecture, city planning, and beauty. In Europe and in Asia, she showed her how citizens should treat their holy and historical places, such as the Basilica of the Sacré-Cœur in Paris, or Westminster Abbey in London. Driscoll learned that a great city balanced respect for the past while allowing people to enjoy modern lives.

On the journey home, Driscoll's mother died from a sudden illness. Crushed, Driscoll brought her body to San Antonio for interment. Unsure what to do afterward, she walked the city. Often she found herself at the Alamo church. She thought it a shamble, with a garish grocery store tacked to one side. This was the cradle of Texas legends. Why wasn't it San Antonio's Notre-Dame, its Taj Mahal?

She felt so strongly she penned a letter to the *San Antonio Express*. "There does not stand in the world today," she wrote of the

Alamo church, "a building or a monument which can recall such a deed of heroism and bravery. . . . How do we treat it? We leave it hemmed in on one side by a hideous barracks-looking building, and on the other by two saloons. . . . All the unsightly obstructions should be torn away, and the space utilized as a park."

Afterward Driscoll returned to Europe, where she remained for three years, adrift. She returned to Texas only in 1903, and was staying at the Menger that day when the front desk said someone named Adina De Zavala wanted to meet her. They had tea. The two women bonded easily and immediately, recognizing a shared purpose and complementary skills, a pair of strong, educated Catholic single women ready to challenge a male-dominated world.

There and then, Clara Driscoll joined the Daughters, agreed to chair its fundraising committee, and, more important, pledged to do anything possible to buy the Long Barrack. From the Menger, the two women headed to a meeting with Driscoll's attorney and Charles Hugo, whose family owned the Long Barrack. A few days later, Driscoll handed over a $500 check for a thirty-day option to buy the property for $75,000. If the Daughters could furnish another $4,500 within thirty days, Hugo would let them pay off the balance over five years.

The De Zavala Chapter mobilized, mailing hundreds of letters across the state asking for donations. The results were underwhelming: They raised a grand total of $1,021.75. Driscoll wrote another check, extending the option a year. De Zavala embarked on a spree of mailings and appearances, explaining to potential donors the importance of the Long Barrack. Even then too many Texans, she realized, mistakenly believed the Alamo's defenders fought to the last inside the church.[10] De Zavala wanted to rebuild the Long Barrack into a Hall of Fame to preserve the hallowed ground of the battle and create a place where Texans could learn the full, true story of the Alamo.

When the Texas legislature convened, the Daughters converged on the capitol in Austin and lobbied lawmakers to contribute at least a portion of the purchase price. But when lawmakers threw in $5,000, the governor, W. T. Lanham, vetoed the bill. Driscoll had to write another check.

This bit of philanthropy opened the first small gap between the two women. The newspapers lavished praise on Driscoll, anointing her the "Savior of the Alamo," even as De Zavala kept busy with the scut work, collecting documents and compiling analyses underscoring the Long Barrack's importance. For the moment no one dwelled on the fact that the two women leading the charge to save the Alamo had sharply different views of what to do with it. De Zavala sought to return everything to the way it looked in 1836. Driscoll? Not so much. She wanted it all to serve as the centerpiece of a beautiful park-like shrine.

Driscoll leveraged her new status as the Alamo's "savior" into celebrity. In Austin she was a whirlwind on the capital society circuit, seemingly gaining political allies with every dance. Few were as useful as her beau, Henry Hulme "Hal" Sevier, a gentlemanly newspaperman. They were married in New York's St. Patrick's Cathedral. Together Driscoll and Sevier emerged as a persuasive political force, slyly questioning why poor Governor Lanham couldn't understand the importance of the Alamo. Why, Clara purred, even schoolchildren knew it as the cradle of Texas liberty. Didn't he realize how every Texas man — um, every Texas voter — aspired to Bowie's bravery, to Travis's gallantry? Didn't he remember the Alamo?

In time Driscoll prevailed upon Representative Samuel Ealy Johnson Jr., Lyndon Johnson's father, to introduce a bill to buy the Long Barrack. De Zavala drafted it herself. Lawmakers passed the bill, and Lanham, thoroughly outmaneuvered, was obliged to sign it. It was everything they could have hoped for, two women who couldn't even vote forging an unprecedented partnership — at least in Texas — to bend the machinery of government to their will. No one was happier than De Zavala. The ink on the spending bill was not yet dry, though, when Driscoll betrayed her.

The daughters celebrated the state's purchase of the Long Barrack at their annual meeting in April 1905. The De Zavala Chapter put forward a resolution giving themselves custodianship. De Zavala, after all, had pursued this fight for years; supervising the Alamo seemed a just reward. But out of nowhere, the executive committee circulated a different proposal. Driscoll had been lobbying behind the scenes, and given that she financed everything, she expected to take control. Worse, from De Zavala's point of view, was Driscoll's stated intention to tear down the Long Barrack to make way for her park.

After a heated debate, the executive committee, dominated by Driscoll, was given the final word. It handed everything to Driscoll. The vote represented the nastiest possible split between De Zavala and Driscoll, one that triggered a lifelong enmity. Neither woman ever spoke meaningfully of the split, but their hatred was evident to all. When the *San Antonio Express* ran a story featuring De Zavala's picture, Driscoll scribbled "Get her out" across her face.[11]

Thus began what's known in Texas as the Second Battle of the Alamo. Driscoll had won the opening round, but De Zavala wasn't giving up. The next round occurred in September 1905, when the governor planned to formally convey the church to the Daughters with a proclamation. Driscoll, however, was scheduled to leave for a long trip to New York. In her absence the executive committee agreed to give control of the Alamo to her assistant. That's when De Zavala declared war, in the simplest way possible: She showed up first and took the keys. De Zavala told reporters she intended to give them to Driscoll, but — wouldn't you know it — she couldn't be found. De Zavala's victory, however, was illusory. When she hired an attorney, he told her to return the keys.[12]

Still De Zavala wouldn't give up. At the Daughters' 1906 annual meeting, she prevailed upon the membership to give her chapter control of the Alamo in a vote. Two weeks later, the executive committee reversed every single component of De Zavala's victory. Her amendments, they ruled, violated state law.[13] De Zavala learned of this when she received a letter from one Charles Reeves, representing the Vanderventer Hotel Company of St. Louis.

Mr. Reeves informed De Zavala of the executive committee's plan to demolish the Long Barrack and transform the area into a park. Next door, Mr. Reeves went on, his company intended to build not just a hotel, but a "winter theater" and a convention center. De Zavala fired back a letter saying, in essence, over her dead body. Mr. Reeves's reply was a triumph of mansplaining. Her plan to save the Long Barrack, he wrote, would "result in preserving indefinitely an eye-sore which would be a source of humiliation and regret to the people of San Antonio for all time."[14] If it was not removed, he said, "we will dispose of the property and invest our capital elsewhere." Mr. Reeves and his company ended up walking away anyway.

The battle between De Zavala and

Driscoll resumed at the 1907 convention, which descended into a byzantine struggle over bylaws and Robert's Rules of Order. When the Driscollites walked out, the Texas governor, Thomas Campbell, had to step in. He declared them the Daughters' legitimate authority.[15] A judge granted the Driscoll faction temporary control pending resolution of a lawsuit.

This is when things begin to get weird. The Daughters were scheduled to take control of the Long Barrack in February 1908. Once again, though, De Zavala showed up early and, amazingly, proceeded to barricade herself inside the building. The Driscollites howled. When the sheriff tried to evict her, she put her fingers in her ears and refused to budge. Nonplussed, the sheriff decided to starve her out, posting two deputies outside with orders to make sure she received no food or water. De Zavala had anticipated such a move. On the siege's second day, her friends began running up to the building and tossing oranges and sandwiches through the windows.[16] Finally, on the third day, the governor sent an aide to take control of the building; pending resolution of the court fight, he announced, neither faction would run things.

De Zavala left the next day, declaring victory.

By this point the gentlemen of San Antonio were sick of the whole thing; the only time the city got mentioned in the national press, it seemed, was to report the latest outburst between Driscoll and De Zavala. It made the city look, well, provincial. "We do not want to appear sacrilegious," a fellow named L. J. Hart was quoted saying. "But we realize that the time has come to stop mentioning the Alamo in the same breath with San Antonio. This has and is still being done to a most harmful degree for by doing it we are advertising San Antonio not as a modern and enterprising city . . . but are associating her with a name that carries with it the idea that San Antonio is still a Mexican village. . . . Let's let the people abroad forget the Alamo."[17]

Later that year a Houston court made its long-awaited ruling: Driscoll won control of the Daughters, and of the Alamo. She had the executive committee promptly expel De Zavala and her supporters. But still this wasn't over.

Three years later, in 1911, a new governor took office, and he had ideas of his own about the Alamo. Oscar Colquitt was a paunchy Georgia-born lobbyist whose enthusiasms ran to white supremacy and Kaiser Wilhelm's Germany. His reasons to remember the Alamo had more to do with politics than history. During the 1910 Mexican Revolution, violence had broken out on the border, and when Colquitt sent in the Texas Rangers to preserve order, they ended up massacring Mexican and Tejano civilians by the dozens. Playing up the Alamo, he mused, was a way to glorify the victory of Anglo Texas over the hated Mexicans. It served the governor's tough anti-Mexico talk and, he hoped, would subtly excuse the Rangers' atrocities.[18]

When Colquitt persuaded lawmakers to give him money for improvements to the Alamo — the Driscollites had made no significant improvements in the interim — De Zavala rushed him like a linebacker, arguing for preservation of the Long Barrack.[19] Seeking a consensus, Colquitt invited De Zavala and the Daughters' leadership to a meeting at San Antonio. In large part, he told the startled Daughters, he agreed with De Zavala; he announced his intention to restore the site to its condition as of March 6, 1836.[20]

Clara arrived fashionably late, forcing the governor to repeat his remarks. One senses she knew what was coming, for she promptly played a new card guaranteed to give Colquitt pause. "I don't think the Alamo," she ventured, "should be disgraced by this whisky house, which obscures the most remarkable relic of the world."[21] The key word here was "whisky"; Hugo & Schmeltzer had sold its share. Why this mattered was the mushrooming strength of the state's prohibition movement; the Prohibition Party, in fact, controlled both houses of the legislature and loathed Colquitt. Invoking "whisky" was a threat.

When the Driscollites raised the question whether the Hugo building was in fact the original Long Barrack — there were questions how much the grocers had altered the building — De Zavala too came prepared. Using a series of letters and maps, including Reuben Potter's description of the Long Barrack in 1841, she showed the governor beyond any doubt that, whatever Hugo & Schmeltzer's wares, its building was the Long Barrack. She had measured the walls; they were the same height as in 1836. The Texas State Historical Association agreed. This was enough for Governor Colquitt.

"If I can find out how this building looked when Travis lost his life," he said, "I will spend every dollar at my disposal to make it look like it did then. No power can budge me from my determination."[22] The governor, alas, hadn't reckoned with Clara Driscoll.

Driscoll and the Governor promptly went to war. The Daughters issued a statement proclaiming that if he recommended anything other than the Daughters' planned park, they would consider his action a usurpation of their legal authority as custodians of the Alamo.[23] The governor was unamused and, as an opponent of women's suffrage, tired of women interfering in men's business.[24]

Days later, he issued a statement saying that the Daughters had done nothing to improve the property over the previous six years. He announced that he was terminating the custodianship agreement; the state would take permanent control of the Alamo.[25] He would hire an architect to draw plans for reconstructing the Long Barrack as a museum.

The Daughters got an injunction stopping it, but because the state owned the property, the governor ordered laborers in the spring of 1912 to remove the wooden structure around the Long Barrack's stone walls, wiping away the Hugo & Schmeltzer building.

He asked lawmakers for more money, arguing that a restored Alamo would boost tourism. San Antonio had begun marketing the March 6 anniversary with ceremonies, and they had proven popular.

Then, in late 1913, a district judge and an appeals court ruled in the Daughters' favor. Colquitt realized he had lost. What happened next has a long tradition in Texas politics. Colquitt left the state on business and, faced with a political loss, left Lieutenant Governor William Harding Mayes as acting governor to do what was necessary. Mayes allowed San Antonio officials to demolish the upper walls of the Long Barrack, as the Daughters desired, claiming that rain had damaged them. The workers left behind eight-foot walls that resembled an old ruin just as Driscoll had imagined.

De Zavala was crushed. She had not only lost control of the Alamo, her beloved Long Barrack was now a shell. She tried to move on, forming a new group, the Texas Historical and Landmarks Association. They focused on placing historical markers throughout the state and renaming schools after Texan heroes. But every good preservationist knows that what can be torn asunder can be rebuilt. De Zavala would keep fighting to teach the truth at the Alamo, even if

Driscoll's shrine to the Heroic Anglo Narrative had prevailed for the moment.

CHAPTER 14
THE WHITE MAN'S ALAMO

It is currently reported that there has been employed and included in the faculty of said University those who are out of touch and not in sympathy with the traditions of the South.

— STATE REPRESENTATIVE
ALEXANDER HENSLEY, 1897

Fifty years after the fall of the Alamo, Texas pride was already very much a thing. Writers such as Yoakum, Potter, and Pennybacker had created a rich folk history of the revolution and inculcated a collective memory of how the state came into being, what modern scholars sometimes refer to as the Texas Creation Myth. Anglos embraced the folklore with gusto, proud of their unique history. And as far as most were concerned, every word was gospel truth.

Which became a bit of a problem after the first academic historians arrived in Texas with the opening of the University of Texas in 1883. The professional study of American history in the late 1800s was very much in its infancy, at least in Texas, and after 1893 was heavily influenced by the so-called frontier thesis advanced by a University of Wisconsin professor named Frederick Jackson Turner. In a paper delivered before the American Historical Association that year, Turner argued that the Anglo conquest of the American West generated a spirit of freedom, democracy, and egalitarianism and created a uniquely American culture. This was history by, for, and about the white man; Native Americans, Black people, and Latinos were marginal characters at best, two-legged buffalo at worst. To Turner, America's exquisite society more than justified the barbarous means used to achieve God's will. Practically overnight it became law in history departments nationally. It would remain so for decades.

The first chairman of the University of Texas history department, George Pierce Garrison, was a rigorous Turnerian who founded the Texas State Historical Association in 1897, edited its quarterly journal, and introduced professional historical research to Texas. Which was all well and good, until it became apparent that Texans didn't want their folklore challenged by pesky facts. The trouble started when Garrison hired a sharp young professor named David Franklin Houston — no relation to Sam — who arrived in Austin after turning his master's thesis at Harvard into a book, *A Critical Study of Nullification in South Carolina.* The problem with Houston, and his book, was that word "critical." Houston challenged the idea, widely accepted in the South, that the Constitution allowed states to reject or nullify the federal government's actions.

A first-term state representative from Bay City, Alexander Hensley, was not going to stand for such nonsense. Hensley had grown up under Reconstruction and took pride in defeating an emancipated slave who had held the seat before him. On June 9, 1897, he rose from his desk on the floor of the Texas House of Representatives to ask precisely what those eggheads at the university were teaching the impressionable youth of Texas. "It is currently reported that there has been employed and included in the faculty of said University those who are out of touch and not in sympathy with the traditions of the South, but hold our traditions and our institutions in contempt, and circulate and teach political heresies in place of the system of political economy that is cherished by our people," Hensley's resolution said.[1]

Hensley persuaded his fellow lawmakers to require that university regents only hire faculty "who are known to be in sympathy with Southern political institutions," and to fire any "faculty not so in sympathy." An investigative team interviewed everyone involved, all of whom insisted that no one was teaching anything "that would be objectionable to Southern people." As for Houston's book, the lawmakers admitted they didn't have time to actually finish reading the thing. "From a casual reading [the committee] would pronounce it to be unacceptable from a Southern standpoint as setting forth principles contrary to Southern teachings," a report concluded. "We questioned Professor Houston, who is South Carolinian, with regard to the book, and he stated that it was written before he came to Texas, and that in his teaching here it was not used."[2]

In the end, university regents promised the committee always to hire Texans first, Southerners second, and faculty from anywhere else only when absolutely necessary. It wouldn't be the last time Texas politicians intervened on behalf of the Heroic

Anglo Narrative. David Houston survived, going on to serve as president of what is now Texas A&M until Woodrow Wilson named him secretary of agriculture. The message to those he left behind was clear: Stick to the folklore, to "Southern traditions," and you'll keep your job. Mess with Texas, mess with its myths, and you may not.

One of the students who learned this lesson well was a University of Texas sophomore named Eugene C. Barker.

In the 1990s, when historians finally got around to seriously explaining Texas history in new ways under the umbrella term "revisionism," one of the questions everyone wanted answered was why the field had lagged so badly, why so many of its beliefs, its ceaseless glorification of the revolt's heroes, seemed mired in the nineteenth century. There were plenty of reasons. In 1991 the historian Paul D. Lack came up with a fun new one. He blamed Eugene C. Barker.

Lack's thesis, as laid out in an essay titled "In the Long Shadow of Eugene C. Barker," was that Barker had intimidated three generations of academics from questioning the underlying conclusions in his University of Texas faculty's decades of work. The problem wasn't that Barker was a kook. Far from it. In fact, Lack goes on, it was "because he advanced scientific or objective history" that "few have acknowledged that Barker's work rested essentially on an ideological foundation similar to that of the Texas chauvinists and romanticists who came before him." It was Barker more than anyone, Lack laments, who allowed Texas history to be overwhelmed by "the suffocating power of its heroes."[3]

Maybe it's unfair to criticize Barker for being a man of his time, but that he was. Born in East Texas in 1874, he came of age during an era when white Southerners were at once still angry over Reconstruction and fascinated by a flood of published remembrances from Civil War and Texas Revolt veterans. A poor young man, he had gone to work at fourteen and began hearing these stories while toiling in railroad yards. Intrigued, he dreamed of history as a vocation, and after seven years managed to save enough to begin studying at the University of Texas. He was a sophomore when Alexander Hensley launched his investigation.

Barker spent the next twenty years completing his master's, teaching in the history department, briefly lecturing at Harvard, and gaining a doctorate at the University of Pennsylvania before returning to the University of Texas at Austin in 1908. Under his mentor George Garrison, the department he rejoined was on its way to an enduring dominance of Texas history scholarship, amassing valuable archives of papers, including Stephen F. Austin's. While their work is reliably lauded for its impartiality and professionalism, Garrison's faculty, it must be said, taught and produced a history that assumed Anglo superiority over other races. Garrison's *Texas: A Contest of Civilizations* argued that the Texans' superior moral stock practically guaranteed victory over underdeveloped Mexican and Native American cultures. The writings of his colleague Charles William Ramsdell, a veteran of the Dunning School of Reconstruction scholarship, assumed the inferiority of African-Americans.

When a heart attack felled Garrison in 1910, Barker was elevated to department chair, a position he held for forty years. For much of this period, he would also serve as editor of the influential *Southwestern Historical Quarterly,* a position that in essence made him commissioner of the Texas history league. Stern and aloof, Barker brought the study of Texas history fully into the twentieth century, demanding the rigor, intellectual discipline, and evenhandedness his predecessors often lacked. Yet as advanced as his methods were, his worldview remained firmly entrenched in the late nineteenth century.

Early on, Barker went on a hiring spree, bringing in star professors such as Walter Prescott Webb. All embraced a romantic and Anglocentric version of Texas. In his writings, Barker worked hard to shake off the stink of slavery. He firmly rejected assertions that the Texas Revolt was a fight to establish a slavocracy. Barker termed slavery a constant "dull, organic ache" that plagued the Anglos' relationship with Mexico, but otherwise minimized its importance.[4] He and the era's other Southern historians were trying to redefine their ancestors not as oppressors of people of color, but as defenders of liberty. That was, after all, what the Texas legislature demanded.

By the 1930s, Barker had begun passing his baton to a second generation of Texas chroniclers, especially Webb and the folklorist J. Frank Dobie, who joined the faculty in 1914. As the state's preeminent men of letters at midcentury, Webb and Dobie devoted their careers to popularizing a romanticized version of Texas history, Webb most notably in his pioneering 1930 study of the Texas Rangers, Dobie in a series of books in which he lamented the passing of rootin', tootin' frontier virtues. Some modern writers find their work vaguely embarrassing.

The Heroic Anglo Narrative these men enshrined was all that generations of Texans learned of their history. Barker, Webb, and Dobie became the state's first public intellectuals, icons who taught thousands of students, who in turn populated the faculties of colleges and high schools across the state. Their longevity, and their failure to change their views over time, meant that the ways of teaching Texas history they learned before World War I were still being widely used after World War II.

"Inbreeding ruined the vigor of the herd of Texas historians," a pair of Texas A&M historians, Walter L. Buenger and Robert A. Calvert, argued in their 1991 book, *Texas through Time.* "How can eighty years go by with so little change? Why has the shelf life of truth been so much longer in Texas? A partial answer is that the family trees of many historians writing on Texas still go back in an almost straight line to Garrison, Ramsdell, Barker, Webb, and Dobie."[5] Their acolytes, in fact, dominated Texas history faculties well into the 1970s and '80s.

For this, no one deserves more credit, or blame, than Eugene C. Barker, who died in 1956. Unsurprisingly, one of Barker's protégés would be responsible for the first serious — and seriously troubling — study of the Alamo.

The woman destined to become the Alamo's first academic chronicler, Amelia Williams, was born on her family's cotton plantation in Central Texas in 1876. Her father had come from South Carolina after the Civil War. While Williams's teachers recognized her as a precocious student — she attended private schools in Austin and Nashville — her parents' deaths meant she was obliged upon graduation to supervise operations and her four younger sisters on the family's two-thousand-acre farm. Only in 1910, once her sisters were grown, and Williams was well into her thirties, did she earn a teaching certificate. She spent the next fifteen years working in area schools. Then, in 1925, at the age of forty-nine, she did something few women of her age were doing in the 1920s: She enrolled at the University of Texas to study history.

Williams was, by all accounts, an excellent student. Her master's thesis focused on the men from Gonzales who reinforced the Alamo. Barker was so impressed that, when she began work on a PhD, he urged her to devote her dissertation to the broader Alamo narrative. Study of the siege, after all, remained a gaping hole in the literature. Williams embraced the challenge, diving into libraries and archives, writing letters to the defenders' descendants and trundling all over Texas in her battered Model T to take delivery of letters, diaries, and remembrances kept in attics and family Bibles. She corresponded with everyone who was anyone, from Susanna Dickinson's grandchildren to Adina De Zavala. And she got results. Sam Houston's family had resented Barker's criticisms of Houston in his Stephen F. Austin biography, but Williams prevailed upon them to donate his papers to the university. None of it was easy; many men she contacted had little use for a female graduate student.

It would be heartwarming to tell you that Williams's dissertation, issued in 1931, was a triumph. It wasn't. What it was, was the first academic narrative of the battle compiled with professional rigor, jammed with original documentation, so thorough it dissuaded two generations of academics from attempting to improve upon it. But Williams's full-throated endorsement of the Heroic Anglo Narrative cripples the work. To Williams, the Texians rebelled because "self-government, liberty, freedom of conscience and of speech were as necessary as the air they breathed. . . . Furthermore, these colonists were of Anglo-Saxon descent, and it is the nature of the Anglo-Saxon man to refuse to be dominated by an inferior race."[6]

It gets worse. Williams declares that the Mexicans who settled Texas were "absolute failures" and that Mexican soldiers were convicts and "the worst class of men." The Mexican government's abolition of slavery, meanwhile, she judges "hateful to the colonists," not the principled act of a sovereign republic.

But that's only the half of it. Modern researchers have been withering in their contempt for Williams's accuracy. Writing in 1986, Paul Andrew Hutton dismissed her work as being "of stunningly poor quality."[7] In his 2003 book, *Alamo Traces,* Thomas Ricks Lindley identified more than fifty errors and distortions in a forty-five-page takedown of Williams.[8] "Sometimes Miss Williams relies on pure trash," the author Walter Lord wrote in 1968.[9]

Despite some pointed questions by faculty

reviewers, none of this mattered, certainly not to Barker, who pronounced Williams's dissertation the definitive account of the battle. And indeed for almost four decades, until Lord began raising questions in the late 1960s, it was widely considered exactly that, the go-to source for every Alamo history, novel, and movie.

The real damage Williams did was to enshrine the Anglocentric dogma that Barker, university regents, and Texas lawmakers demanded. Empathetic readers may defend her as a product of her time, which is probably fair, and as a woman struggling to earn a place in a male-dominated field. Even if she had wanted to, she probably couldn't have prevailed against the era's academic norms. But whatever you think of her work, there's no denying that she and Barker gave the Heroic Anglo Narrative a professional seal of approval — just in time, as it happens, for it to find a much wider audience. Via, of all things, a comic strip.

In a state that was no stranger to white supremacists, few cities were as open about their racism as Dallas in the 1920s, years in which the Ku Klux Klan controlled almost every significant position in local government. Looking back decades later, *D* magazine termed '20s-era Dallas "the most racist city in America," and it's hard to argue.[10]

It's ironic that the newspaper that eventually brought the Dallas Klan to its knees, *The Dallas Morning News,* would give birth to a creation that probably did as much as any to popularize the Anglocentric myths of the Alamo. It was a comic strip, a hugely popular component of metropolitan newspapers at a time when editors triggered bidding wars to see who got to print the latest episodes of *Barney Google and Snuffy Smith.*

The owner of the *Morning News* was a proponent of public education, and in 1926 an editor suggested the paper develop its own comic strip devoted to Texas history. A columnist named John Rosenfield Jr. wrote it, and the paper's cartoonist Jack I. Patton drew it. They called it *Texas History Movies* — at the time, comic strips were sometimes called "movies in print." Between October 1926 and June 1928, the paper cranked out 428 episodes, a sizable number of which were stunningly racist. *Texas History Movies* referred to Mexican-Americans as "greasers" and "tamale eaters," mocked African-Americans as stupid, and called Native Americans "redskins." One panel declared that Lipan, the name of an Apache tribe, meant "vagabond or bum."[11] It portrayed

Texas slaves as "unwittingly happy," as one modern reviewer puts it, and stated that all enslaved Black people were fully educated and free to change masters at will. Seriously. This was in a major Texas city in 1928.

The Alamo narrative comprised twelve strips, and they all presented a version of the Heroic Anglo Narrative that even then must have struck some as a caricature. Travis draws his line. Rose the coward runs away. Crockett jauntily plays a fiddle. A crazed Santa Anna defeats the Texians only by threatening to kill any of his men who don't fight.[12]

The strip became one of the paper's most-read features, so popular that Texas school-teachers began using it in the classroom. The *Morning News* actually suspended its publication in the summer of 1927 because kids were out of school. They decided to conclude the strip's run in June 1928, but the impact of *Texas History Movies* was only beginning to be felt. The P. L. Turner Company bought the rights, and in partnership with Magnolia Petroleum, published the series in a book Magnolia donated to every seventh grader in Texas — and would keep doing every single year until 1959, when Magnolia disappeared into a merger with Mobil Oil.

Texas History Movies, as such, became a Texas institution. Think about that: For going on thirty years, every Texas seventh grader was fed comic strips calling Latinos greasers. And many of those kids were Latino.

Even after 1959 the thing wouldn't die. A new edition was issued in 1970, and three years later the *Houston Chronicle* urged the Texas State Historical Association to distribute it to seventh graders again. It was only at that point that someone said, You know, this is 1974, you can't say this crazy shit anymore. So the association formed a board to strip out the overt racism and put out an updated edition. There was another in 1986, and still another in 2007, thankfully now devoid of references to tamale eaters.

Once Adina De Zavala was vanquished in 1913, Clara Driscoll took full control of the Daughters and thus the Alamo, intent on having the church recognized as the centerpiece of the grand park she envisioned. Though she never was able to realize it — developers snapped up much of the land lining the original compound — what the Alamo remains today can almost all be traced to Driscoll. She purchased several small adjacent lots and in the 1930s enclosed it all with a stone wall, creating the quiet little garden behind the church that thousands of tourists still shuffle through every year. To play up the church's importance, Driscoll had the Daughters issue fanciful tales of fighting inside it, while the scene of the serious fighting, the Long Barrack, languished alongside, an afterthought. To make sure Texans were paying attention, the Daughters began holding annual commemorations of the battle every March 6.

The final act of the Alamo's long transformation, and amazingly, of the decades-long feud between Driscoll and Adina De Zavala, arrived in 1936, on the occasion of the Texas Centennial. Clara was fifty-five at this point, just back from her husband Hal's posting as ambassador to Chile, and still at the height of her power. The all-day commemoration she oversaw was a masterpiece, bringing together every conceivable ethnic and religious group, plus a Who's Who of the state's hoi polloi, to pay respects to the dead on Alamo Plaza in front of the church. There were Catholic nuns and eighteen bishops, Baptist preachers and Episcopal priests, even a group of rabbis chanting Kaddish. Old prejudices remained. When a speaker read the names of those who had died, she excluded the Tejanos.

Three months later, Driscoll topped herself, arranging for the Roosevelts to visit the site. The president toured the church, laid a wreath, and read a statement proclaiming the importance of the defenders' sacrifice. Newspapers across the country ran his comments. The Alamo, heretofore a fairly obscure regional shrine, was beginning to enter the American imagination. Having the Roosevelts glide through the church while ignoring the Long Barrack, however, was too much for De Zavala.

"Would any other place in the world have permitted the Alamo history to be misstated and camouflaged for so many years?" she asked a reporter. "And would any other place have permitted the main building of the Alamo, where our heroes died, to be dismantled and unroofed and desecrated? . . . No visitor really sees the place where our heroes died. . . . The president did not."[13]

It didn't matter. This was Clara Driscoll's Alamo now. She had one final project left to complete, a monument to the defenders. During the Centennial, Texas lawmakers provided $100,000 for the work, and De Zavala's old friend Pompeo Coppini helped create it. When it was unveiled in a ceremony in November 1940, the Alamo Cenotaph towered sixty feet above the plaza, a colossus hewn from Georgia marble and Texas granite, Coppini's statues of Travis, Crockett, Bowie, and James Bonham clustered at its base. The names of 187 defenders were chiseled into it. Alas, they used Amelia Williams's list, which ended up causing all kinds of problems. Later research showed that some of the men listed were never there. Others, to the anguish of their families, were left off.

In the end, Driscoll got almost everything she wanted, a smaller Alamo but a celebrated one, one in which the Daughters enforced rules of etiquette, ensuring the hushed respect of a mausoleum. After building a lakeside mansion on land Stephen F. Austin once owned in the capital — today it's Austin's Laguna Gloria, an outdoor art museum — Driscoll died in 1945 in the penthouse of a hotel she built in her native Corpus Christi. Her body lay in state in the Alamo.

Adina passed away in 1955. The Daughters refused to allow her body to lie in state at the Alamo; instead, the funeral procession made do with driving past it on the way to the cemetery. The legislature passed a resolution saluting her contributions. De Zavala's dream of a museum in the Long

Barrack would finally be realized in 1965 when workers stripped the vines off the old stone walls and used them to create a small, single-story museum. The Daughters, of course, maintained the emphasis on the church.

In 1994, in a gesture designed to heal old wounds and prevent new ones, they unveiled a marker dedicated to the two women. It's a tiny thing, stuck in the ground in the garden. Below their names, it reads, "Two loyal members of the Daughters of the Republic of Texas, each in her own way responsible for preserving this historic site." That's one way to look at it, certainly the diplomatic way. Another is that Driscoll's victory represented the triumph of myth-making over historical accuracy. It's a tension, as we'll see, that the Alamo grapples with to this day.

CHAPTER 15

THE ALAMO GOES GLOBAL

Not only for Texas does the Alamo have meaning, but for the nation as a whole, it stands as a towering memory to Anglo-American achievement in a world dominated by force. The Alamo spells out large the word — Liberty!

— *THE ALAMO,* 1956

By the time Driscoll and De Zavala passed from the scene, the Alamo narrative was already migrating from the written page to the new venues of film and television. This would do more to spread the Heroic Anglo Narrative than anything before. There had already been a number of Alamo movies by that point, the first a now-lost 1911 film called *The Immortal Alamo,* which features a fictional Mexican spy who tries to seduce and then abduct Susanna Dickinson, playing on America's anxieties about interracial sex at the time. But the towering achievement of early Alamo films is hands down 1915's *Martyrs of the Alamo,* easily the most perversely distorted version of the Alamo narrative ever told.

A paean to early twentieth-century racism, *Martyrs of the Alamo* was the brainchild of the filmmaker D. W. Griffith, who the year before had directed the single most racist blockbuster film in U.S. history, *The Birth of a Nation,* replete with African-American rapists — actually wild-eyed white actors in blackface — and avenging Ku Klux Klansmen. *Martyrs* was its spiritual sequel, written by Griffith and directed by a gent named W. Christy Cabanne. It portrays the Texas Revolt as an Anglo revolt against the sexual predations of Santa Anna and his soldiers. Forget liberty, forget Mexican tyranny. The Alamo was actually about the perils of miscegenation.

The film opens with scenes of Mexican troops in the streets of San Antonio leering at Anglo women and raiding their homes, creating smoldering resentment among the Texians. Santa Anna merrily engages in orgies, indulges in opium, and forces himself on a blond woman, the girlfriend of one of the heroes, "Silent Smith," a character probably based on the Texian scout Deaf Smith. The Texians cannot take it anymore, so they take up arms and drive Santa Anna back to Mexico. The Tejano population, naturally grateful for liberation, bows before them in awe.

Santa Anna is not gone for long, though, and soon returns with a massive army to attack the Texians in the Alamo. Mexican troops kill Crockett, Travis, and Bowie in accordance with the prevailing folklore. The racism is breathtaking. Mexican soldiers are cowards; their officers shoot those who retreat. At one point, a Mexican soldier bashes a little blond girl against a wall, killing her. Later, Sam Houston gains the white man's revenge by riding into San Antonio with a Texian army and capturing the evil Santa Anna amid a drunken Mexican orgy. When the movie was rereleased a decade later as *The Birth of Texas,* a Mexican-American audience in Baytown got up and walked out.[1]

The Texas Centennial prompted a pair of Alamo films in the 1930s, neither of note. Republic Pictures made Sam Houston the main character of *Man of Conquest* in 1939, which, rather than showing Houston humiliated by his divorce and fleeing Washington, depicts Andrew Jackson sending him to Texas to seize the territory, through either diplomacy or revolution. By the 1940s, the

Alamo had become a story that filmmakers trotted out from time to time when a period drama was needed. Outside Texas it had no special audience, no community of hobbyists, no existential meaning.

All that began to change in 1948, when the Hollywood titan Walt Disney, angry at left-leaning labor unions, decided his films needed to do a better job shoring up "traditional" American values: patriotism, courage, self-sufficiency, and individual liberty. To do that, Disney decided, he needed to begin making movies about genuine American heroes. He told his screenwriters to find some.[2]

The Alamo narrative has always been a challenge for storytellers, in part because everyone knows how it ends, and the "bad guys" win. Another problem is the ensemble cast. Who to feature? The puffed-up Travis? The brooding Bowie? Crockett was the best-known name, but he played a soldier, not a leader, and as such deserved third billing at best. That's what he got in 1937's *Heroes of the Alamo.* Other films told Crockett's life story but, intimidated by the Alamo's dramatic challenges, left the battle out entirely, preferring to focus on his bear-hunting days.

Nor were modern history books exactly putting him front and center. Neither Barker nor Williams gave him much thought. In 1945's *The Age of Jackson,* Arthur Schlesinger Jr. called Crockett a "phony frontiersman" and a con artist who wasn't smart enough to cut it in Washington.

But alone among the Alamo's "heroes," Crockett had star potential. He'd shown it during his lifetime. He had been a stalwart of comic books and children's literature for more than a century. All you had to do was ignore the historical David Crockett, the failed congressman, and embrace his alter ego, Davy. The rugged individualism, the frontier populism, the quips, the *bears* — not to mention a heroic death at the Alamo. It was all there, waiting for a clever storyteller to bring it to a wider audience.

Which is where Disney comes in. In 1948, the chairman of Disney Studios was in a funk. Hollywood had been plagued by labor strikes for years, and Disney had suffered his share. Like a lot of studio bigwigs, Disney was convinced Communists were behind it all. It was driving him nuts. Because Disney hated union members, many of the studio's best animators were leaving. Meanwhile Disney's animated films, once considered technological wonders, were losing audience to live-action movies, especially action-packed westerns. Disney hatched an idea to solve all his problems at once, by making live-action movies and imbuing them with "traditional" American values centered on families and patriotism. He wanted dramatic story lines with a hero who faced adversity, experienced self-discovery, and instilled viewers with a moral. He wanted heroes who battled a more powerful foe, a corrupt government, a tyrant, a criminal.[3]

Disney's writers pored over history books and folklore. Their first discoveries, such as Don Diego "Zorro" de la Vega, were featured in live-action shorts that played before Disney's animated films. These shorts were the perfect length for a new medium, television, that was sweeping America. Most studios were dismissing it as a fad. Walt Disney sensed it was far more than that.[4]

Disney produced its first television programming, a pair of Christmas specials, in 1950 and 1951, and saw how Disney television could drive viewers to Disney movies. It was Walt's introduction to corporate synergy, and he proved a genius at it.[5] His brother Roy approached executives at NBC and CBS in 1953 offering a television series if they would help finance a Disneyland theme park, creating another revenue stream. Both passed.[6] But ABC, the perennial last-place network, was desperate. The two sides cut a creative deal for the era: In return for ABC buying a third of the stock for Disneyland, Disney agreed to produce an hourlong weekly television show for the network.

Walt Disney's Disneyland debuted on ABC on a Wednesday evening, October 27, 1954, and proved an immediate hit. When the producers proposed an episode based on Crockett, Disney was skeptical. Crockett was no longer what you would call a household name. The writers, though, crafted a story line Disney could not resist.[7] The trick was to treat all of Crockett's boasts as fact, and then make his death at the Alamo the climax of a three-part miniseries. Part one would focus on Crockett's time killing Native Americans, and of course bears, the next would cover his time in Washington, and the final episode would end with glory at the Alamo. The miniseries showed little resemblance to the facts of history, but there was no doubt it was a great story, that of an honest man betrayed by the world who nevertheless sacrificed himself so others might live. If that sounds a little familiar, a little, shall we say, biblical, well, that was very much on purpose.

When the miniseries' first episode, "Davy Crockett: Indian Fighter," aired December 15, 1954, American families saw hunky Fess Parker portray Crockett not as a boastful bumpkin but as a saintly stoic who, whether striking a deal with a Native American chief or President Andrew Jackson, was always fair, principled, and above all committed to liberty. "We had no idea what was going to happen to Crockett," Walt said years later. "Why, by the time the show finally got on air, we were already shooting the third one and calmly killing Davy off at the Alamo. It became one of the biggest one-night hits in TV history, and there we were with just three films and a dead hero."[8]

Crockett fever hit with gale force after the second episode, in January 1955. Within days boys across America were imitating the Tennessee frontiersman, gunning down imaginary Native Americans and singing the show's bouncy theme song. By the time the third and final episode aired the next month, Disney was raking in millions from Crockett memorabilia, none more iconic than coonskin caps. The price for a pound of raccoon tails — yes, that's apparently a thing — spiked from twenty-five cents a pound to eight dollars.[9]

The third episode brought a Disneyfied version of the Alamo into millions of American living rooms. Disney taught the world the myth of Travis drawing a line in the sand and showed Crockett crossing it first in the name of liberty. When the Mexican troops charge, Crockett is on the wall, shouting, "Here they come!" He fights to the last, swinging Old Betsy at Mexican soldiers as they overwhelm the Texians. Most Americans had little sense that they were being sucked into what was essentially a biblically inspired fable meant to prepare Americans for the Cold War.

Within two months, Americans spent $100 million on Crockett merchandise; an astounding 10 percent of all children's clothing sold in 1955 was affiliated with Crockett. The craze didn't last long; seven months later, raccoon tail prices had returned to pre-Disney levels.[10] For a moment, though, "Davy was the biggest thing since Marilyn Monroe and Liberace," *Variety* reported.[11]

Snobby writer types tried their darndest to explain that the Disney Crockett was hooey, but it was no use. In *Harper's*, the Texas-born John Fischer termed the historical Crockett a "juvenile delinquent," a deserter "who weaseled his way out of the

329

army," an "indolent and shiftless" farmer, "an unsuccessful politician; a hack writer" and king of nothing save maybe "the Tennessee Tall Tales and Bourbon Samplers Association." Fischer even poured water on the Alamo. In one of the earliest-known examples of Alamo revisionism, he portrayed its defenders as drunken bigots too stupid to retreat from what became "the worst military blooper in American history, short of Pearl Harbor." In their defense? "They died well," Fischer sniped. "From a military standpoint, that is about all that can be said for them; and it is the only solid fact about the Alamo which most Americans ever hear."[12]

Crockett fans reacted to this kind of disparagement with outrage, a foreshadowing of the coming culture wars. As described in the book *A Line in the Sand,* all the critics got angry letters; when the *New York Post*'s liberal columnist Murray Kempton deigned to author a four-part series debunking the Crockett legend, fans actually picketed the paper. "Davy killed a b'ar at 3," one placard read. "What did Murray Kempton ever shoot — except the bull???" The modern conservative movement had begun in the early 1950s, and its de facto founder, William Buckley, placed the attacks on Crockett in a political context. "The assault on Davy," he said on a radio show, "is one part a traditional debunking campaign and one part resentment by liberal publicists of Davy's neuroses-free approach to life. He'll survive the carpers."[13]

Despite the haters, Disney's Crockett clearly gave mainstream America something it needed in the mid-1950s, a measure of comfort in frightening times. The Cold War was under way, and after fighting to a draw in Korea, Americans worried about the spread of Communism. Looking across the oceans at Russia and China, the United States appeared surrounded and outnumbered, just like the men at the Alamo. Americans found comfort in Disney's fanciful Crockett and, strangely, inspiration in his martyrdom. The message, a not too subtle one, was that dying in defense of freedom was a heroic act.

Somewhat like *Texas History Movies,* Disney's Davy Crockett lived on for years. After each episode was rebroadcast, the miniseries was edited into a full-length feature film called *Davy Crockett: King of the Wild Frontier.* It remains a souvenir of a time when the needs of Anglo myth-making justified racial insensitivities such as the bumbling Native Americans Fess Parker predictably outsmarted and outgunned. And Disney's success didn't go unnoticed. At Republic Pictures, one Alamo fan in particular couldn't have been happier to see Crockett rehabilitated. Like Walt Disney, he too was a political conservative preoccupied with halting the spread of international Communism. He'd wanted to make a movie about the Alamo for more than ten years. His name was John Wayne.

John Wayne, born Marion Morrison in 1907, was already an established star when he first imagined making an Alamo movie in 1945. He had been acting in films for fifteen years by then, emerging as a bankable leading man in John Ford's 1939 classic, *Stagecoach*. From the beginning, the Alamo was more than just another film project for Wayne. It was a cause. Biographers have suggested his motivation was twofold. During World War II he had been granted repeated deferments and thus avoided military service. Stars like Jimmy Stewart, meanwhile, were returning home with medals on their chests. Wayne, it's said, was more than a little insecure about this. And like Walt Disney, Wayne keenly feared that the world, and Hollywood itself, was being overrun by Communists.[14]

What thirty-eight-year-old John Wayne knew how to do best — it was what he had done during the war — was make patriotic movies, and in the Alamo he sensed a parable for uncertain times. In his eyes, Travis, Bowie, Crockett, and the rest embodied the best in American values. In Santa Anna and his soldiers he saw the ideal villains, dark, swarthy foreigners fighting for a proto-dictatorship to wipe out God-fearing white Christian Americans; blink and they could have been Russian or Chinese Communists.[15]

Wayne envisioned his film as a crowning achievement, an epic on the scale of *Gone with the Wind.* He persuaded his studio, Republic Pictures, to hire a screenwriter and a research assistant, and the trio began doing research in San Antonio between drinking bouts in the Menger Hotel bar.[16] Soon they had a script. But Republic got nervous when Wayne started talking about building a scale model of the Alamo in Panama. He was the studio's biggest star, so its chief, Herbert Yates, coddled him for a time, but when Wayne proposed a $3 million budget, Yates worried it could bankrupt the company. Things got so heated Wayne quit the studio. He had to leave the script behind.

Fast-forward ten years: Disney's Davy

Crockett rules the land, and suddenly Hollywood was bubbling with talk of new Crockett and Alamo movies.* It wasn't Wayne, though, who struck first. It was Republic. A new studio chief ordered up a rewrite of his decade-old script and put it into production as the unremarkable if surprisingly accurate *The Last Command,* released in 1955. The release of two major Alamo films did nothing to suppress Wayne's zeal. But in retrospect, he took too long finalizing his plans for an Alamo film. By the time he presented it in 1956, Crockett's moment had passed. ABC had produced a television series about Bowie — it focused on his days in Louisiana and Arkansas — but it flopped.† Warner's, having

---

* The decade had actually already produced one Alamo-related movie, the unusual *Man from the Alamo,* released in 1953. It was the fictionalized story of Moses Rose, played by actor Glenn Ford. The film has Rose avoiding the battle when he is dispatched as a courier; afterward he is branded a coward, managing to salvage his reputation only after saving a wagon full of settlers under attack from outlaws.

† Here is what may be our favorite Alamo factoid of all: The Bowie television series was broadcast in England. Among its fans was a London boy

concluded that audiences were tiring of westerns, decided to pass.[17]

Wayne took the idea to United Artists, which expressed interest but blanched at a proposed budget of $7.5 million. At the time, Wayne was planning to produce and direct the film but take a secondary acting role, maybe portraying Sam Houston. United Artists offered $2.5 million, but only if Wayne agreed to a multipicture deal, threw in money of his own, and took a starring role. Wayne accepted. But that still left him $3 million short. Luckily, he knew exactly where to find rich people who cherished the Alamo and loathed Communists: Texas.[18] Wayne flew to Austin, where the governor suggested he talk to a trio of millionaire oilmen, Clint Murchison and the McCullough brothers. Murchison and company agreed to furnish the money if the movie was shot in Texas. Wayne eagerly agreed.

By 1958, *The Alamo* was to be a big, big film: big actors, big money, big ideas. The

---

named David Robert Jones. The boy grew up to be a singer, and at the age of eighteen, fearing he would be confused with Davy Jones of the Monkees, he adopted the frontiersman's last name as his stage name. Thus David Bowie was born.

script was a three-hour meditation on Wayne's worldview: America stands for freedom, socialism is oppression, and American men must sacrifice for freedom. It spends not a minute questioning why Anglo adventurers were in Texas, much less the importance of slavery to all these brave white fighters, or why Santa Anna felt entitled to send them home. Wayne was trying to draw parallels with the Soviet Union; all he wanted was a bloodthirsty dictator trying to crush good men fighting for self-determination.

That he got. But Hollywood's biggest names — Clark Gable, Charlton Heston, Rock Hudson, Burt Lancaster — proved unavailable. He ended up hiring up-and-comers instead: the British actor Laurence Harvey as Travis; the perpetually angry Richard Widmark as Bowie; the singer Frankie Avalon as a messenger who, of course, sang. The script was built around Crockett, and Wayne took the role, assigning the veteran Richard Boone to portray Sam Houston.

He built his Alamo on a ranch outside Brackettville, two hours west of San Antonio. It took a year to complete, and was actually a marvel of accuracy; one history terms it "the most authentic set in the history of the movies." Wayne even had his contractor bring in laborers from Mexico who still knew how to use building techniques the missionaries had used 250 years before.[19]

The shoot, spanning the fall of 1959, proved a rough one. This was Wayne's first attempt to direct, and it showed. Fortified by endless cups of coffee and up to a hundred cigarettes a day, he had an unmatched work ethic, but no patience for imperfection or delays. He frequently lost his temper; the most frequent focus of his anger was a plague of crickets. They were everywhere, hopping onto actors and chirping in every take. "Goddamnit!" Wayne would bark. "Shut those crickets up!"[20]

He was no kinder to the cast. While Wayne knew how to compose an image and obsessed over details of the set, he had little sense of how to direct actors. One complained that his go-to advice was to act like him. Widmark was a notorious hothead, and he and Wayne were soon at each other's throats. Widmark tried to quit more than once.[21] More serious trouble arrived in October when a bit player named Charles Harvey Smith, embroiled in a tempestuous backstage romance with an actress named LeJean Ethridge, got drunk and plunged a butcher knife into Ethridge's chest, killing her. Shooting was suspended for a week.

They wrapped on December 15, just three weeks behind schedule. Wayne returned to Hollywood having shot a half million feet of film. The three-hour, thirteen-minute movie that resulted was, shall we say, not exactly *Gone with the Wind*. The best thing about it was the cinematography, which ably captures the beauty of South Texas, and its stirring score, which would earn an Academy Award.

But Wayne's desire to turn the battle into a Cold War parable led him far from the truth and beyond much of the myth. The names are right, but the actors portray entirely different people. Wayne mimics Fess Parker's portrayal of Crockett as a fatherly figure. Laurence Harvey buys into Amelia Williams's conjecture that Travis was a foppish, narcissistic boor. Widmark comes closest to the mark with Bowie as an angry drunk. We certainly don't get a sense of the real men: Bowie the con artist, Travis the preening politician, Crockett the washed-up politico. Santa Anna, meanwhile, gets almost no screen time, and neither do the Mexican commanders and troops. The Seguíns and the Tejanos are bit players.

The script was, to put it bluntly, a snooze.

338

As Wayne's biographers Randy Roberts and James S. Olson observe, a better director — a William Wyler, say — would have focused on character development: Travis's maturation as a leader maybe, Bowie's humbling, the feckless Crockett's decision to stand and fight. Wayne, instead, made do with "a combination of action, physical humor and preachy, stilted dialogue."[22] Wayne didn't play Crockett so much as he indulged the preachiest version of himself. He drones on about the glories of living in a republic, which "means that people can live free, talk free, go or come, buy or sell, be drunk or sober, however they choose." He warns against big government, with too many rules or powerful leaders. Wayne takes every opportunity to reinforce headshakingly simplistic views of gender: Women are baubles, madonnas, or whores, but all have hearts of gold. The film promotes what future generations would call toxic masculinity. His depiction of combat, meanwhile, could have only come from someone who'd never seen it.

By this point, Wayne had developed a kind of grand fantasy for his movie's release. Superstardom had left him with a messiah complex, and *The Alamo* was his chance to use American folklore to change the direction of the country through cinema. "I want to remind the freedom-loving people of the world that not too long ago there were men and women in America who had the guts to stand up and fight for the things they believed in," Wayne said in a press release. "The people of the Alamo realized that in order to live decently a man must be prepared to die decently. There were no namby-pamby pussy-foots, malingerers or skedaddle in that brave band."[23]

But Wayne wanted to use the Alamo to change not just American culture but American politics. Which is why he decided to release *The Alamo* just before the 1960 presidential election. Wayne honestly believed his Alamo had a chance to sink the career of a certain Catholic senator from Massachusetts, a man Wayne feared would ruin America with his effete liberal ways: John F. Kennedy.

CHAPTER 16
THE ALAMO SUPREMACISTS

The Alamo will remind a forgetful world
what kind of people Americans really are.
— JOHN WAYNE, 1960

The Alamo did, in fact, play a role in the
1960 presidential campaign between John F.
Kennedy and the former vice president
Richard Nixon, but as you may have
guessed, it wasn't exactly the one John
Wayne envisioned. The high point came on
September 12, 1960, six weeks before *The
Alamo* was to be released, when Kennedy
gave a speech at the actual Alamo. Behind
him sat the usual coterie of notables, including Lyndon Johnson. To one side stood
some newspaper boxes, the papers' back
pages already featuring ads for Wayne's
much-anticipated "epic."[1]

Kennedy's appearance was notable for a
couple of subtle things. Aware of Wayne's
intentions, fantastical or not, he began his

speech by cheekily quoting the movie's tag line, calling the Alamo "the mission which became a fortress — the fortress which became a shrine." But then, in yet another moment that presaged the coming culture wars, Kennedy invoked it as a symbol not of reflexive patriotism but of the Mexican Revolution that led to the war in Texas. "If this place is dedicated to freedom — this day is also a landmark of liberty," he said. "For one hundred and fifty years ago this Friday, Father Hidalgo made his famous plea for liberty when he asked his people 'will you have freedom' and they responded by beginning Mexico's war for independence." Having hitched the Alamo to the revolution — a clear hat tip to Mexican-American voters — Kennedy launched into a speech about the need for closer ties with Latin America.[2]

It's what happened afterward that folks in San Antonio remember. Kennedy was in a hurry; he had a big speech in Houston later that same day. He was in the church, trapped by crowds outside, when he supposedly asked whether it had a back door. "Senator," someone replied, "there are no back doors at the Alamo. Only heroes."*

* For the record, there are several back doors.

Get it? Years later, one of the Daughters and a local congressman took credit for the line, but it may have been apocryphal.[3]

It was actually in Houston where Kennedy overtly played the Alamo card. This was the speech, given to a group of Protestant ministers, where he sought to end speculation that if elected the first Catholic president, he'd be taking orders from the Vatican. After noting the persecution of Jews and the Pilgrims' discrimination against Baptists, Kennedy compared those who had fought religious intolerance to those who had "fought at the shrine I visited today, the Alamo. For side by side with Bowie and Crockett died McCafferty and Bailey and Carey — but no one knows whether they were Catholic or not. For there was no religious test at the Alamo."[4] No one had ever used the Alamo as a symbol of Catholic tolerance among Protestants before, but it worked. Historians say this was the moment Kennedy put "the religious issue" to rest.

Not to be outdone, Richard Nixon attempted, awkwardly, to use the Alamo as well. On the last weekend of the campaign, he told a crowd there that should Kennedy be elected he would be taking orders from the head of the United Auto Workers, not

Pope John XXIII.[5] Which was where things stood when John Wayne's *The Alamo* made its debut.

Wayne's publicity campaign for *The Alamo,* masterminded by the publicist Russell Birdwell, was a strange combination of straightforward Alamo primers and veiled political appeals. To educate audiences, Birdwell persuaded seven governors to declare an Alamo Day and sent Alamo instructional kits to middle and high school teachers.[6] At the same time, he took out a full-page ad in *Life* magazine calling on voters to reject professional politicians who relied on speechwriters and strategists. The copy, under Birdwell's byline, invoked the defenders of the Alamo as the archetypes of American manhood.[7] "These men left a legacy for all who prize freedom above tyranny, individualism over conformity," he wrote. The ad drew national attention, spurring reactions from editorial writers, who mostly felt Birdwell had a good point.

The Alamo had its star-studded premiere on October 24, 1960, at the Woodlawn Theatre in San Antonio. Hundreds piled into the streets for the festivities. By and large, San Antonians liked what they saw. Critics, not so much. Wayne, noted *The New*

Yorker, "turned a splendid chapter of our past into sentimental flapdoodle. . . . Nothing in *The Alamo* is serious . . . nothing in it is true . . . a model of distortion and vulgarization." *Newsweek* was just as dismissive: "*The Alamo's* place in history will probably be that of the most lavish B picture ever made . . . B for banal."[8]

Wayne and Birdwell took these as fighting words. They responded with an ad that noted, among other things, "*The Alamo* will remind a forgetful world what kind of people Americans really are . . . savagely cruel against injustice, willing to carry their share of disaster — *and at all times on the side of God-fearing people!*"[9] The more coastal elites called out *The Alamo,* the more Birdwell saw a chance to recruit an audience in the heartland. "I deplore the garbage now being splashed on the screen," Wayne said. "It is giving the world a false, nasty impression of us."

In the end, the film's legacy was less political than cultural. (Kennedy won, we've heard.) Even as a critical and box office disappointment, it spread the Heroic Anglo Narrative to the wider world, planting itself deeply into the minds of many, especially young men, whose newfound passion for the battle would turn the Alamo into an international icon. Talk to Alamo-heads today, often white men of a certain age, and most trace their zeal to a boyhood viewing of Fess Parker or Wayne, usually both.*

But Wayne's movie also marked a turning point in the way the Alamo was viewed, what it symbolized, a kind of American fortitude, especially military fortitude, a sense that patriotic Americans, as in the traditionalist view of the Alamo's defenders, were willing to fight and die to defend their freedoms. Texans and their politicians seem to have started this kind of talk, repeatedly invoking the Alamo in speeches and editorials during World War II. But it was only once international Communism seemed to threaten the West that the references truly began flying. Things ramped up during the Vietnam War, when the Alamo was the site of repeated pro-war rallies, with aging veterans singing "God Bless America" while holding placards saying things like "Down

* We sometimes wonder whether many of these folks are more interested in the cinematic Alamo than the real one. When the Alamo hobbyist community began organizing during the 1970s, in fact, its early newsletters often contained as many articles about Parker and Wayne as about the Crockett of history.

346

with Protesters" and "Better Dead Than Red." Antiwar protesters actually viewed the Alamo in much the same way; in a 1971 protest march, Vietnam veterans threw their service medals at the church doors.

But Disney and Wayne were only the first two members of the cultural triumvirate that transformed the Alamo into what it represents today. The third was a Texan who invoked the Alamo as often as some folks blink: Lyndon Johnson.

The Alamo was a hallowed place for Johnson, who was a child of the Texas Hill Country and a third-generation Texan. All his adult life, he loved little more than boasting of his family's ties to it. A great-great-uncle, John Wheeler Bunton, fought at San Jacinto.[10] Johnson was a schoolboy in 1917 when his father sponsored the legislation to take ownership of the Alamo.*

* He told this story well into his presidency. "I received a good deal of my political philosophy right here in San Antonio. Before I was born, my father was writing the bill — my grandfather wrote it because my father asked him to, as he wasn't a lawyer — my father was introducing a bill and speaking for the bill that saved the Alamo. It was being torn down and a hotel would have replaced

347

In fact, his father's role in saving the Alamo was the only one of his credentials LBJ cited in his first congressional campaign, in 1938; during his first Senate campaign, in 1948, he boasted endlessly that Clara Driscoll was among his financial backers.

Throughout his career, Johnson returned again and again to the Alamo narrative, especially when America was at or near war. As a congressman, he rallied support for fighting the Nazis by asking Texans to "step over the line"; everyone knew what he meant. But it was during the Vietnam War that Johnson's preoccupation with the Alamo emerged as a kind of obsession. Identify a wartime challenge, and Johnson had an Alamo analogy ready. "Hell, Vietnam is just like the Alamo," Johnson once

---

the Alamo. And he got a good lady to put up enough money long enough to hold the structure until the legislature could pass a bill to preserve the Alamo. That was in 1905. I was born in 1908, I believe." (Lyndon B. Johnson, Remarks in San Antonio at the Signing of the Medicare Extension Bill, April 8, 1966, online by Gerhard Peters and John T. Woolley, The American Presidency Project, https://www.presidency.ucsb.edu/node/239400.)

said.[*] "Hell, it's just like if you were down at that gate and you were surrounded and you damn well needed somebody. . . . I thank the Lord that I've got men who want to go with me, from [Defense Secretary Robert] McNamara right on down to the littlest private who's carrying a gun."[†] At

[*] Johnson wasn't the only one to invoke the Alamo in service of the Vietnam War. According to Christopher Sharrett, "The Alamo: Fact, Fiction and the Last Stand of History," in 1969 Johnny Cash sang "Remember the Alamo" at Madison Square Garden before addressing President Nixon, who was not in attendance, "Mr. President, these are the odds we face today!" Nixon must not have taken offense, because the following year Cash was invited to perform in the East Room of the White House. (Sharrett, "The Alamo," *Cinéaste* 29, no. 4 [2004], 14–17, http://www.jstor.org/stable/41689771.)

[†] Fess Parker, who played David Crockett in the Disney television series, visited the troops in Vietnam in 1968. "I suddenly realized that all these kids fighting this war were the Davy Crockett generation," he told Stephen Harrigan in a 1986 interview for *Texas Monthly.* "That was very painful. Some of those guys I was talking to flew off in their planes the next day and didn't come back." (Stephen Harrigan, "The Ballad of Fess Parker,"

one point, Johnson explained that he had "gone into Vietnam because, as at the Alamo, somebody had to get behind the log with those threatened people," meaning the Vietnamese.

Early on, journalists took notice. *Life* magazine's Hugh Sidey famously dubbed it Johnson's "Alamo syndrome"; the writer Larry L. King called the framework through which Johnson saw every war as an opportunity for valor "the Alamo mind-set." At White House dinners the president was known to recite a poem his mother had taught him as a child. "And Travis, great Travis, drew sword, quick and strong," Johnson would say. "Drew a line at his feet. . . . 'Will you come? Will you go? I die with my wounded, in the Alamo!' " It always got applause.

Eventually Johnson's "Alamo syndrome" got him in trouble. On November 1, 1966, while addressing troops in South Korea, he suddenly announced, "My great-great-grandfather died at the Alamo."[11] This was, needless to say, not the truth. Hugh Sidey was probably the first to cite Johnson's fib, attributing it to the president's wanting to

---

Texas Monthly, November 1986, https://www.texasmonthly.com/articles/the-ballad-of-fess-parker/.)

draw from the "wellspring of courage [that] was the Alamo," he wrote. "Johnson longed for some blood connection to those dead heroes, but he had none. Finally, that did not stop him. . . . It was something that should have been, at least in Johnson's mind, and so he just said it was so."[12]

Until John Wayne infused his culture war allegory with his vendetta against Kennedy, the Alamo had always been considered Texas property — literally and, more to the point, figuratively. The Alamo had been the story that made Texans, or at least many of them, feel special. But if Disney had turned Crockett and the Alamo into international symbols of American exceptionalism, Wayne's movie had turned the Alamo into a national political symbol, a romantic bulwark against shifting political winds.

As a political Rorschach test, the Alamo had always symbolized two distinct yet intertwined concepts: kicking ass and taking names. In the conservative telling, it's an inspiration to send troops into the fight, no matter the odds, for victory or death. But after Kennedy used it to talk about spreading freedom in Latin America and tolerance for religious and ethnic differences, politicians could look at the Alamo and see something else: a willingness to go against orthodoxy* and to take a broader view of history that includes Mexico as a partner and not an enemy.

Together, Disney, Wayne, and LBJ transformed the Alamo from a quaint Texas shrine into a potent symbol of American nationalism. The final brushstrokes in this portrait were applied by a book published in Johnson's final year in office, a mammoth, 767-page history of Texas called *Lone Star,* which became so beloved — some might say notorious — that it is still widely known in Texas literary circles simply by the author's last name: Fehrenbach.

Lone Star is the Torah of the Heroic Anglo Narrative, the most popular and best-selling

---

* In 2011, historian Paul Andrew Hutton noted that author James Simon Kunen credited Davy Crockett in part for the student takeover at Columbia University. Kunen wrote in his memoir *The Strawberry Statement:* "I realize that my conception of the philosophy of law comes not so much from Rousseau as from Fess Parker as Davy Crockett. I remember his saying that you should decide what you think is right and then go ahead and do it. Walt Disney really bagged that one; the old fascist inadvertently created a whole generation of radicals."

book of Texas history in living memory, a swash-buckling, triumphalist pulp narrative in which Native Americans are "Stone Age savages," women are submissive, and Comanche are termed "Red Niggers." Spanning prehistory to the twentieth century, the book's core is the Texas Creation Myth: the Alamo, Goliad, San Jacinto. It celebrates the Anglo Texan's violent conquest of just about everyone and everything, for the simple reason that this is what white men did.

But dismissing *Lone Star* as amateurish or ham-handed does it a great disservice. Its author, the Princeton-educated T. R. Fehrenbach, a gruff, cigar-chomping San Antonio insurance man turned bestselling writer, brought an eloquence and literary sophistication unmatched by almost any book in the Texas canon. Fehrenbach understands Anglo Texans at a primal level. He celebrates the Alamo's leaders not as shining heroes but as deeply flawed men of their time. And, let's just admit it, the book is a fabulously entertaining read. Bloody, brawny, and unapologetically lurid, its sentences flow like water, unblocked by a single source note, the better to move things along, Fehrenbach explained in a foreword.

Even in 1968, reviewers hated it. "Fehrenbach does not have the inhibitions which plague professional historians in their quest for accuracy," one reviewer noted. "In fact, he seldom allows facts to hamper his interpretations."[13] *The Texas Observer* sniped: "The legend of the Textosteroned Anglo Male versus Practically Everyone Else is gospel to Fehrenbach. Unlike academic historians, he ignores any pretense of objectivity and simply preaches — sometimes until he is possessed by the voices and cojones of the machos he lauds."[14]

None of this carping mattered. More than anything written by beloved Texas historians such as J. Frank Dobie, *Lone Star* would go down as the crowning achievement of Texas history on the page, a book that so dominated the field it all but killed the market for more — a phenomenon one modern reviewer terms "the curse of Fehrenbach."

The Alamo's journey from fact to legend was now complete — just in time for an unlikely squadron of naysayers to begin tearing it all apart.

CHAPTER 17
THE RISE OF
ALAMO REVISIONISM

Davy Crockett's [death], it's sort of like a
Chicano version of the Jewish Christ killers. If you're looking at the Alamo as a
kind of state religion, this is the original
sin. We killed Davy Crockett.

— RUBEN CORDOVA,
CHICANO ART HISTORIAN

For 150 years, the Heroic Anglo Narrative
of the Alamo reigned pretty much unchallenged. By vanquishing Adina De Zavala,
Clara Driscoll enshrined not just the Alamo's remaining buildings, but also the accepted narrative of what happened there
into a metaphor for the triumph of Anglo
Texans over legions of insidious Mexicans.
Eugene Barker and his acolytes, most notably Amelia Williams, encoded this doctrine
into academia so thoroughly that few dared
follow, leaving the field free for two generations of writers to spread the legend in

popular books, a process capped by Fehrenbach's opus *Lone Star.* Buoyed by Disney's
Davy Crockett, John Wayne and LBJ
brought it to the world.

This traditionalist narrative was zealously
guarded by generations of Driscoll's cult-
like Daughters of the Republic of Texas,
which by the 1960s had evolved into a kind
of paramilitary Junior League. The Daughters were the humorless schoolmarms of the
Alamo, forever shushing tour groups and
tossing out anyone who marred its sanctity.
A *Texas Observer* writer claimed he was
ejected for questioning the veracity of a
locket of Crockett's hair.

The Daughters' signature crusade was the
war it declared in 1969 against a Hollywood
movie planned for filming at the old mission. *Viva Max!* was a farce that imagined a
hapless Mexican general invading modern-
day Texas to retake the Alamo. Apoplectic
at the prospect of its despoliation, Daughters marched on city hall, demanding all
filming be banned, arguing at one point that
allowing it would "lead civilization down
the twilight trail to oblivion."[1] When the
city council voted to allow filming anyway,
the Daughters sought court injunctions in
vain. As one columnist put it, they "did
everything but pull out their muskets and

Bowie knives." *Viva Max!* was released in 1969. Civilization endured.*

Smaller moments were just as telling, as in an awkward encounter between several Daughters and a young *Texas Monthly* writer named Stephen Harrigan in 1975. As Harrigan wrote:

> [One] asks me what my views are on the battle of the Alamo. And, because I feel it is my job, I summon forth all my reserves of smart-ass sophistication and introduce the notion that the Texas Revolt might, after all, have had as much to do with land speculation and slave holding as with Truth, Justice, and the American Way.
>
> Silence. I have just thrown a rattlesnake on the conference table.
>
> Mrs. Davis shakes her head and quotes

---

* One or two historians have attempted to cast *Viva Max!* as an early example of Alamo revisionism. It's not. The movie, like the 1966 novel it is based on, has nothing to say about its symbolism or importance to Anglos or Latinos. "Oh no, I had no political motive, nothing really profound to say at all," recalled the novel's author, James Lehrer, a cub reporter at *The Dallas Times-Herald* at the time who went on to anchor the *PBS News-Hour.* "I just wanted to write a good story."

Ronald Reagan: "You can't have freedom without prosperity and profit."

"Maybe these men came here seeking freedom for themselves," says Mrs. Dibrell in a fine, quavering, indignant voice, "but they did not have to stay. They did not run away. They stayed and gave their lives." She abruptly leaves the room and returns with a copy of a speech given at the Alamo by a general several months earlier: "Here 186 men stood, fought and died — that others, as yet unborn, might live, free of tyranny."

The women are slowly recovering. But it has been a shock to all of us that one of those "as yet unborn" people should speak such heresy.

"They died for something they believed in, and that is a fact!" Mrs. Davis says.[2]

This kind of reactionary stance might have been dismissed as harmless parochialism had it not proven so destructive to the identity of an ethnic group that fifty years later is poised to become a majority of Texas citizens: Latinos. For generations Mexican Texans simmered mostly in silence, suffering the indignity of an Anglocentric narrative that implied they were the murderers of Travis, Bowie, and Crockett. Even today, many Tejanos describe the history class Texas children take in middle school as a humiliating experience. Among themselves, they often tell a different story of the Alamo. In the turbulent 1960s this narrative began to surface publicly, and in it lay the seeds of what is known as Alamo revisionism, a school of thought that periodically roils the state to this day.

Andrés Tijerina, a retired college instructor in Austin, vividly remembers that day in 1957 when the history teacher called him to the front of the classroom. "He said, 'It was the Mexicans that killed Davy Crockett,' " he recalls. "It's like Andy's grandfather killed Davy Crockett." Tijerina shakes his head, uttering the words you hear from many Texas-raised Latinos, especially those of a certain age. "It's the first time I found out I was a Mexican. It's the first time I found out I was different."

Tijerina's wife, Juanita, had an identical experience in her South Texas classroom in the 1950s. "We felt like crawling under the desks," she remembers. "We didn't know we were different until they told us we killed Crockett."

For Richard Flores, a professor at the University of Texas, it happened during a third-grade field trip to the Alamo itself. Even at that age he considered Travis, Bowie, and Crockett heroes. It wasn't until he returned outside that the other children began teasing him. "You killed them!" one jabbed. "You and the other 'mes'kins.' "[3]

"I remember that being really uncomfortable, that you don't want to own whatever this past was that has been assigned to you," remembers Diego Bernal, a Texas state legislator, of his own childhood trip to the Alamo. "That sucked. That wasn't fun at all. I just remember being a little bit uncomfortable because the sense was that my folks were on this side who were bad, and we lost, and your folks were on this side and you're good and you won."

A California professor named Rosa-Linda Fregoso writes of the shame she felt during her middle school Texas History class in Corpus Christi:

Mrs. Roy gave interminable, heart-wrenching lectures, reenacting with melodramatic detail the Anglo-Mexican struggles leading to Texas independence. . . . The noble letter-writing campaign of Stephen F. Austin versus the "bloody dictator" Santa Ana's [sic] wrath; the memorable deeds and bravery of Travis, Crockett, and

Bowie versus the atrocities of the "treacherous" Mexicans; the high-powered artillery rifles and canons [*sic*] of the "villainous" Mexicans versus the handful of muskets, revolvers, and the bowie knife of the heroic Anglos. . . . [Sometimes] she gazed at me, the only Tejana in the class, and I felt her whiteness overpowering me each time she mentioned "the cruel streak in the Mexican nature . . ." By the eighth grade, I had internalized . . . a self-hatred equal to the hatred Anglo teachers of Texas history felt for Mexican Texans.[4]

Talk to Latinos raised in Texas and you hear this same kind of story over and over. Many grew up with Anglo friends and considered themselves no different, until that fateful day when a telling of the Alamo story altered their identities forever. Now, we should make clear, this is not exactly a hot-button issue for most Latinos. Ask about the Alamo and many will shrug. But ask a bit more and you often find the shame is there, a psychic wound lying beneath the surface.

"Everyone has the seventh-grade story where, you know, they make the field trip and then all the white kids start treating them differently," says Ruben Cordova, a

San Antonio art historian. "Davy Crockett's [death], it's sort of like a Chicano version of the Jewish Christ killers. If you're looking at the Alamo as a kind of state religion, this is the original sin. We killed Davy Crockett." It's the kind of talk, Cordova goes on, often used to put Latinos in their place. He remembers the story his father told of working on an air force base and being hazed by Anglos, who would walk by, punch him in the arm, and say with a smirk, "Remember the Alamo."

"The way I explain it," says Andrés Tijerina, "is Mexican-Americans are brought up, even in the first grade, singing the national anthem and the Pledge of Allegiance and all that, and it's not until the seventh grade that they single us out as Mexicans. And from that point on, you realize you're not an American. You're a Mexican, and always will be. The Alamo story takes good, solid, loyal little American kids and it converts them into Mexicans."

Inevitably, there is a second chapter to the Latino "seventh-grade story" that comes when the shamed student asks his parents what really happened at the Alamo. Rosa-Linda Fregoso remembers asking her father. "Just imagine," he explained, "that one day you invite a guest into your home and you allow them to live in your home on the condition that they follow certain rules. Then one day, your houseguests decided that they don't agree with your rules and so they decide to take your house and kick you out. That's how it happened in Tejas."[5]

It isn't just Latinos who recoil from the Heroic Anglo Narrative. A retired San Antonio teacher named Dan Bolen, an Anglo, remembers how he used to pile his fifth graders into buses every year for a trip to the Alamo. He quit doing it when one of them announced to the class, "I hate Mexicans." A San Antonio academic named Linda K. Salvucci has written of uncomfortably encountering this sentiment in her own family when her five-year-old went through a Davy Crockett phase. One day she returned home to find him crouched atop their jungle gym firing an imaginary gun and yelling, "Kill Mexicans!"

His Latina babysitter stood by in silence.

"Why do you want to kill Mexicans?" Salvucci asked.

"Because they killed Davy," came the reply.

For Salvucci, enough was enough. "Right across our own backyard," she has written, "I drew my line in the sand — against history-as-hero-worship that, however unwittingly, demonized an entire culture."[6]

This kind of story is so commonplace among Mexican-Americans in Texas you'd think it would be a staple of the literature. It's not. In fact, you have to look hard to find examples of Latinos saying things like this publicly. The reason, one suspects, is what happens when they do.

Take the case of Rosie Castro. Castro is a veteran Latina activist in San Antonio, probably best known as the mother of Julián Castro, the 2020 presidential candidate, and his twin brother, Joaquin, a U.S. congressman. In 2010, when Julián was housing secretary during the Obama administration, *The New York Times Magazine* asked her what she thought about the Alamo. She held nothing back.

"They used to take us there when we were schoolchildren," Castro replied. "They told us how glorious that battle was. When I grew up I learned that the 'heroes' of the Alamo were a bunch of drunks and crooks and slaveholding imperialists who conquered land that didn't belong to them. But as a little girl I got the message — we were losers. I can truly say that I hate that place and everything it stands for."[7]

For her candor, Castro was publicly savaged, especially in conservative venues. She hasn't spoken much publicly since.* "You don't question the Alamo," says María Berriozábal, the first Latina to serve on the San Antonio City Council. "This is a story that, growing up here, there's always been this thing, this resentment, this pain that that's not the [true] story. . . . How would you start saying that's not the story? So what you do is kind of know there are others who feel like you do. You kind of all just know, and then you don't talk about it."

Little of this, we should say, is apparent to many Anglo Texans. In researching this book, in fact, we couldn't find a single white friend who knew of this widespread Latino sentiment. This ignorance, we might venture, lies at the root of much of the resistance toward updating the Alamo narrative. If Texas Anglos truly understood what the Alamo represented to their Latino neighbors, would they be so resistant to change? Certainly the sentiment remains widespread. There's anecdotal evidence that this kind of feeling — that the Alamo is not

* When asked about the Alamo, Julián tends to shrug off anti-Alamo sentiments, commenting more than once that his generation is "less burdened" by its narrative than his mother's generation has been.

something that's safe to talk about outside one's family — remains common among Latinos. All the way back in 1960, an activist named Adela Sloss-Vento dared to write a letter to Lyndon Johnson protesting John Wayne's movie. "Everytime [sic] the words 'Remember the Alamo' [are] mentioned," she wrote, "the blood of the Mexican boils. We too have had to suffer the consequences of the hatreds of Texas history."[8]

Not for years, though, would such sentiments begin seeping into public view. That's when the trouble started.

Mexican-Americans raised in Texas were long aware they were being slighted by history books, but it wasn't until the 1920s that a handful of Latino intellectuals began trying to do something about it. Not counting Adina De Zavala's writings, none spent much time examining the Alamo, preferring instead to address the larger problem of their people's removal from *all* Texas history. The two most energetic, a politician and a South Texas schoolteacher, were both deeply ashamed by, and deeply committed to correcting, the Anglocentric narratives popularized in the principal textbook of their youth, Anna Pennybacker's 1888 *A New History of Texas.*

The politician was José Tomás Canales, a legislator and lawyer in the Rio Grande Valley who had made his name investigating the World War I–era massacres of Tejanos by Texas Rangers on the Mexican border. A founding member of the League of United Latin American Citizens, known as LU-LAC, a kind of Latino NAACP, Canales believed the roots of Tejano discrimination lay in the belief among many Anglos that Tejanos sided with Santa Anna. Determined to present a "counter history," he spearheaded LULAC's plans to highlight Tejano contributions to early Texas during the 1936 Texas Centennial. This effort resulted in a pamphlet, likely the first of its kind, called *Viva Tejas: The Story of the Mexican-Born Patriots of the Republic of Texas*.[9]

The pamphlet amounted to a Depression-era shout in the wind, but it was a start. In those days, LULAC members suggested that Seguín's portrait be hung in the Alamo, and that Latino Boy Scouts be allowed to lead tours. You can guess where those efforts led: nowhere. Somewhat more successful was a South Texas schoolteacher, Maria Elena Zamora O'Shea, who like Canales kept up a lively correspondence with De Zavala about efforts to push Tejanos back into the history books. Her crowning achievement was a novel, *El Mesquite,* published in 1935, that presented the history and culture of Tejanos narrated by perhaps the only living thing that had seen it all, a mesquite tree.

This kind of consciousness awakening, including memoirs written by Canales and others, took the revisionist impulse embedded in Tejano oral traditions and introduced it, however gingerly, to the broader world. Probably the first significant work of true revisionist scholarship was a book written in 1949 by an Anglo liberal in California named Carey McWilliams. *North from Mexico* was a sympathetic history of an "invisible people" just beginning to struggle, much like African-Americans at the time, to overcome centuries of Anglo oppression and discrimination. It takes only a glancing swipe at Texas and Alamo revisionism, noting how Mexican-Americans at the time called the Texians " *'los diablos Tejanos':* arrogant, overbearing, aggressive, conniving, rude, unreliable, and dishonest." It portrays the Alamo's defenders as "filibusters" invading a sovereign Mexico. It wasn't much, but it was a start.

North from Mexico was ignored by reviewers, taken out of print, and forgotten. But in 1961 two of McWilliams's publishing friends decided to reissue it, and to everyone's surprise it sold well. It was the third edition, issued in 1968, that became a sensation with a new generation of militant Chicano students and thinkers emerging in California. The union leader Cesar Chavez once said he recommended it to everyone interested in Chicano issues.*

North from Mexico became the template for a school of new Mexican-American scholars who in the early 1970s set to work producing an array of Latino-centric books and academic papers, many of them focused on labor and migration issues. What appears to be the first significant work of Alamo

---

* A new edition of *North from Mexico* was issued in 2016, and it remains in print today, though its availability in Texas libraries can be spotty. As the authors of a 1998 appreciation of McWilliams note, "Every year it is still removed from scores of library shelves in institutions of learning, especially in conservative regions of Texas." In 1994 librarians in the Texan town of San Benito complained they continually needed to replace the book because of "individuals who keep destroying them." As a professor at the University of Texas–Edinburg explained at the time, *North from Mexico* "has a way of making people feel uncomfortable with their ignorance and prejudice."

revisionism, *Olvídate de El Alamo,* or *Forget about the Alamo,* arrived just as this wave was forming, in 1965.* Issued in Spanish by a Mexico City publisher, *Olvídate* was authored by a prolific Mexican-born playwright in Los Angeles, Rafael Trujillo Herrera.† Forgotten today, it is an idiosyncratic yet passionate jeremiad that prefigures every component of Alamo revisionism. It portrays the Texas Revolt as a conspiracy orchestrated by Andrew Jackson and Sam Houston; Santa Anna's Texas expedition as a justified response to American aggression; Bowie as a slave trader; and Travis as a fugitive who fled to Texas after committing a murder. "Should Mexico permit the continuation of a dark legend that also harms the sentiments and friendship of both nations?" he writes. "Does the battle cry 'Remember The Alamo' not just become a restless insult

* No, we didn't name our book in honor of this one. We learned of it much later.

† Not much is known about Trujillo, who was born in Durango in 1897; a history of American Hispanic theater says he began writing plays for the radio and stage in the late 1920s, published a series of Spanish-language novels and histories in Mexico, taught drama, and eventually established a community theater, Teatro Intimo, in 1974.

and accusation?"

Olvídate is a rank outlier in the Alamo canon.* Trujillo gives no clue to its origins, but the book clearly circulated in the Mexican-American community. Rosa-Linda Fregoso, the self-described Tejana who survived Mrs. Roy's Texas History class, remembers a copy her father gave her that forever changed the way she viewed history.

Both *North from Mexico* and *Olvídate* were strong influences on a young radical at Cal State Northridge named Rodolfo "Rudy" Acuña, who in 1966 created one of the first university-level courses in Chicano studies. Acuña's 1972 textbook, *Occupied America: The Chicano's Struggle toward Liberation,* is a scorching history of Anglo oppression, portraying Mexican-Americans as a conquered and abused people. The book's first chapter is a philosophical blowtorch aimed squarely at conventional Anglocentric Texas history. Building on the ideas of McWilliams and Trujillo, Acuña paints the Americans who died at the Alamo as nothing more than mercenaries staging an illicit rebellion

* Thanks to Santiago Escobedo for reading *Olvídate* in our stead. Santiago is a talented young Austin artist. Check out his work at santiagoescobedo.com.

to seize sovereign Mexican territory.

But what angered Acuña most was the way in which generations of Anglos created myths that, he argued, served only to justify the oppression of Mexican-Americans.

Anglo-Americans in Texas were portrayed as freedom-loving settlers forced to rebel against the tyranny of Mexico. The most popular of these myths was that of the Alamo, which, in effect, became a justification to keep Mexicans in their place. According to Anglo-Americans, the Alamo was a symbolic confrontation between good and evil; the treacherous Mexicans succeeded in taking the fort only because they outnumbered the patriots and "fought dirty." This myth, with its ringing plea of "Remember the Alamo!" colored Anglo attitudes toward Mexicans, as it served to stereotype the Mexican eternally as the enemy and the Texas patriots as the stalwarts of freedom and democracy. . . . Such myths, as well as the Anglo-Americans' biased versions of Mexican-American history, helped to justify the inferior status to which the Chicano has been relegated — that of a conquered people.[10]

Acuña takes swipes at Fehrenbach and says Eugene Barker's work "is simply justifying Anglo-American racism." To Acuña, the Alamo is the symbolic cradle of Mexican-American oppression. The Alamo "is probably the single most important source of racism toward Mexicans in this country," he told the *Los Angeles Times* in 1995. "Its purpose," he said in 1990, "is to hate Mexicans."

One might have thought Acuña's fiery revisionist take would have inspired follow-up research from the Latino PhDs who began emerging from Chicano Studies and similar programs in the 1970s. By and large it didn't. "We didn't care about the Alamo; the Alamo was an Anglo phenomenon, an Anglo construct," recalls Andrés Tijerina, a 1977 University of Texas PhD. "Sure, we knew the truth, but as scholars we were more concerned with our basic legitimacy as Americans. I didn't give a damn about the Alamo. You didn't see Mexican-Americans writing about the Alamo."

Nor did Anglo academics seem eager to fill the vacuum. For almost twenty years after Fehrenbach, in fact, not a single book appeared on the Alamo or the Texas Revolt that could be considered academically significant, much less revisionist. "Although an amazingly large body of historical and popular literature has been generated on the battle, there has never been an adequate serious study of it by a professional academic historian," the historian Paul Andrew Hutton marveled in 1986. "Academic historians have thus deserted the field, leaving the battle to the popularizers and propagandists."[11]

This, it appears, was the real problem. In the academic world, study of the Texas rebellion, and especially the Alamo, was considered hopelessly déclassé. As the historian Gregg Cantrell put it in 2015:

Looking for a way to get labeled "provincial" as a historian? Announce to the world that you plan to write about the Texas Revolution. Your book, then, for which you will easily find a publisher, can take its place alongside such dramatic titles as *Blood of Noble Men* or *Blood of Heroes,* or perhaps even share a shelf with *The Mystery of the Alamo Ghost, The Alamo and Zombies,* or *Custer at the Alamo.* But if looking to be taken seriously as a scholar . . . there are probably more promising career strategies than writing about the Alamo.[12]

The few revisionists who dipped their toes into Alamo waters in the 1970s and early 1980s, meanwhile, were enveloped in scorching denunciations — from the political right, as you'd expect, but also from the left. A case in point was the Chicano director Jesús Treviño's 1982 *Seguín,* a public television biopic of Juan Seguín. "I was interested in telling the Chicano side of American history, which both John Wayne and American textbooks have ignored," Treviño said. "In Wayne's version, Mexicans are portrayed as either bandidos, dancing señoritas, sleeping drunks, or fiery temptresses."[13] A critic on the left, meanwhile, Rudy Acuña, an adviser to the film, actually resigned over Seguín's portrayal, calling him a traitor to Mexican-Americans and comparing his alliance with the Texians to that of France's Vichy government with the Nazis.

Given the tumult of such political currents, one can understand why a young associate professor seeking tenure at Texas Christian University or Texas A&M might think twice before plunging in. Few did.

By the 1970s, it was clear that two schools of Alamo revisionism were emerging, the cultural revisionism of Rodolfo Acuña and left-leaning scholars who sought to recast its causes and meaning, but also a second, narrower school intent on reexamining what actually happened that day in 1836. Both challenged cherished Texas myths. Oddly, it would be the narrower school that initially incited the most heated passions. For traditionalists, cultural revisionism could be dismissed as the tinny, political musings of obscure academics. But the notion that Davy Crockett surrendered? In Texas, these were fighting words.

For those studying the Alamo, the main challenge is the spotty historical record. It's the same problem scholars of the West run into. Billy the Kid was too busy shooting people to keep a diary, and few Harvard professors were riding around Tombstone after the shootout at the O.K. Corral. The long delay in the onset of Alamo research made things worse. "With few facts available on an event of such epochal proportions," an early modern researcher, Walter Lord, wrote in 1968, "legend naturally filled the vacuum."[14]

Academics as early as Barker and Williams had done yeoman's work correcting the historical record, while being careful to preserve the Heroic Anglo Narrative. It was Lord, a suave New York author best known for *A Night to Remember,* his 1955 book on the *Titanic,* who upon beginning his own Alamo book in the late 1950s started asking the kinds of questions that made the Daughters squirm. Eschewing secondhand accounts, he crisscrossed Texas and traveled to Mexico collecting eyewitness statements, and was among the first to incorporate the writings of Santa Anna's soldiers.

In his 1961 Alamo book, *A Time to Stand,* Lord was the first writer to raise serious questions about the Alamo legend. Among other things, he dismissed the "line in the sand" as an easily disproven myth — by the 1960s, even Fehrenbach admitted that — and openly asked whether Crockett had really gone down fighting. At the time, his questions prompted little in the way of controversy.

In the '70s, they would.

As snippy as the debate over Travis's line could be, nothing in the history of the Alamo can compare with the explosion of anguish and invective that erupted in 1975. It was Crockett. The circumstances of his death had always been the Alamo's greatest mystery. In the 1970s, it was popularly accepted that he had gone down pretty much as Fess Parker had, fighting until his last bullet, then swinging Old Betsy until he was overpowered. But Crockett's death wasn't always viewed this way, and when an older version of events surfaced, all hell broke loose.

Alamo revisionists love to diss traditionalists for clinging to myths born in the nineteenth century. The Crockett myth, however, turns out to be far more recent. The story of his surrender was widely reported in 1836. No one questioned Crockett's bravery at the time. His execution, in fact, was often held up as evidence of Santa Anna's barbarity. Biographers through the 1800s cited the surrender as fact. As late as 1934, when the New York publisher Charles Scribner's Sons published *The Adventures of Davy Crockett,* its frontispiece was a painting of a bloodied Crockett led before Santa Anna.

Barely twenty years later, however, when the book was reissued in 1955, the painting had disappeared, a change first noticed by the modern researcher James E. Crisp. "What had changed?" Crisp asks in his wonderful 2005 book, *Sleuthing the Alamo.*[1] The answer, of course, was that thanks to Walt Disney, by 1955 Crockett had emerged not only as a hero to millions of American boys, but as a symbol of American resistance to Communism. The Crockett of the 1950s, Scribner's had presumably decided, would never surrender to the Commies.

Things began to get strange that same year when, out of nowhere, an obscure Mexican antiquities dealer named J. Sánchez Garza published a manuscript in Mexico City. He called it *La Rebelión de Texas.* The book purported to be the wartime diary of one of Santa Anna's junior officers, José de la Peña. De la Peña, it seemed, was a federalist with no love for Santa Anna, and his narrative of the Texas campaign, and especially of the battle itself, was not only packed with riveting detail, it pulled no punches about Santa Anna's blunders. At a glance, it was easily the most authoritative version of the battle ever published.

The bombshell, albeit one with a very slow fuse, comes as de la Peña is describing the battle's aftermath. Bodies still lay bleeding around the plaza as Mexican soldiers gathered to hear Santa Anna give his victory speech. This section needs to be quoted at length:

Shortly before Santa Anna's speech, an unpleasant episode had taken place, which, since it occurred after the end of the skirmish, was looked upon as base murder and which contributed to the coolness [I] noted. Some seven men had survived the general carnage and, under the protection of General [Manuel Fernández] Castrillón, they were brought before Santa Anna. Among them was one of great stature, well proportioned, with regular features, in whose face there was the imprint of adversity, but in whom one also noticed a degree of resignation and nobility that did him honor. He was the naturalist David Crockett, well known in North

America for his unusual adventures, who had undertaken to explore the country and who, finding himself in Béjar at the very moment of surprise, had taken refuge in the Alamo. . . . [Manuel Fernández Castrillón asked for mercy.] Santa Anna answered Castrillón's intervention in Crockett's behalf with a gesture of indignation and, addressing himself to the sappers, the troops closest to him, ordered his execution. The commanders and officers were outraged at this action and did not support the order, hoping that once the fury of the moment had blown over these men would be spared; but several officers who were around the president and who, perhaps, had not been present during the moment of danger, became noteworthy by an infamous deed, surpassing the soldiers in cruelty. They thrust themselves forward, in order to flatter their commander, and with swords in hand, fell upon these unfortunate, defenseless men just as a tiger leaps upon his prey. Though tortured before they were killed, these unfortunates died without complaining.[2]

Publication of the de la Peña book, and its account of Crockett's fate, went unnoticed outside the academic world, and even there it made no waves; though a vivid account, this was pretty much what everyone might have expected. As word spread, though, you could see writers getting squeamish about portraying Crockett this way. Three years after the manuscript appeared, when the Dallas newspaperman Lon Tinkle published the stoutly traditionalist *13 Days to Glory* — the basis for the John Wayne movie — he mentioned the de la Peña diary but included no mention of Crockett's death. Either he actually never read de la Peña, which is likely, or he was the first cautious victim of what might be called "Scribner's disease."

Even Walter Lord, writing in 1961, caught the bug. Lord was the first to address the subject head-on, in a back-of-the-book section titled "Did Davy Crockett Surrender?" After weighing the evidence, Lord concluded, "It's just possible." In the end he hedged, noting, "There's a good chance that [he] lived up to the legend."[3] The new legend, that is, the one of Disney and John Wayne.

There matters lay, unexamined, for thirteen years, until 1974, when a Texas philanthropist named John Peace bought the de la Peña manuscript and smuggled it out of

Mexico.* He hired a former director of the Alamo library, Carmen Perry, to translate it. A year later, Texas A&M University Press published Perry's work as *With Santa Anna in Texas: A Personal Narrative of the Revolution.*

One suspects this little book would have drifted into an eddy of academic obscurity if not for that bane of Spanish manuscript translators everywhere — *People* magazine. How on earth the editors at *People* pulled themselves away from exposés of Shaun Cassidy's latest crush long enough to find poor Carmen Perry is lost to history, but they did. "Did Crockett Die at the Alamo? Historian Carmen Perry Says No," read the headline.[4] The magazine press-ganged Mrs. Charles Hall, who chaired the Daughters' Alamo committee, into the kind of pearl-clutching denunciation you'd expect. "We don't believe Davy Crockett ever surrendered," she chirped. "We feel he went down fighting. And by 'we' I mean all Texans."

Smart-aleck headline writers had a field day. "Has the King of the Wild Frontier Been Relieved of His Coon-Skin Crown?" asked one paper. "People don't want to

* Fehrenbach too wanted nothing to do with questions surrounding Crockett's death. He ignored it.

believe [this] account because they don't want to believe it," Perry sighed. "We prefer to live by legend."

All this was prelude, however, to the storm that blew in three years later, when a Corpus Christi accountant named Dan Kilgore published the first book-length examination of Crockett's death, a slender volume called *How Did Davy Die?* Kilgore, an amateur historian and former president of the Texas State Historical Association, identified the statements of seven Mexican soldiers that appeared to confirm that Crockett had, in fact, surrendered and been executed.

For this, he was all but hanged in effigy. "Them's Fighting Words: Davy's Legend Smudged" was the headline in the Corpus Christi paper.[5] No less a source than the Associated Press opined: "Any Texan worth his pointy-toed, ringtail lizard–skin cowboy boots knows better than to smear the legend of Davy Crockett."[6] News of the controversy zinged from Austin to New York (*The Wall Street Journal!*) to Canada and London.

It went on and on. On a Memphis radio show, someone called him a "smut peddler." Those who complained loudest seemed to view the controversy as political, sensing that anyone who challenged a symbol of

American pride must be a Communist. The supermarket tabloid *Weekly World News* — admittedly, not the sanest literary critics out there — called the book "a commie plot to trash our heroes."[7]

Things got so bad that at his book party, the publisher actually offered Kilgore police protection. In time, of course, it all blew over. And despite the grumblings of the Daughters and a handful of amateur historians, Kilgore's conclusions came to be broadly accepted. For the time being.

The de la Peña and Crockett controversies, while limited to a single controversial assertion, demonstrated to a generation of historians that the Alamo's story was not set in stone, that the Heroic Anglo Narrative championed by everyone from Barker to Fehrenbach was not only ripe but long overdue for reinterpretation. This process did not happen overnight; it would take years, in fact, for serious works of revisionism to be published.

A turning point arrived with the Alamo's sesquicentennial in 1986, which renewed interest in the battle and the events that led to it. Still, other than a notable exhibition examining revisionism at Southern Methodist University in Dallas, an anticipated flurry of revisionist literature failed to show. What arrived instead was a skimpy, traditionalist 1987 television miniseries, *The Alamo: 13 Days to Glory,* featuring battle scenes lifted from 1955's *Last Command,* rubber bayonets that could actually be seen bending onscreen, and a dashing young Alec Baldwin as Travis drawing one more cinematic line in the Alamo dirt.

Up to this point, talk of revisionism amounted to a bunch of academics wringing their hands that *someone* needed to take a new look at the Alamo. Which was a far stretch from anyone actually doing it. As so often happens, it would take a complete outsider to get the ball rolling.

The winds of change were already beginning to blow in 1985 when a struggling young writer in far-off Colorado, a Texas refugee weaned on John Wayne's movie, began work on what he thought would be a quick, easy Alamo book,* "just the old hoary tale jazzed up for a modern readership." His name was Jeff Long. The son of a wandering petroleum geologist, Long was born in Texas and as a boy fell in love with Fess Parker's Crockett, becoming an Alamo-

* There is no such thing, take our word for it.

head years before there was a word for such a thing.

In the early 1980s, while working as a stonemason in Boulder, Long sold his first book, a true-crime thriller set in Utah. When an editor urged him to try something more ambitious for his second, his thoughts drifted to his childhood fascination with the Alamo. "I had no intention of writing a 'revisionist' history," Long says. "I got a whopping $20,000 advance and a one-year deadline. My initial plan was to draft in the wake of other Alamo books. I was going to update the story with more contemporary scholarship and retell [it] with new-fashioned language."

He checked into a San Antonio hotel and spent six months immersed in the Alamo's archives, logging long days hunched over primary documents. What he found astounded him. In Travis's diary, he discovered notes on his sexual conquests and his efforts to combat syphilis. He learned that Bowie and Fannin had been illegal slave traders. He began to understand the importance of slavery to the conflict, to see how the conflict was less a "revolution" than a secessionist revolt intended to defend Texas's slave-based economy against the creeping threats of Santa Anna's centralism and the government's deep-seated abolitionist tendencies.

"The Alamo consumed me, it changed me," Long says. "All these incredible facts, versus fictions, were lying like gold on the ground. For over a century, historians simply gave the Alamo myth a free pass. It continually shocked me that my book had never been written. . . . To me the earlier tales about the Alamo were the revisionism. What came later was the history, a weird inversion."

After a year of work, his advance money all spent, Long had to decide whether to discard the quickie book he had envisioned for the far more ambitious revisionist history he was now seeing. He decided to go for it. For the next five years he worked on patios and retaining walls around Boulder to subsidize his book. He saved enough at one point to spring for a trip to Mexico City, where he spent days combing through government archives.

Published in 1990, Long's *Duel of Eagles* was a screaming banzai charge against everything John Wayne and T. R. Fehrenbach held dear. The tone was urgent and almost angry, a brash young outsider shaking his fists at his ignorant elders. In *Duel* the defenders of the Alamo are "mercenaries," "pirates," and "fanatics," "Manifest Destiny . . . killers with dirt under their fingernails, lice in their hair," and "the stink of ignorant, trigger-pulling white trash." Ordinary Texans, the book suggests, raised weekend spending money by prostituting their wives.

Long's depictions of almost everyone involved were so over the top, it was as if he were physically stomping on everything written before. Crockett he termed "an aging, semiliterate squatter of average talent," "an arrogant mercenary" who surrendered and then begged for his life. Sam Houston he judged a drunken cocaine addict and — wait for it — a budding transvestite fond of wearing corsets and girdles. To Long, Bowie was utterly without merit, a "frontier shadow creature," a thug fleeing a "lifetime" of "frauds and hoaxes." Travis, well, Travis he got about right. But then no one likes Travis.

Book reviewers in Texas have a long history of snarling at Yankee authors who deign to swim in Lone Star waters, but the abject horror that greeted *Duel of Eagles* was a thing to behold. "If he isn't careful, Jeff Long may become the Salman Rushdie of Texas," the *Houston Chronicle* warned. "Students of Texas history may pray for a hurricane to blow Long's house down." Even such sober academics as Paul Andrew Hutton seemed almost personally offended, terming Long a "rather shallow young author. . . . There is, in fact, nothing new about this book at all beyond its stridently revisionist tone."[8]

Duel of Eagles was little noticed outside Texas, where a number of reviews praised it, but reaction within the state left Long shaken. "Fairly soon I started getting threatening phone calls, including death threats," he remembers. "It seems like they passed around my phone number. Then the Houston newspaper wondered why my house was still standing. It was meant as a joke, but I was starting to get a little concerned. Eventually it died down, enough for me to not fear walking by my window."

The 1990 publication of *Duel of Eagles* is the big bang of Alamo revisionism, an event that signaled a rush of works that in short order transformed the 1990s into the golden age of Alamo reassessment. Suddenly, it seemed, all anyone wanted to talk about was Texas history. Panels and symposia sprouted like bluebonnets, with professors, journalists, and amateur historians debating everything from how Travis, Bowie, and Crockett died to the Daughters' proper role to what the Alamo truly symbolized. *The Texas Observer* termed it all a "literary assault."

National publications such as *The New York Times* and *Christian Science Monitor* took notice, introducing these issues to the rest of the country. "When I was young, you could never have this kind of discussion about Texas history," enthused Lawrence Wright, the Austin writer who led a 1994 discussion titled "Dibs on the Alamo." "There was an orthodoxy of belief, and nothing was more orthodox than the story of where we came from."[9]

Revisionism did not waltz into Texas unchallenged. For every Jeff Long there were ten Fehrenbach adherents willing to push back. A *San Antonio Express-News* columnist sneered at the revisionist tone of a National Association of Chicano Studies convention, noting, "It doesn't really take much to ignore the adolescent mental masturbation of the politically correct." *The New Yorker*'s Michael Lind, defending Crockett's bravery, actually issued a 274-page poem, *The Alamo: An Epic*. Veteran Texas media types could only shake their heads. "If the Alamo had had that many defenders in the spring of 1836," one quipped, "Santa Anna would have turned tail and run."[10]

Driving the process was a new school of academic thought called New Western History that inveighed against "gunsmoke and bullshit" history, which is to say, the entire Heroic Anglo Narrative of the American West. Popularized by a group of upstart professors and graduate students at Yale, it sprang from experiences during the 1960s — with Vietnam, racism, poverty, and the environment. New Western History strove to demolish hoary myths and highlight the stories of those long neglected: women, Latinos, Native Americans. It raised their status to that of actual human beings with rights and inner lives. "What was missing," one adherent explained at the time, "was a frank, hard look at the violent imperialistic process by which the West was wrested from its original owners. . . . It was time for historians to call such violence and imperialism by their true names."[11]

The tension between traditionalists and revisionists produced a string of important new works on the Alamo and the Texas Revolt. Randolph B. Campbell and Paul D. Kirk published the first books exploring slavery's role. Stephen Harrigan issued probably the greatest work of Alamo fiction, the massive *Gates of the Alamo*. Stephen L.

Hardin authored the first military analysis. One favorite was *Three Roads to the Alamo,* William C. Davis's 816-page warts-and-all tri-biography of Travis, Bowie, and Crockett, a book you can still find in many Texas homes.

By the turn of the century, the revisionist take on Alamo history had established itself as a legitimate alternative to the Heroic Anglo Narrative, at least in the academic world. The real world, alas, was another matter. *Duel of Eagles* and *Three Roads* aside, revisionist books were mostly issued by scholarly presses, and easily ignored. Their authors muttered about the "curse of Fehrenbach," who remained alive and well, happy to jeer at the revisionists when a reporter came calling.

Efforts to push revisionist thinking into the mainstream got off to a wobbly start. The most active theater was the naming of schools. If you live elsewhere, you may not appreciate how pervasive Travis, Houston, Austin, Bowie, Crockett, and even Fannin remain on the streets of Texas. In the Austin area alone, citizens live in Travis County, in the neighborhood of Travis Heights, and have children attending Austin High, William B. Travis High, James Bowie High,

Crockett High, and Lake Travis Middle School. It's like living in Alamo Land.*

Every year or two beginning in the late 1980s, some group somewhere in Texas has tried to get a school renamed, usually one of the Bowies or Travises. In 1988 the NAACP picketed the Austin school board over Bowie High, saying African-American children "should not have to attend a school named after a man who smuggled slaves." They lost. Similar efforts failed in Dallas and Houston.

The classic case came in the city of Bryan, next door to Texas A&M, when the school board wanted to name a new school after Travis. One board member — a Michigan transplant — proposed naming it instead after Mary Branch, an African-American woman who was the first female college president in Texas. Another member — from Connecticut! — brought up the soft-core portions of Travis's diary and, after that, well, it was Katy, bar the door.

The controversy quickly became a flame

* And don't even get us started about San Antonio. The comedian Albert Brooks, in an unattributed snippet found in the Alamo archives, actually once wrote a poem about it. See the full poem at the end of the chapter.

394

for media moths. "School Bypasses Name of Slave Owner Travis," read the *Houston Chronicle* headline. From there it was on to wire services, London tabloids, and the Paul Harvey radio show. As the school board considered what to do, Texas columnists kept the issue alive for weeks; several seemed most upset by the fact the board members pushing the change were born out of state. In the end a compromise was struck. The school was named after Branch. An administration building was renamed after Travis.

By 2000, then, revisionism had gained a foothold in the public imagination. Our favorite example is the time Texas Public Radio put Travis "on trial" for being a deadbeat dad. But the Heroic Anglo Narrative remained strong. Fehrenbach, in other words, was still winning the battle. A new century was dawning, though, during which the competing narratives of traditionalism and revisionism would take center stage in a series of cultural and public debates unlike anything Texas had seen.

■ ■ ■ ■

Everything in the town is named after it.
Every human!
Every building!
Every everything!

"Alamo Drug Store! . . .
No, no thank you!"

"Alamo Dry Cleaner!"
Eight-thirty, ten-thirty, twelve-thirty, yessir!

"Alamo mortuary! . . ."
No, he's dead!
Thank you!

Every person walking the streets:
"There's Alamo Bradley and his wife
 Alamina!
Little Alamo Junior!"

CHAPTER 19
THE ALAMO UNDER SIEGE

One reason the story of Ozzy Osbourne urinating in Alamo Plaza struck such a chord back in 1982 was that he wasn't the only one doing it. By the 1980s, the Alamo and its environs had devolved into a dingy curiosity in the heart of downtown. Panhandlers and the homeless were ever present. Every morning tourist buses lined up alongside the Long Barrack, all but hiding it from view. Their exhaust billowed into the church and the museum. "Certainly at night, it was just not a safe place," remembers Davis Phillips, whose family opened a wax museum in a graffiti-spattered storefront across the plaza a few years later. "It was dark, there were no successful businesses around, and it was not somewhere families would come."

As early as the 1950s the San Antonio papers had decried the jarring juxtaposition of the "hallowed" Alamo and the cheesy amusements around it. "Vendors, Nude Girls Battle for Tourists' Attention at Shrine," read one 1958 headline. In the early '80s, what little debate enveloped the Alamo had more to do with urban renewal than identity politics. That was the situation at least when a Chicago man named Gary Foreman stepped into Alamo Plaza.

In a way, everything that's happened in the years since, all the controversies swirling around the Alamo today, began that morning with Foreman, just six weeks after Ozzy did his business back in February 1982. At the time, he was a thirty-one-year-old aspiring documentary filmmaker who had worked on Bicentennial events and spent his weekends reenacting Revolutionary War battles. He'd felt a connection to the Alamo since boyhood, gorging on viewings of Fess Parker and John Wayne dying their heroic deaths. Like Phil Collins, he had developed a sense that he had been at the Alamo in a previous life.

"For a lot of us who are really wrapped into the Alamo, I'll just say it: We know we've been here," Foreman says today. "And I don't care what people think of that."

Those were the days when much of Alamo Plaza, a matrix of streets, sidewalks, and seating areas roughly approximating the old compound walls, was still open to traffic. Foreman remembers standing in it snapping photos when he spied a taxi bearing down on him, obliging him to dive to the curb. Gathering himself, he sat on a low wall, and that's when it happened. "I sat down, and this may make sense to some people, some they'll never understand," he recalls. "But there are these moments from time to time in your life when all of a sudden something major happens, and you get a voice. And this little voice popped into my head and said, 'You gotta do this.'"

Somewhat as Reuben Potter must've felt on his first visit 141 years before, Gary Foreman knew he was destined to save the Alamo. He glanced around. Its neighbors included a tattoo parlor, a video arcade, a military surplus store, and a weary Burger King. There was little sense that the church and the Long Barrack once stood at the heart of a compound, other than a set of thin lines carved into a sidewalk where Crockett was thought to have defended the south wall. The only information sign in the area read: "No Parking Bus Loading Zone — 10 Minute Limit." The Alamo's other approaches were just as neglected. "The only information sign on the backside of the grounds," Foreman says, was "Do not feed the squirrels."

Inside the hushed, dimly lit church, stern Daughters patrolled with index fingers seemingly fused to their lips. There was no interpretive signage and no guides, nothing that had the faintest whiff of living history, just some amateurish dioramas and paintings of dubious merit. The little museum they'd opened in the Long Barrack seemed designed to celebrate not the historic Alamo but John Wayne, complete with a promotional poster and an award Wayne's movie had won. One popular exhibit featured Crockett's coonskin cap, which upon closer inspection turned out to be a replica Wayne had worn. Those in need of more information could sit through a ten-minute black-and-white movie that seemed made by a ninth-grade film class.

Out back there was a jaunty gift shop that sold "Kiss the Cook" hot plates and enormous Texas mosquitoes in brightly colored felt. Most visitors sailed through the whole place in less than twenty minutes. "How many times have we all taken visitors there to show them the Alamo and they ask, 'This is it?' " one business leader asked a few years later.[1] Foreman just shook his head. He recalls attending a museum conference in San Antonio around that time in which a speaker announced, "If you want to see how to not run a museum, go to the Alamo."

Seven months later Foreman presented the Daughters, the city, and the state with an unsolicited twenty-page plan to rescue the Alamo. He proposed restoring the 1836 footprint of the Alamo, a slew of new exhibits, tour guides in period costumes, multimedia presentations, and historically accurate battles for tourists to watch. He thought it could all be done for maybe $2 million.[2]

"I want to enhance the Alamo so people go there and consider it more than a wayside, more than a place to buy a Coke and go to the bathroom," Foreman told a reporter for *People* magazine.[3]

The Daughters rolled their eyes. No one had ever heard of Gary Foreman. He wasn't even from Texas. They sent him a polite letter thanking him for his interest. But Foreman would not give up. He began presenting his plan to business groups, historical societies, and arts commissions. The most common reaction was surprise that the old mission had once been an enormous compound. Even lifelong residents thought "the Alamo" referred only to the church.

Along the way Foreman gained his first ally, the Chicana city councilwoman María

Berriozábal. More than a few local leaders thought they were onto something. "We believe Foreman's ideas have some merit," the *San Antonio Express* editorialized. *Texas Monthly* went a step further. "It is time," its editor wrote, "to save the Alamo from the way it's preserved today."[4] Sensing momentum, Foreman embarked on a national media blitz, explaining his plans to scores of reporters. *USA Today* put a drawing of his vision on its front page. *The New York Times* and the *Chicago Tribune* noted that the Alamo's aging walls were beginning to crumble. Foreman tried to remain polite, but when he termed the Daughters "a tea club running a historical site," things got testy. The article everyone remembers ran in *People*. "Mr. Foreman doesn't understand that this is a sacred shrine," Peggy Dibrell, chair of the Daughters' Alamo Committee, told its reporter. "He wants to turn the Alamo into a tourist trap." Besides, "Mr. Foreman is not a Texan."[5]

Foreman realized, with the sesquicentennial of Texas's independence approaching, that the time was ripe for some kind of commemoration. The Daughters held a quiet service inside the church each year on the battle's anniversary. Foreman met with city leaders and pitched an outdoor spectacular featuring speeches, live music, fireworks, and historical reenactments on the plaza — at sunrise. Amazingly, he was given the green light to stage it.

On March 6, 1986, the city of San Antonio held the first "Dawn at the Alamo" commemoration, an alternately moving and kitschy celebration that continues to this day. The Daughters, amazingly, boycotted it. But no one else did. That morning the plaza was jam-packed. Foreman remembers that NBC's *Today* show ran part of the show live, as did CBS, and even the Christian Broadcasting Network's *700 Club*.

"They're all there. I mean it was huge," said Foreman. "I mean, television trucks were everywhere and over three hundred reenactors all showed up."

It was, however, the high point of Foreman's influence. He kept pushing his plans, even getting Fess Parker himself to back them, but with the Daughters firmly opposed, his efforts slowed.* By 1990, Foreman had given up to produce documenta-

* The Daughters' resistance to developing the plaza was as much commercial as philosophical. There were twenty-one parking spaces in front of the Alamo in those days. Losing those, the Daughters feared, meant visitors to the all-important gift

ries for PBS and later the History Channel. "What happens in this town is so primitive," he says today. "Anything they don't like, anything new, they call revisionist history."

Savvy businessmen, struck by the sesquicentennial's success, began to revive the plaza. That wax museum opened, along with offerings from Ripley's Believe It or Not! and Guinness World Records. A new mall went up, complete with a spiffy IMAX theater, and that's when the trouble began.

A city councilman named Walter Martínez started it. Like many Tejanos, Martínez didn't give a rat's — well, let's just say the Alamo had never been a major focus of his life. "I think the Alamo has always been a big issue for Anglo Texans, and it's always been a big attraction mostly [built around] that John Wayne myth, that depiction of heroism," he allows. "For Latinos, it's never been a big issue. Yeah, we know it's there. But so what?"

The trouble began when a friend slipped Martínez the script for a movie called *Alamo: The Price of Freedom,* billed as "the

shop, their only source of outside income, would have no convenient place to park.

definitive and authentic account of the Alamo."[6] It was to be a permanent feature of the IMAX theater. Martínez saw it was rife with inaccuracies. Bowie is seen up and around, even giving a stirring speech when he was known to be bedridden. Crockett goes down fighting. The wrong flag flew over the Alamo. But that wasn't what got Martínez worked up: There were no significant Tejano characters anywhere in the film. The minor Tejano characters that did appear were wholly subservient.

Worst of all was a scene involving a "Pretty Señorita." It depicted a seventeen-year-old Tejana girl making out with what appeared to be a drunken Kentuckian in the belfry of a Catholic church. To Martínez, this was deeply offensive. He called a press conference, denouncing the film as "demeaning and degrading." The filmmakers fought back, trotting out the Daughters to give it their seal of approval, which only made things worse. When Martínez pushed, the filmmakers agreed to cut the Pretty Señorita scene, but otherwise drew their own line in the sand. "History," the producer argued, "is debatable."

Martínez assembled a coalition of Latino and allied groups and protested the premiere at the theater in March 1988. "We have seen these movies with their distortions for so many years," a LULAC activist told reporters. "This is the first time the Hispanic community draws the line." A professor named Gilberto Hinojosa read off the names of the nine Tejanos who died at the Alamo, and after each, the crowd shouted, "Presente!"[7]

None of it mattered. The IMAX theater at San Antonio's Rivercenter Mall shows the film to this day. But in the protest's wake, many around San Antonio, especially in its Tejano majority, began viewing the Alamo in a new light. Consciousnesses, as they say, had been raised. LULAC, denouncing the Alamo as a symbol of Anglo oppression, began periodically calling for the Daughters to cede control. "The traditional attitude of the Alamo needs to be changed," argued LULAC's José Garcia De Lara, "so our children may grow up with the pride that they were part of the fight for freedom."[8]

This kind of talk brought out the worst among traditionalists. A letter writer in a Houston newspaper said that turning the Alamo over to LULAC "makes about as much sense as giving control of the Pearl Harbor memorial to the Japanese." In El Paso an editorialist proposed giving Harpers Ferry, the site of John Brown's 1859 abolitionist raid, to the Ku Klux Klan. "We don't need another battle of the Alamo," complained a *Houston Post* writer. "The Anglos have it and aren't going to give it back — to the Tejanos any more than to the Mexicans."[9]

The next shot fired against the Daughters came eight months after the premiere, when a pair of state legislators, Jerry Beauchamp and Orlando Garcia, threatened to remove the Alamo from the Daughters' control if they didn't allow state officials to review their books. In a hearing, Garcia took issue with the Daughters' $1.7 million reserve fund, suggesting it might contain irregularities. Richard Santos, who had analyzed the IMAX script, actually attacked the Daughters' cash cow, the Alamo's tacky gift shop. "I fail to see what coonskin caps — made in Taiwan or wherever — have to do with Texas during its Republic," Santos complained, calling it "a glaring example of what could be construed as a misuse of public funds."

Mayor Henry Cisneros backed the Daughters, who ended up opening up the Alamo's books to any state lawmaker, but that wasn't the biggest change.[10] A sense was developing, in San Antonio and around the state, that changes were needed at the Alamo and that the Daughters were not only the reason, but a roadblock.

The Imax tempest of 1988 was a political moment, and like most political moments, it passed. But the early 1990s, as we've seen, brought Jeff Long's *Duel of Eagles* and a slew of works that pushed Alamo revisionism into mainstream discourse. The Daughters were soon feeling the heat.

This time it started with San Antonio's county archivist, a man named John Leal. Descended from an old San Antonio family, Leal had been translating the records of the city's Franciscan missionaries from the 1700s.* What he found stunned him: The land all around the church, including much of Alamo Plaza, had been a cemetery. It was all there in black and white, records showing the burials of 1,006 people, including 921 people of Native American or mestizo descent.[11]

This, we should say, was not exactly a state secret. Over the years, just about any time workers dug anywhere around the

* Among other things, Leal discovered that one of his ancestors, a Canary Islander immigrant named Juan Leal Goraz, had been the first mayor of the settlement that became San Antonio.

Alamo, they had found old bones. The remains of three adults and a child had been uncovered on the grounds as recently as 1936. A report in 1976 established that the plaza lay atop the old cemetery. The state confirmed the finding a year later. In the days before Alamo activism, no one much paid attention. But because Texas law explicitly forbade anyone building anything atop cemeteries, the state never got around to designating the plaza as such, as had been done at San Antonio's other Spanish missions. To do so, of course, might have meant digging up or even tearing out the plaza, then still a main thoroughfare.

In the 1990s, though, Leal's discovery was a hand grenade waiting to be tossed. The man who ended up throwing it was Gary Gabehart, president of a Native American group called the Inter-Tribal Council of American Indians. In early 1994, Gabehart issued a report called *Alamo Cemetery* laying out Leal's results and requesting that at least some of the plaza be closed to traffic. "I think we've got troubled ground," he told reporters. "We've had cars, buses and horses running over that cemetery for years. And what goes around, comes around."[12]

The Daughters, as was their wont, scoffed. "There have been rumors of bodies, cannons and gold buried in and around the years," a spokesman said in a chilly prepared statement. Until someone "can produce irrefutable proof, we will expect the street in front of the Alamo to remain open."[13] But the days when the Daughters could blithely steamroll their opponents, especially those with views rooted in identity politics, had passed.

By the mid-1990s, the Daughters were keenly aware that they had an image problem. The local newspaper columnists were now taking regular potshots at the Alamo's management. When a human skull was found inside one of the old walls, the Daughters plastered it over without further examination. Headline! When someone peered closely at the single tiny photo of Adina De Zavala in an exhibit case, it turned out it was actually of her sister. Headline! One columnist went so far as to compare the Daughters' propaganda machine to that of the Nazis' Joseph Goebbels.

At wit's end, the Daughters hired a foundation to study their plight, and it came back with a smart suggestion: The Alamo should hire an official historian. To their credit, the Daughters agreed. But there was not, shall we say, a rush by noted academics to seize the job. They ended up hiring a PhD recipient fresh out of Texas Christian named Bruce Winders, a reenactment buff whose dissertation covered the Mexican-American War.

"There were many in the historical profession that when I told them, they'd say, 'Oh, you poor thing, that's horrible,' " says Winders. "Kind of like going to San Quentin because the idea was, you're the Daughters' hired gun, you're gonna be telling their story."

At the Alamo, Winders encountered the skepticism you'd expect. Hiring him "was a slight to them, because everybody there [considered themselves historians]," he says. "Because I had a book coming out on the Mexican war it was like, 'He's a Mexican historian, he don't know nothing about Texas.' I actually had a board member come up and say, 'This is Texas history, not Mexican history.' "

Looking back today, though, it's clear Bruce Winders was the right man for the job. He understood the Alamo needed to embrace revisionist viewpoints, and, crucially, he had a gentle way of urging change on the Daughters. Under Winders's guidance, the Alamo opened its first education department, teaching schoolchildren not just about the Anglo defenders but their Tejano allies and the motivations of Santa Anna and his army. The Daughters erected a sign out front noting, "The Alamo has a long and diversified history," placed a marker on Adina De Zavala's grave, and installed a plaque celebrating both her and Clara Driscoll.

"They saw that I worked with them, that I wasn't pushing a real extreme narrative," Winders says. Historically accurate programming "essentially serves as a sword and shield, a defense against people saying all we do is John Wayne history. You've got to tell an evidence-based story because you've got to be able to defend your position."

Maybe the cultural high point came after new bones were unearthed during renovation work. Assuming they were Native American, the Daughters actually allowed members of the Tāp Pīlam Coahuiltecan Nation, a member of the Inter-Tribal Council, to hold reinterment ceremonies inside the church. They even initiated a program heralding the contributions of Tejanos and Native Americans. Much of this programming remained in place for years.

San Antonio, and the broader community of Alamo-heads, was impressed. Some of the pressure on the Daughters began to ease. By now debate over their administration had become a staple of Texas political discourse, but in 1995 the state's new governor, George W. Bush, a man who loved Alamo analogies as much as Lyndon Johnson, emphasized that he would veto any bills removing their custodianship.

Things began to quiet down. The Daughters' embrace of revisionism had disarmed their critics and bought them time. In the end, though, it would not save them.

CHAPTER 20
THE SISTERS OF SPITE

Traditionalism did not go quietly into the night. Far from it. As the American Right began its march to power in the 1970s, the Alamo emerged as one of its touchstones, a symbol not only of American patriotism and determination but of the conservative movement's sense that it was besieged by condescending liberal elites. By the '90s, whenever a conservative cause came under fire, you could be sure someone somehow would invoke the Alamo.

It's proven especially popular on the Far Right. In 1997, the leader of a militia group calling itself the Republic of Texas walled himself inside a ramshackle trailer east of El Paso after a shootout with police and pledged to stage a "second Alamo" if they didn't leave him be. "He believes he's Davy Crockett," a bystander sighed. Like Crockett, this chap too declined to go out fighting. He agreed to surrender after a week or so, but only to a Texas Ranger, not the FBI, when, according to a version we'd like to believe, he ran low on beer.[1]

As a new century dawned, the reigning champion of the Heroic Anglo Narrative was George W. Bush, the Connecticut native who as Texas governor in the 1990s was especially fond of Alamo references. When, during a trip to the Baseball Hall of Fame, someone asked him about a fistfight involving his fellow Texan Nolan Ryan, Bush inexplicably chirped, "Remember the Alamo." Hands down his most memorable invocation came when the professional golfer Ben Crenshaw invited him to address the U.S. Ryder Cup team during a 1999 match against a European team outside Boston. The United States was trailing badly that morning when Bush walked into the clubhouse and simply read aloud Travis's letter, the one that finished with "Victory or Death." He then said "Godspeed" and left. The moment had the intended effect. "Let's go out and kill them!" one player blurted. When the Americans rallied to an improbable win, Governor Bush and the Alamo legend reaped a share of the credit.[2]

The terrorist attacks of 9/11, as you'd expect, brought a new rush of heroic Alamo references. It also spurred Hollywood's first serious revisit of the legend since John Wayne's. After the success of Disney's *Pearl Harbor* suggested a thirst for patriotic epics, the studio in 2002 fast-tracked an Alamo movie starring the actor Billy Bob Thornton as Crockett. The first director, Ron Howard, was cut loose when he sought something grittier than what Disney had in mind. His replacement, the Texan John Lee Hancock, took pains to craft a script he could defend as historically accurate and culturally sensitive. "You just couldn't make John Wayne's *Alamo* in 2004," notes Stephen Harrigan, an adviser on the film.

The Hancock movie is easily the most accurate celluloid Alamo. He used Santa Anna's actual field manuals to train his Mexican soldiers. Tejano defenders stand side by side with Anglos. Enslaved Black people speak of gaining their freedom if Santa Anna wins. Travis is portrayed as a slave-owning adulterer, and he draws no line in the sand. And Crockett is captured and then executed. He goes down screaming. If anything, though, Hancock overdid it. The movie came in far too long, and the deep cuts Disney demanded made a hash of it. Hancock ended up privately disavowing the whole project. Released in March 2004, *The Alamo* tanked at the box office. Disney lost at least $80 million.[3]

In the end, the very ambiguities Hancock prized just didn't strike a chord in a post-9/11 world that yearned for yarns of good and evil. *The Alamo* amounted to a sideshow, both in the canon of post–September 11 films and, as it turns out, in the real world. In the new century's tumultuous first decade, the serious fighting was in San Antonio. The Daughters were about to make their last stand.

Looking back today, all the ugliness, all the infighting and intrigue, all the politics — it really began with the doorknobs. They were in Alamo Hall, the old converted fire station at the back of the Alamo grounds that served as the Daughters' private clubhouse and events venue. It hadn't been updated much since Clara Driscoll grabbed it in 1922, so in 2009 the Daughters were planning a renovation. When word spread that they needed distinctive new doorknobs, a new member named Sarah Reveley thought of a set of nice brass ones her mother had owned.

Reveley, who was destined to become the Daughters' version of Daniel Ellsberg, was a solidly built woman in her mid-sixties with short red hair. A no-nonsense commercial interior decorator, she was a bit unusual among the Daughters, many of whom were wealthy housewives. She was a professional who understood engineering reports and wasn't prone to sugarcoat bad news. That day in August 2009, when she took her doorknobs to Alamo Hall, another Daughter gave her a tour. She found it disconcerting.

For one thing, the existing knobs were original, and distinctive antiques. She couldn't understand why they needed replacing. In storerooms she saw piles of "junk" in towers. In the main room she spied old paintings mounted on nails rather than on professional museum mounts.

"Aren't you gonna museum-mount those?" she asked.

"What's that?" her guide asked.

Reveley was startled by how shabby the place was. "That trip down to Alamo Hall," she says, "just freaked me out." On the drive home, she phoned a friend who worked at the Texas Historical Commission. "You can't believe what's going on down at the fricking Alamo," she said.

"Oh yes I can," the friend shot back, and then suggested she make the connection that would get everything rolling. "You really need to meet Erin Bowman."

Erin Bowman had entered the picture a

few years earlier, when the Daughters recruited her to lead a capital campaign for a proposed $10 million expansion of the Alamo library, a new museum, and two theaters, at an estimated cost of around $30 million.[4] In her fifties, Bowman was not only a Daughter but an elite San Antonio fundraiser. Tall, blond, and immaculately turned out, she agreed to lead the campaign, not realizing she was walking into a rattlesnake nest. At their annual convention in 2007, the Daughters approved the master plan, but at the same time elected an entirely new leadership team that didn't much care for it.

Bowman forged ahead anyway, raising an initial $1.2 million. But she ran afoul of the Daughters' new president general, an imperious doyenne named Madge Roberts who counted Sam Houston among her ancestors, and who didn't like that Bowman called her own meetings, rarely saw fit to keep her in the loop, and refused to share her Rolodex. And so, in May 2008, Roberts and her governing board fired her.[5]

Bowman, though, refused to quit raising money. She formed a splinter group called the Alamo Endowment and kept at it as if nothing had happened. "It didn't bother me," she said later. "The women in charge don't know anything about business. They are living in the dark ages. My blood makes me a Daughter, not them."[6]

Actually, no. Seven months later, Bowman was summoned to a meeting at the posh Barton Creek Resort and Spa in Austin and, along with her fundraising partner, given notice that she was being expelled from the Daughters. This was only the second time in history that the Daughters had kicked someone out, an event notable enough that *The Wall Street Journal* ran a story on its front page. Bowman said she would fight her expulsion and began making the rounds of local leaders.

Which is where things stood in August 2009 when Sarah Reveley got irked about those doorknobs. Reveley found Bowman on Facebook and invited her to her home in Alamo Heights. The two hit it off despite their differences, Bowman the steely corporate Tri Delt, Reveley the makeup-free, T-shirt-wearing technician. "Erin was the one who knew everyone in the world, but I became her researcher," Reveley remembers. "We became a team."

Bowman was out for something like revenge. At least initially, Reveley just wanted to help spruce up the Alamo. That day, when Bowman showed her a copy of the master plan, her eyes were drawn to the engineering report. In it she saw ominous-sounding mentions of cracks and mold in the church roof. Bowman wondered what it meant. "Well," Reveley mused, "that could mean the roof could fall in."

Architects and engineers had warned of cracks in the ceiling as far back as 1979. While the Daughters' new master plan envisioned fixing the roof, Reveley couldn't find that the problem had ever been addressed in any serious way. Worse, she discovered that in 2006 an engineer had warned that the church was infested with mold spores. Leafing through the Daughters' recent financial reports, she saw that the Alamo's entire annual preservation budget — for a site going on three hundred years old — came to the princely sum of $350. She had to check it again before she could believe it.

Using reports the Daughters filed with the state, Reveley dug deeper. What she found startled her. The group made most of its money from the Alamo gift shop and state funds. Not much, though, went to the Alamo. In fact, of the $213,000 or so the state had given between 2005 and 2008, barely $37,000, about 17 percent, was spent at the site. The Daughters actually spent more at a museum they ran in Austin, and nearly three times as much at a far smaller site, the French Legation Museum, also in Austin.[7]

While Reveley dug through documents, Erin Bowman's angry spat with the Daughters caught the attention of the *Express-News'* Alamo reporter, Scott Huddleston, who began snooping around as well. That September he authored a story describing plans by the Daughters' new president general, a flinty woman named Patti Atkins, to halt the flow of "misinformation" by making Alamo employees sign nondisclosure agreements.[8] She later backed off.

Impressed, Bowman and Reveley began sharing their findings with the reporter. "We were Deep Throat to Scott," says Reveley. "If it wasn't for him, none of this would have gone anywhere. Scott was our hero."

The stories Huddleston began writing that fall caught the eye of several Texas politicians. Among the curious was the Alamo district's new state senator, a tenth-generation Tejana named Leticia Van de Putte.

Huddleston's articles were "a defining moment for me," she told *Texas Monthly*. "I didn't understand how the Daughters justify spending so little for the Alamo, which attracts two and a half million visitors a year and is in desperate need of repair."⁹ She sat down with the Daughters' leadership and politely suggested that some transparency might be in order. The Daughters politely thanked her for her interest.

The San Antonio papers kept up a drumbeat of critical articles all through that fall. The turning point came in December, when the Daughters went ahead and, despite obvious opposition in the community, expelled Bowman. This was too much for many people. A week before Christmas the local ABC affiliate excoriated the Daughters in a rare on-air editorial. The Alamo, it charged, had become "a national laughing-stock" because the Daughters were "doing a lousy job taking care of it." It concluded: "The State owns the Alamo, and it's time to take it back."¹⁰

San Antonio's civic discourse tends toward the placid. No one could ever recall any of the major media outlets saying anything like this about the Daughters. Their leaders, never ones to turn the other cheek, responded with a strident YouTube video. Ostensibly an announcement of a new membership drive, the video amounted to a full-throated defense of their management. The Daughters insisted that any suggestion that the site had become a "laughingstock" was "an affront . . . to the memory of the fallen heroes of the Alamo." The head of the Alamo Committee, Virginia Van Cleave, stood before a portrait of Clara Driscoll and spoke of the "literally millions of dollars" the Daughters had spent on preservation efforts over the years, including "several million dollars in just the past few years."[11]

Reveley couldn't believe it. She knew they hadn't spent anything like that much. "That's when I got mad," she says. Reveley put together everything they had — the crumbling roof, the mold spores, the scrimping on preservation, the questionable financial priorities — and rolled it into a sixty-five-page complaint she filed with the Texas attorney general. She charged that the Daughters were in violation of the 1905 law that required the site be maintained "in good order and repair."

Then the roof fell in. Literally. Just ten days later, on February 11, an eight-inch piece of plaster fell from the church ceiling.[12] In Texas, this was akin to one of Michelangelo's works crashing down in the Sistine Chapel. Initially, no one noticed, but each year on February 23, the anniversary of Santa Anna's arrival, the Daughters hold a ceremony in front of the church in which dignitaries walk beneath a line of sabers held aloft by Texas A&M cadets. That year a cold rain forced everyone into the church, where an *Express-News* photographer crouched low and angled his camera high, capturing Patti Atkins, clad in a blue suit crossed by a long violet sash, gliding beneath the sabers.

Opening her newspaper the next day, Reveley barely noticed Atkins or the cadets. All she saw was the damaged ceiling above them. She got on the phone with Bowman, and then she got on the phone with Huddleston. Then she fired off an email to the governor's office that asked, sweetly:

"Couldn't that hurt somebody?"

As it happened, Texas governor Rick Perry was mulling a run for the White House at the time. His chief of staff, Ray Sullivan, immediately sensed the danger when Reveley's email crossed his desk. As he dryly recalled the moment, "The Alamo collapsing on Rick Perry's watch would be bad."

The whole thing ended up with a dogged assistant attorney general named Daniel Hodge. Reveley peppered him with memos all that spring, so many that in the governor's office they began calling her "Darby Shaw," after the whistleblowing heroine of

John Grisham's novel *The Pelican Brief*. The more Reveley dug, the more dirt she uncovered. The most damning arrived from a confidential source — she had "sources" now — who forwarded a set of emails between a Daughters attorney and the leadership revealing that the Daughters had filed to trademark "The Alamo" despite the fact they didn't actually own it.

Hodge politely reached out to ask what they were doing. The Daughters' attorneys argued that they were simply trying to protect the name on the state's behalf.[13] Maybe so, but it smacked of self-dealing, and it looked bad. Despite the state's objections, Patti Atkins inexplicably refused to stop the process. Even worse, Hodge would later determine that the Daughters were using state funds to pay lawyers to fight the state. That's when people began using words like "misappropriation."

Hodge was still hard at work that summer when Reveley decided to out herself, allowing the *Express-News* to reveal her "Darby Shaw" role. Hate email soon followed. Reveley's favorite referred to her and Bowman as the "sisters of spite," a moniker they embraced. The Daughters were not pleased, and shortly after, Reveley became the fourth member ever kicked out of the Daughters.*

"They punish anyone who disagrees with them," Bowman told a *New York Times* reporter later. "It is just sad that a group of stupid, vicious women could hijack an organization with a lot of good women in it."[14]

The Daughters might have outlasted the state's fickle political establishment if not for their dismaying penchant for self-inflicted wounds. In retrospect, the final straw came that autumn, when they announced they were paying the William Morris Agency nearly a million dollars to promote a 175th anniversary concert. The deal eventually fell through, but the governor's office was unamused.

"We," the governor's chief of staff, the laconic Ray Sullivan, noted years later, "had serious concerns."

With the state legislature beginning its biennial gathering in January 2011, Rick Perry quietly slid a single finger across his sinewy throat: The Daughters were to sleep

---

* Another woman, Dianne MacDiarmid, was kicked out with Bowman in 2008 but did not participate in the Bowman-Reveley conspiracy, if you will, to bring down the Daughters from the inside.

with the fishes. Daniel Hodge began writing the proposed bill with State Senator Van de Putte. Citing financial mismanagement, it proposed ejecting the Daughters from the Alamo grounds and placing the shrine under the supervision of the Texas Historical Commission.

By the time the bill was introduced, the Daughters had scrambled to battle stations. They were led by a frosty dynamo named Karen Thompson, who invoked Travis and Crockett with the passion with which Billy Graham invoked Scripture. Thompson mixed harsh language — in one email characterizing Van de Putte's bill as "the worst senate bill ever" — with an old-school feminine touch: baked goods for lawmakers.[15]

Thompson had every right to expect victory. Not only did change-averse Republicans control both the Texas House and Senate, but the Tea Party was in its ascendancy — one of its first rallies had been staged in front of the Alamo. But she overplayed her hand. No one minded the cookies. But folks began getting upset when Thompson and her lobbyists warned legislators they could expect to be "primaried" — challenged by their own party — in the next election cycle if they voted the wrong way. As one senate aide remembers it, "People thought it was a little bit heavy-handed."

In quiet talks all over the capitol, Hodge suggested a likely compromise that would allow the Daughters to continue operating the Alamo under state supervision. If the bill was defeated, though, Hodge made clear the state intended to file suit seeking the Daughters' removal; it would be a long, nasty process. The only way to save the Daughters, in other words, was to have someone watch over them.

The highlight of the bill's voyage was a tumultuous hearing in which Van de Putte pretty much eviscerated poor Karen Thompson. Afterward, Van de Putte was confident she had the votes she needed. On May 3, 2011, when she rose on the senate floor, she knew what she had to do. To ensure her victory, she needed to win over all the Republicans, who were led by a Daughter-friendly San Antonio senator named Jeff Wentworth. What Wentworth needed, she heard, was a way to appear that he had gone down fighting. She picked up a rumor he wanted to give the Alamo to Jerry Patterson, the popular chief of the General Land Office, an Alamo-head who had appeared as an extra in John Lee Hancock's 2004 film.

That day on the floor, Van de Putte announced she was amending her bill to give the Alamo to the Texas Parks & Wildlife Department.[16] Wentworth objected. They argued back and forth, but both legislators knew this was kabuki theater. After a bit, once she felt sure Wentworth had made his needed display, Van de Putte withdrew her bill, at which point the lieutenant governor called the two into a meeting room, as Van de Putte knew he would. There, Wentworth proposed giving the Alamo's supervision to Jerry Patterson. Van de Putte graciously agreed. Wentworth then phoned Patterson, who was in a car driving to Dallas.

"They have the votes, but I want to amend it to give it to somebody else," he told him. "Will you take the Alamo?"

"Well," said Patterson. "Yeah."

The amended bill sailed through the senate, and then the house, before landing on the governor's desk. Perry signed it into law. Life at the Alamo went on largely as before, but now under the GLO's watchful eye. Bowman and Reveley were triumphant. A few years later, a new Daughters administration asked them to rejoin the group. The two women ended up on Reveley's living room couch. Bowman said she would consider rejoining if Reveley did.

"Erin, I don't want to go back," Reveley said.

"I'm not going back until you go back," Bowman said.

They ended up rejoining together. Things were a little strained, of course, but both women were happy. They loved Texas history, they loved the Alamo and its legends, and being in the Daughters made them feel connected to it all.*

The drama at the Alamo, however, was far from over. In 2014, Jerry Patterson left the GLO and made an unsuccessful bid for lieutenant governor. In his place arrived a new face, a handsome young man whose ambitious plans would plunge the Alamo

---

* Bowman passed away in 2019 after a long hospitalization following a heart attack. The previous year, she had given Reveley an orchid for her birthday, but it had died. Reveley could not bear to go to the funeral, but on that day she noticed a bud on the supposedly dead orchid that looked like it would open. The following day, when Bowman was buried, "it opened a beautiful bloom. She was telling me she was okay," said Reveley, who drove the next day to the cemetery and put a brass Alamo ornament on her friend's grave.

into a new circle of Texas history hell.
His name was George P. Bush.

CHAPTER 21
"THIS POLITICALLY INCORRECT NONSENSE"

Stop political correctness in our schools. Of course, Texas schoolchildren should be taught that Alamo defenders were 'Heroic'!
— TEXAS GOVERNOR GREG ABBOTT, TWITTER, 2018

One reason the Heroic Anglo Narrative endures is that those who disagree with it, especially Texas Latinos, have rarely captured widespread attention. The occasional objections from LULAC and activists like Rudy Acuña have been easily dismissed, and the voices of Latino artists, writers, and intellectuals have seldom found purchase in the state's Anglo-dominated media.

In early 2002, Ruben Cordova wanted to change that. Cordova was not born in Texas, and contrary to what the country song might suggest, he did not get here as fast as he could. He is not, as they say, a good ol' boy. He made stops at Brown University and Berkeley, where he earned a doctorate in art history from the University of California. He wrote his dissertation on Picasso, but he taught classes on political art by Chicanos (a term he prefers over "Mexican-American," "Hispanic," "Latino," or the geographically specific "Tejano").

Cordova* arrived in San Antonio without the indoctrination Texans call seventh-grade Texas History. But he had rudimentary knowledge of Texas's myths and legends. He knew the story of the Alamo, and he'd experienced the associated racism, but as an art history instructor at Texas universities, he knew he needed to catch up. He admired a collective of Texas-based Chicano artists and wrote a monograph titled *Con Safo: The Chicano Art Group and the Politics of South Texas*. Most members of Con Safo lived in San Antonio and had created photography, paintings, and sculpture critical of the Alamo narrative since the 1960s.

In the first years of the century, Con Safo members organized a series of exhibits called "Forget the Alamo." Organizers

* After interviewing Cordova and reading his catalog, we recruited him as an early reader of our manuscript. We are grateful for his insight and advice.

invited artists to contribute many types of work for the show, which happened every other year for six years. For the second edition in 2005, Ramón Vásquez y Sánchez curated the show at the Centro Cultural Aztlan in San Antonio. Rolando Briseño created a performance to comment on how slave traders auctioned African-Americans in front of the Alamo in the 1850s. He had a sombrero-clad assistant manipulate an Alamo piñata, draped in red, white, and blue. Then he paid an African-American actress, dressed as a slave, to invite the audience to take a swing. After a few hits, the piñata disgorged brown plastic dolls. Briseño said the piece, *The Alamo Hatches Brown Babies,* symbolized the birth of the Chicano. Most of the work for Forget the Alamo, though, was more generic political commentaries on current events, if they were political at all.

Which is how Cordova came to organize an art show commemorating San Antonio's three hundredth anniversary: *The Other Side of the Alamo: Art against the Myth.* For the exhibition's catalog, he dived deep into the rabbit hole of Alamo lore, a journey we have come to know all too well.

"The Texian Revolt — and the Battle of the Alamo in particular — are bitterly contested subjects," he wrote in the opening line of the show's catalog. "Interpretations of them are not infrequently based on sheer fantasy and wholesale misrepresentation, which, unfortunately, dominate treatments of these topics in popular culture."

For the exhibit staged at the Guadalupe Cultural Arts Center, Cordova selected existing works and commissioned others. But more important, he began researching the Alamo's history and symbolism. "I think the Alamo is absolutely the only subject that is adequately represented at the San Antonio library," Cordova said with a chuckle. He read more than five hundred books and articles. His goals for the show were twofold: to provoke Anglos to consider the truth, and to give Chicanos a history they would not normally encounter because most avoided the Alamo. "I provided them with information that they would never access in any other way. They trusted my scholarship and I think it was a revelation to all the artists and all the people who read the catalog," Cordova told us.

The show included a photograph from 1971 by César Martínez that shows a United Farm Workers flag spray-painted on the Alamo cenotaph. A new work by Ed Saavedra proclaims "Davy Crockett died for your sins," an homage to *Custer Died for Your Sins,* the American Indian Movement manifesto by Vine Deloria Jr. from 1969. A photograph made for the exhibit by Daniela Riojas shows a Native American girl's tears falling on the church. Perhaps the most illustrative is a painting by Enrique Martinez depicting a Native American, a Spanish priest, a Mexican soldier, an Anglo cowboy, a fat-cat businessman, and Clara Driscoll fighting over the Alamo. The arms of slaves and their manacles float like ghosts in the background.

To top off the show, he had something special in mind. "I wanted a big mural on the main wall, of the Confederate flag with the Alamo as the center star," Cordova said. The image became the show's central work.

Unfortunately, Cordova said, the center's director feared the show was too provocative. She limited the marketing and did not allow the public performances Cordova had planned. "Texas is a violent place," Cordova said. "There was a lot of fear, especially on the city's part, because when they took down the Confederate statues all these people with weapons of mass destruction showed up at City Hall. They were just terrified."

The years since have only crystallized his

view that city and state leaders have little idea how to properly recognize the Alamo's history. "In a way, just like Germany has to confront its racist past, San Antonio, Texas, and the United States has to do the same," Cordova said. "It has all this beautiful rhetoric about freedom and the rights of man, but it's predicated on slavery, and it was imperial from its inception."

The art historian in him has even less time for what's happened to the Alamo compound. "Taking an unfinished, deserted church, and making it into a shrine for white power, while claiming you are a preservationist and knocking down the second wall of the Long Barrack so the Alamo will seem bigger?" he asks. "Then building an insane cenotaph that dwarfs that agglomeration of contradiction? The army kind of ruined it, you know, by making the hump. Then celebrating the hump because it's the thing that is the most foreign thing to add to a genuine colonial church you can do?"

The Daughters call the hump "the symbol of the quest of freedom." It's really just bad architecture.

Last, there is the slogan: Remember the Alamo. He will never forget how white men on the air force base randomly punched his father in the arm before saying it. We remember it too. It was a thing back in the day. "It's something that's understood as anti-Mexican even without anybody having to say anything about it," Cordova said.

Cordova's show was subversive and nothing like any art show before in San Antonio. But just when the revisionists thought they were gaining ground, forcing Texas to confront the truth about its past, the traditionalists struck back.

Ground zero in the conflict between traditionalism and revisionism would be the State Board of Education, the agency that decides what Texas schoolchildren learn in public school. There's a stereotype about Texas and its textbooks, of course, one that portrays the state as a place where children are taught the world is flat and climate change is a liberal hoax. While there are a fair share of, um, "outliers" among those who oversee Texas textbooks, and you'll meet a couple, the caricature is mostly not true. Back in 2000, in fact, the Texas History curriculum was almost what you'd call inclusive.

The Heroic Anglo Narrative had dominated in the 1950s, but in the '60s Texas history textbooks began including sections on racial and ethnic minorities. By the '70s, women were being written into the story. By the '80s, one academic judged, the curriculum was "doing a good job of including information about minorities, ethnic groups and women."[1] In the '90s, under the conservative Governor Bush, things actually got even more inclusive. In 1997, the legislature adopted standards that did not whitewash the state's origins. Teachers weren't required to say anyone was "heroic," and teaching Travis's letters was optional, along with biographies of people like Lorenzo de Zavala. Teaching children about Juan Seguín, however, was required. Crockett and Bowie weren't mentioned at all.[2]

The zenith of this march toward liberalism came in 2003, when the state board approved a textbook called *Texas!* This was Texas history for everyone. Seguín was given an entire story arc. *Texas!* even devoted a page to "the issue of slavery in Texas," including one of those letters from a Southerner asking Stephen F. Austin if he could bring his slaves. The book asks its thirteen-year-old readers: "Do you think the writer would go to Texas if he could not keep his slaves?"* It concluded with a

---

* No, he wouldn't.

discussion of Mexican abolitionism. *Texas!*, in other words, was beginning to challenge the Heroic Anglo Narrative.[3]

The first salvos in the coming textbook wars were fired in 2002 by a conservative think tank called the Texas Public Policy Foundation, known as TPPF, founded in 1989 by a Christian businessman named James R. Leininger. TPPF formed a coalition of nine conservative groups to police Texas textbooks. Among its first targets was an environmental science text it condemned as "anti-technology," "anti-Christian," and "anti-American" for claiming there was a scientific consensus on global warming. Soon after, TPPF made its first attempt to "amend" Texas history standards. "Texas' students are cheated by watered-down, politically-correct social studies that replace history education," the TPPF claimed.[4]

For the moment, the conservatives found no traction. But curricula are reassessed every seven years in Texas, and in the next two cycles there would be two public dust-ups over the Alamo. Both were short but sharp, both ended in landslide victories for one camp, and both involved a long-suffering onetime history teacher named Stephen Cure.

There's a joke you sometimes hear about Texas History classes. Walk up to a Texan of any age and say, "I know the name of your seventh-grade Texas History teacher." When the Texan expresses skepticism that this could be possible, you smile and say, "Coach." This is no knock against coaches, but it's to say that in the ranks of teaching jobs, Texas history has never exactly been what you'd call a plum assignment. All the way back in 1979, in fact, an academic paper noted that, "in general, teaching Texas history is regarded as a low-status, temporary task, and minimal teacher interest and preparation almost assures poor teaching of [it]."[5]

Stephen Cure had actually enjoyed his time teaching it for eight years in an Austin suburb, and by 2008 had stepped up to become director of educational services at the Texas State Historical Association, the TSHA. A seventh-generation Texan with ancestors who fought at San Antonio and San Jacinto, Cure reminds you a bit of the late actor James Gandolfini, a gentle bear whose calm, measured opinions were prized among those who made education policy in

Texas. He was the force behind the modernized *Texas History Movies* comic book the TSHA issued in 2007.

In the early 2000s, as conservative attacks on textbooks demonstrated, Texas was moving to the right, and angry right-wingers had replaced moderates and Democrats on the State Board of Education. A 2007 brawl over whether to force science teachers to teach the theory of "intelligent design" convinced Cure he needed to get involved in the upcoming assessment of the state history curriculum, and so in mid-2008 he volunteered for a working group tasked with making recommendations to update Texas History classes.

At the group's first meeting in January 2009, the dozen or so teachers and professors were told simply to brainstorm, and they did, tossing out dozens of half-cooked ideas they collected in spreadsheets. That's when the trouble started. You know how we said the clichés about Texas educational policy weren't entirely true? Well, there are people who stand as exceptions, and one was the new chairman of the state board, a dentist named Don McLeroy.

McLeroy was a caricature of the angry archconservative, the kind of Bible-thumper who advocated teaching creationism in public schools. Asked once how he evaluated history textbooks, he replied, "We are a Christian nation founded on Christian principles. The way I evaluate history textbooks is first I see how they cover Christianity and Israel. Then I see how they treat Ronald Reagan — he needs to get credit for saving the world from communism . . ." and oh my God he keeps talking.[6]

In an unprecedented move, McLeroy shared the spreadsheets prepared by several working groups with the TPPF, which released a report blasting their work for "repeated examples of bias against individualism, against the free enterprise system, and against personal responsibility." The report gave McLeroy cover to appoint a shadow committee composed of reliable conservatives to review the working groups' recommendations. "Somebody's got to stand up to these experts," McLeroy proclaimed.[7]

By the time Cure's group handed their full recommendations to the state board, Cure was pretty pleased. They hadn't overloaded the curriculum — a teacher's time is a key concern — and suggested a greater diversity of examples "in terms of race, geography, gender, and ideology." Cure thought there was a chance this would all go smoothly. We have

Nope.

In January 2010, the fifteen members of the Texas board of education gathered in their intellectual Thunderdome, Room 130 inside the William B. Travis State Office Building in downtown Austin. They sat in a circle, each in a high-backed burgundy leather chair behind a wooden desk. This meeting, the first of three sessions in which the state's new social studies standards would be ironed out, ended up revolving around the American History standards, though the Alamo did prompt one memorable exchange.

It was initiated by a liberal named Mary Helen Berlanga, a longtime board member from Corpus Christi, who proposed a requirement that fourth graders be required to learn the names of the nine Tejanos who died at the Alamo. A Beaumont businessman named David Bradley, best known for loudly doubting evolution, argued instead for Travis, Bowie, Seguín, Crockett, Santa Anna, and Susanna Dickinson, an idea Cure volunteered might "become a significant burden. After all these are fourth graders." Stymied, Berlanga swore to "fight to the bitter end" to get Tejanos written back into

Alamo history. "We have ignored their names for a long time in our textbooks and schools," she said. "They deserve their place in history."[8]

Round two came at the board's second meeting in March. Berlanga came loaded for bear, adorning her desk with photocopies of racist Jim Crow signage, including one that warned, "No dogs, negroes, Mexicans."[9] Once again, Texas History was overshadowed, this time by one of the more notorious moves in board history, the excision of Thomas Jefferson from the American History standards. Jefferson's transgression? Advocating the separation of church and state. The board's move would be lampooned by everyone from *The Huffington Post* ("Texas Textbook Massacre") to Jon Stewart's *Daily Show*.[10]

In a long, rancorous meeting, Berlanga once again pushed for inclusion of Tejanos in the Alamo curriculum. "Listing the names of the Tejanos who fought in the Alamo can instill pride in Hispanic children," she wrote in an op-ed. "This is a feeling that all Texas students should experience upon hearing the story of the defenders of the Alamo."[11]

Pat Hardy, a Fort Worth Republican, objected. "They were just among the other people who died at the Alamo," she said. Other conservatives piled on, arguing the Tejanos weren't the narrative equals of Travis, Crockett, or Bowie. "What did James Bowie and Davy Crockett do that the Tejanos did not do?" Berlanga asked. "This is a disservice to the Hispanics who fought . . . at the Alamo."[12]

Then came a moment whose eventual significance appears to have been lost on everyone. Studying the Texas History standards, Barbara Cargill, a Republican science teacher from Conroe, moved that they strike the phrase "the Tejanos who died at the Alamo" in favor of "the 189 heroes who gave their lives there." Remember that word: heroes. In the audience, Steven Cure didn't notice it.

Berlanga was outnumbered. The new language, essentially replacing the word "Tejanos" with the word "heroes," passed on a party-line vote, subject to approval at the board's third and last meeting. Between Thomas Jefferson and her defeat on the Tejano front, Berlanga got so exasperated she left the meeting, soon to be followed by the other Democrats. "We can't just pretend that this is White America, that Hispanics don't exist," she said. "It's like Nazis all over again. Burn the books, you know. Basically, that's what they're doing."[13]

Republicans, in turn, were exultant. Afterward one walked over to Cure and crowed, "American exceptionalism is back!" The wording at issue underwent one final tweak at a final meeting in May. Because Cure objected to the number 189 in the phrase "the 189 heroes who gave their lives there" — the exact number who died has never been agreed upon — the final wording was changed to oblige the teaching of "all the heroic defenders."[14] They thought they'd fixed the problem, when they'd created a far bigger one. A land mine had fallen off an army truck; it was just a matter of time before someone stepped on it.

Eight years passed.* Across the state, Texas History teachers began noticing their students actively engaging with the curriculum, especially the funhouse reflection of Santa Anna's Mexican government trying to halt Anglo immigration. With President Trump promising to build a wall, Texas history never seemed so relevant.

Still, teachers had to be careful. Lance Simon, who taught at Bettye Myers Middle

* The curriculum reassessment was delayed one year after a budget crisis.

School near Denton, tried to avoid teaching what he calls "value-charged words" like "heroism" — even though he was required to teach just that. He wanted students to understand all the viewpoints of what had been, after all, a complex struggle. Berlanga would have smiled at his firm emphasis on Tejano contributions, explaining how the revolution was never simply an ethnic conflict between Anglos and Mexicans. "I am very careful to say there were Tejanos," says Simon.

When it was time to again reassess the Texas History curriculum in 2018, a new working group assembled at a DoubleTree hotel in Austin.[15] Steven Cure was back, this time as chairman. Simon was there too. This time around, the state board, still dominated by conservatives, thoroughly vetted the group's members; even Cure was obliged to sit through an hourlong interview. The committee's goal, as before, was to craft a series of tightly written standards, typically no more than a paragraph each, outlining what was to be taught on every aspect of Texas history. The existing précis on the Texas Revolt, for instance, was all of sixty words, fleshed out with a list of topics and historical figures that could be, or must be, taught.

For almost ten years Texas teachers had been complaining they had been given entirely too much to explain. The central problem in the Texas Revolt précis, Cure saw, was its insistence on teaching about "all the heroic defenders" who died at the Alamo. That's just four words, one of which was destined for controversy. At the time, the word that worried Cure, though, was "all." It was too much. " 'All' does not say 'all groups,' 'all people,' " Cure explains. "It says 'all defenders.' That's the guys fighting on the ground, regardless of ethnic makeup. You can't teach all. All is stupid. It would be the 'Defenders of the Alamo course' and not Texas History."

Everyone had lobbed in comments beforehand, most of them gathered into a spreadsheet. They decided to toss out "all the heroic defenders" because it was an impossible task. Quietly, Cure didn't mind losing the word "heroic," either. He was increasingly aware that the state's Latino community, soon to be a majority of the population, might not see the defenders that way. "We've got to understand we're teaching to different cultures now," he says.

The ensuing controversy might have been avoided if not for a single comment someone made that was incorporated into the

450

spreadsheet. Some say Lance Simon made it; he doubts it. Whoever did, the comment explicitly challenged whether "heroic" was a "value-charged" word. Meaning that the defenders' heroism was open to debate.

Had Cure studied the spreadsheet more closely, he admits he would've deleted the freighted comment before sending it to the board. But he didn't, and after several months of honing their recommendations, Cure submitted them to the board in August 2018. He was happy they had managed to trim the Texas Revolt précis from sixty words to thirty-nine. They had cut the number of issues teachers would be required to teach, even deleting Travis's famous letter; anyone teaching the Alamo, they reasoned, couldn't help but mention that. Some of the most controversial issues they dodged. The whole study of the revolt had been deeply influenced by Andrew J. Torget's 2015 book, *Seeds of Empire,* which emphasized the centrality of the colonists' slave-based cotton economy. Cure justified ignoring it by reminding himself they were there to streamline standards, not add to them. As for "heroic," he felt sure he could negotiate any changes the board might want.

"Unfortunately," Cure sighs, "the shit hit the fan before we were able to make those changes."

It started with a tip someone gave Carlos Sanchez, *Texas Monthly*'s political editor. The source, Sanchez says, was a "historical purist who knows Texas history well and loves to point out the absurdity of those who don't," which could mean almost any Texan living in liberal Austin. Sanchez, while noting the Travis letter would no longer be required, focused on the sexiest bit, elimination of the word "heroic," zeroing in on the comment on the spreadsheet. His story, posted online on Thursday, September 6, ran beneath the red-meat headline: "Should Texas Schoolchildren Be Taught That Alamo Defenders Were 'Heroic'?"[16]

Cure had heard a story was brewing, but still, sitting in his office that day, he wasn't prepared for what he read when the Google alert hit his inbox. It was a face-palming moment. "Oh, shit," is all he remembers saying.

In the debate between Alamo revisionists and traditionalists, only the latter camp tends to vent its spleen in public. By that evening, the angry comments had begun to pile atop Sanchez's story like a game of Tetris. Many sounded like this one by an especially splenetic commenter calling himself FiftycalTX: "The battle of the ALAMO has been taught for close to 200 years and no ISIS REVISIONISM is going to get it 'untaught.' Any 'teachers' that have a problem with calling the patriots that FOUGHT AND DIED at the Alamo 'heroic' need to return to New Germany or where ever they came from."[17]

That's the kind of over-the-top comment writers tend to cite to make you think all traditionalists are ungrammatical lunatics. In fact, some were more lucid, as in this comment from someone calling himself Keith Smith: "The good people of Texas need to see this for what it really is: an insidious attempt by leftist radicals and hand-wringing American apologists to rewrite our proud Texas history and twist our struggles for freedom into unspectacular yarns of Yankee colonialism and thinly veiled white supremacy. They want to make us the oppressors and bad guys in the eyes of our children."*

---

* Others were actually thoughtful. "They were heroic, no doubt about it," wrote Oblate Spheroid. "Inspirational, admirable, and legendary, too. But that's for us to decide on our own, and not for a textbook to tell us. Textbooks provide facts and context. Heroism is not a fact, but an opinion

The real fireworks came the same afternoon the article went live when Texas governor Greg Abbott tweeted, "Stop political correctness in our schools. Of course Texas schoolchildren should be taught that Alamo defenders were 'Heroic'! I fully expect the State Board of Education to agree."

It's entirely possible that the conservative politicians who leapt onto the governor's Friday afternoon bandwagon were genuinely offended by the proposed changes and did not consider the political advantage in expressing this grievance two months before an election. It's also possible that a diet solely consisting of refined sugar, tobacco, and whiskey is good for you. The first in, George P. Bush, chimed in just sixteen minutes later.

"This politically correct nonsense is why I'll always fight to honor the Alamo defenders' sacrifice," Bush tweeted. "[Travis's] letter & the defenders' actions must remain at the very core of TX history teaching. This is not debatable to me."

The state's bellicose conservative lieutenant governor, Dan Patrick, tweeted "its [*sic*]

based on one's perspectives and values. The committee is right."

454

time to draw a line in the sand on political correctness in our schools." The onetime presidential candidate Mike Huckabee weighed in with a tweet blaming the whole thing on "some whack job" who "wants to purge" the teaching of the Travis letter.

By Monday morning, a day before the state board was to convene, the Alamo media tsunami showed no signs of ebbing. In Washington, a Houston-area congressman named Ted Poe rose on the floor of the house to deliver a speech called "Victory or Death": "To quote Travis, I have a value-charged word or two to say about that: 'Victory or death,' " Poe said in words that he would later repeat at the board meeting. "Those elites who want to rip the Travis letter from our Texas history books dishonor the sacrifice" of the Alamo defenders. Senator Ted Cruz of Houston, never one to miss a good scandal, weighed in with a similar op-ed on the Fox News website.

Cure, a quiet man, actually raises his voice when he recalls how exasperating all this was. "The word 'heroic' hasn't been required since we started teaching Texas History in 1936!" he fumes. "You didn't need to tell teachers or kids what happened at the Alamo was heroic! It's freakin' obvious!"

Still, Cure realized he had to do something. In the final hours before the board's meeting that Tuesday, he reached out to everyone in his working group and several board members. He ripped up the thirty-nine-word Revolt précis and wrote a new one, sixty-seven words long, this one stating the Travis letter must be taught to every seventh grader. He pulled off a deft bit of compromise that seemingly pleased everyone, requiring seventh graders to be taught "the heroism of the diverse defenders."

The 2018 board, it turns out, didn't have its predecessors' thirst for controversy, and in a bid to deflect this one they put Cure on as the first speaker at the hearing that Tuesday. He explained what had happened, then walked the board through the implications of the words "heroism" and "diverse," clarifying that teachers would be required to "show contributions of groups, other than Anglo men, to the defense of the Alamo."

When he finished, people in the audience actually applauded. They clapped louder when one of the board members said they would unanimously adopt his language. Sixty members of the public, many angry traditionalists, had shown up to speak that day. By the time Cure finished, half had left. Everyone, even the governor, appeared satisfied. "GREAT NEWS," the governor tweeted. "Thanks to all the Texas patriots who weighed in."

Afterward, Cure returned home, happy it was over. He had only one regret. "I missed the opportunity to congratulate Congressman Poe for calling me something I've never been called before, an elitist," he says. "My family thought that was hilarious."

CHAPTER 22
THE ALAMO REIMAGINED

The protesters, maybe fifty of them, began gathering that cool Friday morning, December 27, 2019, for the kind of demonstration that by now had grown commonplace on Alamo Plaza. Many wore camouflage. Several wore tactical gear and carried AR-15s. They assembled around the base of the sixty-foot-tall Cenotaph, which has been standing outside the Alamo since 1940. In its latest revitalization effort, the city was planning to disassemble and repair the aging monument, then move it five hundred feet south. The protesters were calling this a desecration and pledging to prevent it, using "physical force" if necessary. For now, they were promising to "occupy" the site overnight.

Maybe it was inevitable that the rise of Alamo revisionism would end up stirring the pot of right-wing politics in the Trump era. Certainly there was more than a whiff of white supremacy in the air that day. One gent held a placard calling a Tejano city councilman a "Caucaphobe" and a "left-wing, racist, white people–hating" person. Another wore a red MAGA ball cap. Still another wore a cap emblazoned with the name of a Texas militia group.

Their leader was Brandon Burkhart, a beefy bellower who called on Governor Abbott to put the matter to a vote. "Our numbers will keep on increasing," he told reporters, "and if they try to move that Cenotaph, or bring cranes in anywhere near it, we're going to be there to stop them."

This, we should say, is just one glimpse of the craziness that has enveloped the Alamo in recent years. Maybe the most bizarre moment came just two weeks earlier, when another fervent Alamo traditionalist went on Facebook to charge that the politician who now oversees the site, George P. Bush, was planning to adorn Alamo Plaza with a statue of Santa Anna. That Bush was planning no such thing didn't convince Burkhart and his followers.[1]

If the demonstration that day was the opening scene of a movie, this is the spot where you would read the phrase "ten years earlier." Because an awful lot has happened to get to this point, and all of it — the protests, the lawsuits, the over-the-top Trump-era name-calling, the nasty online campaigns — is in a very real sense the culmination of the decades-long clash between revisionism and traditionalism. What began as an obscure scholarly debate in the 1970s, what mushroomed into a literary and academic brouhaha in the '90s, has finally spilled messily into the strange new political world of twenty-first-century America. By and large, it hasn't been pretty.

A good place to start this story is with the terribly nice little man who began showing up at the Alamo in the 2000s. He was slight and balding and usually wore a black T-shirt. He chatted with gardeners and maintenance men. Before long the security guards and gift-shop ladies knew him by name. Everyone liked him. Everyone called him Phil.

Yes, this was Phil Collins. The singer, as we've mentioned, had been fascinated with the Alamo since boyhood. He had begun collecting Alamo artifacts years before and was on his way to assembling the largest collection of Alamo-sourced items in the world. By 2014 he was musing about finding a museum to hold his 206-piece collection, which included everything from Jim Bowie's Bowie knife to a shot pouch said to have been Davy Crockett's. Collins wasn't getting any younger and wanted to ensure the collection was in safe hands before he passed.

But he couldn't find the right place. One day in 2014, when Collins was in San Antonio visiting his collecting partner, an artifact-shop proprietor named Jim Guimarin, Guimarin mentioned it to Kaye Tucker, who worked for the General Land Office, the state agency overseeing the Alamo.

"Would you like to meet him?" Guimarin asked.

"Yeah," Tucker said. "We'd like his stuff."

The moment she said it, Tucker almost clapped her hand over her mouth. She was a midlevel government bureaucrat with precisely zero authority to discuss the subject of Collins's collection, much less its acquisition. The three of them ended up having lunch at El Mirador, a place in the King William district that always gave Collins a private dining room. "So, Kaye," Guimarin said at one point, "was there something you wanted to talk to Phil about?"

Tucker, who seldom found herself lunching with British music superstars, made a stammering mention of the collection. "I wondered," she said, "if you would entertain the idea of giving it to us." The GLO. The Alamo. "He looked at me, and he kind of turned his head, and he goes, 'I didn't even think you would want it.' "

"Why would you think that?"

"I mean, where would you put it?"

Everyone in the GLO knew the Alamo needed a new museum. In the back of her mind, Tucker felt sure Collins's collection would not only be a fabulous centerpiece for any new facility but would spur donations to build it.

A few days later, Land Commissioner Jerry Patterson sat down with Collins for a government-budget lunch of sandwiches and Diet Cokes. They quickly reached an agreement for Collins to give the GLO his collection. He had just two conditions. He wanted everything displayed in one place, and if this was to be a new museum, as everyone assumed, he wanted ground broken within seven years. That would give the GLO until 2021. Patterson agreed. On June 26, 2014, Collins announced the deal at a press conference on Alamo Plaza. "This completes the journey for me," he said. "These artifacts are coming home."[2]

The clock began ticking.

The politics of San Antonio, like that of

many American cities, has grown steadily more progressive over the last thirty years. As the Latino community has grown — it's now nearly two-thirds of the population — postwar accommodationist politicians like Henry Cisneros have been replaced by a new generation of assertive, liberal Latinos. In 2011 one of the best examples of this was Diego Bernal, a garrulous onetime social worker and civil rights lawyer with three degrees from the University of Michigan. Elected city councilman for the Alamo's district that year, Bernal found himself working with a middle school chum, the new mayor, Julián Castro.

Like Castro and many of the city's Tejanos, Bernal had never spent much time dwelling on the Alamo or its meanings, especially after his own distasteful encounter with it in seventh grade. But the more constituents he spoke with about reviving downtown, the more he realized it was about burnishing the city's top tourist attraction.

"One of the people on my staff was like, 'You know what, the Alamo sucks,' " Bernal recalls. " 'It's got all this crap around it. It's supposed to mean a lot to us. It doesn't.' As the councilman you hear over and over again how disappointed people are in their

463

experience there. Like you just feel there's been some sort of failing on your part to make people's trips there worth it."

But Bernal's deeper motivation was reclaiming the Alamo narrative for his fellow Tejanos, both those who understood their people's history there and those who didn't yet. "You keep meeting [Tejanos] who are like, 'My family fought there, my family was there.' And I realized that there's all these Mexican-American families talking about having family members who fought in the revolution on the *winning* side. And I'm like, 'Why do you sound like a conspiracy theorist?' Because what we've always been taught was there's no way that was possible, that all of us were on the losing side, that we are the bad ones. I realized it all had more depth and dimension than what I remember from being a kid. I realized there is a way for every person, every San Antonian, to see themselves in a way that doesn't sort of elicit shame. And I wanted that for them."

Bernal saw that the main reason previous redevelopment efforts had failed was the yawning gap between the largely Anglo Daughters and the Latino community. "We're saying, 'Fuck you,' you're saying, 'Fuck you,' to us, we're both so preoccupied with who owns it, nothing is happening," he says. He manages a mischievous grin. "I've learned there's nothing like public shaming to get people to do shit."

And so he tried. With a pointed 2013 op-ed in the *Express-News,* Bernal asked whether it was finally time to upgrade the Alamo.[3] Five months later, he persuaded Mayor Castro to form a committee to once again consider a revitalization plan. Everyone got a seat at the table: Tejanos, Anglos, the Daughters, Native Americans, the GLO, businesspeople who operated shops on the plaza.[4]

From the beginning, it was clear to everyone involved that however they chose to "reimagine" the Alamo, its message needed to go far beyond the Heroic Anglo Narrative. Revisionist sentiments, in fact, infused deliberations from the outset. "Everyone accepted the fact that we're going to have to change the narrative, to start developing museums and tourism based on the facts and no longer the old anti-Mexican bludgeon that we always used to club the Mexicans with," Andrés Tijerina, the revisionist Texas historian hired to advise the committee, explained later.

The moment everyone remembers was Tijerina's impassioned first presentation.

After walking the committee through an overview of Texas history from Indigenous peoples through colonization to the revolt, he laid down a gauntlet. "Texas is the most brutally racist place in the United States," he said. "And the Alamo is a big part of that. There shouldn't be the victors and the losers, but a balanced approach showing virtues on both sides. All Texans should be proud of the site and the battle." He scanned the room. "Until you get little Mexican American fifteen-year-old girls doing their quinceañera* at the Alamo, you're never going to own it, and you'll never get anywhere. They should claim it. This is theirs."[5]

This was unprecedented talk, at least for this kind of government committee: For the first time since 1994, an official group

---

* A quinceañera, which is less often called "quinceaños," "quince años," or "quince," is the name for the religious and social celebration of a girl's fifteenth birthday, observed in Mexico, Latin America, and the Caribbean, as well as Latino communities in the United States. It is common for the quinceañera (the term refers to both the celebration and the celebrant) to pose in a brightly colored formal dress in public places, such as the Texas Capitol, for formal portraits.

backed by a government body addressed the most sensitive issues about the Texas Revolt head-on. Whose Alamo was it anyway? San Antonio's? Or the world's? After all, 95 percent of its visitors came from out of state.[6] And if the Heroic Anglo Narrative was to be replaced, by what exactly? Was the Alamo a stage to retell only the narrative of the siege and the battle? Or of the mission's entire history, going back to the days when Franciscan fathers baptized all those Native Americans?

The businessmen on the committee argued that the battle narrative must take precedence. That's why people come, Davis Phillips, the owner of Ripley's Haunted Adventure and Tomb Rider 3D, insisted. The committee "wants to talk about who all was here before and they want to make it just as important as the battle," Phillips recalls. "Sometimes I said, 'Guys, that's a mistake.' It makes you happy, but you're not the ones coming to spend the money. If we end up with a big boring history lesson and a thousand Texans lose their jobs and people stop spending as much time here and as much money, that's not a win."

In the end, the committee found a way — it thought — to please almost everyone by recommending the battle as an "entry point" to tell the longer history of the old Spanish mission that could be peopled prominently with Tejanos and Native Americans, a story of "racial understanding and healing." Revisionism, in other words, would define the new Alamo experience. At a public hearing, questioners seemed about evenly split on the committee's ideas. Gary Foreman — still active thirty years after his heyday — argued it would be a mistake to deemphasize the battle. "The story of what took place in 1836 resonates across the planet," he said. "It resonates with every ethnicity, every culture, every nation, because it's the story of sacrifice. It's why people come here."[7]

The *Express-News* agreed. "This telling needs to be inclusive but let's not fool ourselves about what point of the site's history will be the biggest draw," it editorialized. "After all, one doesn't go to Gettysburg to learn about a quaint Pennsylvania town's history."[8]

The committee ended up softening its final language, and in December 2014 the city council adopted it.[9] Just about everyone, even onetime outliers like the Native Americans, was pleased. It had been five months since Phil Collins announced his gift. By this point everyone assumed his collection would go into some new museum this process would build. "We had ten years to go," recalls Ramón Vásquez, executive director of American Indians in Texas at the Spanish Colonial Missions, "and we were on track."

By January 2015, the Alamo's political deck was being reshuffled. Julián Castro had joined the Obama Administration, and Diego Bernal was headed to the state legislature. Elections had swept a new crop of hard-edged conservatives into state office, and with them came a rush of strange new conspiracy theories about the Alamo. UNESCO was poised to designate San Antonio's four Spanish missions, including the Alamo, a World Heritage Site, and it didn't take long before protesters were in front of the Alamo waving Texas flags, swearing to fight the coming UN takeover. In Austin, a Tea Party state senator introduced a bill to ban foreign ownership of the Alamo;* this was too nutty even for the Texas legislature. The General Land Office

* To be fair, the idea of a "foreigner" trying to buy the Alamo wasn't completely batty. A Saudi sheikh had expressed interest in doing exactly that in 1975, saying he wanted to purchase it for his son,

got so tired of fielding questions and complaints it ended up starting a website to refute the rumors, alamotruth.com.

Among the new faces in Austin that January was thirty-eight-year-old George P. Bush, oldest son of Jeb, nephew to George W., and grandson of the first President Bush. Raised in Miami, Bush came to Texas to attend Rice University in Houston and the University of Texas law school, then spent a few years piddling with real estate and private equity before, inevitably, filing to run for his first public office to replace Jerry Patterson at the General Land Office. He won.

Every land commissioner in the last fifty years has gone on to run for higher office, and because Bush was half Hispanic — his mother was born in Mexico — he held out the promise of broadening the Republicans' appeal. But no one had a clue what to expect when he took office. The Alamo was the only sexy item in his portfolio. Fixing up the Jerusalem of Texas must've seemed like the perfect addition to his résumé. Then, on March 12, 2015, the day after the legislature named Phil Collins an honorary

---

who had undergone training at a San Antonio-area air force base and fallen in love with the place.

Texan, Bush dropped the bomb: After 110 years, the Daughters were to be ejected from the Alamo. A state audit cited ten minor breaches of their contract, but that was a fig leaf. Long story short, Bush didn't think the group was up for the complex revitalization project he envisioned.*

The Daughters did not go quietly into the Texas night. They refused to hand over the contents of the Alamo library, a limestone building in the garden across from the gift shop. Later that summer, Bush made clear he was not fooling around. When the Daughters' Alamo archivists came to work, their keys wouldn't fit in the lock.[10]

The handover was made official in an emotional ceremony that July. A line of men

---

* Former aides of his tell us the move originated with Patterson, who after contracting with the Daughters to manage the Alamo under his oversight came to accept that they were not up to the job. "When we were in charge, we had started that separation with the Daughters," said one aide. "We actually knew before we left office that there was going to have to be a clean break." The Daughters didn't have any infrastructure in place to run the Alamo like a world-class historical site, much less a business. Bush simply executed the Patterson plan he inherited, albeit without grace.

in period dress flanked a crowd of Daughters standing in front of the church. After a series of prayers, the Daughters' American and Texas flags were lowered, and another Texas flag was raised. There was a drumroll, then someone called for three cheers. A bagpiper played "The Yellow Rose of Texas." The assembled women then sang the state song, "Texas, Our Texas." Many had tears on their faces as they did.

Bush moved swiftly to consolidate the GLO's idea of building some kind of museum around the Phil Collins collection into San Antonio's emerging revitalization plan. After forty years of dead-end dreaming, things finally appeared to be falling into place. More advisory boards were named, and the legislature ponied up $5 million for repairs and then another $25 million to begin buying some of the surrounding buildings and paying all the architects and engineers and lawyers who would devise the actual plans. The city chipped in $31.5 million. Just about everyone, from Collins to San Antonio politicians to the Tāp Pīlam Coahuiltecan Nation, seemed not just satisfied but excited.

"This will happen," the new state representative Diego Bernal promised, "and it will be magnificent."[11]

They called it "reimagining" the Alamo, which sounded great to San Antonio, where "reimagining" was interpreted as a place-making term for fixing up the run-down Alamo Plaza. The word would eventually encounter resistance, especially in rural Texas, where many took it to mean that the Heroic Anglo Narrative was undergoing a remodel. For the moment, though, everyone involved just seemed so darned happy something was finally happening. Bush named a team of "Texas Titans," headed by the billionaire San Antonio car dealer Red McCombs and prominent real estate developer and Republican donor Gene Powell, to lead the fundraising efforts.

For almost two years, with the notable exception of the occasional protests against the United Nations, everything at the Alamo was pretty much sweetness and light. In July 2016, archaeologists working with the Tāp Pīlam Coahuiltecan Nation began the most extensive excavation ever undertaken on the plaza, near the base of what was once the Alamo's south wall. As is common in construction projects, the archaeological work was required before they could finally repair the Alamo. The dig turned up dozens of remains, each turned over to the tribal community for reburial.

When Bush made his first unscripted remarks about the upcoming Alamo master plan at a conference in Austin in 2016, what's notable is how thoroughly he had embraced revisionism. "The Alamo can be a centerpiece for taking on the controversial issues of the past," Bush said, mentioning slavery. "I think the opportunity for this re-imagining of the Alamo Master Plan is for us to take that to another level."[12]

Still, all good things come to an end. When the master plan was finally released in April 2017, it was met with an outpouring of dissent. Designed by a set of architects in distant Philadelphia, a glass wall was to enclose much of the original compound. Inside, what's now Alamo Plaza would become a shaded courtyard, entered via a new entrance on the south, roughly where the main gate was in 1836. Three buildings on the west side, including Davis Phillips's haunted house, would be demolished to make way for a four-story museum topped with an open-air restaurant. The Cenotaph would be repaired and moved to a café-lined promenade just outside the entrance. Millions were to go toward repairing the church and the Long Barrack.

Everyone found something to dislike.

Some balked at the price tag, $450 million. Vásquez objected to the museum's proposed entrance fee and termed the idea of building a courtyard over the cemetery "cultural genocide." Just about everyone hated the glass wall, preferring something that evoked 1836. Conservatives considered the relocation of the Cenotaph a desecration of the Texians' mass graves. "It was like the battle was just going to be a footnote. This whole thing is just a money boondoggle in furtherance of a politically correct Alamo," said a retired Fort Worth firefighter named Rick Range.

Range, a passionate Alamo traditionalist armed only with a flip phone and a Rolodex, launched a website, savethealamo.us, and began attacking the master plan online and in appearances across the state.* He

---

* Range has often attacked George P. Bush for tweeting, "We have to take the focus at the Alamo off of the battle in order to promote racial unity and not division in our society." We have not been able to find evidence that Bush ever tweeted that, and when asked, none of his former aides could recall that. When we asked Range if he could share proof that Bush had ever tweeted that, he emailed, "We will try to find the original tweet but we have used it numerous times ever since so I know it is

claimed the redevelopment plans relegated exhibits about the Battle of the Alamo to the museum's basement[*] and would rename the Alamo the Misión San Antonio de Valero.[†]

Critics on the right accused Bush of using the Alamo as a political stepping-stone.

"The Republican Party of the state of Texas wants to present George P. Bush as the political savior of the Alamo," said Dr. Betty Edwards, who was president of the Daughters of the Republic of Texas when they were kicked out. "So everybody, and especially you Hispanics because his mom's from Mexico, needs to vote for George P. Bush forever because he saved the Alamo."

By September, five months after the plan's unveiling, the conservative anger Range stoked had begun to seep into Texas politics.

---

correct." He never provided proof to back up his accusation.

[*] They did not.

[†] This is, of course, the Alamo's original name and was referred to often in the "reimagining" plans in the proper historical context, but as far as officially renaming the Alamo, one highly placed Alamo insider confirmed that this was complete horsepucky, emailing, "This would NEVER HAPPEN and is a complete fabrication."

A Tea Party activist named Ray Myers was told he would need to raise or donate $250,000 if he wanted to join the GLO's star-studded Alamo fundraising committee, a common ask. Myers went public, claiming that the Alamo campaign had asked him for a bribe.[13] Myers, also a member of the Texas Republican Party's executive committee, won passage of a nonbinding resolution demanding that any Alamo redevelopment effort abandon revisionist elements and focus instead on the traditional narrative of the battle.[14] At the GLO, Bush and his people could only roll their eyes.

Soon, though, they began to feel the heat, in part because Bush seemed politically vulnerable. When someone leaked an internal audit critical of the way the GLO was running the site, Bush blamed Patterson loyalists and cleaned house. His purge created a supply of angry insiders eager to leak embarrassing tidbits to the press. He shot himself in the foot when he got on a conference call with his father's presidential campaign advisers and lamented that he couldn't join them on the Republican primary trail because he was "stuck here in Texas" after "running for dogcatcher like I did."[15] Oof. And it didn't help when the GLO's number two man at the Alamo had to resign after using his official credit card at Hooters, among other places.

All of which Bush might have waved away except that he was running for reelection, and the Republican primary — the only election that really mattered in Texas politics at the time — was coming up in March 2018. In short order, opposition to the Alamo's redevelopment plans became all about Bush, and Bush's reelection contest became all about the Alamo. An October protest against moving the Cenotaph — the first of many to come — morphed into a series of angry denunciations of Bush's stewardship.

With heat rising on his right, Bush began distancing himself from the master plan's revisionist DNA to emphasize the Heroic Anglo Narrative. Gone, by and large, were references to slavery and Native Americans and bothersome cemeteries. Every Bush appearance was peppered with references to 1836. "We must restore the battlefield to honor the Alamo's gallant defenders," he said at a press conference on the plaza just a week after that Cenotaph protest. "We must respect this sacred space. We must and will ensure that 1836 lives here every single day."[16]

Nothing Bush said, though, could calm

traditionalists. Morale in the Bush camp sank, a mood that only darkened when Jerry Patterson announced he would challenge Bush in the primary. It was clear the campaign would be a referendum on Bush's plans for the Alamo. Everywhere he went that winter, it's all people asked about. "George," every wealthy donor would ask, "what are you going to do about the Alamo?" And Bush would try to explain, and the donor, inevitably uninspired, would sigh and say something like, "God, the Alamo, that's all I hear about. Y'all need to back off." *Texas Monthly* headlined its assessment of the race: "George P. Bush's Last Stand at the Alamo."

"The real source of Bush's problems . . . ," the magazine concluded, "is that he has so far failed to understand the signs and symbols of this state — the foundation of the story — and that may now cost him everything."[17]

Patterson adorned all his campaign literature with Alamo illustrations; it was even on his new business cards. The Taco Bell roofline of the Alamo church dominated his campaign logo. Bush had no choice but to fight the Alamo fight. He assigned an aide named Bryan Preston to be his Mr. Alamo, and that winter Preston was everywhere, on radio shows and at luncheons, gently explaining that no, "reimagining" the Alamo didn't mean telling the narrative any differently than before. It meant updating and safeguarding the site, getting rid of the gassy traffic and tacky wax museums, and turning it into a world-class venue Texans could be proud of. They ran explanatory Alamo ads on radio across Texas, printed glossy handouts and mailers featuring the shrine in full color, and started a Facebook page called "Save the Alamo." Preston wanted to believe it was working.

But they couldn't be sure. And so, just after Christmas, they took a poll. Afterward, the pollster, a tall, high-energy young man named Chris Perkins, sat with Bush and his top advisers at campaign headquarters in downtown Austin and went over the numbers. The initial ones weren't encouraging. Perkins first showed a word cloud, a graph in which the size of words corresponds to how often people mentioned them. The word "Alamo" loomed in the middle, three times larger than any other. Bush and an aide exchanged glances. This didn't look good.

When was the last time you heard anything about the Alamo? Most people answered six months to a year, meaning they weren't paying close attention. Did you enjoy your last visit to the site? A whopping 60 percent said no. The last question was the most important. Do you want to see the Alamo transformed into a "world-class tourist attraction"? Almost three-quarters said yes. Perkins smiled. The far right might be angry over plans for the Alamo, he said, but mainstream Republicans simply weren't. "Don't worry about it," he said. "You guys are fine."

From that moment on Bush could relax, confident the Alamo was a winning issue. In every speech, he emphasized the importance of the battle, avoiding any hint of revisionism. In the March 6 primary, he received twice as many votes as Patterson.* The Bush who emerged victorious, however, seemed a changed man. At the state Republican convention in San Antonio that August, it was clear his conservative brethren hadn't forgotten all that talk about slavery and Indian burial grounds. When Bush blamed criticism of his Alamo stewardship on "fake news" in the "liberal media," the

* Rick Range and land surveyor Davey Edwards were also running in the Republican primary, both campaigning against George P. Bush's stewardship of the Alamo as their top issue.

line was met with an outpouring of boos that echoed off the concrete walls in the convention center. Dozens of people began shouting, "Remember the Alamo!" Bush spread his arms wide, grinned, and then shrugged. "I did win, right?" he asked.[18]

Those who disagreed with Bush began to question whether he still embraced the idea of an Alamo, as he once put it, "in which every Texan can be proud." Bush put Preston back on the road, and his message was 100 percent undiluted Heroic Anglo Narrative. "We are Texans doing a Texas thing," Preston explained. The Alamo is "our superhero origin story, and it happens to be true."

Team Bush's newfound embrace of traditionalism notwithstanding, the reimagining of Alamo Plaza proceeded just as Bush's critics feared thanks to some smart lawyering by the city of San Antonio. The city leased the Alamo Plaza to the GLO on the condition that they move the Cenotaph or the city could cancel the lease, which Roberto Treviño, the city council member who succeeded Bernal, promised to do. "We're not going to leave the Cenotaph there," he said. "This is not a bargaining chip."

The committee listed five goals that struck both traditional and revisionist notes:

restore the Alamo church and Long Barrack, delineate the original footprint, create a sense of arrival, restore reverence, and build "a world-class visitors center and museum that tells the story of the Alamo and its more than 300 years of history."[*]

Turning the focus of the Alamo from a battle site into a multicultural epic spanning centuries was exactly what Bush told Republicans he would not allow — and exactly what was required in the contract he signed to get control of the plaza. "They don't want to hear that we're telling the complete story of the Alamo," said Treviño.

As far as the actual designs for the Alamo went, well, those were still largely secret. The conceptual drawings depicting shaded promenades and sidewalk cafés were just that — conceptual. Regardless of what was happening behind closed doors, it became obvious that those doors were getting closed on former insiders. Alamo descendants' organizer Lee Spencer White was frozen out first after she publicly criticized Bush dur-

[*] To Sarah Reveley, the Daughter who brought down the Daughters from the inside, even the nod toward "restoring reverence" was not enough. Says Reveley: "Say historical and nowhere do they say REMEMBER THE ALAMO!!!!!!!"

ing his reelection campaign and sued to prevent the Cenotaph's removal. The GLO refused to allow her descendants' group to hold its annual candlelight vigil in the church. At a press conference in October 2018, White announced that she was the first of the major Alamo players to file suit against Bush, over the vigil.[19] She would sue again two years later, trying to block the Cenotaph's relocation. "The Alamo Cenotaph is our family headstone," she told a reporter. "The Alamo Plaza is our family graveyard." Why not have the Cenotaph where the defenders "bled and died, where their souls left this earth to heaven"?[20]

Then the Native Americans decided they could not, as Sam Rayburn liked to say, go along to get along. They sued to force the GLO to acknowledge what everyone knew — the Alamo was a cemetery. The Alamo's interpretation plan included symbolic markers to signify where the remains had been found, but they would not allow an archaeological investigation, much less the reburial of Native Americans. "In San Antonio, we have a frickin' cemetery in the middle of downtown," Ramón Vásquez noted. "We do our best to cover it up to promote genocide and build a $450 million state-of-the-art museum to promote slavery."

The GLO claimed the lawsuit made it harder to raise money. Maybe, they even speculated, legal delays would cause them to miss their 2021 deadline. And in what Vásquez believes was retribution for the lawsuit, for the first time since 1995, the Tāp Pīlam Coahuiltecan Nation was not allowed to hold El Llanto, their ceremony in the church to honor the memories of their ancestors buried there.* When about five dozen Native Americans and a couple of state lawmakers showed up for the twenty-fifth annual Sunrise Ceremony, they found the doors to the church chained.[21]

For many, the Alamo's new tack toward traditionalism was personified by Douglass McDonald, a former CEO of the National Underground Railroad Freedom Center,

---

* Alamo insiders tell a different story. To provide equal access to the Alamo, which is a public facility, they required that all events be open to the public in partnership with the Alamo. An exception was made for El Llanto, which drew a lawsuit from Lee Spencer White's Alamo Defenders Descendants Association on the grounds of religious discrimination in favor of the Native Americans and the disfavor of Christians. To make that lawsuit go away, the Alamo removed Tāp Pīlam's exception.

who was hired as the Alamo's CEO in 2017.* From his first public comments, McDonald made clear his team would emphasize the narrative of the 1836 battle over the pre-1836 contributions of Tejanos and Native Americans. "The facts are that the centrality of the 1836 battle will always be central to the Alamo — always has been, always will be," McDonald said in October 2017. "We are not reimagining the history of the Alamo. We are reimagining the experience people have when they come to the Alamo."[22]

With McDonald paying lip service to traditionalism, just about everyone who embraced a revisionist viewpoint began complaining. "He treated me like I was a nobody, like he was too valuable to even speak to me on the phone," recalls Vásquez. The Alamo's historian, Bruce Winders, felt the chill as well. He was dismayed when McDonald began making cuts to education programming. "I've talked to Doug Mc-

* In June 2020, McDonald, then sixty-eight and with a new granddaughter he had seen only three times, announced he was stepping down as CEO of the Alamo in September 2020. "People would rather fight about the Alamo than fight for the Alamo," he said.

Donald and I said we're going backward in the interpretation," Winders said. "We've essentially been on the cutting edge. We pushed that story for years. I see us going backwards from there. And he says, 'Well, you've got to understand.' " Meaning: You've got to understand that the people we're asking to donate to fix up the Alamo — and by extension George P. Bush — want nothing to do with Alamo revisionism. Winders was forced out in 2018.

If it seemed that every conceivable ethnic group had found a way at some point to oppose the plans for the Alamo, by 2019 another had emerged: African-Americans. Black leaders in San Antonio began lobbying city council members to save the old Woolworth Building, one of the three structures slated for demolition to make way for the museum. Today the home of Ripley's Haunted Adventure and a Jimmy John's sandwich shop, the site is where Woolworth's operated a lunch counter in March 1960. After a protest march, its lunch counter became one of the first San Antonio restaurants to begin serving Black patrons. "African-American history is embedded in Alamo Plaza," a local historian named Everett Fly said. "We simply cannot segregate our collective history and culture and be considered serious stewards of Alamo Plaza and Texas history."[23]

When a local conservation group floated the idea of preserving a section of the building as a civil rights section of the museum, Alamo CEO Douglass McDonald rejected the idea. He had privately questioned the authenticity of the Woolworth's lunch counter story, but at the time the public civil rights hero myth went unquestioned in San Antonio. His tone-deaf response was more evidence, to opponents at least, of how far Bush's GLO had moved from its embrace of inclusive elements in 2016.[24]

The $450 million Alamo revitalization project, complete with the museum to be built around the Phil Collins collection, remains controversial. The San Antonio City Council formally approved everything in 2018, and in June 2019 hired an architect to design the museum. After the Texas Historical Commission refused petitions by Lee Spencer White and Ramón Vásquez to designate Alamo Plaza as an "unverified cemetery,"[25] the groups filed suit in federal court.

The protests at the Cenotaph continued. One day Burkhart's This Is Texas Freedom Force would be guarding the Cenotaph with their coolers, snacks, and assault rifles against cranes that never came, and the next Lee Spencer White would be rallying her descendants of the Alamo defenders with her impassioned talk of spilled blood and sacrifice.

Rick Range keeps fighting the plan, publishing the startling revelation that Bush planned to erect a statue of Santa Anna in the Cenotaph's place.* Bush, not known as a political brawler, finally got out of his defensive crouch and onto Twitter.

"One must ask themselves, why am I being accused of honoring the murderous dictator Santa Anna? Is it because my mother (now a naturalized citizen) is from Mexico? I was born in Houston, my wife is from San Angelo, and my boys were born — you guessed it — here in Texas. . . . The idea that I would EVER place a statue of Santa Anna at the Alamo is patently false. Enough is enough. This is an outright lie, and is quite frankly, flat out racist."[26]

Into that breach leapt Lieutenant Gover-

---

* "I am not making this up. We know that parts of the Bush plan were going to be horrendous, but it now looks like it will be worse than we ever dreamed," Range wrote in a Facebook post. According to a fact-check by the *Austin American-Statesman,* he was making it up.

nor Dan Patrick, a Tea Party darling and the Texas co-chairman of Donald Trump's 2016 campaign. Patrick reasoned that since the Texas Senate had passed a bill to make it harder to remove historical monuments such as the Cenotaph, then Bush was obviously calling every state senator a racist. Patrick seized the opportunity to slam both Bush and the redevelopment plan, even threatening to transfer management of the Alamo to another state agency. The manufactured outrage was widely considered Patrick's opening gambit to keep Bush from challenging him in a future Republican Party primary election.

Meanwhile, *Fox & Friends* cohost Brian Kilmeade came out with what might be the best-selling Alamo book of all time, *Sam Houston and the Alamo Avengers.* To say he hewed to the traditional view of things understates the matter; he referred to slaves as servants. Allen West, the former Tea Party congressman from Florida, moved to Texas and won his insurgent campaign for the state Republican Party chairmanship. His main issue? The Alamo.

And if it wasn't clear that the Heroic Anglo Narrative had again become a conservative keystone,* in February 2020 Donald Trump promised a "great American comeback" in his State of the Union address. "This is the country where children learn names like Wyatt Earp, Davy Crockett, and Annie Oakley. This is the place where the pilgrims landed at Plymouth and where Texas patriots made their last stand at the Alamo," he said, continuing through the applause, "the beautiful, beautiful Alamo."

For the 2020 anniversary of the battle, Alamo-heads gathered in San Antonio for the Dawn at the Alamo ceremony that Gary Foreman had started all those years ago. There were more people wearing Davy Crockett backwoods outfits than MAGA hats, but both were easily outnumbered by the more than one hundred Sons of the Republic of Texas in their blue blazers and pale felt Stetsons. More than a dozen wreaths stood along the wall by the Long Barrack. Later, descendants would bring

---

* In March 2020, 97 percent of Texas Republican primary voters voted for a nonbinding resolution stating: "Texans should protect and preserve all historical monuments, artifacts, and buildings, such as the Alamo Cenotaph and our beloved Alamo, and should oppose any reimagining of the Alamo site."

them up one at a time to remember the Texian dead. A high school choir sang "Texas, Our Texas," and someone, with evident sincerity and good humor, called out "Yee-haw" when they finished.

But the ceremony began with the voice of Gary Foreman, whom McDonald had brought back to be the master of ceremonies. His voice, projected over speakers in the chilly darkness, rang with a showman's air, heightening the moment's solemnity.

"Welcome to sacred ground.

"Welcome to the cradle of Texas liberty.

"Welcome to the Alamo."

CHAPTER 23
THE PROBLEM WITH PHIL

As of this writing, and despite all these irksome lawsuits, the $450 million Alamo revitalization effort remains very real, its centerpiece the new museum to be built around the collection of artifacts and documents Phil Collins donated to the state in 2014. Everyone involved — George P. Bush, the GLO, the city of San Antonio, and the Alamo itself — has a lot riding on this. Finally, they promise, the Alamo will be a "world-class destination."

There's just one problem. According to a dozen prominent antiquities dealers, collectors, and archaeologists, not to mention the Alamo's longtime official historian, the Collins collection is not what it's cracked up to be. The historian, Bruce Winders, who was the first to review the collection's authentication papers in 2014, tells us its documentation is so sketchy he repeatedly warned his superiors about it. Asked about his level of concern, Winders replies, "There's enough to make you think that there is some deception going on here."

Numerous private collectors we spoke with also question the star items in the Collins collection, the ones associated with the Alamo's holy trinity.

"I have had the opportunity to study, appraise, and value numerous collections," says Compton LaBauve, a prominent Louisiana collector. "No collection is totally devoid of at least a couple of items that are questionable, at the very least. But the Collins collection contains more questionable pieces, with more than questionable provenance, by far, than any collection I'm aware of."

To understand how this came to be, it's crucial to understand how Collins built his collection. The story begins in 2004, when the singer brought his wife and son to visit the Alamo after a performance in Houston. As we've mentioned, he was a lifelong Alamo fan, and had already begun collecting a few things, mostly documents.

Bruce Winders, who met Collins about this time, recalls thinking that he seemed emotionally adrift, as if he were searching for a new purpose in life after his singing career had peaked in the 1990s. "He had been a rock star, and as you age, that all started to go away," Winders says. "He was kind of at a loss. He was trying to figure out who he was now. And the Alamo filled that void for him. It was a phase for him. His Alamo phase."

After Collins toured the Alamo that afternoon, he walked around the corner to the History Shop, a touristy storefront boutique that sold a variety of old documents and a handful of Alamo artifacts. Its owner, a tough, leathery gent in his seventies named Jim Guimarin, had discovered a lucrative niche in the collectibles business. People would often wander into the Alamo hoping to sell something — an old gun or document — but the Daughters had no budget to buy such items. Instead, they would suggest the collector take their find to Guimarin's shop.

"And the people would come over," he says, "and if I wanted it, I'd buy it." He kept those items in the glass cases for other tourists hungry to possess more from the Alamo than a coonskin cap or T-shirt. He also got good at spotting fakes.

"I've had people bring me maps and things that were not real. And I've seen a few documents that are very suspicious. But if you've got a knowledge of the history, know a little something about paper or metal, you can spot things," Guimarin said.

Guimarin did a decent trade selling rare books, guns, and the odd collectible, but his real expertise and income came from documents. Over the years, he had emerged as the go-to expert for restoring and preserving the trove of antique papers and maps the city, county, and the Daughters had amassed over the years.

That day when Collins wandered into the shop, the two struck up a conversation. "He was interested in documents, and I had a Sam Houston document," Guimarin says. "He bought that later, but he left me his information and said whenever I got something, that he would like first look at it. He was interested in anything to do with the Alamo."

Guimarin understood the history bug; he'd become interested as a child when he learned his great-grandfather owned a slave plantation in Haiti. In his twenties, Guimarin traveled to St. Thomas looking for more information and came across his great-grandmother's passport. He became hooked on collecting historical documents and maps.

Guimarin was never a big collector of Alamo artifacts. In fact, major collectors rarely bought anything from Guimarin and didn't think much of the History Shop's minor bits and bobs, such as a Mexican uniform button or an old knife. But the shop's location guaranteed foot traffic from tourists like Collins. Guimarin knew a good customer when he saw one, so he started seeking out items for Collins, who complimented him on his reasonable markups. The business relationship became a friendship.

Guimarin introduced Collins to a new world of Alamo history buffs, most of whom did not recognize him as a rock star. What mattered to the Alamo-heads was what you knew and what you owned. Collins soon wanted to own just about anything that could even remotely be connected with the Alamo. To help his top customer fulfill his dreams, Guimarin recruited a young man who hoped to one day take over the History Shop. Intense, motormouthed, and desperate to please, Alex McDuffie understood the world of rifles, swords, knives, bullets, cannonballs, and paintings. He'd been dealing in antiques for a few years and had a talent for finding rare objects. Guimarin also recruited his old friend Sam Nesmith, a former Alamo curator, to look over everything Guimarin and McDuffie found and to certify its authenticity. Soon the Collins collection began to grow exponentially. Phil was thrilled.

The relationship went to another level in 2007, when Guimarin, concerned about the security of his collection, tried to install a floor safe beneath his building. There, workers found an adobe wall from the Alamo's original irrigation canal, or acequia. Around it, they found uniform buttons and metal objects easily attributable to the Mexican army. Guimarin wanted to dig further, but he didn't own the building. That's when he got the idea. By this point, Collins was visiting San Antonio three or four times a year, wandering the Alamo, coming into the shop, perusing Guimarin's latest finds. Over margaritas, Collins listened to Guimarin's pitch. He immediately loved it.

Which is how Collins came to purchase Guimarin's building, and financed a dig. They started in January 2008 with a six-foot-deep hole down to the limestone bedrock. Then workers dug horizontally until someone would spot an object and call Guimarin over. He would take a photo of the rusty chunk of iron, brass, or bronze, then carefully extract it.

In addition to the small items, they found three firepits evenly spaced in a straight line, the kind of thing soldiers might do. Mexican accounts reported that cavalrymen had camped near the History Shop's location, and the excavation turned up bullets, some easily attributable to the Mexican army because they were made from bronze. The diggers also found cannonballs, belt buckles, hat insignia, and countless horseshoes. Guimarin is convinced the firepits and artifacts are all from the March 1836 battle.

What Collins didn't keep, Guimarin sold. "A lot of people came through, and they're paying seven or eight hundred dollars for a horseshoe," Guimarin says. "I sell these things at atrocious prices, but where else are you going to get it?"

During a visit to his middle-class home outside San Antonio, Guimarin took us on a tour of his one-acre compound. He showed off the workshop where he still restores books, the shed where he uses electrolysis to get the crud off the stuff from the History Shop dig. And he showed off his antique map collection. He still assembles little archival boxes filled with rusty horseshoes and has set boxes aside for his grandkids.

Guimarin provides a booklet of documents with every sale, attributing the objects to the Collins dig. The state, which has since bought the building, has approved a historical marker explaining that Santa Anna's cavalry camped there.

Collins had rarely felt so fulfilled. Collecting artifacts, financing a dig, and hanging out with a bunch of other old men obsessed with the Alamo made him happy. "I have to say it was one of the most exciting projects I've been involved with," he wrote later in his book.* "I managed to get my hands dirty on the few occasions I was able to get there, and it was very exciting knowing I was digging in earth not seen since those fateful days back in 1836."

Collins and Guimarin shared their work with the *Express-News* in a brief item published in March 2009 that reported the unearthing of "hundreds of cannonballs, documents and other artifacts from the Alamo," but gave little detail. "Basically, now I've stopped being Phil Collins the singer," Collins told the newspaper. "This has become what I do."

The History Shop became Collins and

* We made more than a dozen attempts to interview Collins, and asked Alex McDuffie to contact him on our behalf. Collins sent a message through McDuffie saying that he has nothing more to add than what is in his book, and declined to answer any questions.

Guimarin's unofficial headquarters, a kind of Alamo Central. When Guimarin heard that a fifteen-foot-square diorama of the mission complete with a sound show depicting the battle was available in Atlanta, Collins wrote a check. Once it arrived, Collins recorded a voiceover, which drew hundreds of tourists.

McDuffie, meanwhile, was poring through auction catalogs, meeting with collectors, and researching objects to sell Collins. An aspiring museum curator who admits he was never a good student, McDuffie spent eight years searching for Alamo artifacts and collected commissions on the resales. McDuffie estimates he discovered and acquired 80 percent of the artifacts in Collins's collection. "He's like a hound dog," says Guimarin. "He gets the scent and, boy, he stays after it."

McDuffie invited us to his small ranch-style home near Lake Travis. It's decorated with McDuffie's Texana collection, including portraits that might be — maybe — of Sam Houston and Jim Bowie. McDuffie was a ball of nervous energy, with long wet hair parted down the middle that dried as we talked. His obsession started during his junior year in high school outside Houston when his mother gave him *13 Days to Glory,*

Lon Tinkle's thirteen-chapter story of Santa Anna's siege of the Alamo. The book is a fast-moving retelling of every Alamo myth, beloved by many Alamo enthusiasts, and ridiculed by historians.

"I was just fascinated, just really absorbed. This is really the first book that I read cover to cover without it being an assignment for school," McDuffie said.

McDuffie was designing and building websites in 2000 when a notorious collectibles dealer named Alfred Van Fossen hired him. Before his death in 2006, Van Fossen was renowned for selling questionable and even fake items supposedly associated with the Alamo. Among the disputed items was a knife he claimed was Jim Bowie's that has since gone missing. In the late 1990s, still nurturing his boyhood fascination with the old mission, McDuffie quit his website business to work alongside Van Fossen. "He had some really great pieces, but he also, I didn't know at the time, had a lot of fakes," McDuffie says. "And so that was my first exposure to antiques. I found out he was a real scoundrel."

McDuffie fell out with Van Fossen and started dealing antiques on his own. He found a mentor in Guimarin's friend Sam Nesmith, who gave him some out-of-the-box advice. Documents proving an artifact's authenticity are crucial, Nesmith counseled. But in the end, you have to trust your gut. "Why do you care what other people think?" he recalls Nesmith saying. "What do you think? What does your gut tell you? When I started listening to my own gut, that's when I really started finding pieces that were just really great."*

The four-man team hoovered up just about every Alamo artifact that came on the market over the next decade. Guimarin spent $750,000 of Collins's money at just one Dallas auction. McDuffie was the scout and procurer. Nesmith vetted what he found. Guimarin sold the best to Collins, who jetted in several times a year to review their progress. They would have margaritas at El Mirador and walk the Alamo grounds at night. Guimarin once took Collins to Goliad, where the State of Texas rents out the priests' quarters in the old mission. They sat on the walls there and tried to imagine the massacres of 1836.

None of this is unusual in the world of

---

* Sam Nesmith died in 2018. A memorial website includes dozens of photographs of him posing with Guimarin, McDuffie, and Collins, and includes a warm note from Collins.

wealthy collectors, who have curators and dealers waiting on them hand and foot. Exclusive tours, special access, and VIP treatment are part of the package. Ultra-wealthy collectors are called whales, and you do everything possible to keep them happy, which means a constant supply of objects to satisfy their obsession. McDuffie knew a guy from his days working with Van Fossen who had something Collins would certainly want: Jim Bowie's personal knife. But the Bowie knife owned by Los Angeles–area collector Joseph Musso had become so controversial that collectors had named it after him. Depending on whom you believe, the "Musso knife" either belonged to Bowie or is an elaborate hoax. Thanks to Collins, it now belongs to the people of Texas.

The legend goes that Bowie and his brothers started commissioning fighting knives after the Sandbar Fight in 1827, which made Jim famous for his big blades. The Bowie brothers' designs evolved from a minor variation on a Spanish-style butcher knife to the curved version most people think of today. As Bowie's fame spread, hundreds of knife makers across the country started approximating Bowie's design. They became a must-have for any greenhorn looking for adventure. There are so many, and they are so common, that there are thousands of collectors and they formed the Antique Bowie Knife Association to argue about what's what.

One highly debatable version of the legend goes that Bowie created the iconic design in 1830 and paid Arkansas blacksmith James Black to make it. Bowie purportedly met Black at a little tavern near the town of Washington called Stuart's, where he was plotting the takeover of Texas with Davy Crockett and William B. Travis. That part is probably not true, but Bowie did visit Arkansas and probably met Black.

Fast-forward to California in 1970. Musso, who won a lifetime achievement award from Hollywood's Art Directors Guild, is at a gun show and spots a handsome Bowie knife that looks like it could date to the nineteenth century. The feature that sets it apart is a strip of brass that extends from the handguard to the dip in the knife, called the clip. The brass back supposedly helps parry an opponent's knife and reinforces the blade. Purists in the Antique Bowie Knife Association believe brass-backed knives came along in the 1850s. Musso says he did not think much about it until eleven years later when he was cleaning some of his guns and decided to rub a little solvent to clean the crud off his Bowie knife.

"In doing so, I found it had the initials J.B. on it," Musso told us. "I had to sit down and have a long talk with myself because I knew that I didn't put it on it."

Anyone could have scratched those letters into the metal, so Musso paid companies to metallurgically determine the age of the knife. The report, he says, revealed that the steel was from the 1830s, made in a relatively primitive charcoal furnace. Another lab determined the brass was consistent with a small workshop, with trace elements matching those found in a green sand deposit 250 yards from Black's Arkansas workshop. Musso says that's when he began to question the Bowie knife association's dogma about brass backs. He knew Bowie's ancestors were Scots and wondered if he might have been inspired by seventeenth-century Scottish dirks featuring brass backs. Musso took the knife to a psychic, who confirmed it belonged to Bowie.

"Metallurgically, I have a knife that belonged to an American officer with the initials J.B., of Scottish descent, that was made by this blacksmith around 1830," Musso claims.

Musso hunted for documentary evidence

and came across the illustrated 1855 memoirs of Sam Houston. In one sketch, Houston is holding a Bowie knife that appears to have a strip of metal along its spine.

"I can't say 100 percent that it's Jim Bowie's knife, but there is a lot of evidence for that," Musso said. "But I would say it's a very important knife."

McDuffie thinks Musso is too modest. By his standards, he believes there is more than enough evidence to attribute the knife to Bowie. Guimarin is more circumspect. "Is it the same kind of knife that they used? Yes, it is. But is it THE knife? I don't know," Guimarin said.

Nevertheless, Guimarin and McDuffie arranged for Collins to buy the knife for a rumored purchase price of $1.5 million. "I really never planned to sell it," Musso said. "But I'm kind of grateful that Phil did approach me because he agrees, and if things go through, it can be shared with the world."

McDuffie learned from Musso, and soon he had eerily similar good luck with a saber, which he calls one of the best pieces in the Collins collection.

McDuffie was attending an antique show when another seller offered what he called "an Alamo sword." The dealer relayed how the nineteenth-century saber had belonged to a U.S. soldier who had told his family that he was ordered to fight with the Texians at the Battle of San Jacinto. According to family lore, this young soldier brought the saber home as a war prize after the battle. McDuffie called Nesmith and Guimarin for advice, but they dismissed the story as hearsay. McDuffie's gut convinced him to buy it anyway. When he got it home, he decided to apply a little solvent, just as Musso described.

"I noticed something on the spine," McDuffie said. "I called Joe Musso because, you know, I didn't want to mess up the patina. He said, put some Hoppe's bore solvent on it and let it sit for a day."

After letting it soak for two days, McDuffie made out an inscription: "J. Bowie."

McDuffie took it to a metallurgist, who determined the sword was from the right period. The next question was: Who had found Bowie's saber? McDuffie researched the surname of the family that sold it and found that General Edmund Gaines had listed their ancestor as a deserter from Fort Jesup, Louisiana. Then his name also showed up on the Battle of San Jacinto muster rolls. McDuffie became convinced a Mexican soldier took the sword off Bowie at the Alamo, then lost it at the Battle of

San Jacinto, where this soldier acquired it.

"It's like the story wanted to tell itself," McDuffie said. "I sold that to Phil."

A little dab of solvent has helped McDuffie make several more significant discoveries. "So many pieces that I've bought over the years that they advertise or say it's unmarked, you can't really make out anything," McDuffie explained. "But if you put a little oil on it and you take it out in the sunlight, and you look at it at angles, a lot of times you'll find that the engraving — maybe identifying somebody's name or a maker — is just filled in with grime."

In the space of a few years, Team Collins found and purchased objects thought lost to the ages, or at least to Mexican soldiers eager to collect as much booty from the battlefield as possible. Guimarin purchased many items at public auctions on behalf of Collins, a number of which have their own set of authentication challenges. At one Heritage auction, for instance, Guimarin bought a "sword belt" purported to have belonged to Travis. The seller, an Arkansas dealer named Gary Hendershott, promised to send along documentation connecting the item to Travis but never did. In the small world of Alamo artifact collectors, he became Guimarin's and McDuffie's archenemy. Collins kept the belt anyway and, in his book, claims it belonged to Travis.

While perusing another auction catalog, McDuffie spotted a consignment lot that included a pistol, a small knife, a powder horn, and a pouch. Hendershott listed them as a "New Mexican Hunting Pouch, Pistol & Knife, ca. 19th century," and he was selling them on consignment for Jeff Hengesbaugh, an antiquities dealer in Glorieta, New Mexico. McDuffie would have preferred to buy the lot directly from Hengesbaugh, but his fellow collector had already listed it with Hendershott. McDuffie overcame his reluctance to deal with Hendershott because his gut told him this could be something special. The bag was embossed with the initials E.S., and McDuffie was convinced it belonged to Erastus "Deaf" Smith, the scout who rode out of the Alamo for help.

Nesmith initially rejected McDuffie's theory because he doubted Smith would have owned the percussion cap pistol, which was a new technology uncommon in 1830s Texas. But then McDuffie found an eyewitness account from the Battle of San Jacinto describing Smith firing a percussion cap pistol. McDuffie took the handgrip off and found a Mexican milagro charm that he theorizes Smith's Mexican wife put there for his protection. McDuffie then applied his solvent technique to the knife and, he says, the initials WBT revealed themselves. He believes they stand for William Barret Travis and theorizes that Travis gave the knife to Deaf Smith when he left the Alamo seeking reinforcements. Collins bought the whole lot.

In our conversations with McDuffie and Guimarin, they provided vivid descriptions of their hunt for rare objects.* One adventure involved a trip to Mexico, a mysterious intermediary, and a suspected drug cartel murder.

McDuffie says the lead on Davy Crockett's pouch, powder horns, and musket balls came from a Mexican waiter and seminary student living in Colorado. His name was Heriberto Delgado Mujica, and his family sent him to Colorado after his brother was kidnapped and beaten to death. The Delgado family owned a collectibles shop in

---

* Recently McDuffie has worked on another Bowie knife that also appeared to have no markings. His oil technique revealed "J. P. Bayless" engraved on the blade, which McDuffie says is evidence the knife belonged to Joseph Pleasant Bayless, who also died at the Alamo.

Mexico City, and they claimed to be in contact with the descendants of Mexican soldier and memoirist Enrique de la Peña. They also claimed to have a stash of Crockett items their ancestor had taken from the Alamo after the battle.

After securing Collins's approval, Guimarin says, he traveled to Mexico City. "I know it was de la Peña's people," he insists. "They gave me enough things to know that I was dealing with the right people, but I never could get to them direct."

McDuffie, however, was not so sure. "Heriberto had previously sent me pictures of that stuff, and it didn't really do anything for me," he says. "Jim comes back with it. Maybe it was [Crockett's], I don't know. Did it come from the de la Peña family? Yeah, it did. Was the de la Peña family being honest about it? I don't know."

None of which, of course, amounts to anything close to actual authentication. Oh, and before we move on, there's just one quick coda. Heriberto Delgado was murdered in 2016 by "assassins" who burst into his apartment and shot him. No one's quite sure why, and his friends and family are not answering questions.

If any of this — or all of this — seems a tad

far-fetched to you, well, you're not alone. Even Guimarin acknowledges having doubts about some of the collection's marquee items, including a rifle said to have belonged to Crockett. "I wasn't involved in that, Phil just told me about it," he says. "I mean, it was a rifle, it wasn't at the Alamo, but it belonged to Crockett, so they say. Who's to say?" This, we should point out, is not the kind of authentication many collectors insist upon.

Winders acknowledges he had heard disquieting rumors about Guimarin, McDuffie, and their work with Collins, but says, "It really wasn't my role to ask about any of that." Besides, he goes on, "we liked Jim, he was a business partner for the Alamo at one point, and it just becomes one of those things where you didn't ask questions."

In fact, when the General Land Office got into the lawsuit with the Daughters, the agency hired Guimarin and Nesmith to assess and appraise the Alamo collection. Guimarin shared an anecdote about appraising a knife someone had donated to the Alamo fifty years ago. The knife as an antique was worth $5,000. But if you could connect it to the Alamo, it was worth $60,000. The value relied on believing a story, and piecing together stories to somewhat plausibly connect artifacts to the Alamo's most famous fighters was Guimarin's and McDuffie's specialty. But what Guimarin and McDuffie say is sufficient evidence to back up Collins's claims in his book, others consider circumstantial at best and potentially fraudulent at worst.

When we asked Winders whether McDuffie's name set off any warning bells, he replied: "Bells? All the bells. Yeah, kind of like Notre-Dame. People are amazed at some of the artifacts he comes up with. How does he find so many choice artifacts?"

Serious Alamo collectors watched Collins build his collection from a distance with bemusement, wondering if he had more money than sense. Why wasn't he reaching out to them or other prominent dealers? Why was he trusting these three men so much? Why not get independent assessments? While the idea of spending millions to purchase suspicious collectibles is offensive to many, Collins was only harming his own bank account. After all, if the crown prince of Saudi Arabia can spend $450 million on what many people believe is a fake Leonardo da Vinci, then why can't Collins spend a few million on some old knives that he wants to believe were at the Alamo? But then Collins decided to publish a book touting his collection, one filled with bold claims. And then he gave his collection to the State of Texas and required the state to spend millions on a new museum to house it. The Collins collection suddenly demanded greater scrutiny, so we started asking questions.

By 2010, working closely with Guimarin, Nesmith, and McDuffie, Collins had amassed what appeared to be the world's most extensive collection of Alamo-sourced artifacts. It was at this point that he approached a small Texas publisher known for its Alamo offerings, State House Press, with an idea of publishing a coffee-table book. State House was enthusiastic; this would be by far the most visible book it had ever published. *The Alamo and Beyond: A Collector's Journey* is a gorgeously illustrated book describing the Collins collection in detail. But as we discovered, the book is also a source of ridicule and horror in the Alamo collecting and archaeological world.

"I could actually write a book lampooning this book," says Thomas Nuckols, an archaeological consultant to the Texas Historical Commission and an expert on Alamo-era artifacts. "Just about everything they said was used at the Alamo, these are not Alamo-related items. This book, it embarrasses collectors. It embarrasses me. A lot of us enjoyed the book just because of the silliness of it. You have to understand. A lot of people believe the Collins stuff is the real thing. It's not. And that's a problem."

Two professors from McMurry University in Abilene signed on to oversee the book project. Even before meeting with Collins, though, they had concerns. Not so much about the collection's historical documents, everything from Bowie's 1830 application for Mexican citizenship to letters signed by everyone from Crockett to Stephen F. Austin; those seemed authentic. The artifacts, though, especially those attributed to the Alamo trinity, were another thing.

"I was kind of in charge of quality control, and I knew that provenance on some of these artifacts was, uh, well, not too solid," recalls Stephen L. Hardin, probably best known for his 1994 book *Texian Iliad*. "I said, 'You know, Phil, we can't just say this is Davy Crockett's shot pouch.' It very well could be, but, well, we asked a lot of tough questions. He was always very cooperative and was very receptive. He doesn't want to be embarrassed either. I can't speak for Phil, but my sense is that he knew that some of the artifacts might not be the genuine article. But if he bought literally all of them, some would be. There for a while, you know, he was buying literally everything that came on the market. When you got a guy out there that buys everything, to people who manufacture bogus artifacts, that's a bird's nest on the ground."

As they readied the book's text, Hardin says he urged Collins to couch his claims for authenticity wherever possible. "If you go through the book carefully, you will see a lot of qualifiers, and that's on me," he says. "That's a standard academic practice called hedging. There's a lot of couching. That's because we didn't want this to come back and bite us in the ass. All we're saying is, 'This is the Phil Collins collection.' Beyond that . . ." Here Hardin's voice trails off. "Beyond that," he goes on after a moment, "and with further research, let's just say we have heard the same reservations that you have."

The episode is touched on in a lengthy 2012 Collins profile in *Texas Monthly* written by John Spong (a friend of ours). In it, Hardin argues that even if certain items couldn't be definitively linked to Bowie, Travis, or Crockett, they still had value as period pieces. "Take the belt that suppos-

517

edly held Travis' sword," Hardin said. "That's really hard to prove. But it's an 1830's sword belt from the Texas Revolution, and that's significant." He added: "We had some very frank conversations with Phil. Sometimes he convinced us, and sometimes he didn't."

When Spong asked Collins about the belt, the smiling, easygoing mien the singer had consistently displayed to that point vanished. "This is all bullshit," Collins vented in an email. "Whoever described that to you has no idea of what went on and should mind their own business! I have as much provenance as you could hope for. In my book, I have a question mark in the title of the essay relating to the belt because its origin, like most Alamo artifacts, is hard to prove. Then if you do try to prove it, there are people lining up to shoot you down in flames."[1]

Still, no one involved seems to have suggested that concerns were severe enough to merit canceling the project. It was, after all, the biggest, most expensive book the publisher had ever put out. Winders agreed to write a glowing introductory essay. He's a bit sheepish about that now. "At the time I wrote the essay, I only knew about the Musso knife," he says. "I didn't have major

concerns. His collection was still in Switzer-
land."

In the end, the book is rife with contradic-
tions. While the text is dotted with hedges
and couched claims, the titles above the
individual items are not.* The description
of the shot pouch and powder horns attributed to Crockett, for example, claims
they came from de la Peña's family but
acknowledges "some things are not known"
about the items.

No one seems to have publicly questioned
the collection when *The Alamo and Beyond*
was published in 2012. But across the
clubby world of antiquities dealers and collectors, jaws began to drop. "I've dug the
sites, I know what weapons were used and
the artifacts Phil has just don't fit," says
Nuckols. "He says he has cannonballs shot
by the Twin Sisters at San Jacinto. Nobody
knows what caliber those cannons were! We
just don't know enough about them to find
a cannonball at San Jacinto and say it was
fired from one of the Twin Sisters. He shows
pictures of rusted metal and says these were
shot out of Texas cannons. It's just rusty
metal! It could be literally anything."

* The one exception: that Travis belt. Its title is
followed by a question mark.

What incensed Nuckols, though, was the description of items from the dig Collins would include in his book. On page 209, to cite just one example, Collins writes that given the array of equine artifacts they uncovered, "it seemed indisputable" they had found a campsite used by the Mexican cavalry commander Juan José Andrade.

"They found horseshoes," he says. "Collins says they were from Santa Anna's cavalry. In fact, we know that in the late 1800s, there was a blacksmith shop on that site — everything they found there they attributed to the Alamo. I've been to the shop; I've been to the plaza. And they're just not. Those artifacts could be from any time period."

Mark D. Zalesky, the longtime editor of *Knife Magazine,* was floored by claims Collins made for knives in his collection, including a folding knife Collins said Bowie wore in his boot. "There are seven knives in the book, and one, the Sam Houston knife, may be authentic," Zalesky says. "Every other knife is either fake or misrepresented. The boot knife is a laugher. It's a joke. It's an old knife, but it's unlikely it even would've been in this country. How is that associated with Jim Bowie?"

Zalesky, who has followed the controversies surrounding the Musso knife for more than twenty years, has no doubt it too is a fake. When Musso first began showing it in the late 1980s, Zalesky says, "very quickly the experts on this reacted negatively to the knife and were sort of beaten back with threats of lawsuits from Joe. Many battles were fought over this during the '90s, in 'Antiques Digest,' that sort of thing. Over a period of time, it got to where the knife magazines, and the knife community, more or less, rejected this knife, while its owner continued to push the knife and finally found a community that accepted it, and that community was the Alamo community. Musso cultivated this community that accepted his knife and his story. And finally, he found a fellow" — Collins — "who had a lot of money and wanted Jim Bowie's knife.

"This knife was probably made in England in 1971 or 1972. I have a photo of the knife in London in '72, from the London *Daily Telegraph*, [held] by the girlfriend of a dealer who is a known associate of the most notorious Bowie knife counterfeiter of all, a man named Dickie Washer," Zalesky says. "I can trace that exact knife from 1972 to how it got to Joe. And we have Joe's lab reports, including all the juicy bits Joe always left out. Among other things, they clearly show that it's not [made from] the steel they used during that period. . . . It's fake."

If the skeptics are right, Collins's explanations suggest a serious level of gullibility. To cite just one of many examples, he actually acknowledges the Bowie boot knife's skeptics in his text, but says he puts his faith in a yarn that Bowie may have given it to a woman in Missouri when both lived there; her family supposedly kept it for decades. "All we can do with provenance is digest, analyse, dig further, and make conclusions without too much cynicism and a little bit of trust," Collins writes. "Adding up the evidence given, I have little reason to doubt that this possibly was James Bowie's folding knife."

Little reason to doubt it possibly was the knife? There's some twisty reasoning for you. Read the book's text carefully, though, and you can find any number of places where Collins all but admits he is taking provenance on faith, something no reputable collector would ever do. On page 303, for instance, in the description of a Brown Bess musket "taken from the San Jacinto battlefield," Collins comes right out and acknowledges it: "Of course, like many things associated with the battles of the Texas Revolution, there's little hard proof of this — just speculation."

Hendershott was stunned to see the lot he sold to McDuffie attributed to Travis and does not mince words. He never saw the knife in person because Hengesbaugh sent it directly to McDuffie, but when we gave him the available facts about the WBT engraving, he said the knife guard had clearly been altered. "It's a fake!" he emailed us. "I've seen this a 100 times."

In page after page of the book, Collins attributes hundreds of artifacts to people and places that do not add up. In the opinion of the experts and collectors we spoke to, the collection's centerpiece items — those said to have belonged to Bowie, Crockett, Travis, Sam Houston, and the courier James Bonham — are all of highly questionable authenticity. There are fifteen in all, including two knives attributed to Bowie, the Crockett shot pouch, the Travis belt, and a Crockett rifle. We asked Hardin whether even one of these items has anything like solid provenance. He lowered his voice.

"No," he said. "No."

Both Guimarin and McDuffie acknowledge they've heard widespread doubts about the collection. They dismiss it all as professional jealousy. "Every single enemy that I've made has been because they've valued their ego over the truth," McDuffie says. "Someone brings you something, and you tell them, 'I'm sorry, I don't think it's right because of X, Y, and Z,' and they just have it out for you." He singles out Hendershott as someone trying to ruin him to settle an old grudge. Guimarin also accuses collectors critical of the Collins collection of envy. "Everything is fake to them, unless, of course, it's in their collection."

McDuffie shared with us the provenance document he provided Collins when he sold the Deaf Smith items, and the document offers no solid proof. Since McDuffie and Guimarin claimed the controversy was nothing more than bad blood within the Alamo community, we went outside it and asked Henry Yallop, the Keeper of Armour and Edged Weapons at the United Kingdom's Royal Armouries, about properly authenticating artifacts. He agreed to speak generally about the field but could only offer an opinion on a specific object after viewing it, and then only to the legal owner. He deferred some of our technical questions to the museum's conservators.

Yallop said armies sometimes engraved a

unit identifier or a weapon number on early nineteenth-century edged weapons for inventory purposes. Additional decorations were sometimes used to denote that objects were used at specific battles and turn them into presentation pieces. For irregular forces he couldn't really comment or think of examples in which weapons were personally marked in this way, beyond presentation arms and the like. The Royal Armouries conservators said that in their experience, engravings could be obscured by dirt and grime, but they were "not aware of an instance where the application of gun oil and solvents made inscriptions magically appear."

Yallop said he knew of no instance where an obscured engraving led to the attribution of a weapon to a famous warrior. "On its own, an object being of the right date and having relevant initials would not be considered as definitive 'proof' by most people," Yallop wrote in a reply to questions. "In certain circumstances, this would enable further research to be done which could help build evidence."

For centuries, unscrupulous dealers have altered historic objects to make them more valuable, Yallop added. "It should be noted that such engraving could have been added many years ago, but that does not necessarily mean they are from an object's 'working life,' " he wrote. "In the past people may have added engravings or other decoration to an object that was already thought/known to be associated with something. Or they could have been added with no such association, to deliberately deceive." After the book's publication in 2012, flaws in the Collins collection became an open secret in the collecting world. Yet no one appears to have communicated any of this skepticism to the GLO's Jerry Patterson when he began negotiating with Collins in early 2014. After the formal announcement that July, in fact, the donation process went forward without a hitch. Winders remembers that everything arrived at the Alamo that October. He worked with an Alamo-GLO team tasked with cataloging it all.

"He had everything professionally removed from its frames and boxed up, very nice plywood boxes, furniture-grade plywood, it was pretty spectacular the way it came," Winders recalls. "We spent about two months unpacking everything."

After that, Winders turned his attention to the four books of receipts Collins furnished laying out where he had acquired his items as well as their provenance — their proof of authenticity. Nesmith and Guimarin had drafted many of these reports detailing the items' history and discovery. What Winders read left him deeply concerned. "It was kind of painful because I was finding things that were just somewhat disturbing, you know, this isn't right," he remembers. "What I saw was, the big things are gonna be connected to the Big Three, Bowie, Crockett, and Travis, right? What I saw were items that said they were of this type; they *could've* been at the Alamo." But again and again, Winders leafed through the documentation and found no proof. "The fact was," he says, "they only *might* have been at the Alamo."

It was at that point, Winders goes on, that he voiced concerns to the Alamo's board and the GLO's deputy director of archives and records, Mark Lambert. "I told Mark Lambert, I told our Alamo people past and present, that this is gonna have to be addressed at some point," he says. "There was a lot of conversation going back and forth. Mark Lambert was concerned. . . . He was kind of in the same position as I was when I talk to my management. It was always, 'We'll deal with that when the time comes.' "

The problem is that the time didn't come.

Once the collection was donated, "we inventoried it and pumped it up and put it out in the press releases," recalls a onetime GLO staffer. "I'm not aware of any due diligence, honestly. Our job was to get the most [press coverage] out of that as we could. It wasn't to make sure that that knife that he was holding was actually Jim Bowie's knife."

Guimarin and McDuffie, meanwhile, dismiss any concerns Winders or the GLO may have. Winders, Guimarin says, is "super conservative." McDuffie scoffs at the GLO's expertise. "The General Land Office doesn't know their head from their ass with their stuff," he fairly snorts. "They don't know what they're looking at." He says he provided Guimarin and Nesmith with detailed reports providing evidence of the objects' authenticity, including metallurgical reports and photos showing how he revealed the inscriptions.

We asked the General Land Office to let us see Collins's receipt books. The agency declared them confidential, but we won a ruling from the Texas Attorney General's Office that made them available under the Texas Public Information Act with only the prices paid redacted. Sam Nesmith signed most of the certificates of authenticity, and they are a master class in how to weave fairy tales while using enough hedge words to stay out of jail.

Each certificate begins with a detailed professional description of the object but then launches into prosaic storytelling. A U.S. military hat insignia, which collectors call a shako plate, offers an example of the form:

"This style of plate would have been in use by some of the U.S. Army veterans who came to Texas with the volunteer units in 1835 or 1836. It would be a natural thing for them to wear their old, military shako whenever they were 'going off to war,' " Nesmith writes.[2] "This type of plate could have been worn by any of the volunteer units at the Alamo, Goliad or San Jacinto. This particular specimen was dug up in Mexico and probably represents a souvenir that was taken back home by a Mexican soldier."

Nesmith is extra vague when it comes to certifying Crockett's shot pouch. He uses many passive sentences, reports well-known facts, but then avoids explanation for his attribution.

"The pouch appears to have a most interesting history and was recovered from the personal effects of Colonel José Enrique de

529

la Peña. It is listed in an inventory of his property at the time of his death in 1840. It is also stated that these items were given to Don José Enrique de la Peña, while serving at the Alamo during the war in Texas, by 'D' David Croquet in appreciation of de la Peña's attempts to save his life," recalled Nesmith.[3]

Yes, every Alamo-head is aware of the probate document, but how does Nesmith know this particular pouch belonged to Crockett? He never explains. "As the pouch appears to be authentic, it is truly a historical, American artifact carried by Crockett during the Battle of the Alamo in 1836," he writes.

Nesmith's imagination truly takes off when it comes to what he describes as de la Peña's sword, which he says bears the marks of battle. With absolutely nothing to back up his claims, Nesmith testifies: "It is quite likely that de la Peña carried the sword in the heaviest of the fighting during the Battle of the Alamo."

Nesmith joins with McDuffie and Musso to certify the authenticity of the knife engraved with the initials WBT. "Collectively, an unbiased conclusion can be drawn that the group is true Texana material," the certificate says. "More importantly, when considered as a whole, research into the clues left behind on each artifact suggests a common point of origin, a definite association with a specific individual within a very narrow historic window; the attribution is solid and beyond probability."[4]

Nesmith's most bizarre testament, though, is reserved for the Musso Bowie knife. The first page is titled "Sam's Psychic Impressions on JB's Knife."

Nesmith tells the story of a young Mexican soldier discovering a brass-back knife after the Battle of the Alamo and his sergeant confiscating it. The sergeant's commander takes it for himself. And so the absurd story goes on until the knife ends up in California, where Musso can buy it at a gun show.[5]

Another authenticator, described as "a descendant of one of the martyrs of the Alamo and a forensics analyst," offers his independent psychic impression. "There is an overwhelming sadness associated with the knife," he declares. He then provides a complementary explanation for how it left the Alamo.[6]

Nesmith concludes: "It is most probably the knife carried by Bowie during his encounter with Comanche Indians at the Battle of Calf Creek, while searching for the

Lost San Saba Mine. It is also the knife carried by Bowie during the Siege of the Alamo and probably the last object he held prior to his death."[7]

Nesmith, Guimarin, and McDuffie provided the only authentication for most of the Collins collection's items. If Collins sought outside opinions, he did not include them in his files. But you can see the collector's fever rise over time. What started in 2001 as a staid, legitimate collection of early Texas documents becomes increasingly fabulist between 2008 and 2011. To judge from the claims made in his book, Collins wants to believe the fantastical stories attached to these objects, and he's happy to spread them even though he knows many experts have serious reservations.

We asked on several occasions for an interview with Bush or Lambert, but Bush's communications director never got back to us.

"By the time you get to Bush, it's 'We're gonna build this spectacular museum worthy of the collection,'" Winders said. "Both me and Mark had raised our concerns, that was about all we could do. I figured I would still be at the Alamo, and I could handle some of these concerns." He stops, then sighs. "But it didn't work out that way."

Winders was forced out in 2018, robbing the Alamo of an influential voice advocating a vetting of the collection. "I don't think the GLO or [the Alamo] are prepared for or have any idea the ruckus the collecting world is going to raise once the collection is made public," Winders says. "I've warned them, but they see the collection as a big draw for the future museum." Voicing doubts, he goes on, doesn't simply risk tarnishing the collection's reputation; it puts the entire $450 million museum project in jeopardy.

"There has always been the fear that Phil would take the collection back," Winders says.

That's exactly what happened in June 2020, when Collins began losing patience with the slow pace toward building his museum.

"I have to admit I'm getting more than a little discouraged with the speed and urgency that is being displayed regarding my collection and related museum. Please update me with a likely museum date," Collins wrote to Hector Valle, one of Bush's lieutenants. "I don't want my collection sitting in boxes in a basement. This is the situation now it seems. I realize there are more pressing things on P's list, but on my list, my hard earned collection is important to me. Please let me know the situation . . . the REAL situation."

After we contacted Collins about how he authenticated his collection, to no response, he dropped a bomb in an email to the GLO.

"I would like you to consider the real probability of me withdrawing my collection and giving it back to me," Collins wrote to Valle. "I'll be happy to donate it when the museum is ready, but right now, I'd like to bring it back. I don't want to bring lawyers in, but I will if need be. Plus I'm getting flack on what's 'real' and what's not. Please let me know . . . PC."[8]

The Bush team scrambled to soothe Collins and persuade him to change his mind.

"Please know that your collection is extremely important to the entire State of Texas and we would not be where we are in this process if not for you and your generosity. You sparked this entire Alamo Plan and we owe you so much," Valle replied.[9]

A week later, apparently after a phone call, Valle followed up with news that the GLO was replacing the executive director at the Alamo and offered to put the Collins collection on display as soon as possible, if Collins did not want to wait for the museum. Valle also promised a phone call with Bush, but Collins would prove too busy.[10] He canceled five calls with the land commissioner at the last minute. But we obtained Bush's talking points for when he did connect with Collins.

"I share your frustrations and want you to know that I am committed to making sure your collection is displayed and that we meet the requirements of our agreement," Bush's notes said. "My staff tells me that we have been trying to schedule a meeting to hear your thoughts on the proposed design and want you to know that we will make the designers available at your convenience."

When it became clear the GLO would not complete a museum in time to meet the conditions of Collins's contract, Bush proposed constructing a smaller building on the Alamo grounds to house the collection. As this book goes to press, the GLO declined to answer our questions about whether Collins was pacified. We emailed Collins, but he also declined to answer questions.

"Life is busy at the moment, with music rehearsals and personal stuff, so I'll have to pass on your request," Collins wrote. "Of course I'm totally interested but I cannot deal with this right now. Many thanks, PC."

Bush was in a bind because the Collins collection and the Alamo were entangled with his political ambitions. "He wants this to be a feather in his cap," says Hardin. "Everyone knows this is a stepping-stone job for him. He wants to be president someday; he wants to prolong the family dynasty. He will never publicly admit, and he will never allow anyone in the GLO to admit, that they accepted the donation of a pig in the poke. He won't admit that. Ever."

What bothers Tom Nuckols is the prospective power of a flawed Collins collection. He once helped excavate one of the retreating Mexican army's camps in Wharton County. The guns, cartridge boxes, and dozens of other artifacts they found were put on display inside the Alamo gift shop. "And it wasn't a very popular display," he says. "But that stuff Collins has, they're gonna say, 'This gun was owned by Travis, this knife by Bowie,' and that's gonna be bad. It's just gonna be bad. The tourists, they'll believe that nonsense over what's in an archaeological exhibit. That's what's gonna be popular, I promise you."

EPILOGUE:
ANOTHER BATTLE
OF THE ALAMO

George P. Bush, the GLO, the city of San Antonio, and the Alamo itself have a lot riding on the rehabilitation of the Alamo and its surrounding plaza. Tourism remains one of the city's main employers and sources of income, and the Alamo is the city's crown jewel for attracting tourists. Building a new, state-of-the-art museum could raise the number of visitors from two million a year to more than eight million, according to the Alamo Trust's fantastically optimistic projections. The key is to offer an experience that makes everyone feel welcome. The problem, though, is that the Heroic Anglo Narrative, a myth held dear by the older, conservative whites who vote in the Republican primary, is rooted in white supremacy.

There is, however, another group of Texans, many of them young and people of color, who are just learning about the plan to spend $450 million of taxpayer and donor money to glorify a nineteenth-century battle in the nation's poorest large city. For them, the Alamo is a troubled symbol of crimes against Indigenous people, and they are offended by the idea of spending nearly half a billion dollars on a monument to so-called Anglo heroes who fought for the perpetuation of slavery and the villainization of Mexicans.

Those passions rose after a Minneapolis police officer killed an African-American named George Floyd by kneeling on his neck while horrified bystanders watched his last breaths. Around midnight on May 29, 2020, a young Hispanic man, angered by the police killing, walked up to the Cenotaph with a can of red spray paint. Across the base, he scrawled downward-facing arrows next to "white supremacy, profit over people, the ALAMO." The next day, protesters marched onto Alamo Plaza calling for an end to police brutality and racism.

Texas's changing demographics and culture were on stark display over the next few weeks of daily protests. Young people on the march declared the Alamo no different from a Confederate war statue. Self-appointed Alamo defenders, including the group This Is Texas Freedom Force, showed up in fatigues and body armor with assault rifles strapped across their chests. They formed a cordon around the Cenotaph and lined up in front of the church, promising to prevent any further defacement. When the shoving started, San Antonio Park Police and the Alamo Rangers squeezed between the two sides, acting as human shields. When protesters became rowdy, shouting and gesticulating threats, city riot police fired tear gas.

The protest was the first physical confrontation over the Alamo's symbolism since the Ku Klux Klan demonstrations of the 1980s against revisionism and multiculturalism. Four days later, the GLO installed an eight-foot-high barrier across the front of the Alamo to keep people and vehicles from getting close enough to do any damage. Officials said they would maintain the wall indefinitely and keep the compound closed to the public until further notice.

"The Alamo is the Shrine of Texas Liberty. And it will be defended," Bush tweeted in a statement released on June 13, 2020. "Rest assured we have already deployed, for several weeks and will continue to do so, the Alamo Rangers in partnership with SAPD, The Department of Public Safety and The National Guard to protect this sacred site. My message to the protestors is simple: Don't mess with The Alamo."

Dan Patrick, the lieutenant governor aligned with the Tea Party, said Bush was the greater threat. "Nobody has put the @OfficialAlamo at more risk than @georgepbush with the outrageous 'reimagining' plan, lousy management, lack of transparency and moving the cenotaph," Patrick said on Twitter. The lieutenant governor has also threatened to use his power in the legislature to stop Bush from watering down the Heroic Anglo Narrative.

Insiders say this was a proxy war for their political futures. Bush, as is customary and polite, asked Patrick if he was planning on running for reelection in 2022, by way of expressing his own interest in that office. Patrick assured him that he was staying put, which should have ended the matter. But shortly thereafter Bush admitted at a private fundraising event that he was still considering running for lieutenant governor. Patrick, who has a scale model of the Alamo and memorabilia from the John Wayne movie in his state office, was instrumental in the Texas legislature's providing $70 million for the Alamo project in 2017. In January 2020, he had approvingly toured the site and reviewed Bush's redevelopment plans, expressing no serious objections. After Bush's faux pas, Patrick turned on Bush, and the Alamo plan. To defend himself, Bush became a backer of the Heroic Anglo Narrative.

Gene Powell, whom Bush appointed to raise the $100 million plus needed in private philanthropic funding, stepped away from the Alamo Foundation. He could see where this was headed. "All of a sudden, after years of agreement on telling the story of all the layers of history of the site, everyone now seems to want this to be John Wayne's Alamo," he said.

One thing is clear, though, Bush is surrounded on all sides: San Antonio's city council, Chicanos, Native Americans, African-Americans, white conservatives, and the business community are all opposed to his plan to renovate the compound, for different reasons. The heir to the Bush dynasty doesn't want to make his last stand at the Alamo, but Patrick plans to end Bush's political career there.

It is too early to know whether the summer of 2020's awakening to racial injustice will change the course of the Alamo renovation. We hear rumors that the uproar is giving some donors cold feet. Conservative supporters are angry that the Alamo Trust wants to accommodate the Tāp Pīlam Coahuiltecan cemetery and commemorate the

African-American request to restore the Woolworth's lunch counter. Some state lawmakers want to outlaw any criticism of the defenders on the Alamo grounds, guaranteeing that the myths are maintained within at least one city block. City and state politicians are worried about getting on the wrong side of history with a younger generation of Texans who are mostly Latino and have no sympathy for the old lies and false histories.

Patrick won a major victory against Bush's renovation plan in September 2020 when he convinced the Texas Historical Commission to deny the application to move the Cenotaph five hundred feet down the plaza. City officials had promised that the entire plan relied on relocating the Cenotaph and declared the project at an impasse. As this book goes to press, the state and city remain deadlocked.

If history is any guide, though, there is a good chance this latest attempt to turn Alamo Plaza into a "world-class attraction" will fizzle out like all the others. As the generation that grew up with coonskin caps and John Wayne begins to pass on, the number of people who share their love of these legends is shrinking. School boards can only insist on teaching the myth in seventh grade for so long. While some will always remember, most young Texans are ready to forget the Alamo.

AFTERWORD:
WE ARE WHAT WE REMEMBER

We define ourselves in the stories we tell, the people we honor, and the enemies we choose. As we age, learn, and live, we change the stories to reflect our evolving understanding of the world and what it means to us. Neuroscientists tell us that every time we recall a memory we will re-remember it a little differently, and therefore the story will change over the years with every retelling, like a decades-long game of telephone. The same is true for societies, nations, and cultures.

"Remember the Alamo" was a battle cry intended to inspire a blood-thirsty rage in a group of rebels attacking a national army. The Battle of San Jacinto was as much as anything a brilliant piece of psychological warfare. Position your troops where there is no retreat, inflame their racist hatreds, and attack at an unexpected moment. Sam Houston's victory was impressive, but Texas is a different place now. We are seven generations past the Texas Revolt. We no longer keep humans as chattel. We — most of us, at least — no longer believe white skin is superior to brown. When Texans celebrate the bicentennial of Texas independence in 2036, Hispanics will make up the majority of Texans, and Anglo rule will have come to an end. Will we need to Remember the Alamo differently?

Of course. It's said that those who do not know their history are doomed to repeat it, but there are plenty who remember the Heroic Anglo Narrative and want to endlessly repeat this version of history, seeing themselves under siege by tyrannical rule to take away their guns or commit any number of cultural atrocities. And there are others who remember the history as a land grab followed by ethnic cleansing that robbed Tejanos of their rights and land and Blacks of their emancipation. And even in remembering, they see history repeat itself. Remembering the Alamo has not stopped history from repeating.

The challenge is to tell a story about our past grounded in historical fact. The Battle of the Alamo in 1836 is an integral part of Texas history, and the myth circled the globe in books, poems, songs, television shows, and movies. What must change, though, is the story we tell about the Alamo. To learn the real lessons of the Texas Revolt, we need to learn the truth about Bowie, Travis, and Crockett. Bowie was a murderer, slaver, and con man; Travis was a pompous, racist agitator and syphilitic lech; and Crockett was a self-promoting old fool who was a captive to his own myth. They can no longer be the holy trinity of Texas, nor can the Alamo be the Shrine of Texas Liberty. But all three men did believe in liberty and self-determination, and Travis was one hell of a letter writer. They fought for freedom, just not everybody's freedom. We also need to remember the people intentionally left out of the Alamo myths and legends, like Juan Almonte, the Mexican revolutionary who fought against the Texians to abolish slavery. Or Juan Seguín, the Tejano leader whose fight for federalism was coopted into a secessionist movement by the Texians. If we shift the frame just a little bit, the whole story of the Alamo is transformed. And, frankly, a lot more interesting.

As for what is left of the Alamo, the structure itself? Well, it's a Spanish mission, a Coahuiltecan burial ground, a segregated lunch counter, as well as a site of a dozen battles, including one in March of 1836.

When we focus on only thirteen days and leave out the other three hundred years, we forget a history that is equally important, if not more so.

For the past fifty years, the United States and Texas have struggled, imperfectly and inconsistently, to address the white supremacy that underpinned our social, economic, and spiritual life since the first enslaved person arrived in North America in 1619. After decades of debate, officials and protesters are removing statues to Confederate leaders across the nation. Groups ranging from the Department of Defense to NASCAR are banning Confederate symbols that many white people consider badges of their heritage. We must recognize that the Battle of the Alamo was as much about slavery as the Civil War was about slavery. But we should preserve the Alamo exactly as we do the other Spanish missions that make San Antonio a World Heritage Site.

In 2019, the Texas legislature debated whether to protect Confederate monuments, and one lawmaker, with all benevolence toward the Shrine of Texas Liberty, amended the bill to clarify that the Alamo and the Cenotaph would also be protected from the politically correct revisionists. That bill did not pass, but in doing so that legislator proves our point. The Alamo, long used in a myth that demonized and gaslit Mexican-Americans and Indigenous people, might as well be a Confederate monument in the minds of conservative adherents to the Heroic Anglo Narrative.

It doesn't have to be that way and won't be for much longer.

Our book will be called a history book. We call it a historiography, that is, a history of the history. In those first weeks and months after the battle, many knew the truth and argued over it even then. You have read how the Battle of the Alamo created waves of storytelling and revision, always updated to serve the needs of the storyteller. You have learned how the official Alamo story became entrenched by the state and eventually embedded into national politics and foreign policy, with disastrous results, starting with Lyndon Johnson's inability to see military conflict outside of an Alamo framework and continuing into the wars that followed 9/11.

Dr. Bruce Winders, the deposed Alamo historian, was at the Alamo on 9/11, and the wars went on long enough for him to also be there when troops would visit from one of San Antonio's military bases. And those soldiers would show him, often as not, photographs from a war zone where they had given their encampments a familiar name.

"There's one Alamo here in Texas, you know, there's countless Alamos in Iraq and Afghanistan," said Winders. "I think what's interesting is it's become a symbol that people use. Sometimes they forget where it came from. So, they put a meaning to it, but they don't — they don't know what that meaning is."

The Alamo is a story we've learned to tell ourselves to justify violence, both real and threatened, first against Mexicans, then Tejanos, then Mexican-Americans, and eventually the Vietcong and al-Qaeda. "Remember the Alamo" was a battle cry that we recycle long past the fight's utility. How Mexican-Americans were shamed in Texas History classes, how politicians and bureaucrats have changed that history over the years, and any number of other episodes that make up the back half of this book tell us more about who we are now than what we thought we knew about what happened over thirteen days in 1836. That is the history that we need to learn, because we are repeating it ceaselessly.

Maybe it's time to forget the Alamo, or at least the whitewashed story, and start telling the history that includes everyone. Problems arise when there's an official version of events. Texas is big enough to tell an expansive, inclusive story about the Alamo, what really happened before, how it really went down, how we wrestled over who had the right to tell the story, and why we're still fighting about it today. We do not and will never agree completely on the events. It'd be a strange place if we did and one we're sure we wouldn't like.

From a practical perspective, we must do something with Alamo Plaza. It desperately needs a refresh. But spending $450 million to build a monument to white supremacy as personified by Bowie, Travis, and Crockett would be a grave injustice to a city that desperately needs better schools, jobs, and services. If Phil Collins wants to "Remember the Alamo," he is welcome to do so in the privacy of his own home. The rest of us need to forget what we learned about the Alamo, embrace the truth, and celebrate all Texans.

ACKNOWLEDGMENTS

This book began at a Sunday breakfast on Austin's South Congress Avenue, three writer friends chatting about their latest work, bouncing ideas off one another, gauging the reaction. It was a routine morning, until Chris began talking about one of his *Houston Chronicle* columns, this one about the Alamo. At some point, probably around the time he began describing how so many Latinos viewed conventional Anglo narratives about the famous siege as twisted myths used to oppress generations of Mexican-Americans, Bryan and Jason sat up straight and began to listen. "Really?" one of us asked.

Chris leaned in. "Everything you think you know about the Alamo," he said, "is flat-out wrong."

He went on. And on. He had done his homework, that much was clear. Finally, in one of those moments that occur often when writers tell their tales, Bryan slapped his hand on the table.

"That's a fucking book!" he exclaimed.

It's the kind of thing literary types say all the time. Ninety-nine times out of a hundred, nothing comes of it. But this time, well, something has. Two years after that breakfast, what we originally envisioned as a quick, book-length essay has resulted in a full-blown Alamo historiography, a project that consumed us pretty much seven days a week, much of it during the COVID pandemic. Of necessity our breakfast talks eventually evolved into socially distanced discussions in Chris's yard.

There's a lot of folks to thank on a book like this, but our biggest thank-you goes to our fourth Beatle, the indefatigable Maggie Walsh, PhD, who had the unenviable job of spearheading and organizing the yearlong research effort for (gulp) three authors at once. She tells us she loved the work, and she must have, because she also played the role of umpire when we could not easily agree on things. But more important, the book wouldn't be what it is without her persistence in pelting us with ideas, from surprise characters she turned up by combing through decades of handwritten letters and manuscripts to key points she found in obscure journals and books. Her stoic judgment and fierce dedication to provable fact elevated this enterprise. She demanded the best of us in every way. She made this a better book. She was our partner. Full stop. Thank you, Maggie. We couldn't have done it without you.

Thanks as well to the estimable Ruben Cordova of San Antonio, who gave us invaluable real-time feedback on the manuscript in an effort to help three hopelessly Anglo authors responsibly represent Latino viewpoints. And to Andrés Tijerina, who gave us a master class in Texas history. We highly recommend spending an afternoon or several watching his lectures on YouTube. He opened up our thinking and we cannot thank him enough.

Among our most indispensable sounding boards, none proved more valuable than Bruce Winders, the Alamo's longtime official historian. At breakfasts in San Antonio, and in innumerable emails and phone calls, we swarmed poor Bruce like linebackers after a quarterback. One or two parts of this book simply would not have been possible without his help — and patience.

At the University of North Texas, Andrew Torget was of immense aid explicating the economic forces that buffeted colonial

Texas; as we note in chapter 1, our first three chapters are keenly reliant on the pioneering work he did in the 2015 book *Seeds of Empire.* In Austin, our great friend and rabbi Steve Harrigan, author of among other things the wonderful *Gates of the Alamo,* gave us the unofficial go-ahead for this project, and allowed us to pepper him with dumb questions.

An undertaking like this always requires days looking for nuggets of primary source material that others have passed over. Our expert guides included Donna Guerra at the Sisters of Charity of the Incarnate Word in San Antonio, who patiently helped us with the Adina De Zavala archive, and Carolyn Taylor, who manages the Clara Driscoll archive for the Driscoll Foundation. Thanks too to Misty Harris, who oversees the *San Antonio Express-News* library and archival materials and who provided invaluable advice for tracking down articles and sources; also to Marc Duvoisin, the newspaper's editor, for his support. A special mention is owed the Austin Public Library for the resources it makes available online. And while we accessed it remotely during the pandemic, we cannot recommend highly enough visiting it in person. That library is a treasure.

Thanks to Santiago Escobedo for reading and briefing us on the Spanish-language *Olvídate de El Alamo.* And to our pal Jim Henson for a special favor. Thanks to Bill Groneman, Jeff Long, and the late Jim Lehrer for sharing their stories. For our reporting on the Phil Collins collection, thanks to Compton LaBauve, Thomas Nuckols, Stephen L. Hardin, and Mark D. Zalesky, as well as several prominent dealers and collectors who preferred their guidance remain discreet. Thanks also to Jim Guimarin and Alex McDuffie for sharing their stories with us.

For the sections on the modern Alamo, thanks to Lee Spencer White, Bryan Preston, Ash Wright, Betty Edwards, Jerry Patterson, Gary Foreman, Roberto Treviño, Diego Bernal, María Berriozábal, Ramón Vásquez, Davis Phillips, Dr. Gilberto Hinojosa, Stephen Cure, Sarah Reveley, Denise Hernandez, Harold Cook, Laura Hernández-Ehrisman, Juany Torres, Tomas Larralde, James Aldrete, Eddie Aldrete, Jesús F. de la Teja, PhD, David McLemore, Scott Huddleston, Paul Stekler, Kaye Tucker, Justin Renteria, Carlos Sanchez, Dr. Cynthia E. Orozco, Chris Perkins, Gene Powell, John Pritcher, and William Thornton. Because of the highly charged politics

surrounding the Alamo, many folks re-
quested that we keep their identities private.
Every effort was made to corroborate their
accounts, and we thank them for their contributions.

Jason wishes to thank his employer,
Hill+Knowlton Strategies, for patience and
support while he worked on this book. Parts
of it were written in guest houses owned by
Robin Summers, Debbie and Braxton Mon-
cure, and Ginger Durdan-Shaw and Bob
Shaw, for whose hospitality Jason is grateful.

A big thank-you to Ben Kalin, who fact-
checked the manuscript. Ben's a pro; if
you're looking for a skilled fact-checker,
he's at ben@factcheckpros.com. At the
Wylie Agency, Andrew Wylie and Jeffrey
Posternak handled our business affairs with
their typical aplomb. Special thanks to John
Silbersack at the Bent Agency for his patient
and sage counsel. At Penguin Press, Scott
Moyers and Mia Council were top-tier editors who gently guided us through the har-
rowing process of trimming our original
submission by almost a third. Thanks too to
Penguin's Tyler Comrie for crafting the
book's memorable cover art.

And last, we'd like to thank our families.
Bryan would like to thank his parents,

John M. and Mary Burrough, and his sons, Griffin and Dane, for their love and support. Jason would likewise like to thank his dad, Phil Stanford, his mom, Pililani Meyer, and his sons, Henry and Hatcher, who he hopes enjoy the book, as well as his wife, Sonia Van Meter, to whom he owes a great debt of time he looks forward to repaying. Chris would like to thank his good friends Philip Gourevitch and Keri Blakinger for keeping him sane, and his mother-in-law, Lakshmi Ramanathan, for daily lessons in joie de vivre. But all his love goes to his partner, Shalini Ramanathan, without whom his participation in this book would have been impossible.

NOTES

Introduction

1. Alison Boshoff and Annette Witheridge, "I Remember the Alamo: How a Psychic Cook Called Carolyn Convinced Phil Collins He's a Reincarnated American Hero," *Daily Mail,* November 26, 2010, https://www.dailymail.co.uk/femail/article -1333165/How-psychic-cook-called -Carolyn-convinced-Phil-Collins-hes -reincarnated-American-hero.html.
2. Ozzy Osbourne with Chris Ayers, *I Am Ozzy* (New York: Grand Central Publishing, 2009), 9.
3. Dan Solomon, "A Brief History of Peeing on the Alamo," *Texas Monthly,* February 5, 2014.

Chapter 1: Bloody Texas

1. Paul Andrew Hutton, introduction to Susan Prendergast Schoelwer with Tom W. Gläser, *Alamo Images: Changing Perceptions of a Texas Experience* (Dallas: DeGolyer Library and Southern Methodist University Press, 1985), 4.
2. Cited in Andrew J. Torget, *Seeds of Empire: Cotton, Slavery, and the Transformation of the Texas Borderlands, 1800–1850* (Chapel Hill: University of North Carolina Press, 2015), 35.
3. Kevin Brady, "Unspoken Words: James Monroe's Involvement in the Magee-Gutiérrez Filibuster," *East Texas Historical Journal* 45, no. 1, article 14 (2007), 58–68.
4. Raúl A. Ramos, *Beyond the Alamo: Forging Mexican Ethnicity in San Antonio, 1821–1861* (Chapel Hill: University of North Carolina Press, 2010), 40.
5. From letters between Governor Antonio Martínez and Viceroy Juan Ruiz de Apodaca, cited in Torget, *Seeds of Empire,* 39.
6. Torget, 48.

Chapter 2: The Americans, Their Cotton, and Who Picked It

1. Cited in Andrew J. Torget, *Seeds of Empire: Cotton, Slavery, and the Transformation of the Texas Borderlands, 1800–1850* (Chapel Hill: University of North Carolina Press, 2015), 67.
2. Gregg Cantrell, *Stephen F. Austin: Empresario of Texas* (New Haven: Yale University Press, 1999).
3. Stephen F. Austin to Samuel M. Williams, April 16, 1831, cited in Cantrell, 190.
4. Torget, *Seeds of Empire,* 73.
5. Torget, 73.
6. Torget, 75.
7. Torget, 86.
8. Torget, 86.
9. Charles Douglas to Stephen F. Austin, February 25, 1825, cited in Torget, 90.
10. Torget, 95.
11. Stephen F. Austin Proclamation, May 1, 1824, cited in Torget, 80.
12. Torget, *Seeds of Empire,* 95.
13. Stephen F. Austin to Coahuila y Texas State Legislature, August 11, 1826, cited in Torget, 104.
14. Cited in Torget, 111.

Chapter 3: The American Middle Finger, Extended

1. Cited in Andrew J. Torget, *Seeds of Empire: Cotton, Slavery, and the Transformation of the Texas Borderlands, 1800–1850* (Chapel Hill: University of North Carolina Press, 2015), 131.
2. Randolph B. Campbell, *An Empire for Slavery: The Peculiar Institution in Texas 1821–1865* (Baton Rouge: Louisiana State University Press, 1989), 24.
3. Cited in Torget, *Seeds of Empire,* 146.
4. Cited in Torget, 147.
5. Cited in Torget, 152.
6. Cited in Torget, 153.
7. Stephen F. Austin to S. Rhodes Fisher, June 17, 1830, cited in Torget, 154.
8. Stephen F. Austin to Edward Livingston, June 24, 1832, and Stephen F. Austin to Samuel May Williams, April 6, 1831, cited in Torget, 155.
9. Arnoldo De León and Kenneth L. Stewart, *Tejanos and the Numbers Game: A Socio-Historical Interpretation from the Federal Censuses, 1850–1900* (Albuquerque: University of New Mexico Press, 1989), 1–5.
10. Lyndon Orr, "Famous Affinities of History: XLIII — The Wives of General

Houston," *Munsy's Magazine* 47 (April–September 1912), 548. Accessed on Google Books, April 15, 2020.

11. Gregg Cantrell, *Stephen F. Austin: Empresario of Texas* (New Haven: Yale University Press, 1999), 59.

Chapter 4: "The President Santana Is Friendly to Texas . . ."

1. Cited in T. R. Fehrenbach, *Lone Star: A History of Texas and the Texans* (New York: Macmillan, 1989), 181.

2. Stephen F. Austin to Henry Austin, April 19, 1833, cited in Gregg Cantrell, *Stephen F. Austin: Empresario of Texas* (New Haven: Yale University Press, 1999), 264–65.

3. Stephen F. Austin to Samuel M. Williams, November 5, 1833, cited in Cantrell, 275.

4. Cited in Cantrell, 282.

5. William C. Davis, *Lone Star Rising: The Revolutionary Birth of the Texas Republic* (New York: Free Press, 2004), 111–12

6. Cited in Cantrell, *Stephen F. Austin,* 291.

7. Jack Jackson, ed., *Almonte's Texas: Juan N. Almonte's 1834 Inspection, Secret Report & Role in the 1836 Campaign,* trans. John Wheat (Austin: Texas State Historical Association, 2003), 459.

8. Stephen F. Austin to Samuel M. Williams, April 15, 1835, *The Austin Papers,* vol. 3, ed. Eugene C. Barker (Austin: University of Texas Press, 1927), 63.

9. Juan Seguín, *A Revolution Remembered: The Memoirs and Selected Correspondence of Juan N. Seguín,* ed. Jesús F. de la Teja (Austin: Texas State Historical Association, 2002), 20.

10. Cited in Cantrell, *Stephen F. Austin,* 307.

Chapter 5: The War Dogs

1. William Barret Travis, *Diary,* ed. Robert E. Davis (Waco: Texian Press, 1966), cited in Jeff Long, *Duel of Eagles: The Mexican and U.S. Fight for the Alamo* (New York: William Morrow, 1990), 34.

2. Cited in William C. Davis, *Lone Star Rising: The Revolutionary Birth of the Texas Republic* (New York: Free Press, 2004), 118.

3. Cited in William C. Davis, *Three Roads to the Alamo: The Lives and Fortunes of David Crockett, James Bowie, and William Barret Travis* (New York: HarperCollins, 1998), 449.

4. Cited in Davis, 455.

5. J. H. C. Miller to John W. Smith, July 25, 1835, in Henderson K. Yoakum, *History of*

Texas: From Its First Settlement in 1685 to Its Annexation to the United States in 1846 (New York: Redfield, 1855), vol. 1, 345.

6. Stephen F. Austin to Columbia Committee, September 19, 1835, cited in Gregg Cantrell, *Stephen F. Austin: Empresario of Texas* (New Haven: Yale University Press, 1999), 312.

7. Raúl A. Ramos, *Beyond the Alamo: Forging Mexican Ethnicity in San Antonio, 1821–1861* (Raleigh: University of North Carolina Press, 2010), 137–38.

8. Ramos, 144.

Chapter 6: San Antonio

1. Alwyn Barr, *Texans in Revolt: The Battle for San Antonio, 1835* (Austin: University of Texas Press, 1990), 432.

2. Phillip T. Tucker, "Motivations of United States Volunteers during the Texas Revolution, 1835–1836," *East Texas Historical Journal* 29, no. 1 (1991).

3. Paul D. Lack, *The Texas Revolutionary Experience: A Political and Social History, 1835–1836* (College Station: Texas A&M University Press, 1992), Kindle ed., loc 216.

4. Benjamin R. Milam to Francis W. Johnson, July 5, 1835, Digital Austin Papers,

http://digitalaustinpapers.org/document ?id=APB4814.xml.

5. Cited in Sam W. Haynes and Gerald D. Saxon, eds., *Contested Empire: Rethinking the Texas Revolution* (College Station: Texas A&M University Press, 2015), Kindle ed., loc 1199.

6. James Traub, *John Quincy Adams: Militant Spirit* (New York: Basic Books, 2016), 438.

7. Quinton Curtis Lamar, "A Diplomatic Disaster: The Mexican Mission of Anthony Butler, 1829–1834," *The Americas* 45, no. 1 (July 1988), 1–17.

8. Andrew Jackson to Anthony Butler, October 19, 1829, cited in Lamar.

9. Llerena Friend, *Sam Houston: The Great Designer* (Austin: University of Texas Press, 1954), Kindle ed., loc. 986.

10. Marquis James, *The Raven: A Biography of Sam Houston* (Austin: University of Texas Press, 1929), 178.

11. Friend, *Sam Houston,* Kindle ed., loc. 1195.

12. Cited in Gene Brack, "Mexican Opinion and the Texas Revolution," *Southwestern Historical Quarterly* 72, no. 2 (October 1968), 179.

Chapter 7: The Worst Kind of Victory

1. T. R. Fehrenbach, *Lone Star: A History of Texas and the Texans* (New York: Macmillan, 1989), 198.
2. Walter Lord, *A Time to Stand* (New York: Harper & Row, 1961), 74.
3. Jack Jackson, ed., *Almonte's Texas: Juan N. Almonte's 1834 Inspection, Secret Report & Role in the 1836 Campaign,* trans. John Wheat (Austin: Texas State Historical Association, 2003), 347.
4. Antonio López de Santa Anna to José María Tornel, February 16, 1836, published as Document No. 8 in "Santa Anna's Manifesto on Texas Operations," May 1837, in *The Mexican Side of the Texan Revolution [1836] by the Chief Mexican Participants,* 2nd ed., trans. Carlos E. Castaneda (Austin: Graphic Ideas Incorporated, 1970).
5. Santa Anna to Tornel, February 16, 1836.
6. Jackson, *Almonte's Texas,* 358.
7. William C. Davis, *Three Roads to the Alamo: The Lives and Fortunes of David Crockett, James Bowie, and William Barret Travis* (New York: HarperPerennial, 1999), 99.
8. Cited in Davis, 355.

Chapter 8: Countdown

1. Cited in William C. Davis, *Three Roads to the Alamo: The Lives and Fortunes of David Crockett, James Bowie, and William Barret Travis* (New York: HarperPerennial, 1999), 517.
2. Cited in Davis, 520.
3. Walter Lord, *A Time to Stand: The Epic of the Alamo* (Lincoln: University of Nebraska Press, 1978), 87.
4. Jack Jackson, ed., *Almonte's Texas: Juan N. Almonte's 1834 Inspection, Secret Report & Role in the 1836 Campaign,* trans. John Wheat (Austin: Texas State Historical Association, 2003), 367.
5. Jackson, 367.

Chapter 9: The Final Days

1. William C. Davis, *Three Roads to the Alamo: The Lives and Fortunes of David Crockett, James Bowie, and William Barret Travis* (New York: HarperPerennial, 1999), 549–50.
2. Cited in H. W. Brands, *Lone Star Nation* (New York: Doubleday, 2004), 357.
3. Margaret Swett Henson, *Lorenzo de Zavala: The Pragmatic Idealist* (Fort Worth:

Texas Christian University Press, 1996), 26.

4. Henson, 44.

5. Henson, 46.

6. W. S. Cleaves, "Lorenzo de Zavala in Texas," *Southwest Quarterly* 36, no. 1 (July 1932), 38.

7. Cleaves, 34.

8. Henson, *Lorenzo de Zavala,* 91.

9. Henson, 89.

10. Cleaves, "Lorenzo de Zavala in Texas," 34.

11. Henson, *Lorenzo de Zavala,* 93.

12. Henson, 98.

13. Cleaves, "Lorenzo de Zavala in Texas," 38.

14. Cleaves, 37.

15. Walter Lord, *A Time to Stand* (New York: Harper & Row, 1961), 44.

16. Vicente Filisola memoir, cited in Todd Hansen, ed., *The Alamo Reader: A Study in History* (Mechanicsburg, PA: Stackpole Books, 2003), 391.

Chapter 10: The Battle of the Alamo

1. Walter Lord, *A Time to Stand* (New York: Harper & Row, 1961), 157.

2. William C. Davis, *Three Roads to the Alamo: The Lives and Fortunes of David*

571

Crockett, James Bowie, and William Barret Travis (New York: HarperPerennial, 1999), 560.

3. José Enrique de la Peña, *With Santa Anna in Texas: A Personal Narrative of the Revolution,* expanded ed., trans. and ed. Carmen Perry (College Station: Texas A&M University Press, 1997), 47.

4. De la Peña, 48.

5. De la Peña, 48.

6. De la Peña, 50–51.

7. T. R. Fehrenbach, *Lone Star: A History of Texas and the Texans* (New York: Macmillan, 1989), 213.

8. Cited in Lord, *A Time to Stand,* 61.

9. Wallace O. Chariton, *Exploring the Alamo Legends* (Lanham, MD: Republic of Texas Press, 2004).

10. Lord, *A Time to Stand,* 161.

11. Cited in Todd Hansen, ed., *The Alamo Reader: A Study in History* (Mechanicsburg, PA: Stackpole Books, 2003), 370.

12. Cited in Hansen, 370.

13. Davis, *Three Roads to the Alamo,* 562.

14. Jack Jackson, ed., *Almonte's Texas: Juan N. Almonte's 1834 Inspection, Secret Report & Role in the 1836 Campaign,* trans. John Wheat (Austin: Texas State Historical Association, 2003), 421.

15. Jackson, 421.

Chapter 11: A First Draft of History

1. Jack Jackson, ed., *Almonte's Texas: Juan N. Almonte's 1834 Inspection, Secret Report & Role in the 1836 Campaign,* trans. John Wheat (Austin: Texas State Historical Association, 2003), 376.
2. "The Story of Enrique Esparza," *San Antonio Express,* January 22, 1902.
3. Jackson, *Almonte's Texas,* 376.
4. Juan Seguín, *A Revolution Remembered: The Memoirs and Selected Correspondence of Juan N. Seguín,* ed. Jesús F. de la Teja (Austin: Texas State Historical Association, 2002), 108.
5. Sam Houston to James W. Fannin, March 11, 1836, in *The Papers of the Texas Revolution 1835–1836,* ed. John Jenkins (Austin: Presidial Press, 1973), vol. 5, 52–53.
6. Sam Houston to James Collingsworth, March 13, 1836, in Henderson K. Yoakum, *History of Texas: From Its First Settlement in 1685 to Its Annexation to the United States in 1846* (New York: Redfield, 1855), vol. 2, 473.
7. Randy Roberts and James S. Olson, *A Line in the Sand: The Alamo in Blood and*

Memory (New York: Simon and Schuster/ Touchstone, 2002), 74.

8. J. R. Edmondson, *The Alamo Story: From Early History to Current Conflicts* (Dallas: Taylor Trade Publishing, 2000), 393.

9. *Telegraph and Texas Register,* March 24, 1836, 2.

10. *Richmond Enquirer,* May 17, 1836.

11. Cited in Frank Thompson, *The Alamo: A Cultural History* (Dallas: Taylor Trade Publishing, 2001), 106.

12. Cited in Walter Lord, *A Time to Stand* (New York: Harper & Row, 1961), 169.

13. Bill Walraven and Marjorie K. Walraven, "The 'Sabine Chute': The U.S. Army and the Texas Revolution," *Southwestern Historical Quarterly* 107, no. 4 (April 2004), 573–601, https://texashistory.unt.edu/ark:/ 67531/metapth101224/, University of North Texas Libraries, The Portal to Texas History, https://texashistory.unt.edu; crediting Texas State Historical Association.

14. Anson Jones, James M. Day, and John Bowden Connally, *Memoranda and Official Correspondence Relating to the Republic of Texas, Its History and Annexation* (Chicago: Rio Grande Press, 1966).

15. Walraven and Walraven, "The 'Sabine

Chute,' " 573–601.

16. Walraven and Walraven, 573–80.
17. Walraven and Walraven, 573–80.
18. Cited in Todd Hansen, ed., *The Alamo Reader: A Study in History* (Mechanicsburg, PA: Stackpole Books, 2003), 394.

Chapter 12: Remember the Alamo?

1. Laura Lyons McLemore, *Inventing Texas: Early Historians of the Lone Star State* (College Station: Texas A&M University Press, 2004), Kindle ed., loc. 306.
2. Stephen L. Hardin, "David Barnett Edward," *Handbook of Texas Online,* https://www.tshaonline.org/handbook/entries/edward-david-barnett. Published by the Texas State Historical Association.
3. Don Graham, "Remembering the Alamo: The Story of the Texas Revolution in Popular Culture," *Southwestern Historical Quarterly* 89, no. 1 (July 1985), 37.
4. Cited in Graham, 39.
5. Cited in Graham, 42.
6. John Henry Leach, "The Life of Reuben Marmaduke Potter" (master's thesis, University of Texas at Austin, 1939), 36.
7. Leach, 13.
8. "Notes and Fragments," *Quarterly of the Texas State Historical Association* 4, no. 3

(January 1901), 232.

9. Leach, "The Life of Reuben Marmaduke Potter," 76.

10. Leach, 36.

11. Cited in McLemore, *Inventing Texas,* Kindle ed., loc. 91.

12. Henderson K. Yoakum, *History of Texas: From Its First Settlement in 1685 to Its Annexation to the United States in 1846* (New York: Redfield, 1855), vol. 2, 21–25.

13. Yoakum, vol. 1, 285.

14. Yoakum, vol. 2, 32.

15. Reuben Marmaduke Potter, *The Fall of the Alamo: A Reminiscence of the Revolution of Texas, The Texas Almanac* (Austin: Galveston News, 1868).

16. Potter.

17. Cited in Arnoldo De León, *They Called Them Greasers: Anglo Attitudes toward Mexicans in Texas, 1821–1900* (Austin: University of Texas Press, 1983), 32.

18. Jesús F. de la Teja, "The Colonization and Independence of Texas: A Tejano Perspective," in *Myths, Misdeeds, and Misunderstandings: The Roots of Conflict in U.S.–Mexican Relations,* ed. Jaime E. Rodríguez O. and Kathryn Vincent (Wilmington, DE: SR Books, 1997), 95.

19. Juan Seguín, *Personal Memoirs of Juan*

Seguin: 1832 to the Retreat of General Woll (San Antonio: Printed at the Ledger Book and Job Office, 1858), 24.

20. Seguín, 23–25.

21. Cited in David McDonald, *José Antonio Navarro: In Search of the American Dream in Nineteenth-Century Texas* (Denton: Texas State Historical Association, 2010), Kindle ed. See also "The Memoirs of José Antonio Navarro," Sons of DeWitt Colony Texas, http://www.sonsofdewittcolony.org//adp/history/bios/navarro/navarro3.html.

22. Reuben Marmaduke Potter, *The Texas Revolution: Distinguished Mexicans Who Took Part in the Revolution of Texas,* monograph reprinted in *The Magazine of American History,* October 1878, collection of the University of Texas at Austin, 1.

23. William P. Zuber, "Escape from the Alamo," in *The Texas Almanac for 1873, and Emigrant's Guide to Texas,* 1873~, 82, https://texashistory.unt.edu/ark:/67531/metapth123778/, University of North Texas Libraries, The Portal to Texas History, https://texashistory.unt.edu; crediting Texas State Historical Association. The following account and quotations are from pages 82–84 of the same source.

24. Wallace O. Chariton, *Exploring Alamo*

Legends (Dallas: Republic of Texas Press, 2004), 200.

25. Reuben M. Potter to H. A. McArdle, March 19, 1878, The McArdle Notebooks, Archives and Information Services Division, Texas State Library and Archives Commission, https://www.tsl.texas.gov/mcardle/alamo/alamo37-01.html.

26. Zuber, "Escape from the Alamo," 84.

27. Anna Hardwicke Pennybacker, *A New History of Texas for Schools* (Tyler, TX: Published by the Author, 1888), 74.

28. Pennybacker, 75.

29. J. Frank Dobie, "The Line That Travis Drew," *Publications of the Texas Folklore Society* 15 (1939), 14.

30. Thomas Ricks Lindley, *Alamo Traces: New Evidence and New Conclusions* (Lanham, MD: Republic of Texas Press, 2003), 200.

31. Lindley, 200.

Chapter 13: The Second Battle of the Alamo

1. "Chronology," Alamo Trust, https://www.thealamo.org/remember/history/chronology/index.html, last viewed March 28, 2020.

2. *San Antonio Daily Express,* March 6, 1886.

3. Suzanne Seifert Cottraux, "Missed Identity: Collective Memory, Adina De Zavala and the Tejana Heroine Who Wasn't" (master's thesis, University of Texas at Arlington, May 2013), 6.

4. Cottraux, 14.

5. Cottraux, 6.

6. Pompeo Coppini, *From Dawn to Sunset* (San Antonio: Naylor, 1949), 106.

7. Coppini, 107.

8. Coppini, 108.

9. *San Antonio Express,* March 21, 1907.

10. Adina De Zavala, *Anniversary of the Victory of San Jacinto* (pamphlet, 1904), De Zavala (Adina) Collection, B 5/33.

11. "New Custodian for the Alamo Is Miss Eager," *San Antonio Express,* undated newspaper clipping, Clara Driscoll Archive, Corpus Christi, Texas.

12. *San Antonio Express,* November 4, 1905.

13. Daughters of the Republic of Texas Reports 1906, 93–101, De Zavala (Adina) Collection.

14. Charles M. Reeves to Adina De Zavala, September 21, 1906, De Zavala (Adina) Collection, B 5/33.

15. *San Antonio Gazette,* April 20, 1907.

16. *San Antonio Light,* February 11, 1908.

17. *San Antonio Daily Express,* June 16–17, 1908.

18. Gregg Cantrell, "The Bones of Stephen F. Austin: History and Memory in Progressive-Era Texas," in *Lone Star Pasts: Memory and History in Texas* (College Station: Texas A&M Press, 2007), 67.

19. Cantrell, 59.

20. Cantrell, 59.

21. *Dallas Morning News,* December 31, 1911.

22. *Dallas Morning News,* December 31, 1911.

23. *Houston Post,* February 28, 1912.

24. Cantrell, "The Bones of Stephen F. Austin," 61.

25. L. Robert Ables, "The Second Battle for the Alamo," *Southwestern Historical Quarterly* 70, no. 3 (January 1967), 411.

Chapter 14: The White Man's Alamo

1. Resolution, June 8, 1897, from Twenty-Fifth Legislature, Called Session, in Harry Y. Benedict, ed., *A Source Book Relating to the History of the University of Texas at Austin* (*University of Texas Bulletin* 1757, October 10, 1917), 406.

2. Statement, June 17, 1897, from Twenty-Fifth Legislature, Called Session, in Bene-

dict, 407.

3. Paul D. Lack, "In the Long Shadow of Eugene C. Barker: The Revolution and the Republic," in *Texas through Time: Evolving Interpretations,* ed. Walter L. Buenger and Robert A. Calvert (College Station: Texas A&M University Press, 1991), 134–64.

4. Eugene C. Barker, "Public Opinion in Texas Preceding the Revolution," *Annual Report of the American History Association for 1911* (Washington, DC: Smithsonian Institution, 1913), 217.

5. Walter L. Buenger and Robert A. Calvert, eds., *Texas through Time: Evolving Interpretations* (College Station: Texas A&M University Press, 1991), xx.

6. Amelia Worthington Williams, "A Critical Study of the Siege of the Alamo and of the Personnel of Its Defenders" (doctoral dissertation, University of Texas at Austin, 1931), 14–15.

7. Paul Andrew Hutton, introduction to Susan Prendergast Schoelwer with Tom W. Gläser, *Alamo Images: Changing Perceptions of a Texas Experience* (Dallas: DeGolyer Library and Southern Methodist University Press, 1985).

8. Thomas Ricks Lindley, "A Critical Study

of a Critical Study: 'Puzzling Questions,' "
chap. 2 in *Alamo Traces: New Evidence and New Conclusions* (Lanham, MD: Republic of Texas Press, 2003), 37–81.

9. Walter Lord, "Myths and Realities of the Alamo," in *The Republic of Texas* (Palo Alto, CA: American West Publishing, 1968), 18.

10. "When Dallas Was the Most Racist City in America," *D* magazine, June 2017.

11. Mike Zambrano Jr., "Texas History Movies," *Handbook of Texas Online,* last visited November 3, 2020, https://www.tshaonline.org/handbook/entries/texas-history-movies. Published by the Texas State Historical Association.

12. John Rosenfield Jr., *Texas History Movies* (Dallas: Magnolia Petroleum, 1928), 97–102.

13. *San Antonio Express,* June 13, 1936.

Chapter 15: The Alamo Goes Global

1. Don Graham, "Remembering the Alamo: The Story of the Texas Revolution in Popular Culture," *Southwestern Historical Quarterly* 89, no. 1 (July 1985), 48.

2. Steven Watts, *The Magic Kingdom: Walt Disney and the American Way of Life* (Bos-

ton: Houghton Mifflin, 1997), 287, 393.

3. Watts, 287, 393.

4. Watts, 287, 393.

5. J. P. Telotte, *Disney TV* (Detroit: Wayne State University Press, 2004), 4.

6. Telotte, 4.

7. Randy Roberts and James S. Olson, *A Line in the Sand: The Alamo in Blood and Memory* (New York: Simon and Schuster/Touchstone, 2002), 239.

8. Roberts and Olson, 243.

9. Paul F. Anderson, *The Davy Crockett Craze: A Look at the 1950's Phenomenon and Davy Crockett Collectibles* (Hillside, IL: R&G Productions, 1996), 49.

10. Anderson, 49.

11. Paul Andrew Hutton, "The Celluloid Alamo," *Arizona and the West* (published by *Journal of the Southwest*) 28, no. 1 (Spring 1986), 5–22.

12. Cited in Roberts and Olson, *A Line in the Sand,* Kindle ed., loc. 4632.

13. Roberts and Olson, Kindle ed., loc. 4659.

14. Donald Clark and Christopher Andersen, *John Wayne's "The Alamo": The Making of the Epic Film* (New York and Secaucus, NJ: Citadel Press, 1995), 9.

15. Clark and Andersen, 9.

16. Roberts and Olson, *A Line in the Sand,* 261.
17. Roberts and Olson, 263.
18. Roberts and Olson, 263.
19. Clark and Andersen, *John Wayne's "The Alamo,"* 20.
20. Roberts and Olson, *A Line in the Sand,* 266–67.
21. Roberts and Olson, 266–67.
22. Roberts and Olson, 269.
23. Clark and Andersen, *John Wayne's "The Alamo,"* 103–4.

Chapter 16: The Alamo Supremacists

1. John F. Kennedy speaking in front of the Alamo, San Antonio, Texas, unidentified photographer, Associated Press, September 12, 1960, https://www.icp.org/browse/archive/objects/john-f-kennedy-speaking-in-front-of-the-alamo-san-antonio-texas, last viewed January 26, 2020.
2. Remarks of Senator John F. Kennedy, the Alamo, San Antonio, Texas, September 12, 1960, https://www.jfklibrary.org/asset-viewer/archives/JFKSEN/0911/JFKSEN-0911-025, last viewed January 26, 2020.
3. Tom Shelton, "Presidential Nominees Visit San Antonio," *The Top Shelf* (blog), October 10, 2016, https://utsalibraries

topshelf.wordpress.com/2016/10/10/presidential-nominees-visit-san-antonio/, last viewed October 27, 2019; Randy Roberts and James S. Olson, *A Line in the Sand: The Alamo in Blood and Memory* (New York: Simon and Schuster/Touchstone, 2002), 341. See also https://www.barrypopik.com/index.php/texas/entry/alamo_has_no_back_door_maury_maverick_jr/.

4. Address of Senator John F. Kennedy to the Greater Houston Ministerial Association, September 12, 1960, Rice Hotel, Houston, Texas, https://www.jfklibrary.org/archives/other-resources/john-f-kennedy-speeches/houston-tx-19600912-houston-ministerial-association, last viewed October 24, 2019.

5. W. H. Lawrence, "Nixon Forecasts Reuther Control If Kennedy Wins," *New York Times,* November 4, 1960, https://timesmachine.nytimes.com/timesmachine/1960/11/04/issue.html, last viewed January 26, 2020.

6. Donald Clark and Christopher Andersen, *John Wayne's "The Alamo": The Making of the Epic Film* (New York and Secaucus, NJ: Citadel Press, 1995), 103–4.

7. Russell Birdwell, "There Were No Ghost

Writers at the Alamo," *Life,* July 4, 1960, 5.

8. Quoted in Roberts and Olson, *A Line in the Sand,* 275.

9. Roberts and Olson, 275.

10. Jan Jarboe Russell, "Politician of the Century — Lyndon Johnson," *Texas Monthly,* December 1, 1999, https://www.texasmonthly.com/politics/politician-of-the-century-lyndon-johnson/, last viewed February 1, 2020. Bunton is pictured in William Henry Huddle's painting *Surrender of Santa Anna.*

11. "Remarks to American and Korean Servicemen at Camp Stanley, Korea," November 1, 1966, The American Presidency Project, https://www.presidency.ucsb.edu/documents/remarks-american-and-korean-servicemen-camp-stanley-korea, last viewed February 1, 2020.

12. Hugh Sidey, *A Very Personal Presidency* (New York: Atheneum, 1968), 22–23.

13. Ben Procter, book review in *Pacific Historical Review* 38, no. 4 (November 1969).

14. Debbie Nathan, "Lone Done Gone," *Texas Observer,* January 16, 2004.

Chapter 17: The Rise of Alamo Revisionism

1. Randy Roberts and James S. Olson, *A Line in the Sand: The Alamo in Blood and Memory* (New York: Simon and Schuster/ Touchstone, 2002), 286.
2. Stephen Harrigan, "The Alamo? Sure. Two Blocks, Turn Right, and It's Right Across from the Five and Ten," *Texas Monthly,* September 1975.
3. Richard R. Flores, *Remembering the Alamo: Memory, Modernity, and the Master Symbol* (Austin: University of Texas Press, 2002), xiii.
4. Rosa-Linda Fregoso, *MeXicana Encounters: The Making of Social Identities on the Borderlands* (Berkeley: University of California Press, 2003), Kindle ed., loc. 727.
5. Fregoso, Kindle ed., loc. 765.
6. Linda K. Salvucci, " 'Everybody's Alamo': Revolution in the Revolution, Texas Style," *Reviews in American History* 30, no. 2 (June 2, 2002), 236–44.
7. Zev Chafets, "The Post-Hispanic Hispanic Politician," *New York Times Magazine,* May, 6, 2010, https://www.nytimes .com/2010/05/09/magazine/09Mayor-t .html, last viewed March 1, 2020.
8. Cynthia E. Orozco, *Agent of Change:*

Adela Sloss-Vento, Mexican American Civil Rights Activist and Texas Feminist (Austin: University of Texas Press, 2020), 163.

9. Omar Valerio-Jiménez, "Refuting History Fables: Collective Memories, Mexican Texans, and Texas History," *Southwestern Historical Quarterly* 123, no. 4 (2020), 390–418.

10. Rodolfo Acuña, *Occupied America: The Chicano's Struggle Toward Liberation* (San Francisco: Canfield Press, 1972), 10.

11. Paul Andrew Hutton, introduction to Susan Prendergast Schoelwer with Tom W. Gläser, *Alamo Images: Changing Perceptions of a Texas Experience* (Dallas: DeGolyer Library and Southern Methodist University Press, 1985).

12. Cited in Sam W. Haynes and Gerald D. Saxon, eds., *Contested Empire: Rethinking the Texas Revolution* (College Station: Texas A&M University Press, 2015), Kindle ed., loc. 165.

13. Paul G. Levine, "Remember the Alamo," *American Film,* January–February 1982.

14. Walter Lord, "Myths and Realities of the Alamo," in *The Republic of Texas* (Palo Alto, CA: American West Publishing, 1968), 18.

1. James E. Crisp, *Sleuthing the Alamo: Davy Crockett's Last Stand and Other Mysteries of the Texas Revolution* (New York: Oxford University Press, 2005), 68.

2. José Enrique de la Peña, *With Santa Anna in Texas: A Personal Narrative of the Revolution,* expanded ed., trans. and ed. Carmen Perry (College Station: Texas A&M University Press, 1997), 53.

3. Walter Lord, *A Time to Stand* (New York: Harper & Row, 1961), 207.

4. "Did Crockett Die at the Alamo? Historian Carmen Perry Says No," *People,* October 13, 1975, people.com/archive/did-crockett-die-at-the-alamo-historian-carmen-perry-says-no-vol-4-no-15/.

5. Cited in Randy Roberts and James S. Olson, *A Line in the Sand: The Alamo in Blood and Memory* (New York: Simon and Schuster/Touchstone, 2002), 291.

6. Dan Kilgore and James E. Crisp, *How Did Davy Die? And Why Do We Care So Much?,* commemorative ed. (College Station: Texas A&M University Press, 2010), 59. (The book, with Kilgore as author, was originally published in 1978.)

7. Susan Prendergast Schoelwer with Tom W. Gläser, *Alamo Images: Changing*

Perceptions of a Texas Experience (Dallas: DeGolyer Library and Southern Methodist University Press, 1985), 16.

8. Paul Andrew Hutton, review of *Duel of Eagles: The Mexican and U.S. Fight for the Alamo* by Jeff Long, *Southwestern Historical Quarterly* 96, no. 1 (July 1992), 134–35.

9. "For Alamo's Defenders, New Assault to Repel," *New York Times,* March 29, 1994.

10. Eddie Weems, quoted by Clay Reynolds, review of *The Gates of the Alamo* by Stephen Harrigan, *Texas Observer,* December 24, 1999.

11. Cited in Roberts and Olson, *A Line in the Sand,* 299.

Chapter 19: The Alamo under Siege

1. David Anthony Richelieu, "Alamo Supporters Disagree over $2 Million Facelift," *San Antonio Express,* December 8, 1983.

2. Richelieu.

3. Lianne Hart, "The Daughters of Texas Have a Curt Rebuke for a Yankee Who Remembers the Alamo — Forget It," *People,* June 4, 1984, https://people.com/archive/the-daughters-of-texas-have-a-curt

-rebuke-for-a-yankee-who-remembers-the
-alamo-forget-it-vol-21-no-22/, last viewed
June 25, 2020.

4. "Alamo Changes Deserve Study," *San
Antonio Express,* undated; Gregory Cur-
tis, "Behind the Lines," *Texas Monthly,*
February 1984.

5. Julie Morris, "Texans Split over Alamo
Revamping," *USA Today,* December 27,
1983; Bruce Buursma, "Plan Pursues an
Alamo Worth Remembering," *Chicago Tribune,* April 23, 1984; Wayne King, "Alamo
under Siege: Defenders Standing Firm
against Illinois History Buff," *New York
Times,* April 12, 1984; Lianne Hart, "The
Daughters of Texas Have a Curt Rebuke
for a Yankee Who Remembers the Alamo
— Forget It," *People,* June 4, 1984.

6. "Film Details: *Alamo: The Price of Freedom,*" Giant Screen Cinema Association,
https://www.giantscreencinema.com/
Films/Film-Database/FilmDatabaseDetail
View/movieid/10, last viewed September
7, 2020.

7. "The Premiere of a Movie about the
Alamo Sparked . . . ," UPI, March 7,
1988, https://www.upi.com/Archives/1988/
03/07/The-premiere-of-a-movie-about-the
-Alamo-sparked/3533573714000/, last

viewed January 11, 2020; interview with Professor Gilberto Hinojosa.

8. Randy Roberts and James S. Olson, *A Line in the Sand: The Alamo in Blood and Memory* (New York: Free Press, 2001), 302.

9. Roberts and Olson, 303.

10. Associated Press, "Legislature to 'Remember the Alamo' and Its Profits," *Brazosport Facts,* November 14, 1988.

11. "Vault to Hold Bones Found in Alamo," *San Antonio Light,* January 6, 1937.

12. Marty Sabota, "Man's Search for His Roots Unearths Hidden Past of Alamo: Hundreds of Indians Buried at Mission," *Gazette Telegraph* (Colorado Springs), April 10, 1994.

13. *Dallas Morning News,* January 26, 1994, 28A.

Chapter 20: The Sisters of Spite

1. Sam Howe Verhovek, "Texas, Where History Stings," *New York Times,* May 4, 1997, https://www.nytimes.com/1997/05/04/weekinreview/texas-where-history-stings.html, last viewed September 7, 2020.

2. Oliver Holt, *Miracle at Medinah: Europe's Amazing Ryder Cup Comeback* (London:

Headline, 2013); Nicholas Lemann, "Remember the Alamo," *New Yorker,* October 11, 2004, https://www.newyorker.com/magazine/2004/10/18/remember-the-alamo, last viewed September 7, 2020.

3. "Best Movie about the Alamo?," HornSports, May 31, 2014, https://www.hornsports.com/forums/topic/6884-best-movie-about-the-alamo/, last viewed December 8, 2019; interview with John Pritcher, December 9, 2019; "How Much Did the Alamo Really Cost?" *Slate,* April 14, 2004, https://slate.com/news-and-politics/2004/04/how-much-did-the-alamo-really-cost.html, last viewed September 7, 2020.

4. Report to the Texas Legislature, Investigation of the Daughters of the Republic of Texas, Office of the Attorney General, November 2012, 31.

5. Ben Casselman, "Remember the Alamo? It's under Siege Again — This Time from Within — Daughters of the Republic Manage the Site, but Rebel Group Says They're Stuck in the Past," *Wall Street Journal,* August 20, 2009.

6. Jan Jarboe Russell, "No Retreat! No Surrender!," *Texas Monthly,* October 2010, https://www.texasmonthly.com/the-culture/no-retreat-no-surrender/, last viewed

September 11, 2020; Jeff Winkler, "Never Surrender or Retreat," *Texas Monthly,* April 6, 2015, https://www.texas monthly.com/the-daily-post/never-surrender-or-retreat/, last viewed September 11, 2020.

7. Russell, "No Retreat! No Surrender!"

8. Associated Press, "Gag Order Proposed for Ex–Alamo Backers," *San Antonio Express-News,* September 3, 2009, https://www.mysanantonio.com/news/local/article/Gag-order-proposed-for-ex-Alamo-backers-847392.php, last viewed September 7, 2020.

9. Russell, "No Retreat! No Surrender!"

10. "DRT Alamo," KSAT, December 16, 2009.

11. Allies of the Alamo, "The Alamo Answers," https://www.youtube.com/watch?v=k42B2LZoOsQ&list=FLEgA1v_WdjQVoua4sSUqYtg, last viewed March 22, 2020.

12. Kim Barker, Texas Historical Commission, letter to Dorothy Black, Daughters of the Republic of Texas, February 12, 2010.

13. SB 1841, 82nd Regular Session, Texas Senate Public Education Committee Hearing, April 11, 2010, http://tlcsenate.granicus.com/MediaPlayer.php?clip_id=1392, last viewed September 7, 2020.

14. James McKinley, "Critics Accuse Group of a Serious Texas Sin: Forgetting the Alamo," *New York Times,* December 4, 2010, https://www.nytimes.com/2010/12/05/us/05alamo.html, last viewed September 7, 2020.

15. Karen Thompson, email, March 29, 2011.

16. Senate Journal, 82nd Regular Session, 1696–1703; video of senate session, May 3, 2011.

Chapter 21: "This Politically Incorrect Nonsense"

1. David G. McComb, "Texas History Textbooks in Texas Schools," *Southwestern Historical Quarterly* 93, no. 2 (October 1989), 191–96, https://www.jstor.org/stable/30241292, last viewed October 14, 2019.

2. Chapter 113, Texas Essential Knowledge and Skills for Social Studies, 1998.

3. Larry Willoughby and Dr. Janice C. May, *Texas!* (Austin: Holt, Rinehart and Winston, 2003), 205, 212, 242.

4. "Social Studies Review Finding Problems," Texas Public Policy Foundation, July 2, 2002, https://www.texaspolicy.com/press/social-studies-review-finding

-problems, last viewed December 31, 2019; Alexander Stille, "Textbook Publishers Learn: Avoid Messing with Texas," *New York Times,* June 29, 2002, https://www.nytimes.com/2002/06/29/arts/textbook-publishers-learn-avoid-messing-with-texas.html, last viewed September 11, 2020.

5. Margaret Swett Henson, "Texas History in the Public Schools: An Appraisal," *Southwestern Historical Quarterly* 82, no. 4 (April 1979), 403–22, quotation at 408, https://www.jstor.org/stable/30236865, last viewed October 14, 2019.

6. Mariah Blake, "Revisionaries: How a Group of Texas Conservatives Are Rewriting Your Kids' Textbooks," *Washington Monthly,* January 1, 2010, https://washingtonmonthly.com/2010/01/01/revisionaries/, last viewed June 25, 2020.

7. *The Revisionaries,* documentary written by Scott Thurman and Jawad Metni, directed by Scott Thurman, 2012; "Foundation: Keep Traditional American Values in Texas' Social Studies Curriculum," Texas Public Policy Foundation, May 20, 2009, https://www.texas policy.com/press/foundation-keep-traditional-american-values-in-texas-social-studies-curriculum, last viewed September 11, 2020.

8. "Texts Won't Cover Tejanos at Alamo," *Dallas Morning News,* March 12, 2010, https://www.dallasnews.com/news/education/2010/03/12/texts-won-t-cover-tejanos-at-alamo/, last viewed September 7, 2020; Brian Thevenot, "Civil Civics," *Texas Tribune,* January 10, 2010, https://www.texastribune.org/2010/01/15/sboe-conservatives-and-liberals-try-compromise/, last viewed September 24, 2019.

9. April Castro, "Texas Board of Education Vote Reflects Far-Right Influences; Will Affect Whole US," *Sentinel Source,* March 13, 2010, https://www.sentinelsource.com/news/national_world/texas-board-of-education-vote-reflects-far-right-influences-will-affect-whole-us /article_aee4e75e-9f8d-5703-ac47-4c7ccb270073.html, last viewed September 7, 2020.

10. "Rewriting History in Texas," *New York Times,* March 15, 2010, https://www.nytimes.com/2010/03/16/opinion/16tue3.html, last viewed June 25, 2020.

11. Mary Helen Berlanga, "Board Pushes Its Agenda with No Concern for History," *Waco Tribune-Herald,* May 16, 2010, https://www.wacotrib.com/opinion/columns/guest_columns/mary-helen-berlanga-guest-columnist-board-pushes-its-agenda-with/article_f54e5d47-b0c6

-5ca9-bb91-63c55414cb1d.html, last viewed January 7, 2020.

12. "Texas Won't Cover Tejanos at the Alamo"; Stephen Schafersman, "State Board of Education Continues Debate of Social Studies Standards, Day 3," *Texas Observer,* March 12, 2010, https://www.texasobserver.org/state-board-of-education-continues-debate-of-social-studies-standards-day-3/, last viewed January 5, 2020.

13. "Oral History Interview with Mary Helen Berlanga," The Portal to Texas History, July 12, 2016, https://texashistory.unt.edu/ark:/67531/metapth987558/m1/#track/6, last viewed January 5, 2020.

14. Minutes, Texas State Board of Education, May 2010.

15. Stephen Cure, "Negotiating for Quality: Taking a Proactive Approach to Achieve a Positive Outcome," in *Politics and the History Curriculum: The Struggle over Standards in the Nation,* ed. Keith A. Erekson (New York: Palgrave Macmillan, 2012), 75–87.

16. Carlos Sanchez, "Should Texas Schoolchildren Be Taught That Alamo Defenders Were 'Heroic'?," *Texas Monthly,* September 6, 2018, https://www.texasmonthly.com/news/texas-schoolchildren-taught

-alamo-defenders-heroic/, last viewed June 25, 2020.

17. Sanchez, "Should Texas Schoolchildren Be Taught?"

Chapter 22: The Alamo Reimagined

. Madlin Mekelburg, "No, Texas Has No Plans for Santa Anna Statue at Alamo" ("Rick Range Stated . . . 'George P. Bush to Place Statue of [Mexican General] Santa Anna at the Alamo' "), *Politifact,* December 17, 2019, https://www.politifact.com/factchecks/2019/dec/17/rick-range/no-texas-has-no-plans-santa-anna-statue-Alamo/, last viewed September 7, 2020.

2. Ryan Reed, "$100 Million 'Phil Collins Alamo Collection' in the Works," *Rolling Stone,* October 29, 2014, https://www.rollingstone.com/music/music-news/100-million-phil-collins-alamo-collection-in-the-works-64400/, last viewed June 25, 2020.

3. Diego Bernal, "The Alamo: Restoring Its Grandness," *San Antonio Express-News,* December 8, 2013.

4. Minutes, Alamo Plaza Advisory Committee, May 9, 2014, https://www.sanantonio.gov/Portals/0/Files/CCDO/Maymin%209,%202014.pdf, last viewed April 19,

2020; and May 28, 2014, https://www
.sanantonio.gov/Portals/0/Files/CCDO/
Maymin%2028,%202014.pdf, last viewed
April 19, 2020.

5. Dr. Tijerino based his presentation on
"Constructing Tejano Memory," chapter 7
in his *Lone Star Pasts: Memory and History
in Texas,* ed. Gregg Cantrell and Elizabeth Hayes Turner (College Station: Texas
A&M University Press, 2007).

6. Alamo Comprehensive Interpretive Plan,
https://tnm.me/wp-content/uploads/2018/
10/TNM-Exposing-The-Plan-To-Reimag
ine-The-Alamo.pdf.

7. "Gary Foreman at the Alamo Plaza Committee's Meeting, August 26, 2014,"
posted by Nefarious Ned, August 27,
2014, https://www.youtube.com/watch
?v=RPEeR4HsG7s, last viewed April 23,
2020.

8. "The Alamo Is Why Millions Visit Mission," *San Antonio Express-News,* August
30, 2014.

9. Scott Huddleston, "Plaza Tweaks Goals,
Vision for Alamo Plaza," *San Antonio
Express-News,* September 15, 2014,
https://www.expressnews.com/news/local/
article/Plaza-tweaks-goals-vision-for
-Alamo-Plaza-5757485.php, last viewed
April 26, 2020; "Vision, Guiding Princi-

ples and Alamo Plaza Plan Update," Alamo Plaza Advisory Committee, https://www.sanantonio.gov/Portals/0/Files/CCDO/Resources/Vision-GuidingPrinciples.pdf, last viewed April 26, 2020.

10. "Updated: Temporary Restraining Order Issued against Commissioner Bush in Fight with Daughters of the Republic of Texas," *Quorum Report,* August 24, 2015, http://www.quorumreport.com/Quorum_Report_Daily_Buzz_2015/updated_temporary_restraining_order_issued_against_buzziid24205.html, last viewed September 7, 2020.

11. Scott Huddleston, "Alamo Plan a Team Effort; State Agency and City Will Work Together," *San Antonio Express-News,* April 10, 2015.

12. "Panel Discussion on the Alamo," C-SPAN, September 24, 2016, https://www.c-span.org/video/?415471-1/panel-discussion-alamo, last viewed January 14, 2020.

13. Kenric Ward, "Bush Political Director Offers Alamo Board Position, for a Price," *Texas Monitor,* October 6, 2017, https://texasmonitor.org/alamo-reimagined-george-bush-price/, last viewed April 28, 2020.

14. Jonathan Tilove, "In Remembering the

Alamo, George P. Bush Is Forced to Defend Him-self," *Austin American-Statesman,* October 7, 2017, updated September 25, 2018, statesman.com/news/20171007/in-remembering-the-alamo-george-p-bush-is-forced-to-defend-himself.

15. Christopher Hooks, "George P. Bush's Last Stand at the Alamo," *Texas Monthly,* March 2018, https://www.texasmonthly.com/politics/alamo-george-p-bush/, last viewed June 25, 2020.

16. Tilove, "In Remembering the Alamo, George P. Bush Is Forced to Defend Himself," *Austin American-Statesman,* October 7, 2017; Michael Quinn Sullivan, "Will the Alamo Be Remembered or Re-imagined?" Texas Scorecard, November 15, 2017, https://texasscorecard.com/local/will-alamo-remembered-reimagined/, last viewed April 29, 2020.

17. Hooks, "George P. Bush's Last Stand at the Alamo."

18. Jonathan Tilove, " 'I Did Win, Right?' George P. Bush on Being Booed at the Republican Convention," *Austin American-Statesman,* June 20, 2018; Lauren McGaughy, "George P. Bush Greeted by Boos and Cries of 'Remember the Alamo!' at Texas GOP Convention," *Dallas Morn-*

ing News, June 15, 2018, https://www
.dallasnews.com/news/politics/2018/06/15/
george-p-bush-greeted-by-boos-and-cries
-of-remember-the-alamo-at-texas-gop
-convention/, last viewed April 16, 2020.

19. Brandon Waltens, "Citizens File Suit
against Bush over Alamo Management,"
Texas Scorecard, October 3, 2018, https://
texasscorecard.com/local/citizens-file-suit
-against-bush-over-alamo-management/
?fbclid=IwAR0diy1JbTPcMdpXSSX25B
FHI5rFAKzWMfoqaFkBrQBwnKyx68
_pH1Vn9yU, last viewed April 28, 2020;
ADDA v. Alamo Trust, 18-cv-1030,
United States District Court for the
Western District of Texas, San Antonio
Division.

20. Tilove, "In Remembering the Alamo,
George P. Bush Is Forced to Defend Himself."

21. Vincent T. Davis and Scott Huddleston,
"San Antonio Native American Group
Hosts Sunrise Ceremony at the Alamo,"
San Antonio Express-News, September 7,
2019, https://www.expressnews.com/news/
local/article/San-Antonio-Native-Ameri
can-group-hosts-sunrise-14422225.php#,
last viewed April 25, 2020.

22. Tilove, "In Remembering the Alamo,

George P. Bush Is Forced to Defend Himself."

23. Brendan Gibbons, "Woolworth Building in Spotlight as Architects, Historians Fight to Save It," *Rivard Report,* February 1, 2020.

24. Iris Dimmick, "San Antonio Conservation Society Pitches Alamo Museum 'Compromise,' " *Rivard Report,* May 7, 2019, https://therivardreport.com/san -antonio-conservation-society-pitches -alamo-museum-compromise/, last viewed June 25, 2020.

25. Scott Huddleston, "State Commission Recognizes Alamo Church in Downtown San Antonio as a Cemetery," San *Antonio Express-News,* June 17, 2020, https://www .expressnews.com/news/local/article/ Texas -Historical-Commission-to-take-up -Alamo-15345348.php, last viewed June 20, 2020.

26. Nicole Cobler, "Dan Patrick Criticizes George P. Bush over Alamo Feud," *Austin American-Statesman,* December 17, 2019, https://www.statesman.com/news/20191 217/dan-patrick-criticizes-george-p-bush -over-alamo-feud, last viewed June 20, 2020.

Chapter 23: The Problem with Phil

1. John Spong, "Come and Take a Look at Me Now," *Texas Monthly,* January 2012.
2. Phil Collins, *Phil's Alamo Collection 3,* original receipt book held by the Texas General Land Office, scanned PDF, 103.
3. Phil Collins, *Phil's Alamo Collection 4,* original receipt book held by the Texas General Land Office, scanned PDF, 59.
4. Collins, *Phil's Alamo Collection 4,* scanned PDF, 101.
5. Collins, *Phil's Alamo Collection 4,* scanned PDF, 223.
6. Collins, *Phil's Alamo Collection 4,* scanned PDF, 224.
7. *Collins, Phil's Alamo Collection 4,* scanned PDF, 227.
8. Phil Collins email to Hector Valle, June 15, 2020, obtained under the Texas Public Information Act on July 21, 2020.
9. Hector Valle email to Phil Collins, June 15, 2020, obtained under the Texas Public Information Act on July 21, 2020.
10. Hector Valle email to Phil Collins, June 23, 2020, obtained under the Texas Public Information Act on July 21, 2020.

Acuña, Rodolfo F. *The Making of Chicana/o Studies: In the Trenches of Academe.* New Brunswick, NJ: Rutgers University Press, 2011.

———. *Occupied America: The Chicano's Struggle toward Liberation.* San Francisco: Canfield Press, 1972.

Ames, Bill. *Texas Trounces the Left's War on History.* Dallas: Taylor Publishing, 2012.

Anderson, Paul F. *The Davy Crockett Craze: A Look at the 1950's Phenomenon and Davy Crockett Collectibles.* Hillside, IL: R&G Productions, 1996.

Barr, Alwyn. *Texans in Revolt: The Battle for San Antonio, 1835.* Austin: University of Texas Press, 1990.

Berriozábal, María Antonietta. *Maria, Daughter of Immigrants.* San Antonio: Wings Press, 2012.

Brands, H. W. *Lone Star Nation: How a*

Ragged Army of Volunteers Won the Battle for Texas Independence. New York: Doubleday, 2004.

Brear, Holly Beachley. *Inherit the Alamo: Myth and Ritual at an American Shrine.* Austin: University of Texas Press, 1995.

Brown, Norman D. *Hood, Bonnet, and Little Brown Jug: Texas Politics, 1821–1928.* College Station: Texas A&M University Press, 1984.

Buenger, Walter L., and Robert A. Calvert. *Texas through Time: Evolving Interpretations.* College Station: Texas A&M University Press, 1991.

Buenger, Walter L., and Arnoldo De Léon, eds. *Beyond Texas through Time: Breaking Away from Past Interpretations.* College Station: Texas A&M University Press, 2011.

Burrough, Bryan. *The Big Rich: The Rise and Fall of the Greatest Texas Oil Fortunes.* New York: Penguin Books, 2009.

Campbell, Randolph B. *An Empire for Slavery: The Peculiar Institution in Texas, 1821–1865.* Baton Rouge: Louisiana State University Press, 1989.

———. *Gone to Texas: A History of the Lone Star State.* New York: Oxford University Press, 2012.

Cantrell, Gregg. *Stephen F. Austin: Empresario of Texas.* New Haven: Yale University Press, 1999.

Cantrell, Gregg, and Elizabeth Hayes Turner, eds. *Lone Star Pasts: Memory and History in Texas.* College Station: Texas A&M University Press, 2007.

Cashion, Ty. *Lone Star Mind: Reimagining Texas History.* Norman: University of Oklahoma Press, 2018.

Chariton, Wallace O. *Exploring the Alamo Legends.* Lanham, MD: Republic of Texas Press, 2004. Originally published Dallas: Wordware, 1990.

Clark, Donald, and Christopher Andersen. *John Wayne's "The Alamo": The Making of the Epic Film.* New York and Secaucus, NJ: Citadel Press, 1995.

Coppini, Pompeo. *From Dawn to Sunset.* San Antonio: Naylor, 1949.

Cottraux, Suzanne Seifert. "Missed Identity: Collective Memory, Adina De Zavala, and the Tejana Heroine Who Wasn't." Unpublished master's thesis. University of Texas at Arlington, 2013.

Cox, Patrick L., and Kenneth E. Hendrickson Jr., eds. *Writing the Story of Texas.* Austin: University of Texas Press, 2013.

Crisp, James E. *Sleuthing the Alamo: Davy*

Crockett's Last Stand and Other Mysteries of the Texas Revolution. New York: Oxford University Press, 2005.

Davis, William C. *Lone Star Rising: The Revolutionary Birth of the Texas Republic.* New York: Free Press, 2004.

———. *Three Roads to the Alamo: The Lives and Fortunes of David Crockett, James Bowie, and William Barret Travis.* New York: HarperCollins, 1998.

De la Peña, José Enrique. *With Santa Anna in Texas: A Personal Narrative of the Revolution.* College Station: Texas A&M University Press, 1975.

De León, Arnoldo. *They Called Them Greasers: Anglo Attitudes toward Mexicans in Texas, 1821–1900.* Austin: University of Texas Press, 1983.

De Zavala, Adina. *History and Legends of the Alamo and Other Missions in and around San Antonio.* Houston: Arte Publico Press, 1996. Originally published 1917.

Dillon, Merton L. *Benjamin Lundy and the Struggle for Negro Freedom.* Urbana: University of Illinois Press, 1966.

Dobie, J. Frank. *Stories of Christmas and the Bowie Knife.* Austin: Steck, 1953.

Edmondson, J. R. *The Alamo Story: From Early History to Current Conflicts.* Lanham,

MD: Republic of Texas Press, 2000.

Erekson, Keith A. *Politics and the History Curriculum: The Struggle over Standards in Texas and the Nation.* New York: Palgrave Macmillan, 2012.

Fehrenbach. T. R. *Lone Star: A History of Texas and the Texans.* New York: Da Capo Press, 2000.

Fisher, Lewis F. *Saving San Antonio: The Preservation of Heritage.* San Antonio: Maverick Books/Trinity University Press, 2016.

Flores, Richard R. *Remembering the Alamo: Memory, Modernity, & the Master Symbol.* Austin: University of Texas Press, 2002.

Fowler, Will. *Santa Anna of Mexico.* Lincoln: University of Nebraska Press, 2007.

Fregoso, Rosa Linda. *MeXicana Encounters: The Making of Social Identities on the Borderlands.* Berkeley: University of California Press, 2003.

Friend, Llerena. *Sam Houston: The Great Designer.* Austin: University of Texas Press, 1954.

Gates, Henry Louis, Jr. *Stony the Road: Reconstruction, White Supremacy, and the Rise of Jim Crow.* New York: Penguin Press, 2019.

Gómez, Laura E. *Manifest Destinies: The*

Making of the Mexican American Race.
New York: New York University Press,
2018.

Graham, Don. *Cowboys and Cadillacs: How
Hollywood Looks at Texas.* Austin: Texas
Monthly Press, 1983.

Graham, Don, ed. *Lone Star Literature: From
the Red River to the Rio Grande.* New York:
W. W. Norton, 2003.

Gregory, Jack, and Rennard Strickland. *Sam
Houston with the Cherokees, 1829–1833.*
Austin: University of Texas Press, 1967.

Groneman, Bill. *Death of a Legend: The
Myth and Mystery Surrounding the Death of
Davy Crockett.* Plano, TX: Republic of
Texas Press, 1999.

———. *Eyewitness to the Alamo.* Guilford,
CT: Lone Star Books, 2001.

Haley, James L. *Passionate Nation: The Epic
History of Texas.* New York: Free Press,
2006.

Hansen, Todd, ed. *The Alamo Reader: A
Study in History.* Mechanicsburg, PA:
Stackpole Books, 2003.

Hardin, Stephen L. *Texian Iliad: A Military
History of the Texas Revolution, 1835–1836.*
Austin: University of Texas Press, 1994.

Harrigan, Stephen. *Big Wonderful Thing: A
History of Texas.* Austin: University of

Texas Press, 2019.

Haynes, Sam W., and Gerald D. Saxon, eds. *Contested Empire: Rethinking the Texas Revolution*. Arlington: University of Texas at Arlington, 2015.

Haynes, Sam W., and Cary D. Wintz, eds. *Major Problems in Texas History*. Boston: Houghton Mifflin, 2002.

Henson, Margaret Swett. *Juan Davis Bradburn: A Reappraisal of the Mexican Commander of Anahuac*. College Station: Texas A&M University Press, 1982.

————. *Lorenzo de Zavala: The Pragmatic Idealist*. Fort Worth: Texas Christian University Press, 1996.

Horwitz, Tony. *Spying on the South: An Odyssey across the American Divide*. New York: Penguin Press, 2019.

Jackson, John, ed. *Almonte's Texas: Juan N. Almonte's 1834 Inspection, Secret Report & Role in the 1836 Campaign*. Translated by John Wheat. Austin: Texas State Historical Association, 2003.

Jackson, Ron J., Jr., and Lee Spencer White. *Alamo Survivors*. Waco: Nortex Press, 2010.

————. *Joe: The Slave Who Became an Alamo Legend*. Norman: University of Oklahoma Press, 2015.

James, Marquis. *The Raven: A Biography of Sam Houston.* Austin: University of Texas Press, 1929.

Jenkins, John H. *Basic Texas Books: An Annotated Bibliography of Selected Works for a Research Library.* Austin: Texas State Historical Association, 1988.

Johnson, David R., John R. Booth, and Richard J. Harris, eds. *The Politics of San Antonio: Community, Progress, & Power.* Lincoln: University of Nebraska Press, 1983.

Kilgore, Dan, and James E. Crisp. *How Did Davy Die? And Why Do We Care So Much?* Commemorative edition. College Station: Texas A&M University Press, 2010. (Originally published, with Dan Kilgore as author, 1978.)

Kilmeade, Brian. *Sam Houston & the Alamo Avengers: The Texas Victory That Changed American History.* New York: Sentinel, 2019.

Lack, Paul D. *The Texas Revolutionary Experience: A Political and Social History, 1835–1836.* College Station: Texas A&M University Press, 1992.

Lawrence, Jenny, ed. *The Way It Was: Walter Lord on His Life and Books.* eBookArchitects, 2009.

Leach, John Henry. "The Life of Reuben Marmaduke Potter." Master's thesis. University of Texas at Austin, 1939.

Leach, Joseph. *The Typical Texan: Biography of an American Myth.* Dallas: Southern Methodist University Press, 1952.

Lehrer, James. *Viva Max!* New York: Duell, Sloan and Pearce, 1966.

Lindley, Thomas Ricks. *Alamo Traces: New Evidence and New Conclusions.* Lanham, MD: Republic of Texas Press, 2003.

Linenthal, Edward Tabor. *Sacred Ground: American and Their Battlefields.* Urbana: University of Illinois Press, 1991.

Lloyd, Christopher. *The Texas Chronicles: Educators' Guide.* Greenbelt, MD: What on Earth Books, 2019.

Long, Jeff. *Duel of Eagles: The Mexican and U.S. Fight for the Alamo.* New York: William Morrow, 1990.

Lord, Walter. *A Time to Stand.* New York: Harper & Row, 1961. Also published with subtitle *The Epic of the Alamo.* Lincoln: University of Nebraska Press, 1978.

Martinez, Monica Muñoz. *The Injustice Never Leaves You: Anti-Mexican Violence in Texas.* Boston: Harvard University Press, 2018.

Matovina, Timothy M. *The Alamo Remem-*

bered: *Tejano Accounts and Perspectives.*
Austin: University of Texas Press, 1995.

McCaleb, Walter F. *The Alamo.* San Antonio: Naylor, 1956.

McDonald, David. *José Antonio Navarro: In Search of the American Dream in Nineteenth-Century Texas.* Denton: Texas State Historical Association, 2010.

McEnteer, James. *Deep in the Heart: The Texas Tendency in American Politics.* Westport, CT: Praeger, 2004.

McLemore, Laura Lyons. *Inventing Texas: Early Historians of the Lone Star State.* College Station: Texas A&M University Press, 2004.

McWilliams, Carey. *North from Mexico: The Spanish-Speaking People of the United States.* Philadelphia: J. B. Lippincott, 1948. 3rd edition, updated by Alma M. García. Santa Barbara, CA: Praeger, 2016.

Meier, Matt S., and Feliciano Rivera. *The Chicanos: A History of Mexican Americans.* New York: Hill & Wang, 1972.

Montejano, David. *Anglos and Mexicans in the Making of Texas, 1836–1986.* Austin: University of Texas Press, 1987.

———. *Quixote's Soldiers: A Local History of the Chicano Movement, 1966–1981.* Austin: University of Texas Press, 2010.

Myers, John Myers. *The Alamo*. Lincoln: University of Nebraska Press, 1948.

Nofi, Alfred A. *The Alamo and the Texas War for Independence*. Conshohocken, PA: Combined Books, 1992.

O'Connor, Robert F., ed. *Texas Myths*. College Station: Texas A&M University Press, 1986.

Orozco, Cynthia E. *Agent of Change: Adela Sloss-Vento, Mexican American Civil Rights Activist and Texas Feminist*. Austin: University of Texas Press, 2020.

————. *No Mexicans, Women, or Dogs Allowed: The Rise of the Mexican American Civil Rights Movement*. Austin: University of Texas Press, 2009.

Osbourne, Ozzy, with Chris Ayres. *I Am Ozzy*. New York: Grand Central Publishing, 2009.

Pennybacker, Anna J. Hardwicke. *A New History of Texas for Schools*. Tyler, TX: Published by the Author, 1888.

Phillips, Michael. *White Metropolis: Race, Ethnicity, and Religion in Dallas, 1841–2001*. Austin: University of Texas Press, 2006.

Ramos, Raúl A. *Beyond the Alamo: Forging Mexican Ethnicity in San Antonio, 1821–1861*. Chapel Hill: University of North Carolina Press, 2008.

Rios, John F., ed. *Readings on the Alamo.* New York: Vantage, 1987.

Rives, George Lockhart. *The United States and Mexico, 1821–1848.* New York: Charles Scribner's Sons, 1913.

Robbins, Kevin. *The Last Stand of Payne Stewart: The Year Golf Changed Forever.* New York: Hachette Books, 2019.

Roberts, Randy, and James S. Olson. *A Line in the Sand: The Alamo in Blood and Memory.* New York: Simon and Schuster/ Touchstone, 2002. Originally published New York: Free Press, 2001.

Rodríguez O., Jaime E., and Kathryn Vincent, eds. *Myths, Misdeeds, and Misunderstandings: The Roots of Conflict in U.S.– Mexican Relations.* Wilmington, DE: SR Books, 1997.

Rosenbaum, Robert J. *Mexicano Resistance in the Southwest: "The Sacred Right to Self-Preservation."* Austin: University of Texas Press, 1981.

Schoelwer, Susan Prendergast, with Tom W. Gläser. *Alamo Images: Changing Perceptions of a Texas Experience.* Dallas: DeGolyer Library and Southern Methodist University Press, 1985.

Seguín, Juan. *A Revolution Remembered: The Memoirs and Selected Correspondence* of Juan N. Seguín. Edited by Jesús F. de la Teja. Austin: Texas State Historical Association, 2002.

Taylor, Quintard. *In Search of the Racial Frontier: African Americans in the American West, 1528–1990*. New York: W. W. Norton, 1998.

Timmons, W. H. *The Anglo-American Advance into Texas, 1810–1830*. Boston: American Press, 1981.

Todish, Tim J., and Terry S. Todish. *Alamo Sourcebook, 1836: A Comprehensive Guide to the Alamo and the Texas Revolution*. Austin: Eakin Press, 1998.

Torget, Andrew J. *Seeds of Empire: Cotton, Slavery, and the Transformation of the Texas Borderlands, 1800–1850*. Chapel Hill: University of North Carolina Press, 2015.

Tucker, Phillip Thomas. *America's Forgotten First War for Slavery and Genesis of the Alamo*. Publish-Nation, 2017.

———. *Exodus from the Alamo: The Anatomy of the Last Stand Myth*. Philadelphia: Casemate, 2010.

Turner, Martha Anne. *Clara Driscoll: An American Tradition*. Austin: Madrona Press, 1979.

Wallis, Michael. *David Crockett: The Lion of the West*. New York: W. W. Norton, 2011.

Warren, Robert Penn. *Remember the Alamo!* New York: Random House, 1958.

Watts, Steven. *The Magic Kingdom: Walt Disney and the American Way of Life.* Boston: Houghton Mifflin, 1997.

Weber, David J. *Myth and the History of the Hispanic Southwest.* Albuquerque: University of New Mexico Press, 1988.

Willoughby, Larry, and Dr. Janice C. May. *Texas!* Austin: Holt, Rinehart and Winston, 2000.

Wolff, Nelson W. *The Changing Face of San Antonio: An Insider's View of an Emerging International City.* San Antonio: Maverick Books, 2018.

———. *Mayor: An Inside View of San Antonio Politics, 1981–1995.* San Antonio: San Antonio Express-News, 1997.

———. *Transforming San Antonio: An Insider's View to the AT&T Arena, Toyota, the PGA Village, and the Riverwalk Extension.* San Antonio: Trinity University Press, 2008.

Yoakum, Henderson K. *History of Texas: From Its First Settlement in 1685 to Its Annexation to the United States in 1846.* New York: Redfield, 1855.

Pamphlets

The Alamo. Sovereign Publications, 1960.

Lozano, Rubén Rendón. *Viva Tejas: The Story of the Tejanos, the Mexican-Born Patriots of the Texas Revolution.* San Antonio and Houston: Southern Literary Institute, 1936. 2nd edition, San Antonio: Alamo Press, 1985.

Moffitt, Virginia May. *Remember the Alamo!* 1935.

ABOUT THE AUTHORS

Bryan Burrough is the author of six books, including *The Big Rich, Days of Rage,* and *Public Enemies,* and a coauthor of the number one *New York Times* bestseller *Barbarians at the Gate.*

Chris Tomlinson is a columnist for the *Houston Chronicle* and the *San Antonio Express-News* and the author of the *New York Times* bestselling *Tomlinson Hill* about his family's slaveholding history in Texas. From 1995 to 2007, he reported from more than thirty countries and nine wars for the *Associated Press.*

Jason Stanford is a writer and former communications director for the mayor of Austin. As a political consultant, Stanford has helped elect or reelect at least thirty members of Congress.

The employees of Thorndike Press hope you have enjoyed this Large Print book. All our Thorndike, Wheeler, and Kennebec Large Print titles are designed for easy reading, and all our books are made to last. Other Thorndike Press Large Print books are available at your library, through selected bookstores, or directly from us.

For information about titles, please call:
(800) 223-1244

or visit our website at:
gale.com/thorndike

To share your comments, please write:
Publisher
Thorndike Press
10 Water St., Suite 310
Waterville, ME 04901